The Winter Athlete

The Winter Athlete

SECRETS OF WHOLISTIC FITNESS®
FOR OUTDOOR PERFORMANCE

Steve Ilg

Johnson Books

BOULDER

Published in the United States by Johnson Books, a division of Johnson Publishing Company, 1880 South 57th Court, Boulder, Colorado 80301.
E-mail: books@jpcolorado.com

9   8   7   6   5   4   3   2   1

Wholistic Fitness® is a registered trademark of Steve Ilg.
Cover design by Debra B. Topping
Cover photograph of the author ©1999 by Marc Romanelli
Text design by Mira Perrizo; composition by Trish Wilkinson.

Library of Congress Cataloging-in-Publication Data
Ilg, Steve, 1962–
    The winter athlete: secrets of wholistic fitness for outdoor performance / Steve Ilg
        p.   cm.
    Includes bibliographical references.
    ISBN 1-55566-212-9 (alk. paper)
    1. Winter sports. 2. Physical fitness.   I. Title.
RC1220.W55I44   1999
613.7'11—dc21   98-42787
                                                            CIP

Printed in the United States by
Johnson Printing
1880 South 57th Court
Boulder, Colorado 80301

♻ Printed on recycled paper with soy ink

Contents

PART III
PRESEASON TRAINING ACTIVITIES 113

PART IV
PRESEASON TRAINING PROGRAMS 179

PART V
WINTER SPORTS WISDOM 201

PART VI
SPECIALIZATION TRAINING
PROGRAMS FOR ENDURANCE SPORTS 233

PART VII
SPECIALIZATION TRAINING
PROGRAMS FOR SKILL SPORTS

PART VIII
APPENDICES

Preface

The programs outlined in this book will teach you how to be receptive to sport performance instead of forcing it on you through rigid training blueprints. This is a book about releasing instead of attaining. It offers a style of coaching that runs against many contemporary approaches. My students and I accept this. We prefer to swim upstream, against the tides of fashion. When we swim upstream we get closer to the purer waters, closer to the Source of It All.

Recreational athletes unfamiliar with my brand of workouts may think I take a hard-line approach. Do not be frightened by these training programs. I have worked hard to make them appropriate for both the competitive athlete *and* the fitness enthusiast.

Eleven diverse programs are contained in this book, and each holds unique transpersonal teachings. Each program includes a "Master Sheet," a day-by-day prescription for what type of training to do on a particular day. There is also a "Wholistic Notes" section in each program that describes detailed workouts in each of the Five Fitness Disciplines of Wholistic Fitness®. A Resources section lists specific schools, as well as sources for information and inspiration. Each program ends with a Cycle Summation, allowing the energy of introspection to guide you to your next step.

Part One introduces you to the philosophic and scientific foundations of the Wholistic Fitness way. Parts Two, Three, and Four offer a thought-provoking study of preseason, or "dryland training," activities. Two springboard programs, the Green Tara and the Perfect Power training cycles conclude these sections. These two classic programs represent Wholistic Fitness in vivid color. Between these preseason sports and the programs they serve, the sculpting process of your best winter performance yet will have truly begun.

Part Five addresses winter safety and clothing, and includes an entertaining question-and-answer dialogue between some of my students and me. Parts Six and Seven are the backbone of this book: eleven sport-specific programs that will enable you to develop total fitness for your favorite winter sport.

Part Eight is an extensive Appendix that functions as a comprehensive resource for Wholistic Fitness study. It includes strength-training movements and descriptions, photographs, kinesthetic routines, and recipes that validate my uncompromising effort to produce the most unique, effective, and spiritually relevant form of fitness training in the world.

Parts Three, Six, and Seven contain biomechanical and resource sections. Some of this information overlaps and dances between the various sports. I recommend that you first read this book cover to cover, then use the chapters most pertinent to you as your complete training guide for winter performance.

Acknowledgments

My first round of thanks goes to the following people, for their belief in me and for their support of my work: Stephen Topping and everyone else at Johnson Books; Bill Teel and Cannondale Bicycles; Will Gadd, George Bracksieck, and *Rock & Ice* magazine; Fritz Howard at Atlas Snowshoes; Bobby Rhodes at Unipro Performance Nutrition; Murphy Reinschreiber, Christian Griffith, Dr. Labhriumn MacIan, Governor Gary Johnson, and, especially, Lahra Melton.

A round of special thanks goes to all my students across the world who consider "Ilg" a curse word as they carry on their daily practices, especially Jump Squats! I am very proud of all of you. Wholistic Fitness is here only because of *your* contribution to her flow. Ripples make waves. Think Wholistic and be different—it's okay.

I also wish to acknowledge the few lunatics dumb enough to actually train, compete, and/or perform with me during so many absurdly fun seasons of snow: Ben Greene, for your indomitable spirit; Steve Robards, for your belief in blue whales and Canadian ice; George Watson, for your let's-do-it attitude; Richard and Joyce Rossiter, for your elegance; Chris Hill, for your summit-or-plummet approach; Christoph Schelhaus, my nailing partner; Jennifer Heightley, for your physical and spiritual belays; Gerry Roach, for your inspiration; Ken "Flex" Armstrong, for your quiet conviction; "Racin'" Jason Williams, for our brotherhood; Adam Moss, for your heartspirit; Greg "Lupe" Dodd, for your humor; Michael Dalfonso, for the Ilg wing; Mike Longmire, for your "quivee"; Scott Dupuis, for your potential; Richard and Angela Verderame, for your giving manner; "Fit" Kit Johaneson, for your wolf medicine; Spencer Sandis Smith, for your warmth; and Deborah Ilg, for your commitment higher.

I acknowledge all the sentient beings and, especially, the giving trees upon whose flesh these words appear.

I finally extend my unspeakable gratitude to my family, especially my parents, Marjorie and Henry Ilg, for their loving support.

Introduction

"Perseverance is one of the most difficult disciplines, but it is to the one who endures that the final victory comes."
—Buddha

Snow.

To anyone living in the American Southwest, where I am from, this white stuff is as precious as gold. Winter snows prepare the spring landscape, ensuring the cycle of new life. Snow keeps us alive, as our need to drink never wavers. Yet there are people who disdain its slickness and coldness. Some people even curse the snows.

I, for one, have never understood how anyone could dislike snow. Why curse something that bestows the very gift of your own life? As a child, I recall greeting spring with pensiveness. The snowbanks melting alongside Durango's roads would touch me in sad ways. But then I understood that the melting snows would be recycled and returned to earth at a distant time. Perhaps, as snow.

When I secured the contract for this book, I was in Los Angeles on a hot, humid spring day. Eucalyptus trees waved like seaweed against a coastal breeze. At the time, it was snowing heavily at the Johnson Books office in Boulder, Colorado. I felt a twinge of guilt for not being cuddled by warm clothes in some snowy landscape. Nevertheless, in the market research for this book, I discovered a truth that fascinated me. Winter athletes do not necessarily live where it snows!

Millions consider themselves winter athletes though they do not live in a snowy climate. Accessibility is what makes this so. Los Angeles residents, for example, can reach excellent winter sports areas, such as Snow Summit, in just a few hours' drive. As a child of snowy habitat, this recent enlightenment accelerated my desire to write this book. The explosion of popularity in winter sports has occurred because snow is now the domain of everyone, from Houston to Georgia and points in between.

This book serves four types of people: 1) winter-specific athletes whose primary form of athletic performance is a winter sport; 2) summer athletes who use winter sports to maintain or improve their fitness during the off-season; 3) fitness enthusiasts who wish to explore cross-training activities for year-round conditioning; and 4) those who think winter athletes are whacked out of their mind and want to understand why anyone would even want to go outdoors into the snow and cold.

I have designed this book for many athletes: the nordic skiers who glide across serene fields of snow and sport snowshoers who sling themselves up and down powdery mountainsides. The snowboarder and the alpine skier, whose high-speed dance atop a canvas of white, undulating simplicity reflects individual creativity and expression. The ice climber and the mountaineer, who—by way of rhythmic movement and lightness of breath—harmonize a most inhuman place. This book will teach us not to attack these sports with militant attitude, but to embrace their power and beauty. Finally, these chapters have been written from my perspective as an instructor of Wholistic Fitness. Using the transpersonal teachings of this unique system of fitness training, I will show you how to use winter sports training as a vehicle for personal growth.

For those of us infused with the nordic spirit, it is difficult to understand why some people huddle indoors while sweeping snows douse the landscape. I will not waste space speculating on the psychological fabric of cold-weather versus warm-weather athletes. Instead, I have chosen to write from the premise that the reader of this book loves to frolic with nature dressed in her winter plumage. Perhaps you, like me, crave the opportunity to witness special, sacred winter moments, as when piñon jays flick like blue fire between morning pines or when overnight frosts become visible, fitting like ivory gloves upon sage branches and sparkling in early sunlight. Indeed, this book will only appeal to those of us who know—or who sense—that unique, sacrosanct palace known as winter sports.

In my first book, *The Outdoor Athlete*, many of you sensed my underlying theme; that training for fitness and sport performance is actually an effort to become a better human being. Every aspect of my form of instruction points to the philosophy that there are universal truths at operation within our training. My life has been spent competing in all forms of outdoor sports, in every month of the year. All of nature has been my arena, from Grade VI ice waterfalls in Banff, Canada, to seventy-meter nordic ski jumps in Steamboat Springs, Colorado. From extreme snowboard descents in the Grand Tetons of Wyoming to the World Snowshoe Championships up Colorado's highest peak in the middle of winter. Along the way, I have refined my approach to outdoor performance training so that it enables me and hundreds of others to perform at our peak levels consistently. What is most important, however, is the fact that these years of training, coaching, and performing have helped spur a new form of personal growth ignored by conventional training methods.

I want you to love training outdoors in any weather, in any season. I want you to fall in love with its invisible extensions. Sure, better health and a ton of fun are two reasons to do winter sports, yet more exist.

Out of each winter excursion comes inner reward and, with it, more personal motivation to continue our practice. As we rise to the next challenge, be it learning a more efficient glide on nordic skis, doing a first snowshoe race, or performing a telemark descent of a mountain couloir, we learn more about ourselves.

In the end, that is what matters most.

Racing is not about winning ... it's about ourselves. The author in Rio Rancho, New Mexico.

Part I

Wholistic Fitness®
Training Philosophy

*"In the vaunted works of Art
the master stroke is Nature's part."*
—Ralph Waldo Emerson

1

Wholistic Fitness® History

"Though this be madness, yet there be method in't."
—Shakespeare

Wholistic Fitness® began in the early 1980s, when I worked as the training director at Farentinos Gym in Boulder, Colorado. This position was a source of incredibly rich and colorful inspiration for me. My job was to design training programs for patrons of the facility. These programs ranged from sessions for beginners to complex multicycled routines for the numerous elite-caliber athletes who lived in Boulder. For years, this gift of work enriched my coaching skills and nourished my inner understanding of people. The energetics of so many forms of bodywork, athletic training methods, and alternative health philosophies kept me nearly satiated.

Yet something was missing. I sensed a fundamental element lacking in the fitness training. Conventional athletic training concentrated on specific variables in the conditioning of athletes. In the textbooks I used, there were bar graphs and linear charts. Each depicted a specific endpoint targeted by

a logical method. Yet this straightforward application seemed at odds with the emotional nature of the people I trained. Seldom is life or fitness as uninterrupted as the textbooks would like! Real life is more of a dance than a mathematical formula. I saw the need for a more fluid, more human approach to personal coaching.

WHOLISTIC = WHOLE

In my own training and sport performance, I knew that my cardiovascular fitness had benefited tremendously from my strength training. I also knew that my nutrition patterns could not be separated from the quality of my training, recovery, health, and performance. Flexibility work kept my body expressive and injury-free while my meditation practice imparted depth, clarity, and spiritual meaning to my physical fitness. This five-limbed approach to fitness (strength, cardiovascular, kinesthetic, meditation, and nutrition) seemed commonsense to me. Living it produced a comprehensive, balanced training effect. It produced a "wholistic" reward.

Since its inception, Wholistic Fitness has accurately conveyed the principle of wholeness so critical to my approach. As the years passed, I expanded on the philosophy of Wholistic Fitness so that the work would not be limited to hard-core athletes. I wanted this path to touch everyone, so that even sedentary people could benefit from my work, for they needed guidance the most. That is when I began to synthesize four simple lifestyle principles with the fitness disciplines: breath and posture, mindfulness, appropriate action, and practice.

My budding philosophy of training had finally matured. My goal as a personal trainer was reached. No longer was my work limited to the fanatical or competitive outdoor athlete but was now a transformative lifestyle program that integrated personal growth with long-term health and fitness. My goal was verified by hundreds of students across the country. People from all demographics and all fitness levels were attaining varying degrees of athletic and personal awakening. After more than a decade of refinement, my work has assumed a solid role as a transpersonal fitness system that changes lives for the better.

BIG BASH

Much has been written on the spiritual significance of personal trauma. My contribution follows. One cold day in 1983, a friend and I were attempting an early winter ascent of the East Face of Longs Peak in Rocky Mountain National Park. I was leading a snow-covered section when I pulled off a rock about the size of an office desk. The rock and I sailed down the cliff, hurtling through high-altitude air at thirty feet per second. In what proved a lifesaving gesture, I had attached two large, plastic water bottles to my pack. When I hit the cliff, an explosion of water arced gracefully into the morning sunlight as the shock-absorbing water bottles shattered.

During an epic bivouac on the East Face, complete with a blizzard, I realized that I had evidently fractured my spine. I was unable to move my left side. After a horrible night, the next day finally dawned. With the help of my partner, I escaped the East Face and managed a ten-mile hike out to civilization. What followed was a year-long journey into the realm of physicians, bodyworkers, and spiritual healers. Following months of eclectic healing practices and pessimistic medical prognoses, I began to increase my meditation practice. Through this return to silence, I received information that encouraged me to create my own healing artistry. This integrated philosophy would eventually shape the Wholistic Fitness training system.

WHOLISTIC FITNESS® TODAY

Rinpoche Trungpa said, "Like the river which leads into the ocean, so too does the narrow path of discipline lead to panoramic awareness." Wholistic Fitness is less about sport performance and more about spiritual awakening through the discipline of training. The athletic successes of my students are peripheral to the inner rewards they receive from daily practice. The theory particular to Wholistic Fitness is that sport performance is a by-product of personal growth. In other words, we don't really train for sport performance, we train to live more integrated, balanced lives. Sport performance just comes along for the ride!

The Four Lifestyle Principles and the Five Fitness Disciplines that you will learn in this book affect the emotional, physical, and spiritual bodies. They are easy to learn, but take a lifetime to master. Fortunately, your sport performance will increase immediately upon the application of these teachings. This is a proven path. All you have to do is practice, and your winter sports performance will soar higher than ever before.

THE FOUR LIFESTYLE PRINCIPLES OF WHOLISTIC FITNESS:

- Breath and Posture
- Mindfulness
- Appropriate Action
- Practice

THE FIVE FITNESS DISCIPLINES OF WHOLISTIC FITNESS:

- Strength
- Cardiovascular
- Kinesthetic
- Meditation
- Nutrition

The Wholistic Fitness logo is the yin/yang symbol woven between a dumbbell. It symbolizes the original meaning of the word "fitness," which came from a word meaning, "to knit together." Wholistic Fitness knits together Four Lifestyle Principles and Five Fitness Disciplines for an unmatched transpersonal training effect.

TM

2

The Four Lifestyle Principles

"How you do anything, is how you do everything."
—Zen saying

The central teachings of Wholistic Fitness begin with the Four Lifestyle Principles. These principles may at first seem irrelevant to a winter athlete's training protocol. That is because most athletes follow conventional training methods. Remember, one of the primary differences between Wholistic Fitness and conventional training methods is that Wholistic Fitness does not separate the athlete from his or her daily life. Training is no longer an errand to be run or a chore to be accomplished.

The Four Lifestyle Principles are practical tools for everyday life. Their goal is to awaken the student to a higher level of awareness. But why is this important? When compared with the typical American approach to sport-performance training, this approach may seem ludicrous: "Why do I have to learn about lifestyle principles if I just want to snowboard better?"

The answer can be found in the Zen saying, "How you do anything, is how you do everything." The attention we develop in brushing our teeth, or standing in line at the market, or conversing with others sets the emotional, physical, and spiritual foundation for sport performance. Show me an athlete who is mindless in everyday life, and I'll show you an athlete who gets injured, ill, or is not performing to his or her best ability. Most training methods limit training for sport performance to physical workouts—like an errand to be run. Wholistic Fitness demonstrates that we can train for our sport twenty-four hours a day! We can do this by establishing lifestyle behaviors that transfer directly into all other areas of our life, especially sport performance.

Alpine ski instruction illustrates how my notion of transpersonal sport performance works. Conventional ski instruction requires that we travel to a ski area to apply the techniques on the slopes. We must hire a certified and expensive ski instructor, who

Finding a balanced flow of
energy on the snow begins
by finding it in everyday life.
Wholistic Fitness student
Dr. Anne Sasso, knee deep
in flow.

will teach us about the fall line, angulation, weight transfer, edging, etc., ... the same old stuff that's been taught for years. Oh sure, every year someone or some company reinvents the wheel and comes up with a clever new spin. But it basically remains the same old information. Ski training and conditioning still remain an errand to be run.

BALANCED FLOW

Let us now approach alpine skiing from a Wholistic Fitness perspective. Within the first few moments of starting Wholistic Fitness, you will learn how to examine and adjust the way in which you breathe and hold your posture. There's no need to travel anywhere. No need for expensive new equipment or a ski retreat. How you stand can make you ski better; my coaching philosophy is that simple. Though you may be miles away from the slopes, within a few moments you will have become aware of the two most profound factors

that influence skiing performance: breath and posture. When we bring into alignment our posture and breath, we immediately reach a balanced flow of energy.

A balanced flow of energy. Doesn't that sound like wise ski instruction?

The great thing about a transpersonal approach to sport performance is that the sport we love influences our daily life and vice versa. My students are shocked at how rapidly they pick up their sport-specific fitness after an off-season. Practicing the Four Lifestyle Principles leads to a natural athleticism that becomes an expression of personal growth. When it comes time to participate in a particular sport, the body, mind, and spirit are open and ready to adapt. Let's explore these pivotal Lifestyle Principles. If you are like most of my students, by the time you are finished with this initial section, a mini-awakening will have occurred. You will already have improved your sport performance on the subtle, energetic level.

Wholistic Fitness® Lifestyle Principle #1: Breath and Posture

Only two qualities are continuous throughout our life experience: breath and posture. One connects us with the spiritual plane (breath), while the other grounds our connection to the physical plane (posture). Breath and posture represent our immaterial and material realities. Rarely in our athletic upbringing are we taught how to recognize the awesome potential of these lifelong friends. Besides being *the most overlooked components of long-term health care*, breath and posture create the foundation for sport performance.

BREATH

We began our lives with our first breath, and we will finish our earth journey with the last breath. Breath is the most intimate spiritual "link" humans have with the universe. In many languages, the word for breath and spirit is the same. A true breath assures proper oxygenation throughout the body. The breath is also our way to a clearer, more focused state of athletic performance. The more we consciously return attention to our breath, the less cluttered our mind becomes. Ramana Maharshi said, "One moment of conscious breathing is one moment of purity." Contemplate what a jewel we have access to. If we can befriend an ally who can quell our fear,

quiet our anxiety, and steady our resolve during sport performance, wouldn't you want to cultivate that friendship?

Wholistic Fitness begins its Lifestyle Principles by teaching the belly-breath, or diaphragmatic breath. This breath allows complete expansion of the broad sheet of muscle known as the diaphragm. It can be very subtle. In the yogic traditions breathing becomes very scientific. However, for most Americans I have found the following exercise makes the most difference in the shortest time. To breathe from the diaphragm, do not breathe from the chest. Instead, on inhalation, push out your belly as though making a "beer belly." On exhalation, flatten the belly. Try this for several moments right now and note any mental, physical, and/or emotional differences you may feel.

Did you note a quality of lightness, or a lifting sensation on the inhale? On the exhale did you sense a contracting, a squeezing, or a calming feeling? Try again. Listen to the breath, this time with new awareness. Allow the breath its space. Go again.

STRANGE WORDS, STRANGE WORLDS

Such a breath engages the diaphragm to work as a massaging mechanism for the

spleen, stomach, intestines, and other organs. Diaphragmatic breathing also stimulates meridian, or energy, channels servicing
the body. In some martial arts philosophies,
the breath takes place in the solar plexus, an
area known as the *Hara* (Japanese) or the
Tan T'ein (Chinese). This special point is
considered the storage and generation area
for all inner power. So great are the curative
and performance abilities of this area that
entire healing (*chi kung*) and athletic (*ai-
kido*) systems are devoted to the development of the Hara. In India breath is a science, known as *Pranayama*, that has been
studied for centuries. (*Pran* means life force,
and *yama* means science; thus we know
Pranayamic techniques as the science of
breath.) Compare all this with our American tendency to ignore the breath. We have
been conditioned to disregard the simplicity
of paying attention to our breath. Most of
us simply suck air as we do our sports. This
is not wise for sport performance or for
healthful, vibrant living.

TO-HELL-YOU-RIDE

During the 1995 edition of the celebrated
Melee in the Mines mountain-bike race in
Telluride, Colorado, I was coaching one of
my elite mountain-bike racers, Jim. The
elite racers had to do three laps of a
macabre course (fairly standard for Colorado MTB racing). Jim, whose cycling fitness and race results were earning him
widespread acclaim after only a season of

Wholistic Fitness study, was in the lead
pack. After completing one lap, Jim called
to me that he was "cramping up all over."
I only had time to hand up his water bottle
and check a time split, and he was gone.
His energy, however, was an easy read. His
breath was high in his chest. This happens
often during competition; we forget to
breathe deeply, from the belly. The result is
poor oxygenation of the working musculature and hampered energy flow throughout the body and mind.

As Jim came through on the next lap, he
was truly suffering. I mean, the boy was
hurtin' *real* bad. I jogged next to him, got
as close as I could, and yelled at him, "Get
the breath LOW. Breathe LOW and SOFT,
NOW! BREATHE FROM THE BELLY!"
Within that final lap his cramps disappeared, and he chased down thirteen riders, scoring valuable points for the series.
After the race, another cyclist approached
me. He said, "You know, I wanted to
thank you. I overheard you screaming at
that guy to keep his breath low and soft,
and you know what? It totally saved my
race ... thanks!" Turns out, the guy finished in front of my racer!

FINDING THE BREATH

Recently, one of my students who is training for rock climbing, Doe, wrote in her
Cycle Summation: "The breath work you
prescribed is paying off on my hard routes.
When I'd be on a really gnarly route, my

friends below would tell me to breathe and I *would be*! When I was climbing in Red Rocks [Nevada] I did two routes that I hadn't been able to do before. It was like, 'Wow!!! Oh my God!, I just pulled those moves!!!'"

That's the way "finding the breath" is in sport performance, whether it's a Hang Clean in the gym, pulling some intense moves on a rock-climbing route, or just breathing through an emotionally turbulent moment with a loved one. If we just allow breath its space and respond to it with sensitivity, we discover a whole new world of performance.

Let's go over some of the other benefits derived from deep and mindful breathing:

Physical

- Allows more oxygen to enter the bloodstream and expels old, stale breath and toxic irritants.
- Relaxes the glandular system, allowing the body to redistribute energy in a more productive fashion.
- Balances the nervous system, allowing enhanced organ health and greater kinesthetic relation.

Mental

- Reduces stress, anxiety, and anticipation.
- Can shift states of mind (for example, from one of panic to one of calm).
- Enhances concentration and focus.
- Reduces mind chatter and encourages clear, creative thoughts.

BASIC WHOLISTIC FITNESS® BREATH PRACTICES

There are three basic forms of breathwork that you will find in the programs offered in this book: The Cleansing Breath, the Filling Breath, and Alternate Nostril Breathing. My athletes use periodic sessions of formal breath practice to balance internal and external energy.

The Cleansing Breath

This fundamental breathing technique balances physiological and emotional energy. Sit comfortably with the spine straight. Fill the abdominal cavity by inhaling through the nostrils. At the conclusion of the inhale, begin to exhale through the mouth. Keep the lips mostly closed. Exhale for twice as long as you inhaled.

The Filling Breath

This expands abdominal, thoracic, and clavicular respiration. Inhale assertively through the nose while filling the abdominal, chest, and clavicular (shoulder girdle) cavities to full capacity. When no more air can be taken in, exhale slowly through nose. Exhale for twice as long as you inhaled.

Alternate Nostril Breathing

Our nostrils connect two different nerve paths. Usually, we nostril breathe in an unbalanced fashion, which can lead to numerous conditions of dis-ease. Sit straight and place your right thumb so that it closes

---

**Alternate Nostril Breathing
Quick Reference Guide**

1 = out left nostril
2 = in left
3 = hold both nostrils a few seconds
4 = out right nostril
5 = in right
6 = hold both nostrils a few seconds
7 = out left nostril
ONE ROUND

---

off the right nostril. The right index and middle fingers should be folded into the right palm. Position the right ring finger so that it can close off the left nostril. With the right nostril closed, breathe out through the left nostril. Now breathe in through the left nostril. Close both nostrils and hold the breath for a few seconds. Then, keeping the left nostril closed, breathe out through the right one. Now breathe in through the right nostril. Close both nostrils and hold for a few seconds; then open up the left nostril and breathe out. You have done one round of alternate nostril breathing.

BASIC BREATH PRACTICE SESSION

During any breathing exercise you should remain comfortable and relaxed. Never rush your progress. If you become dizzy or lightheaded during your breath practice,

stop and return to normal breathing. Break into these sessions gently; you may be surprised at how much energy is inherent to mindful breathing. Until your body develops the strength to handle this increased volume of energy, take it easy and never force yourself through any uncomfortable sensations.

Find a quiet space where it is not likely you will be disturbed. Assume a seated cross-legged position with spine straight, or sit tall in a chair with the spine straight. Invoke a sensation of comfort and safety.

- Begin with ten Cleansing Breaths, concentrating fully on the quality of each incoming breath and exhalation.
- Now proceed into ten Filling Breaths, again focusing on inhalation and exhalation.
- Perform ten rounds of Alternate Nostril Breathing.
- End the session with five more Cleansing Breaths.

INTERMEDIATE BREATH PRACTICE SESSION

Assume a relaxed but alert posture as described above. The following is a breath-retention exercise. Remember, the moment you feel dizzy or lightheaded, stop the exercise and breathe normally. With practice, you will develop the capacity to assimilate the energy of these breathing techniques.

Place a notebook near you. Write down any physical and/or emotional changes you experience during the session. Tap into the body/mind. Training for increased sport performance means elevating your body wisdom.

- Perform a slow Cleansing Breath, inhaling through the nose for five counts, holding it for five counts, and exhaling through the mouth for five counts. Do three or more sets.

  Take three full, deep breaths.
- Perform a slow Filling Breath, inhaling through the nose for five counts, exhaling through the nose for five counts, then holding the breath for five counts. Do three or more sets.

  Take three full, deep breaths.
- Perform a slow Cleansing Breath, inhaling through the nose for five counts, holding it for five counts, exhaling through the mouth for five counts, then holding it for five counts. Do three or more sets.

  Take five long breaths.

Experimenting with the above teachings represents another step toward cultivating that beautiful, sweeping exchange of the universe into and out of our being. Many ways exist to use the breath for personal health and athletic progress. Since it so easy to forget mindful breathing, I will outline specific techniques in this book to make sure your breath awareness continues to progress. For now, pay attention to the breath as you continue to read this book. In doing so, not only will you be nourishing your physical health, but you will also be promoting the most powerful site of power: the present moment.

POSTURE

Posture is about being human. It is our most intimate guru. Body-centered therapists like Alexander Lowen, Moshe Feldenkrais, and Ron Kurtz have contributed careful years of study to pioneer the transpersonal aspects of posture. They were among the first to reveal how posture influences our well-being. Like breath awareness, postural integration profoundly affects our health and athletic performance.

Doris Lessing said, "All sanity depends on this: that it should be a delight ... to stand upright, knowing the bones are moving easily under the flesh." As a nation, we have come to accept that sitting slouched and walking stooped over is natural, especially as we age. We endorse that it is somehow okay to be mindless about posture. Well, no student of Wholistic Fitness subscribes to such lame theories!

How we move reflects how we think and feel. As we cultivate our posture, we cultivate our attitude. Through postural awareness, we can achieve equanimity and receptivity to the life force. Our self-esteem expands. One of the best reasons for posture work is to keep our minds anchored in the present moment. The Lifestyle Principles are a path toward athletic enlightenment, and any form of enlightenment requires being present. "Self-observation," said Dennis Lewis, "is the beginning of transformation."

HONED BONES

No matter which winter sports you do, posture is the most crucial factor for performance and enjoyment. Most great winter-sports athletes seem graced with a natural arrangement of bones and joints that allows them distinct advantage over their competitors. Think of Alberto Tomba, Vegard Ulvang, Mike Richter, Shaun Palmer, or Picabo Street. Each of these great winter-sport champions has created a postural sense of what works most efficiently.

When I first began this work, I was one of the few personal trainers who emphasized the concept of structural integrity, or the solidity of the musculoskeletal system. My emphasis on strengthening the whole before training the specifics has driven away more than one client. Many athletes refuse to strength train their entire body, thinking it will make them muscle-bound or too heavy. They quit my approach and jump into a sport-specific program. Weeks, months, or even years later, they often come back to me … injured. Without structural integrity, the joints of the body are prone to inflammation and injury. Only one fitness quality will improve structural integrity and save your long-term joint health and sport performance: posture.

Posture? Why not strength training or flexibility? Without proper postural aware-

ness, strength training, flexibility, or bodywork will not work. If you begin a strength-training or cardiovascular program in poor alignment, you will just be "cementing" your poor posture.

When we work out, we subject our joints to many forces: torsional, tensile, shearing, and compressive. Most winter sports are dangerous to the joints. Broken bones or torn ligaments are too often the symbol of the alpine skier. Unfortunately, the association of these injuries and alpine skiing is accurate, though unnecessary. Many people on a ski vacation have not prepared their joint strength for the high-speed physics inherent to the sport. And to expect an untrained joint to sustain the forces incurred by doing any winter sport is foolish. As we will learn later, injuries are an important guru. They teach us hard lessons about what we need to learn the most. Usually the teaching behind injuries points toward a lack of wholeness. There is a saying along the spiritual journey, "The truth only hurts when it ought to."

POSTURAL WISDOM

What do I mean by "wise" posture? Wise posture means that the body is in alignment and is stable. When I perform a postural analysis with an athlete, it's quite easy to see which areas of the body are tight (or "holding") and which are weak. Many skiers have a posterior pelvic tilt, indicative of tight hamstrings and weak hip flexors.

Nordic skiers and ice climbers have retracted shoulder girdles from overused back muscles and undertrained chest muscles. Therein lies the problem of conventional, sport-specific training compared with wholistic training. Whenever a particular muscle group is used repeatedly, the posturally shortened muscles become tight while the lengthened muscles become loose. Flexibility is lost, and the imbalance results in undercoordinated movement patterns, creating greater injury risk.

My responsibility as a coach is to identify these muscle imbalances and create a long-term fitness plan to bring them into alignment. The first step is bringing postural awareness to the student. I teach a "neutral alignment," which means adjusting the body so that the weight-bearing joints fall within the body's line of gravity.

I usually coach posture while the student holds a "natural" standing habit. I say "habit" because most of us stand and walk habitually. Habits are not to be cultivated in Wholistic Fitness. There is no such thing as a good habit in this work. By definition, a habit is something mechanical and unconscious. Habits get athletes hurt or killed. I am quite serious. There is no way I would have survived ten years of elite-level backcountry, extreme sports if I had chosen to do things out of habit. Awareness is what has kept me alive. In tennis, one can get away with committing unforced errors. In winter sports, especially extreme ones, you can die. That is why I am taking the time in

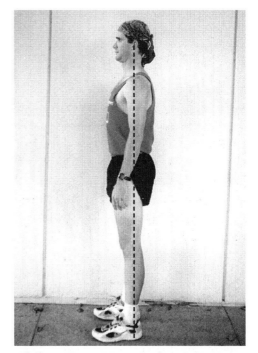

Wholistic Fitness Master Student, Racin' Jason Williams demonstrates an optimal standing alignment. Dotted line indicates alignment of ear, shoulder, hip, knee, and ankle.

these opening chapters to drill these ideas and techniques of awareness into you.

SERIAL DISTORTION

Most of our "natural" postures are in a state of misalignment that can lead to *serial distortion*. An example of serial distortion is a knock-kneed posture. Everything in the body is interconnected. If one part of the body wears down, the body parts around it compensate. This is what gave birth to the chiropractic saying, "As above, so below. As below, so above."

Stand sideways in front of a mirror. Be honest and stand as if you were waiting in a line at the grocery store. If you are like most people, you might have a forward head, rounded shoulders, accentuated lower-back curvature, locked-out knees, and pronated feet. Am I right? Don't feel bad. You've probably never been taught about posture until now! Instead of learning valuable, long-term fitness lessons like postural awareness in Phys. Ed. class in school, we did "jumping jacks." Poor posture is not your fault, but the choice to improve conscious posture is up to you. Do you want to take responsibility for improving your posture and, in turn, your life and sport performance?

BASIC POSTURE CLINIC

This do-it-yourself posture clinic teaches a part-to-whole progression to attain proper postural alignment. I often coach "from the earth up." Thus, step number one identifies where you should place your feet.

1. Stance. Allow your upper thighs to fall naturally down from the pelvic joint. Stand with your toes aligned under each knee, pointing straight ahead. This stance should be narrower than shoulder width for most people. It maintains the Q-angle, the most healthful angle formed by the femur and the pull of the patellar, or kneecap, ligaments.

2. Foot pressure. Now bring your awareness to the bottom of your feet. Feel the earth beneath. Allow the heels to be light. You should feel like you're about to tip forward. Now wiggle your toes up and down to shift your bodyweight toward the mid-foot.

3. Knees. Keep a slight bend at the knees. Never stand on hyperextended knees. Instead, "track" the knees so that they travel directly over the toes when they are flexed (bent).

4. Pelvic control. Position the center of your hips over your heels. Be aware of any anterior or posterior pelvic tilting; the former occurs when the butt sags down, the latter when the arch in the lower back is exaggerated. Try to keep the pelvis positioned between these two extremes, in a neutral position.

5. Heart center. Make sure the heart is in front of your hips. Drop an imaginary plumb line from your heart. Do your hips interfere with the line? If so, push them back and rotate the pelvis downward. The heart = power and love. The hips = fear. In the body/mind tradition, lead from power and love, not fear.

6. Shoulders. Gently squeeze or "pinch" your shoulder blades together. This keeps the back of the heart (the center of relationship energy) open and clear. Keep your shoulder girdle dropped; don't hunch your shoulders or allow them to "creep" forward.

7. Head. Position the head as if it is being

suspended from above. The head should be buoyant, the chin just a little heavy. Do not retract or protract the jaw. Keep your eyes soft and your spine straight. By "soft eyes" I mean to say, let the light of the day flow *into* your eyes. See what happens.

Keep working with the above guidelines until your new posture feels more comfortable. Holding correct alignment arises naturally with time and practice. This may take several months. Don't be discouraged—you are reversing years of unconscious posture! Suddenly you will realize how much effort is required to walk, sit, and stand with mindfulness and gracefulness. It is not enough, however, to be aware of your posture for a moment, then forget about it. From this point on, every workout must revolve around postural awareness. In staying focused on good posture, we attain stability.

Wholistic Fitness uses Lifestyle Principle #1, Breath and Posture, as the primary anchor for developing and maintaining structural and energetic integrity. When practiced consistently, this principle strengthens our connection between the emotional and physical planes. It will also allow you to reap the most benefit from Principle Number Two.

Wholistic Fitness® Lifestyle Principle #2: Mindfulness

According to Wholistic Fitness, mindfulness is the practice of being present. This is incredibly important to health, fitness, and sport performance. If we are not present, we are caught in a continuous stream of random thoughts and assorted fictions of the mind. This chattering, uncontrolled mind is what some spiritual traditions term "monkey mind." Like a monkey, the undisciplined mind is constantly reaching out for new branches, grasping here and there for the next form of ego entertainment. When we are not mindful, contraction and tension accumulate throughout the body/mind/spirit. Without mindfulness, we cannot receive the presence of the moment, be it the energy of a child's smile, the power of a snowy summit, or the kiss of windswept sun across our face.

On the other hand, when we are mindful, we create inner spaciousness and calm. Mindfulness training allows us to become masters of life. As Ron Kurtz has said, "Mastery is the natural result of mindfulness."

We may intellectually understand the need for a more peaceful state of being and the value of being present, but rational understanding does not impart bodily or emotional comprehension. We may say to ourselves, "Oh, I get it. If I am not being mindful when I am listening to my child, then I am not being present for her. That means, I am not really with her at all." This realization is profound, but often fleeting. Inevitably, the myriad of things "needing to be done" snaps us away from mindfulness and soon we are again lost in a hurried state.

SHERRY'S NEW VISION

This is where things get very interesting for athletes. I teach mindfulness as the intermediate lifestyle principle because cultivating it has pragmatic benefits for everyday life, such as not misplacing keys, following through on paperwork, or driving safely, for example. As mindfulness practice increases, we begin to realize that our focus in sport becomes more accurate and persevering. Sherry Jones, a student of mine from Bayfield, Colorado, talks about how mindfulness has transformed her workouts: "The most valuable thing I have learned during this training cycle was learning to pay attention and not let my mind constantly wander to the past and future (well, at least sometimes). I had to focus on what I was doing, especially in strength training, instead of going on autopilot as I used to."

AUTOPILOT

I see many athletes on what Sherry calls autopilot, and it's a shame. They have no spiritual liaison with their workouts. Many people are so zoned out listening to their Walkmans or to their chattering minds that there is no way universal truth or insight can be delivered to them. Because of our techniques, the student of Wholistic Fitness cannot go on automatic pilot during his or her workout. Thus, an awakening occurs. We see the light of transpersonal fitness. We see how mindfully performing mundane tasks translates into improved sport performance via our improved ability to stay present in the moment and attain what psychologist Abraham Maslow would term a "peak performance," when we merge into the harmony of being. A magic arises as we practice mindfulness. Tasks once considered boring by our ego are transformed into moments of joyful serenity and points of power. This is what Kahlil Gibran spoke about in *The Prophet*:

> And to love life through labor is to be
> intimate with life's inmost secret ... Work
> is love made visible.
>   And if you cannot work with love but
> only with distaste, it is better that you
> should leave your work and sit at the
> gate of the temple and take alms of those
> who work with joy.

It's funny how as our society gets more chaotic and "entertaining" we get more bored with it all. The root of our boredom is a lack of mindfulness. As Sherry wrote in her second Wholistic Fitness Cycle Summation, "Being exposed to these lifestyle principles and the variety of training activities made for a very exciting cycle. Definitely no time to get bored." Things are only interesting when we are interested. Through our daily training, we may realize that it is through mindfulness that we escape the mind. Now listen closely, because for athletes, this "no-mind" state could well lead you to attain your next level of sport-performance breakthrough.

Mindfulness training allows us to become masters of life. Photo courtesy of George Neuman archives.

MINDFULNESS LEADS TO NO MIND, A GOOD THING

A cliff, colored by featherlike patches of lichen, sweeps into the sky. Swallows gracefully dare sandstone crowns. Each part of the scene is a profound creation of the divine source. We also possess this simplicity of pure beingness, though human intellect contracts our sense of it. It is this pure beingness that many athletes want. In current terms, an athlete tapped into this unedited, spontaneous flow is "in the zone." Witness Patrick Roy and John Vanbiesbrouck, the goaltenders in the celebrated game four of the 1996 Stanley Cup finals. Their mental fitness was the stuff legends consist of—triple overtime in the championship! Dozens of shots were fired at them by the opposing teams. One goal-tending error—by either goalie—meant failure for their entire

team and their long season of effort. Yet both men reacted flawlessly to ninety mile per hour slapshots and blinding wrist shots. They were, without a doubt, in the zone. Their performance that night was not only love but poetry made visible.

OLD HATS, NEW CLOUDS

When you follow the path of your desire, enthusiasm and emotion, keep your mind in control. Don't let it pull you compulsively into disaster. The best way to control your mind is not to have a mind in the first place. Many pop psychologists and sport "experts" write about how to reach this state of athletic enlightenment. Not as well known is the fact that attaining beingness is old hat to many spiritual traditions.

A meditation teacher once tested me after several hours of sustained sitting during a *sesshin*, or multiday meditation intensive in the Zen custom.

"I understand you are an athlete and a coach."

"I am only a beginner," I replied, feeling my ego swell in the knowledge that this respected teacher had heard of me.

"Show me the coach's mind that sees each athlete as the bird out of its cage."

It has become a trend among the athletic populace to apply varied sorts of mental techniques to enhance performance. Some athletes wire subliminal audio messages into their brains to impart positive affirmations on how great they can become. Others pump loud rock music into their ears to get "psyched." Some athletes pray. I recall two weightlifters during a competition. Before venturing to the lifting platform, they would slap each other in the face "to get their inner power worked up." Whatever.

It could be valuable to test any or all of these techniques. Each supposedly strengthens the mind for optimal performance. Yet each of these procedures will keep the bird in its cage. I coach from a different space.

DANCING SWALLOWS

The ultimate mental state for performance may be what some Eastern traditions term No Mind, a restoration of the natural quietness of the mind. No mind is the mind that does not chatter or create egocentric illusion. Thus, our bodies are free to process intuitive, simple, unimpaired athletic beauty.

Note that I use the word "process" instead of a word like "execute." As with the cliff swallows and the lichen, our bodies reflect absolute truth. We have innate wisdom made up of infinite possibilities and timeless capacity. As athletes, our responsibility is to relax our mental activity so that we open our spontaneous ingenuity. Out of no mind, we dance. When we dance, there is no hesitation, no wavering. There is a fantastic saying by Rumi, the acclaimed Sufi poet, "Dance until you shatter yourself. Men of God dance in their bones."

To reach no mind, do nothing, but *be* everything. Practice stillness. Sit or move, but do not think. Become your breath, and random thought will eventually tire of itself. Dissolve into and merge with the breath, and your mind will relax its dualistic clinch. Recently in the gym, I was working out with a promising young student, Scott. He was struggling with the technique of Repetition Jerks. Instead of jerking the bar overhead using the full-body velocity of his spirit, he was pushing the barbell upward with the strength of his arms. His form was faltering, devoid of spirit and full of overthinking. As he approached his next set, I slapped on another 10 pounds of weight.

"We need more weight so you rely on speed and spirit instead of muscles," I told him. "Do this weight."

Scott looked doubtful knowing how he had struggled with the previous weight. "I'll try …"

"Don't try. Just do."
No mind. Just do.

The wind blows hard among the pines
Toward the beginning
Of an endless past.
Listen: you've heard everything.
　　　　　　　—Shinkichi Takahashi

Everybody hurries in today's society. The reason we rush so much? To be happy. We have been inculcated to believe that happiness is always in the future. Even the Bill of Rights guarantees us the "right to pursue happiness." Not to "be" happy but to "pursue" happiness! Mindfulness practice,

on the other hand, teaches that genuine happiness must reside in the present moment. It cannot linger in some future reality, nor in some amount of accumulated money or material possessions. As mindfulness teacher and psychologist Charles Tart says, "The constant pursuit of happiness in the future is just perpetuating illusions."

Of the Four Lifestyle Principles that lead to transformation, Principle #2, mindfulness, is the most critical for deepening a metaphysical comprehension of all Wholistic Fitness teachings. It also permits a state of mental absorption that gives birth to Principle #3.

Wholistic Fitness® Lifestyle Principle #3: Appropriate Action

Appropriate action represents the most advanced form of lifestyle practice. It is the practice of performing action—mental, emotional, or physical—from contemplative integrity. Remember the trick of counting to ten after stubbing your toe so you don't cuss out of habit or reaction? Well, appropriate action is similar. It means taking a breath before eating junk food or gossiping; it means asking yourself "is this appropriate to becoming a better human being?" Before we think, feel, or do something, we allow that action to be a result of

inner awareness. In Wholistic Fitness, we don't do something to *achieve* something; we do it as an expression of our highest self. Our highest self represents our balanced state of awareness—a balance between ego and soul.

How exactly does one recognize that an action is the result of inner awareness or allow it to be so? The answer to this logical question will arise from your intuitive wisdom that will naturally develop using the techniques presented in this book. Much of appropriate action is common sense, which will become refined through meditation and practice along the path of Wholistic Fitness.

The fourteenth Dalai Lama, Tenzin Gyatso, articulated beautifully the epitome of appropriate action. He said, "Before performing any action or speaking any word, ask this question: 'Is it kind, true, and helpful?'" Can you see just how advanced this principle is? Through self-observation and the repetition of a mantralike question—"Is what I am doing right now appropriate for my highest self?"—we begin to think and behave differently. We discover that things or people we once thought important or "cool" or meaningful lose their appeal and are replaced by something far more precious: self-cultivation. Don't learn by trial-and-error; learn by self-observation. This type of fitness training is completely different from the body- and ego-oriented approaches common in today's personal-fitness scene. In Wholistic Fitness we focus

on the wearing away of the ego, not the on-going construction of it! Live life nakedly, "with no gloves on," as Rinpoche Trungpa used to say, instead of living an illusionary life. Trying to chase happiness by attaining new things or new habits only sets us on a wheel of frustration. Appropriate action is difficult practice, but it is the most powerful tool for self-transformation in the Wholistic Fitness system.

We cannot learn this principle without sufficient training in the former two principles, breath and posture, and mindfulness. Why? Because appropriate action must come from inner spaciousness, not a cluttered mind. Once we discover the joy that comes from performing each action as a step toward our highest self, we will have little desire for superfluous antics of the ego such as overeating, drugging, unhealthy relationships, or laziness. Appropriate action helps us create an inner environment conducive to personal growth.

Wholistic Fitness® Lifestyle Principle #4: Practice

Dogen Zenji, an important Japanese Zen master of the eleventh century, said, "Practice and enlightenment are one." In one sense, the fourth principle involves simply practicing the other Lifestyle Principles: breath and posture, mindfulness, and appropriate action. Until the spirit of our personality animates these principles, they remain but inert fabrications of the intellect. If we practice them with sincere effort, however, self-transformation suddenly becomes a reality from which we live each day. Qualities that once seemed far away, like inner peace, intuitive wisdom, equanimity, clarity, and profound appreciation of life, become allies along our journey. Take each moment as it comes. Do not prejudge it as good or bad, happy or sad, beneficial or adversarial. Instead, practice receiving the moment. Our next lesson toward becoming a better human being lies in the acceptance of this instant.

We do not practice these principles because they are good for us or will make us champion athletes. We do not practice them to attain happiness or riches or to be more alluring to others. Nor do we practice these principles to attain mystic powers or divine celestial information, although these may manifest from our practice. The spirit of practice is to practice for its own sake. Simply use whatever comes our way as a personal enrichment workout.

NOTHING MATTERS, BUT EVERYTHING COUNTS

Early in my spiritual journey a phrase came to me during meditation that still holds truth for me: "Nothing matters, but everything counts." Our practice is nothing special, because nothing really matters in a universal sense. Ten million years from now, will it really matter if you brushed your teeth mindfully this morning? Yet to our own path everything does count because that is all we have. Perseverance in daily practice imparts unwavering even-mindedness through turmoil and stress. It allows us to keep a wide perspective, to witness the comedy of our errors without buying too seriously into the drama of it all.

The practice principle also has a second meaning. It means the practice of the Five Fitness Disciplines: kinesthetic, strength, cardiovascular, meditation, and nutrition. Study of the Wholistic Fitness system introduces the philosophical and interactive teachings of these Five Fitness Disciplines, which have changed the lives of hundreds of people for nearly two decades. The inherent power you gain by the practice of the Five Fitness Disciplines is truly a remarkable experience of personal growth.

3

The Five Fitness Disciplines

*"Mysticism is the basis of all true science and the person who can
no longer stand rapt in awe is as good as dead already."*
—Albert Einstein

MAIN DRIVE

Until the mid-1990s, the Five Fitness Disciplines were the main drive of Wholistic Fitness. When I created this system, these five essentials produced their own dance; I merely listened to the beat. Then, as now, many who come to this path already practice several—if not all—of the Five Fitness Disciplines. I think this has contributed to the success of my approach. Wholistic Fitness feels very "familiar" to many people. According to spiritual principles, this sensation of familiarity is an ethereal manifestation of universal truth, or dharma. Even when I edit the spiritual slant and words from my writings or talks about Wholistic Fitness, people contact me regarding the spiritual strength and underlying metaphysics of the material. It is obvious that Wholistic Fitness operates on a different realm than most fitness training methods.

ZEAL LIFE

During the '80s, when the Five Fitness Disciplines were the mainstay of my work, I continued to distill and extract what I felt were the most effective aspects from a diverse array of scientific, spiritual, and athletic traditions. I also added unique, self-created techniques to produce a comprehensive, versatile, and balanced personal training system.

As the Five Fitness Disciplines became tempered by years of use, it was evident that Wholistic Fitness was functioning as a spiritual resource, opening doors of awareness for its followers. It was not and is not a rigid program that handcuffs students into my particular preferences. The philosophical and structural tenets of Wholistic Fitness stands on their own merits. This is why I refer to "students" instead of "clients." The word "study" is derived from the word "zeal." Ask any Master Student

Through the discipline of training, life bears many dreams. The author as he dreams his way through mile 65 at the Leadville 100 Mile MTB Race.

of Wholistic Fitness and he or she will affirm the fact: Wholistic Fitness study requires much zeal! (To attain a Master Student "Inka," or certification, requires at least one consistent year of formal Wholistic Fitness study.) This is not a hand-holding, cheerleading program in which you become a disciple of the leader. On the contrary, it is an established, proven path that openly welcomes those whose intent is to learn more about themselves through fitness training. The Five Fitness Disciplines function as a natural filter to sift the spiritual warriors from the "wannabes." I

have often said, "You don't come to Wholistic Fitness, it comes to you."

Why did I call them the Five Disciplines? Because the word discipline essentially means learning. This singular quality is the hallmark of any champion athlete or spiritual warrior. If you do not enjoy the intensity of learning, you will not enjoy Wholistic Fitness; it's that simple. Do you have the self-discipline to be a free spirit?

THE FAMILIARITY AND UNFAMILIARITY OF THE FIVE FITNESS DISCIPLINES

As a result of the fitness scene of the '80s, scores of people practiced strength training in the gym and did some sort of aerobic (or cardiovascular) work. Most of these folks were at least aware of a need to stretch and many did some form of stretching, yoga, or dance. Granted, women were more conscious of this area of fitness than men, but by and large, three of the Five Disciplines were already being practiced by many people when I introduced Wholistic Fitness as a professional training system. The components familiar to fitness enthusiasts were strength training, cardiovascular training, and kinesthetic training.

Less common were people who incorporated healthy nutritional patterns into their lifestyle. And the pack thinned considerably when it came to meditation. Very few applicants already practiced consistent meditation. To this day, many Wholistic

Fitness students are quick to respond to the strength-training workouts and highly effective cardiovascular prescriptions. Even the kinesthetic routines are loved by both women and men. Yet the most challenging of the Five Disciplines remain the two softest, most "female" aspects of Wholistic Fitness: nutrition and meditation.

This fact does not surprise me. Where in our upbringing are we taught the value of nutrition and meditation? Our nutritional upbringing, for example, is a joke. As schoolchildren we are force-fed knowledge of nutrition by food corporations who spend millions of dollars to make sure elementary school children are reading about how good beef and milk and pork is for "our growing bodies"! Since television is the main educational vehicle for American children, those same food companies make certain that young minds accept that fast, junk, processed, refined, or flesh food saturated with poisons is "good" food. Few of us were raised to respect and honor food. By the time we are teenagers, we are so distanced from the act of killing the animals we feast upon, so far removed from the act of growing and cultivating the vegetables and grains we eat that we possess an unutterable insensitivity toward those lives that give us our own life. This thoughtless demeanor sets a paradigm of ignorance that affects our entire way of being. Far from being clever and ingenious, our mass production and distribution of processed, frozen, refrigerated, enhanced,

and refined "food" has created an overfat, undernourished, and tactless populace.

What of meditation? Why include meditation as a crucial factor for creating long-term health and optimum sport performance? Because genuine health and certainly sport performance pivot on a wholistic understanding of the human being. The very name of our species underlines my point. We are human *beings*. We are not human *doings*. Physical action is a by-product of our mind, which also includes adjuncts such as imagination, visualization, and neurological patterning.

There is no separation of mind and body; rather we function as a psychosomatic unit, where mental fitness accounts for the majority of our success. For instance, we are nervous about something, and our stomach gets upset. Mind and body, very simple to understand. Or we imagine eating a raw lemon and begin to salivate to neutralize the acid of the lemon. Again, mind and body. Much of sport performance relies upon controlling the mind. Note that I did not say control *over* the mind. The nature of the mind is such that attempted dictatorship over it will always fail. We do not wish to suppress the flow of mind, but rather direct its power. This direction of mental capacity is what I call focus and what a Zen Buddhist might term one-pointedness. One-pointedness does not exclude the world, but uses environmental energy to merge more fully into the object of concentration. For instance, this means really listening to another person speak instead of just "hearing" them talk while your mind is already busy fashioning an answer. Thus Wholistic Fitness training, though it prioritizes mental fitness, is not a mind-over-body attack but rather a mind-with-body philosophy.

TANGERINE DREAMS

Our very own National Mental Health Association informs us that over 46 percent of American adults consider depression a health problem. Forty-three percent consider depression to be a personal weakness. If mental fitness is such a problem, why don't we grow up learning mental training, which is simply another word for meditation? It is not taught in our conventional school system. We don't learn any vocabulary that provides us with the ABCs of mental fitness. Other cultures, such as the Tibetan one, provide such elementary spiritual education to all youngsters. Religion, by the way, is not meditation. The function of organized religion is to provide answers to spiritual questions. The moment we organize spirituality, however, we destroy its nature.

Our medical system, erroneously labeled "health care," is not so much health care (which would certainly include the Five Fitness Disciplines) as disease control. I recall hearing that most Prozac™ prescriptions are written by doctors within ten minutes of meeting their clients; how many medical doctors prescribe meditation to enhance their patients' well-being?

What about the relationship between meditation and sports and fitness training? Here we come closer to receiving some education on how to prepare our psychological health. It is encouraging that most fitness magazines and books now offer a few clues about meditation. However, if you ask your personal trainer if he or she consistently sits in formal meditation, the answer is often buffeted by a rationalization, "Oh, well, not really, but my workouts are a form of meditation." As we will see later, such justification does not pan out.

We discover a growing movement toward meditation as a personal fitness discipline, yet much of that movement is lip service. Most authors of magazine articles on meditation do not meditate. Even yoga instructors, who know that meditation, or *Dhyana*, is inherent to yogic practice, often do not practice what they preach. I have found that most fitness experts love to talk about meditation but rarely practice it themselves. I know of highly paid health instructors at expensive yoga and health retreats who have colleagues sneak in espressos to quell their caffeine addictions. We have a long way to go before meditation becomes a pillar of personal fitness. Until that changes, we risk becoming a pill-popping, ego-oriented society devoid of personal integrity and spiritual prowess.

FINDING YOGA

When you study Wholistic Fitness, you are training several physical, mental, and spiritual variables simultaneously. The Five Fitness Disciplines interweave easily with the Four Lifestyle Principles to produce a unique yoga, or union. No longer will you see sport performance training as something extra to do during time off from work. No longer will you put off personal health and fitness "until the kids are grown up." In fact, the most profound training effect of Wholistic Fitness requires the grist of everyday life in order to flourish. That is the principle behind the Wholistic Fitness saying, "My workout is everywhere."

The strength required to live life as a spiritual athlete is tremendous, and the wind blows strongest against those who stand tallest. However, the beauty of traveling this inner journey results in immediate improvements in self-discipline and self-cultivation. The moment we begin to work on ourselves is when we begin to know ourselves. And to know ourselves is to discover where our mastery resides. Michelangelo said, "If people knew how hard I worked to get my mastery, it wouldn't seem so wonderful after all." To discover and tap the body's performance wisdom, we must be willing to dig deep into ourselves to peel away the layers of ego-conditioned illusions and fear-based emotions. I call this getting rid of the baggage. During the digging we may find many obstacles, but, we may find buried treasures as well. The best way to improved long-term sport performance and a meaningful life is to go right through, not around, your inner obstacles. Zen teacher Dainin Katagiri taught, "Even though you may not like monsters, still, there is some reason they exist."

If you think you have the strength to cultivate your higher self, read further. If at this point in your reading, you think that this approach is too far-out there for a book on sports performance, I will be honest with you: You are not ready for this particular path. Choose another. Remember, you don't come to Wholistic Fitness, it comes to you. This book has landed in your reality because certain spiritual truths are at operation in your life. These truths may be masquerading in the form of sports performance, but spiritual truths they are.

Answer the call. Join us who delight in using performance training as a form of spiritual growth.

Life is either a daring adventure or nothing. To keep our faces toward change and behave like free spirits in the presence of fate is strength undefeatable.

—Helen Keller,
Let Us Have Faith, 1940

Part II

The Five Wholistic Fitness® Disciplines

photo by Roy Wilkinson

4

Discipline 1: Kinesthetic Training

"Think with the whole body."
—Taisen Deshimaru

MORE THAN PHYSICAL

More than a physical fitness component, kinesthetic training is a discipline of physical, mental, and spiritual expansion. In the Wholistic Fitness system, it is a primary discipline that expresses our alignment, posture, and grace. Kinesthetic training also imparts a wonderful, uncoachable transcendent experience. This experience, popularly referred to in sport literature as "being in the zone" refers to a mystical sensation of sudden "oneness," or a complete merging into the moment.

In my writings, I have defined kinesthetic training as "the way the body senses itself." To be classified as kinesthetic activity, a practice should:

- engage whole-body movement;
- involve the breath;
- emphasize meditative facets; and
- have a significant degree of volitional motor-skill involvement.

Kinesthetic training is a discipline of physical, mental, and spiritual expansion. Photo by Marc Romanelli.

37

Some winter sports are very kinesthetic in nature: ice climbing, snowboarding, and alpine skiing. However, winter endurance sports, such as skate skiing, also demand a lot of kinesthesia. Nonsnow activities, or *dryland training*, that increase our winter sport kinesthetic abilities include dance classes, hatha yoga, gymnastics, and martial arts. These activities share a common denominator: They impart sensory or proprioceptive literacy. For athletes, each kinesthetic workout should enhance overall athleticism as well.

Before I discuss the specific physical benefits of kinesthetic training and how it will improve sport performance, I want you to understand that Wholistic Fitness stresses kinesthetic training because of its transpersonal qualities. One such quality is surrender, which includes the type of softness and spiritual receptivity that comes from listening to our bodies, accepting the signals it provides, and, finally, not being afraid to express whatever comes through the dance of our movement. Many of us try very hard to achieve success in areas of our life experience. Kinesthetic training teaches us to try softer, not harder. It is only through softness that our most magnificent and most powerful energy can manifest itself.

Classic examples of surrender can be found in several winter sports, for instance, ice climbing. When leading a difficult ice climb, a climber may easily overgrip her ice tools. This fear-based action wastes a lot of energy through the contraction of the shoulder, arm, and forearm musculature and causes the climber to move rigidly and robotlike (or not at all!). Moreover, overgripping commonly leads to a wicked forearm pump that makes performance less elegant and certainly more dangerous. Through experience, a climber can learn to move through this fear-based attitude and adopt a love-based attitude, which promotes graceful ascension and flawless execution.

MORE SOFT, LESS STRENGTH

More than strength training, the success of an athlete often depends on kinesthetic training. More than a fitness quality that allows you to gain something, kinesthetic training enables you to release something that is already within. I want to make sure I get this point across because many winter athletes come to me seeking to gain something from their training when most of their practice should be centered on releasing something. That something is their own expressive, creative energy that has been covered up by emotional restrictions. Kinesthetic training is the discipline I use to facilitate this transition into a new level of performance.

Alpine skiing, telemark skiing, and snowboarding are also excellent kinesthetic workshops. These sports, contrary to popular instruction, depend more upon release and surrender to the mountain than "attacking" it or "conquering" it. To telemark ski a steep couloir in the backcountry requires a profound sense of what Dan Millman, in his book *The Inner Athlete*, terms "nonresistance," or "flowing with the natural currents of life and making use of whatever circumstances arise." Millman goes on to say that this going-with-the-flow attitude requires "great sensitivity and intelligence." Those who ski the steeps truly recognize just how instantaneous this great sensitivity and intelligence must be, especially when the obstacles include cliffs, avalanches, and bone-crushing falls down rocky gullies! I'll say it again: Winter sports are not like tennis or golf. Mistakes in the outdoor arena, such as being too physically and spiritually rigid, can result in severe consequences.

No human being has ever overcome any mountain. Not Sir Edmund Hillary, not Joe Brown, not Alberto Tomba, not Shaun Palmer, not Wholistic Fitness student Marc Twight. At their best these talented athletes, and others like them, have danced with a mountain, but they have never conquered it. A British Columbia native people have a saying: "Nature is never conquered but one must find one's own strength within her." In my best ascents of peaks and frozen waterfalls, I have never felt particularly kinglike. In fact, on the summits of my most difficult climbs I have most realized utter humility

in the universe. I would like to think all great winter athletes have felt a similar twinge. It is very important for our long-term health to know our place in the universe.

RETURN TO YOUR ROOTS

One of my earliest and most influential kinesthetic teachers was a Native American friend. He bestowed on me a tremendous teaching tool: simplicity. I recall him most often during question-and-answer time at seminars. Typically, a workshop or seminar student will ask, "What's the best way to stay flexible?" I'll reply, "Renounce your furniture." Get rid of chairs and tables. Reduce the amount of desk-top work. Take mealtimes seated cross-legged on the floor. Learn the Asian squat and make use of it. Move with the earth instead of on top of it. Dare yourself to be free! Living close to the earth accomplishes more for long-term muscle and joint flexibility than all the techniques, books, and videos combined.

This earth-friendly lifestyle clicked for me during my years as a climber. For a decade my home was the earth. My base camp was my pickup truck. Mine was a life without clutter: no tables, no chairs. It was simple, basic, and beautiful. Squatting or sitting on the earth was natural and full of humility. Oh, how good it felt to the lower back and hips! Now, retired from climbing, I must doggedly practice kinesthetic

Wholistic Fitness offers the following kinesthetic routines:

Short Form = Basic. Emphasizes lower back and rotary trunk muscles. Spiritual aspects include release of established fears.

Medium Form = Intermediate. Involves more hamstring and beginning gymnastic-type of flexibility. Our most popular and reliable form. Particularly effective for endurance athletes. Spiritual aspects include an opening of the heart center.

Long Form = Advanced. All of the above plus Iyengar yoga – type balance movements. Spiritual aspects concentrate on emotional stability.

WhirlWind Dancer = Advanced. All of the above plus strength/balance moves. A special flow encourages pelvic openness. Energetically based choreography. Spiritual aspects focus on self-reliance.

Breathing Katas = Intermediate. Emphasis on breath and fluidity of movement. Improves earth-merging. Adaptable in nature: calming if you are too excited, energizing if you are feeling lethargic. Include Ten-Sho Breathing Kata and Ai Imawa Sitting Kata.

Ai Imawa Postures = Basic through Advanced. These ancient Taoist healing postures are the historical precursor to Tai Chi Chuan. Emphasis on breath, posture, earth-merging, and inner power development. Meditative as well as kinesthetic.

These forms are available on two Wholistic Fitness videos:

The 4 Kinesthetic Teachings of Wholistic Fitness. Short, Medium, and Long Forms plus the Ai Imawa Postures. This video is included with the purchase of our Basic Correspondence Training Program.

The WhirlWind Dancer. Ai Imawa Postures (non-instructional format), The Ai Imawa Sitting Kata, The WhirlWind Dancer Form, and Ten-Sho Breathing Kata.

training activities more than ever. When I am sitting in a chair behind a computer, the temptation and tendency to slouch and collapse my posture is great. My main sport now is bike racing, a purely locomotive sport without a natural full range of movement and very little "dance." I depend upon yoga and Wholistic Fitness flexibility routines to keep my muscles and joints open, but it is difficult to match the everyday ballet of the climbing lifestyle.

JOINT VENTURE

Kinesthetic training is a forte of the Wholistic Fitness system, designed to keep an athlete injury free and produce higher athletic performance. I have choreographed five Wholistic Fitness flexibility forms in a special sequence to maximize energetic development, spirit, and creativity. Any of these kinesthetic routines can be done fluidly, like a martial art *kata*, or held slowly, as in traditional hatha yoga. The beauty of these forms is that they can be done rapidly, when we don't have much time, or slowly, when we do. The combination is perfect, and hundreds of outdoor athletes have found their best friend—enhanced flexibility—through these forms.

Any aspect of the body inextricably affects and is affected by any/all other aspects of the body. When a client comes to me complaining of a knee injury, for example, I don't consider the knee as the source, but the symptom. From an energetic level, knees often reflect an unwillingness to change. A misaligned pelvis is the root of many knee inflammations or afflictions. I have come to agree with many structural bodyworkers that the postures we assume shape and condition our bodies. Often our lack of mindful posture translates into degenerative or poor body structure. Fortunately, through kinesthetic training we can change both the function and structure of our bodies into an aligned, healthful stance. According to Wholistic Fitness, kinesthetic fitness contains four elements, each of which can be trained to address bodily imbalances and thereby improve performance:

1. neural
2. muscular
3. skeletal
4. spiritual

Neural

Moshe Feldenkrais coined an excellent notion of differentiation, the sorting out of "good" movements and actions over the useless. He taught economy of motion. This is why we are discussing kinesthetic training before the other disciplines; we must rid ourselves of degenerative neural links like poor posture to rediscover our gracefulness and kinesthetic joy. If we are accustomed to poor posture, we don't even realize the extra tension and effort we exert. When we perform winter sports burdened by these degenerative postural habits, it is even more difficult to cull the inconsequential movements and energy from the beneficial. Recognizing our kinesthetic numbness is the first step in replacing that numbness with body sensitivity. The more awake our body is, the easier it becomes to execute effective, fluid movements and postural patterns instead of poor ones.

Muscular

Muscles are well fed by neural service. As we engage in a kinesthetic activity, say stretching or yoga, we are toning muscle via the neural pathway. Strength-training workouts, for example, rapidly improve motor skills. This is how Wholistic Fitness athletes can improve their specific winter-sport performances in the middle of summer! As we nourish the muscles through kinesthetic and strength training, we indirectly enhance sport-specific skills. When the snow falls and we begin practicing our winter sports, those specific skills are much faster to come "on line."

I recall a young nordic skier who wanted nothing more than to become a champion. This youngster ate, drank, and slept nordic skiing. The only thing was ... he did not have much coordination. He didn't seem able to master the integrated movements required of skate skiing. I would watch him put in many kilometers on the ski track, through snowstorm and sun. He spent a fortune on high-tech ski waxes, and he admirably signed up for skate-ski clinics. Yet, it wasn't clicking. This kid was in a kinesthetic cloud without a clue how to get out. One autumn day, I was riding back to town after mountain biking. I saw him roller skiing, getting his head start on another season of frustration. I approached him kindly and asked if he had a coach for the season and if not, would he consider working with me? Since I had solid competitive ski credentials and he knew a little about my work, he jumped at the chance. For his preseason training, I did not change anything in his cardiovascular training. Instead, I designed a strength-training program for him and prescribed our Medium Form flexibility routine, which he was to practice twice daily.

His transformation was dramatic. Within two weeks of the first snowfall, he was executing all the skate-skiing variations with confidence and what could very clearly be termed elegance! At the first race he placed second in his category. The lesson here is that all the sport-specific training in the world will not make up for a lack of synergy. Develop muscles, and nerves are developed. Develop nerves, and coordination is created. By training the neuromuscular system, we create a more efficient motor organization.

Skeletal

Kinesthetic activity must prioritize skeletal alignment. Pioneers of body-oriented therapies such as Ida Rolf, Moshe Feldenkrais, and Joseph Pilates pushed the idea that genuine freedom—emotional, mental, and physical—can only be attained through a discipline of alignment. Like any form of spiritual growth, Wholistic Fitness is ongoing self-study. This process gets boring, tiring, colorless, questionable, and tedious. It requires faith and trust in the process. Where is my posture; how is my alignment? These questions become a mantra to the Wholistic Fitness student. Remember, the goal of kinesthetic training is not for everyone to attain the same ideal of what good posture is, but to cultivate a body/mind/spirit that is free and balanced. It's about creating a body that is not placing undue stress on one area but is in alignment. Feldenkrais described this balanced,

With the Rio Grande River as background, the author performs a "Side Plank," a variation of "Vasisthasana," a yoga pose that requires a balance of strength and concentration. Photo by Scott Dupuis.

aligned state as "the potent posture." Inherent to beautiful performance in any sport is learning how to achieve an aligned state (mental and physical) that is most conducive to powerful, responsive action. Knowing where our alignment is at all times seems to come naturally for gifted athletes, but most of us must cultivate it through training. Fortunately, this training can be practiced during everyday life in any situation. In later chapters, I will describe specific techniques for learning how to attain this everyday kinesthetic training.

Spiritual

Conventional fitness methods do not address spirit as a trainable component of enhanced flexibility. They should. It is in the ancient traditions of the martial and yogic arts that we find time-proven kinesthetic truth. Both the martial artist and the yogin are taught moment-by-moment awareness, for in the act of being present we do not get caught up in mental drama. This mental rattling is not only degenerative to martial-arts performance, but it can actually be dangerous in the high-risk activity of some competitive or combative martial arts.

The yoga tradition has no combative aspect. In the holding of a yoga posture, or *asana*, one is taught to quiet the mind in order to quiet the posture, and vice versa. This quieting of the mind leads to emotional stability, a founding quality of the yogin's journey toward *samadhi,* or awakening, which is the target of many yoga traditions.

The spiritual training common to these two traditions is extremely helpful to the athlete interested in improving his or her approach to winter sports. Those athletes participating in riskier winter sports, such as mountaineering, ice climbing, or extreme skiing and snowboarding, should explore the sciences of martial and yogic arts to enhance their performance. Wholistic Fitness kinesthetic routines combine elements of both traditions to produce a balanced, systematic approach to flexibility training that, instead of ignoring the spiritual aspects of kinesthetic training, includes them as a pivotal principle.

SUMMARY OF KINESTHETIC TRAINING FOR THE WINTER ATHLETE

Kinesthetic training is the conditioning of our athletic expression. It is the study of suppleness in both mind and body. Common kinesthetic training modalities include stretching, flexibility routines, hatha yoga, dance, and martial arts. Receiving bodywork and massage are also forms of kinesthetic training, as they increase the way we sense, and thus relate with, our body.

For the winter athlete, kinesthetic training prevents injury by enhancing muscular and joint flexibility. It is also improves mental fitness by improving concentration, mental quietness, and emotional stability. Finally, kinesthetic training aids motivational abilities, as its softer aspects balance our energy and create a deeper emotional reservoir for creative—and thus athletic— inspiration. The best minute we spend in training is the one we invest in softness. Don't try harder. Try softer.

5

Discipline 2: Strength Training

"Resistance is the creator of all great things."
—Heraclitus

In my first book, *The Outdoor Athlete,* I admitted my obsession with super-strict lifting form and alignment in the gym. According to Wholistic Fitness philosophy, the gym is part yoga studio, part temple. Within these walls a transpersonal power borne from sweat-filled intensity and spiritual valor arises. There is no equivalent for the personal power and long-term health stemming from the practice of strength training.

Read these words from one of my students, Grant, who is from Canada. They are in response to a question regarding his strength-training workouts during his study of my "Cosmic Yang" program: "These workouts felt necessary. The workouts also gave me a sense of calm and peace during daily life. Finding the dance between effort and tension, tensionless effort. There were times in the gym when I was lifting heavier weights than ever before yet using less effort!" Later in the same Cycle Summation

From the gym, transpersonal power and spiritual valor arises. Farentinos Gym, Boulder, Colorado, in the mid-1980s. Photo by the author.

(a questionnaire that my students complete at the end of each training phase), Grant describes his response to one of our "favorite" strength training movements, the Jump Squat: "At one point while I was Jump Squatting, I began to cry. During this whole training cycle, I was always bursting into tears it seems. There was profound joy in this moment of Jump Squatting. I felt compassion and the acceptance of others who do not fit into my vision of 'who' I should give my time to. 'Less beautiful people' if you will. In this Jump Squat moment, I learned that we must say 'yes to it all.'"

As you will learn, Wholistic Fitness is designed so that it affects the subtle energy system in the body. It does so in an "opening" manner, one conducive to spiritual awakening. In this chapter and the ones to follow, I will demonstrate why this transpersonal approach to training is such a beautiful and potent guru of sports performance.

ENERGETIC FOUNDATION

Let's begin at the energetic level, the foundation that is most often ignored. It is little wonder people have negative associations of lifting weights. Why, if I had to "lift" weights, I'd be bumming, too! In Wholistic Fitness we do not refer to the art of strength training as lifting weights. That particular word choice conveys a mechanical, herky-jerky image. Nor do we use the term weight training. Weights seem quite

well trained already. Our preferred word choice is strength training. Doesn't that sound and *feel* better? Strength training implies a wholistic sphere in which we can strengthen more than mere flesh. Every time we step into the gym, we strength train not only our physical body, but our mental focus, our emotional intelligence, our dreams, and our spirit. So from now on, use the words strength training in reference to this transformation. In doing so, a shift to a higher level of awareness remains intact.

STRUCTURE AND FUNCTION

Conventional training offers two reasons for athletes to strength train: to improve physical structure and function. Strength training improves the integrity of ligaments, tendons, and the muscle/fascia system. This strengthening of body structure is a form of health care. The preventive benefits of strength training often go unnoticed. For instance, the strength-trained skier is not as prone to joint inflammations or injuries after a long day on the slopes. And in the long term, the strength-trained athlete runs a far lower risk of joint degeneration.

Functional strength training involves using the gym to cause certain desired biochemical changes in the neuromuscular system. The bodyworker Thomas Hanna recognized a habituated state of muscular contractions and resistance deeply ingrained in our unconscious. Stemming from infancy, these habituated muscular patterns grow into energy-depleting postures. So accustomed we become to this poor posture that we forget easier, more fluid, more powerful ways to sit, stand, walk, and perform. Hanna termed this forgetfulness sensory-motor amnesia, or SMA. Since SMA was a learned response, he theorized, we can un-learn this excessive, degenerative way of being. How? By introducing full ranges of motion in a variety of ways to reawaken the sensory-motor complex. In other words, to become truly free at a functional level, we must introduce a basic and broad integration of neurological patterns. That is precisely what strength training achieves so quickly and profoundly—an integrated neurological pattern.

So these two reasons for strength training—improved structure and function—are the ones that conventional training promotes. In Wholistic Fitness we have a third reason: yoga.

YOGA

Yoga. As in union. Union of the mind and body; union of the separate self and the universal self. Yoga is another way in which to emphasize the transpersonal aspect of physical training that must be honored to perform optimally in winter sports. The ice climber who sees himself separated from the frozen waterfall is not as in sync as the climber who flows up the ice as though he and it were one. The strength-training realm is a sanctuary in which to practice this at-one-ness, or what theologians might know as atonement. It is a place to understand the universal rhythms of patience, failure, victory, and acceptance. Expansive truths inhabit each repetition in the gym. Don't think, "Oh, it's late, and I'm tired. I'm still supposed to go to the gym, but I don't want to." Turn it around and rank feeling over thinking in this situation. Say to yourself, "Wow, I'm pretty strung out from my day. It will feel good to go to the gym and breathe and merge into the workout." As Wholistic Fitness Master Student Lance Zein of Canada says, "My strength training workouts make me whole."

THE THREE AMIGOS

We can select any type of winter athlete and describe how these three strength-training reasons—structure, function, yoga—can benefit him or her.

Snowshoe Racer
Structure: Strength training will help keep knee and ankle joints strong and less susceptible to the inflammatory types of afflictions common to runners. It will also develop upper torso power. Since the arms drive the legs in snowshoe racing, this extra power will be invaluable late in races, when non–strength-trained racers are fatigued. In the final two miles of the 1995 World Snowshoe Championships, when my leg turnover was falling off by

the second due to fatigue, I passed five racers while maintaining a mantra of "Arms drive the legs … arms drive the legs."

Function: Strength training will improve spinal integrity, allowing more efficient neural feed to the legs, resulting in a faster leg turnover. It will increase the upper body as well, preserving a more powerful running gait through the entire race.

Yoga: Strength training will offer a regular refuge of breath and inner power development, wherein the racer can visualize how this training will increase his or her performance. For instance, when pumping out Back Squats, the athlete merges into a visualization of more muscle fibers contracting per foot strike, thus contributing to the ability to make competitor-breaking uphill surges on the snow.

Can you see the value of such a wholistic approach to strength training? Let's take a look at another athlete:

Nordic Skier
Structure: Strength training will increase the strength of the shoulder girdle and back musculature, allowing more effectual poling without fatigue.

Function: Strength training increases the size of the actin and myosin filaments in the muscles used for poling and striding. These filaments are "contact points" for

the electro-chemical reactions responsible for muscle contraction. The more developed the filaments, the more efficient the reaction, and, thus, the greater the endurance.

Yoga: Strength training offers perfect practice for the basic movement skills inherent to nordic skiing through exercises such as Split Jumps, Gunther Hops, and DB Arm Swings. Practicing these movements can restore the spirit of skiing even in summer!

Now you try. Think of any occupation or sport you enjoy. Reflect on how strength training can help you via its structural, functional, and yogic aspects. Go ahead, write in this book—it's yours, isn't it?

Occupation or sport: _____

_____

Structure: _____

_____

_____

Function: _____

_____

_____

Yoga: _____

_____

_____

STRENGTH AND CARDIOVASCULAR TRAINING: BROTHERS, NOT ALIENS

Strength training also improves cardiovascular (CV) fitness, but should be considered only a supplement for elite or competitive CV athletes. Although most coaches and trainers will state that strength training won't work as a substitute for CV training, I have pretty much pushed the envelope on that testimony. But in the end, I agree with them. I used to love using the gym to prepare for endurance and ultra-endurance events. When I lived in Boulder, I once trained for the Doc Holliday ultra-distance trail run just by strength training! I finished in the top twenty in spite of a major bonk a few miles from the finish. I would never professionally endorse such a bizarre training plan for an ultra-runner, but it was a worthwhile experience. It proved to me the underrated value of strength training and its influence upon cardiovascular fitness.

Most scientific studies involving weight training don't use the gym like Wholistic Fitness students do. Sport sciences are still stuck in the three sets of ten repetitions version of strength training. Scientists state that the benefits of weight training are secondary to CV training. They say this because their model of weight training does not sustain an aerobic heart rate. Wholistic Fitness strength training, however, is done in a style similar to that known as *vinyasa* in the yogic tradition. We link our sets and movements together in near continuous flow, never stopping long enough to allow the heart rate to drop below a Zone 1 effort (see Chapter Six). Often we reach Zones 4 or 5 during certain movements!

A, B, & C

A Japanese study was done with three groups of runners. Group A ran. Group B did not run but "did weights" (their terminology, not mine). Group C ran and "did weights." The results showed that Group C performed at higher levels and maintained their fitness over a longer period than did the other groups.

It is not uncommon to come across studies or instances that reveal similar findings. Essentially the thinking behind such findings is that strength training enables the central nervous system to recruit more muscle fibers in an effort, thus improving power. Others believe strength training helps CV fitness from a chemical perspective, such as outlined in the nordic skier discussion above. Perhaps soon, scientists will explore the transpersonal aspects of how the gym helps endurance athletes. I have such high confidence in strength training for cardiovascular performance because my own files are filled with personal records set by endurance athletes after an off-season of Wholistic Fitness strength training.

AMERICAN FLYERS

At the age of 33, I reentered cardiovascular sports after a decade of prioritizing skill sports such as extreme skiing, rock climbing, and ice climbing. Two seasons later, at 35 years old, I finished my experiment having earned a Category 3 road-racing license and an expert license in mountain biking. I

"But I had the gym ..." The author relying on some strength-training fitness while racing through the Death Valley night at 2:30 A.M. during the 508-mile Furnace Creek Ultra Cycling race in 1996. His team would go on to place second. Photo by Jo Anne Swartz.

wore a champion's jersey for the state road bike championships and had a silver medal from the state mountain bike championships. I was racing against many guys who had ten to twelve years of cycling-specific training. But I had the gym. It was certainly not cycling-specific cardio fitness that saw me to the podiums in the super-competitive sport of cycling. It was, instead, the deep-fiber fitness and spiritual tenacity from strength training that got me up there. It will get you up there, too.

Using the multidisciplined Wholistic Fitness approach, I combine the best of both worlds—strength training and cardiovas-cular training—to produce unmatched performance in my students. When combined with the softer disciplines of meditation, nutrition, and kinesthetic training, you'll soon see why Wholistic Fitness will be the training system for the next century.

PLAYING THE NUMBERS

We seem to really confuse things when it comes to the ever-present question in strength training, "Well, how much weight should I use?" First, the *amount* of weight you use in the gym is not as important as is the *form* you use to move it. Think of the sets and reps as the vertebrae of strength training. Your lifting form is the flesh that completes and animates that skeleton. To get stronger, you must carry each set in the gym to momentary failure. I am sure you are familiar with the sensation of momentary failure. It's what happens, for example, when you challenge somebody to a pull-up contest. At some point, you just can't perform anymore pull-ups, no matter how much your mind wants to do another one. This is momentary failure.

The body only adapts to overload. Based on this realization, I teach a simple formula:

Momentary Failure = Number of Reps
+ Failure of Elegance

Each set in the gym needs to be carried to momentary failure *or* failure of elegance. There is an oceanic difference between the two. Let's explore.

FAILURE OF ELEGANCE

If it had not been
For the wind in my face,
I wouldn't be able to fly at all.
                    —*Arthur Ashe*

I often like to spend a few minutes on a "Treadwall®" before doing a strength training workout. I enjoy the way it warms up my joints while imparting a fluid, dance-like energy that I can take into my workout. Photos by Mike Powell.

Let's say we are in the gym performing bench presses, in preparation for a season of mogul-bashing. We need strong shoulder girdle musculature to hold the aggressive fall lines that skiing moguls requires as well as reduce the risk of torn shoulder muscles. Bench presses will help, but we've got to do them in strict form for them to be effective. Now, if we are not students of Wholistic Fitness, we will have this big ego thing about having to lift massive amounts of weight to prove to everyone else in the gym that we are tough. So we start our set, and pretty soon our hips are bouncing off the bench. Our feet and legs are hyperactive like we've got ants in our pants. The barbell is crashing down on our chest, and our spotters are getting fatigued arms just helping us get the weight back up. It's an ugly scene that is played out constantly in gyms all across America, with most strength-training exercises. Now let's examine a set using Wholistic Fitness philosophy instead of ego.

Before we touch the barbell, we place our feet up on the bench or in the air to eliminate the excessive hip involvement that subtracts intensity from the chest. We connect our lower back to the bench, from where it will not waver, no matter what. We take a moderate weight barbell and really concentrate on a slow, controlled yin (or lowering) phase. The bar just "kisses" the chest, whereupon we initiate an explosive yang (or upward) phase. In the top position, we do not lock out our elbows, nor do we pause anywhere during the entire set. Fluidity reigns supreme as the balance between the explosive up (yang) and the controlled down (yin) becomes apparent even to untrained onlookers. This is the classic yin/yang philosophy animated. On reaching rep number seven we realize that our hips have begun to move and that during the yang phase the bar barely made it up. We rack the weight and end the set due to failure of elegance.

BE A MEMBER OF TRIPLE A: AWARENESS, AWARENESS, AWARENESS

Note that it required our *awareness* to sense when our hips were beginning to subtract from the purity of the movement. Strength training is not as much a physical exercise as it is mental. After racking the barbell, we sit up on the bench in good posture, return to our breath, and visualize the next set. All of this in-between-set recovery time is less than thirty seconds. Then we begin the next set. Our heart rate has not had time to fully recover, but the muscles are ready, if prefatigued. Muscle cells recover 50 percent of their contractile components within *two seconds*. Too many people rest way too long between sets.

This mindfulness of elegance permeates all sets and all movements as the entire workout becomes one long meditation session. Meditation means mental training. In the gym we are training the mind. Secondarily, the body is getting the benefits of this mental training. Remember, "less is more."

Be aware of the following three demons that patrol the gym:

1. inelegant or mindless lifting form;
2. too-long recovery times between sets and exercises; and
3. ego reiteration.

Wholistic Fitness considers anything but purity of form to be superfluous and degenerative to true inner power development. By taking on the responsibility to execute strict form during each set, we become masters of the gym and of our sport performance. If we ignore strict form, our ego gets the better of us. Lifting heavy weights for the sake of the ego is damaging to the joints and is symbolic of an impotent and immature higher self. Impotency and immaturity are not qualities to be cultivated in this path!

PERIODIZATION

I do not require my winter sports athletes to strength train year round. Competitive nordic skiers, for example, may not visit the gym at all once racing season begins. However, during the off season they will definitely be cranking out the reps in the gym! We call this cyclic approach to performance training periodizational training. Such an approach ensures productive stimulus for strength gains while acknowledging the importance of regeneration. Wholistic Fitness prioritizes strength training as a fitness discipline for beginning students, particularly for the first two years, to achieve structural and functional integrity, as discussed earlier.

My basic strength-training phases reflect the Wholistic Fitness philosophy of "root-growing." We establish deep and wide roots so that our long-term fitness has a strong support system. I usually prescribe four basic strength-training cycles for athletes interested in increasing their winter performance:

Phase Number One: Transition
(Early Off Season)
Prepares the mind, body, and spirit for deeper work. Here the athlete is encouraged to experience the art of tempo, mental focus, posture, and breath.

Phase Number Two: Basic Strength
(Off Season)
Targets the core musculature with heavy weights done with precise postural control.

Phase Number Three: Basic Power
(Off Season)
Teaches speed strength and the development of fast-twitch fibers.

Phase Number Four: Strength Endurance
(Pre-Season)
Aims for a biochemical training effect that encourages muscular endurance. Some sport specificity permeates this phase.

We follow most of the above phases for about one month: four weeks of active study followed by a recovery week, then the next phase. Later, the student may be allowed to enter the real fun—advanced programs such as Whirlwind Dancer, Spear of Destiny, and the infamous Frugal Realm or Chasm of Fire! For the purposes of this book, you will be introduced to Basic Strength and Basic Power, then a sport-

specific program of your choice that takes the place of Strength Endurance. If you get turned on by the seeds planted by this book, contact my company for a customized training prescription sure to light your inner fire toward self-enlightenment!

Wholistic Fitness has ten copyrighted strength-training techniques. These techniques—referenced in the appendix of this book—are used to give my students an incredibly effective athletic and transpersonal power transfer. The techniques mandate strict postural and breath awareness. They will totally deflate overindulged egos, so be prepared for a little dose of humility. Three techniques are used during the recovery phases of sets. These exclusive techniques are largely responsible for my unmatched success at enabling students to make huge leaps in their sport performance. The sport-specific training programs in later chapters will use these techniques so you can directly experience the color and depth of Wholistic Fitness strength training.

REGENERATE, DON'T DEGENERATE

Most major body parts require twenty-four hours of recuperation before being able to sustain more training. Some body parts have a more speedy recovery process than others. The abdominal muscles, for instance, which have the duty of maintaining posture all day long, have developed a very good recovery process. If done wisely, abs can be trained nearly every day without overtraining them. Paradoxically, the muscles right behind the abs—the lumbar muscles—are the slowest to recover, needing at least two days for recovery. This is why Wholistic Fitness embraces periodization. It allows for full exhaustion as well as complete recovery of the body's musculature over the long term.

Beginning strength trainers recover more quickly than seasoned gym rats. This is because they do not train at the high intensities of a veteran. The harder we train, the more we need to rest. This philosophy, when applied to another discipline, such as CV training, reveals why nordic ski racers don't train much during the season. They race on weekends and basically recover during the week! The notion here is to avoid overtraining. Train with focus and high intensity, push yourself, then back off and recover. Much cellular reconstruction must be accomplished before we can train the body intensively again. As one of my Master Students, Randy Owen, once said after his completion of my Wholistic Fitness Teacher Training Course™, "There is no such thing as overtraining, just under-recovery." Wise kid.

Let's summarize the discussion of strength training by acknowledging the three basic strength-training phases that winter athletes should experience during their off- and pre-seasons.

Basic Strength Phase

Physical Benefits: maximizes structural integrity; balances weaknesses; enhances neuromuscular system; myofibrillization: contractile proteins thicken and increase in number and enzymatic activity. *Transpersonal Benefits:* teaches patience and wholeness.

Basic Power Phase

Physical Benefits: number of cells recruited at moment of contraction is improved; maximum contraction capability is improved; peripheral circulation increases; blood stroke volume increases. *Transpersonal Benefits:* develops timing of yang or go for it attitude and creates depth of personal power.

Strength Endurance or Specialization Phase

Physical Benefits: enhances biochemical activity to resynthesize muscle (phosphate) energy; increases stamina. *Transpersonal Benefits:* teaches acceptance of and perseverance in difficult and repetitive tasks; develops mental fortitude.

6

Discipline 3: Cardiovascular Training

*"To repeat successes of the past, you follow your old program.
Don't get fancy; just be consistent."*

—Bill Rodgers

Wholistic Fitness ombuds-
man Ven Barclay, of Boul-
der, Colorado, getting out
near the Kaibab Plateau.
Ven knows what it takes to
be consistent in training.
Photo by Marcia Murphy.

In my *Bicycling* magazine column came the
following question from a reader,

Hi, Steve—
My strength in mountain-bike racing is
maintaining a solid pace throughout
and passing people one by one. I have
good endurance. The hard part for me
is the "mad dash" at the start of the
race. I usually get to the line early and

get a good starting position but can't
seem to maintain the starting pace as
long as others ... without blowing up.
Last year I experimented at one race
and saw how long I could hang with
the front runners from the sprint ... I
blew up big time about a quarter of
the way through the race, realizing
that's not for me. How long should a

person be able to maintain a sprint and still be able to recover to maintain a "strong" pace for the remainder of the race? Any suggestions would be greatly appreciated!

Thanks—Randy

I decided to use a winter athlete as an example to address Randy's question.

Dear Randy—

Do you know who Vegard Ulvang is? He is a multi-gold medal Olympic and World Champion in nordic ski racing. A Norwegian from Viking heritage, Vegard epitomizes the mental tenacity and unflappable strength and endurance that characterizes what is the planet's most demanding cardiovascular sport. For over a decade Vegard's relentless crushing of his opponents has earned him the nickname, "The Terminator."

As a junior ski racer, Vegard would fire like a missile from the start of his races. Disregarding the race distance, Vegard would ski like a lunatic, creating huge gaps between himself and his competitors. A few kilometers later, however, he'd blow up. Competitors began to depend on Vegard's foolishness. They poked fun at him. Years passed, still Vegard refused to pace himself, much to the dismay of his coaches. What no one seemed to notice, however, was that Vegard blew a little later in each race ...

Then came a cold Norwegian day when Vegard didn't blow up. He simply won the race wire-to-wire. Then came a decade when Vegard didn't blow up. He showed the world what personal fortitude and spiritual tenacity can do; despite what coaches and textbooks say about "mathematically correct" and "physiologically relevant" methods of training.

Randy, I say embrace your weakness. Make it your focus and apply a little Vegard for at least 2–3 seasons. Use regular training sessions to increase your anaerobic threshold. Do this with proper mental training and nutrition and one day ... like Vegard ... you might not blow up.

The essential thing to realize is that MTB starts are a trainable, physiologic quality. You must persevere and KNOW— to the very fiber of your being—that you CAN stay up front. Because, as the saying goes, "If you ain't the lead dog, the scenery never changes."

—Coach Ilg

I open this chapter with that story because I need you to realize that cardiovascular training (or CV) is one of the most highly trainable of all fitness disciplines. Cardiovascular training as used in this book is activity that elevates the heart rate and keeps it elevated for a sustained period. The classic CV winter sports are nordic skiing (backcountry and track), mountaineering, and snowshoeing.

Of the Five Fitness Disciplines in Wholistic Fitness training, CV has the most science behind it. We like to think we know a lot about CV training and performance. The truth is, not a coach in the world can promise an athlete a peak performance on a given day. A coach can only choreograph and arrange training variables. Hopefully that arrangement, when coupled with the dedication of the athlete, will result in a stellar performance on a particular day or time period. This chapter will help you understand what factors create an optimum state of CV fitness. Be patient, however. Learning how to use this knowledge may take years. My friend Don Nielsen, an Olympic biathlete, was fond of reminding me of his training maxim, "TTT," which stands for "Things Take Time."

BASIC CV BENEFITS

I'm not going to spend time convincing you of the benefits of CV training. I will assume that you already realize that it is "good for you." Most likely, you understand that the respiratory, circulatory, endocrine, and other systems of the body are improved by consistent CV training. This book will focus more on the physiology and techniques of CV training and how they affect the preparation for your favorite winter sport.

The heart is the primary beneficiary of CV fitness. Most of the training effects increase or improve the following: blood volume; blood distribution and delivery to exercising muscles via capillary density; stroke volume and cardiac output; and efficiency of respiration. CV training lowers the resting heart rate and increases the lactate threshold. CV training also favorably affects body composition; fat weight is often decreased, contributing to a healthy, lean body weight. Structurally, bones, ligaments, and tendons are positively stressed by wise CV training, thus creating a stronger overall body structure.

BASIC WINTER CV PHYSIOLOGY

Every winter athlete depends on CV fitness to enjoy his or her winter sport. The physiological demands of winter sports range from anaerobic, explosive efforts, such as in alpine skiing and snowboarding, to the aerobic capacity for prolonged exertion required by nordic skiing, mountaineering, and snowshoeing. No matter which winter sport you are training for, however, CV conditioning creates easier and safer performance dividends. For example, most CV training stimulates a type of muscle fiber known as Type I, or slow twitch. This fiber type is used constantly in skiing and other winter sports. The more developed this fiber type becomes through training, the more efficiently it converts chemical energy into mechanical work. Our sports technique improves because we require less overall muscle activity, which means less need for oxygen and more efficient motion. Less muscle involvement and more efficiency means less injury risk and greater long-term health.

The general development of CV fitness also improves the respiratory system, helps the body's thermo-regulatory mechanisms, improves endurance of all muscles, and increases the body's ability to store more carbohydrates for energy. As you can see, all winter sports can be dramatically improved by the development of CV fitness.

AEROBIC AND NOT

The body produces energy for the muscular contractions required to sustain CV training in two primary ways: via the aerobic and anaerobic (without the need for oxygen) systems. The purpose of these two systems is the same: to generate adenosine triphosphate (ATP), a high-energy compound that ignites muscular contraction. Once ATP is broken down, however, we must restore it immediately, because the ATP stored in our muscles lasts only a few seconds. The resynthesis of ATP occurs in three ways: the ATP-PC (phosphocreatine) system, the lactic acid system, and the aerobic system (see chart that follows). The first two methods, the ATP-PC and lactic acid systems, use an anaerobic metabolism,

which is very effective but short-lived and has high acidic waste production. The third, the aerobic system, requires oxygen to function and tiptoes through a twenty-step physiologic process before ATP is even produced! But the good part of the deal is that a greater amount of ATP is generated, with little acid buildup in the muscles.

Generally sports that require more than five minutes of sustained activity derive most of their energy from the aerobic system. CV fitness is intimately linked to effective ATP resynthesis. Since most winter sports require sustained activity longer than five minutes, my emphasis of CV training is probably not surprising. If we do not base training programs upon the correct energy system, we waste time and energy!

If you study the origin of movement, you will begin to understand that a real need exists for CV fitness training across the physiologic continuum. Remember, although the energy for muscular contraction comes from ATP, it is only through aerobic and anaerobic activity that we produce it. When engaging in a low-intensity CV activity—a pleasant snowshoe or nordic ski for example—the delivery of oxygen to the exercising muscles is extremely important to the production of ATP. This is the aerobic system at work. The waste products from the aerobic system include carbon dioxide and water, which we eliminate efficiently through breathing and perspiration. Kick up the intensity factor by running on those snowshoes and our breathing becomes

Three Main Energy Systems for Winter Sports		
System	*Time Span*	*Winter Sport*
ATP-PC	less than 30 seconds	nordic & freestyle ski jumping
Lactic acid	30 seconds to 3 minutes	snowboarding in the half-pipe, alpine/telemark skiing, ice climbing (climbing through cruxes)
Aerobic	more than 3 minutes	snowshoeing, nordic skiing, mountaineering, ice climbing (longer, moderate routes), winter mountain biking, endurance ice skating

labored and our muscles begin burning. This is because the CV system cannot deliver enough oxygen into the muscle cells. Now the body must shift into anaerobic metabolism to generate enough energy for ATP production. The primary waste product is lactic acid, the precursor of that burning sensation in the muscles. The systematic practice of structured CV training, along with a solid strength-training base, can improve each of these systems.

Many winter athletes spend too much training time doing the wrong workouts respective to the energy system they use most. The training programs in this book are designed for the most efficient training in each energy system. That's why so many Wholistic Fitness athletes set new personal records and personal bests in their first year of study. We are training each of their main energy systems, perhaps for the first time in their lives.

OF NADIS, CHAKRAS, AND SWAMIS

Of course, we have been discussing a Western model of movement, and one should not limit the interpretation of movement to just one thought system. The Eastern notion of chi, or "life force," with its flow of energy through the meridians is just as valid as the Indian science of prana, or "universal breath," which is centered around the nadis and chakras. Both of these sciences predate our Western metabolic model by thousands of years and have outperformed the theories of even the most astute Western sport researchers as far as control of the autonomic systems.

At the Menninger Clinic in Topeka, Kansas, in 1970, a famous series of scientific experiments validated control over human physiology that had been previously thought impossible. These experiments, all directed under the strictest Western scientific conditions known, proved that Swami Rama, a spiritual leader from the Himalayas, could control involuntary bodily functions such as heartbeat regulation (the old swami willingly stopped his heart for 17 seconds just for fun), thermoregulatory manipulation (Swami Rama changed the temperature in two spots on his right palm until a difference of ten degrees Fahrenheit was recorded), and brain wave control. His last "trick" was pretty clever. The swami slowed his brain waves to a mere 0.5 cycles per second for twenty-five minutes. (Normal brain activity ranges from fourteen to twenty-eight cycles per second when resting.) After coming out of his meditation, Swami Rama repeated, word for word, the dialogue spoken by the researchers while he was slowing his brain waves.

Wholistic Fitness embraces and uses all available science, not just the Western model. I have studied and integrated Eastern, Asiatic, and Indian models for many of my students. Let's look at the parallels for a moment:

Western model
  aerobic
  anaerobic
Eastern Asiatic & Indian models
  yin/ida nadi
  yang/pingala nadi
Energetic models
  female/endurance/low intensity
  male/power/high intensity

I illustrate this wholistic approach because relying upon just one thought form as absolute truth is dangerous. Much of my coaching success stems from welcoming the larger sphere of knowledge and available science into an individual training program. Just as an extreme skier would be foolish not to use his or her peripheral vision and other senses to rip down a rock-strewn couloir, so, too, would it be equally dangerous for us to assume the validity of only one science when so many are available from which to learn! Throughout this book, you'll find words and terms from diverse sciences in addition to standard Western terms. You can reference all such terms in the glossary.

AGAIN WITH THE YIN/YANG

As previously stated, for optimal sports performance, the winter athlete must develop fitness across a physiologic spectrum. In doing so, he or she embraces the qualities of both male and female, endurance and power, aerobic and anaerobic. For most winter athletes, a CV workout that encompasses both yin and yang aspects offers top-quality training. A "cruise interval" workout is an excellent example of training both yin/yang in one CV session. One of my favorite interval workouts, which I usually do on my snowshoes at a local ski area, is the following (see the chart on the next page for an explanation of the zones):

Yin = ten minutes at easy aerobic effort (Zones 1 and 2)
into
Yin/Yang = five minutes at moderate/high aerobic effort (Zone 3)
into
Yang = two minutes of high aerobic/ anaerobic effort (Zone 4)
repeat cycle

I normally do this three-stage interval set three times. These yin/yang workouts quickly spill into sport performances. The spiritual strengthening that derives from these workouts quickly shifts the athlete into higher realms of self-realization. This type of interval training is difficult to do consistently. It needs to be approached and monitored carefully. Too much, and we risk overtraining. This is why following sport-specific training prescriptions will be important. Pay special heed to the use of zone training.

WORK ZONE AHEAD

Although many formulas have been created to determine CV training intensities, I rely on two. The first is the heart rate–based zone training as structured by the United States Cycling Federation (USCF). The second formula is intuition. Both have their respective places in winter performance training and are included in the graph on the following page.

You should perform an AT determination test for each sport that you do. For example, my AT in classic-style nordic skiing is 188, but my AT in sport snowshoeing is 198. That difference of ten beats per minute changes my zone training mathematics. In the training prescriptions that follow, I use the above zones to describe individual CV workouts.

To make progress in CV training the winter sport athlete must train in Zones 2 to 3 for thirty to sixty minutes four times per week. To maintain that level of CV fitness, he or she will have to train in Zones 1 to 2 for thirty minutes two to three times per week.

SPIRITUAL SIGNIFICANCE OF INTERVAL TRAINING

Wholistic Fitness is not only a performance training philosophy, but also a rewarding path toward self-realization. My athletes go deeper and deeper into their CV training for a simple reason: "to see what is in there." Interval training plays an important role in this work. We consider interval training a spiritual workshop, a time to increase both mental tenacity and emotional

---

USCF/Intuitive Table of CV Training Intensity

Perform an anaerobic threshold (AT) determination test to establish your training zones. The simplest way: 1) warm up; 2) do your sport or CV activity at a steady speed for two minutes, noting your speed and heart rate (HR); 3) repeat step #2 over and over, increasing the intensity until you can no longer speak, your thighs are burning, and your performance plateaus. At that moment, record your HR and use that as your AT high point to determine your CV training zones.

Zone   *Percent of Maximum Heart Rate*
                (Your maximum heart rate equals the AT high point you just determined.)

Zone 1   = less than 65 percent   recovery/warm up/cool down; you can easily speak and whistle during activity

Zone 2   = 65–72 percent   development of aerobic system; you can speak but are winded and can't sustain a whistle

Zone 3   = 73–83 percent   some anaerobic metabolism begins to develop; your effort is forced but sustainable

Zone 4   = 84–90 percent   anaerobic system is in use; you can sustain high intensity for up to three minutes; you feel like you're "sucking goose eggs"

Zone 5   = 91–100 percent   anaerobic system is in use; you can sustain a maximum effort for up to thirty seconds; you're sucking goose eggs *and* feel ready to hurl.

---

vigor. During interval intensities we edge closest to our pure spirit. Interval training is difficult, but but we can either do intervals or experience stagnation of inner power. The choice is ours.

During a snowshoe/yoga retreat, someone asked me, "What's the difference between a recreational athlete and a competitive or serious athlete?"

I answered quickly, "Intervals."

We will be tempted to cheat when following interval workouts. There are a hundred ways to back off or not give 100 percent. But if we cheat in intervals, we will back off in a race. And if we do that, we will cheat and back off for the rest of our lives. We can fool our ego, but we will never fool our higher self. Cheat, and we remain weak inside. Don't try to fool anyone, because no one else will care about you except you! If we wish to become that master winter athlete someday, we must experience and live those anaerobic threshold intensities provided to us by interval training or races. As the saying goes, "Character is what you are when nobody is looking."

Intervals push our mind, body, and spirit into places where conventional preachers, New Age healers, and gurus are often too scared to tread. We must gain control over the ego and find the quality of surrender (see Chapter Four) inherent to each interval. When we do this, we discover a rich inner world full of spiritual insight. One good way to break into an interval workout is a workout on snowshoes that I call riblet intervals. Riblets are those big towers that hold up chairlifts or gondolas at alpine ski areas. They are usually spaced from twenty to seventy-five yards apart. In the winter, you can do riblet intervals by strapping on a pair of sport snowshoes at your local ski area and walking up a lift line to riblet #1. Upon reaching #1, sprint uphill to #2, then walk to #3. Repeat this se-

Intervals are done for a simple reason: to see what is in us. The author "takes a moment" after some inline "ski" intervals near Santa Fe, New Mexico. Photo by Marc Romanelli.

quence until you are just crawling between the riblets toward the top of the mountain. In the summer, you can trade snowshoes for running shoes and ski poles. This exhausting form of intervals is exceptional CV training. It also conditions the muscular system in a way that maximizes gluteal power and frontal thigh drive.

IN DEFENSE OF LACTIC ACID

While we are on the subject of intervals, I wish to defend a much maligned sibling of interval training—lactic acid. In our earlier discussion of the energy systems, we learned that lactic acid is a primary waste product of anaerobic metabolism. Lactic acid has gotten a bum rap for a long time as the terminator of motion. When too much lactic acid accumulates in the cells, muscle fatigue occurs. Well maybe lactic acid is a clumsy metabolic pathway, but that's no reason to rag on it. Lactic acid provides energy in an oxygen-deprived and highly acidic state. Lactic acid must make do in a very difficult situation! When you're telemarking steep bumps at the end of a long ski day and your legs don't have the crispness and speed they did on the first run, don't blame lactic acid. Just breathe into the burn, knowing that the lactic acid system is doing its best.

SOME WHOLISTIC CV MECHANICS

Remember Frank Shorter, gold medalist in the marathon in the 1972 Olympics? Shorter basically started the great running boom of the '70s. Occasionally, I would get to train or race alongside him when I lived in Boulder, Colorado. Two things always struck me about his presence: his meager physique and his ungainly running mechanics. This guy was lean. At the start of one race, I looked over at him. He was shivering from the "cold." Boulder was 69 degrees that morning! What made more of an impression on me, however, was Shorter's running style. He succeeded in his sport in spite of what would be biome-

chanically criticized as an ineffective running motion.

Frank got away with less than optimal CV mechanics because, well, he is Frank! Most of us, however, are not Frank. We need to practice beauty and gracefulness in our CV training because where there is beauty and grace, there is efficiency. Efficiency means energy conservation, a most vital quality in the CV journey. To master this discipline—or just to enjoy it more fully—we must find our path of least resistance.

The first quality we should seek in a CV sport or activity is beauty. We want to master this sport or activity and be so beautiful that we don't even burn one calorie in an hour of doing it. This never happens, of course, but we are performing artists, and it's the ideal we are after, not necessarily the reality. If we study the great masters of winter CV sports—the nordic skiers, the speed skaters, the sport snowshoers—we will see a very streamlined energy output.

BEAUTY AND GRACE

Bjorn Dahlie is a national hero of Norway. He is a nordic ski champion in several distances. When Bjorn races, it looks as though he has been set to music. His tremendous effort is poetically camouflaged by his smooth technique. We see only a skier dancing upon snow, a choreographed interplay of arm and ski pole. There is such grace to his skiing style that when he crumples across the finish line with lungs heaving, snot flying, and sweat frozen upon his face, it seems out of place!

In the way Michael Jordan seemingly floats forever in the air above "the paint," so too does Bjorn seem to float on his skis. Each stride held for an eternity, maximizing his glide. The poetry!

We, too, must pursue such masterful qualities. Never do a CV activity mindlessly. Mimic the champions who make their art available for study. In time, we will create our own beauty, our own grace. Too many of us enter our CV training mindlessly, yet think we deserve immediate and long-lasting results! It is only through daily CV practice that we learn from the spirit of repetition. What the unenlightened call boring, the sun and moon call rising, the trees call growing and the Wholistic Fitness student calls opportunity. It is only through the spirit of repetition that we can hammer out character flaws. There is a Norwegian proverb, "Life without discipline means death without honor." You've got to want to learn. You've got to love to suffer as much as you love the feeling of having done it. Much knowledge lies within the orchestration of lung and leg.

WHOLISTIC FITNESS® CV MEDITATIONS

Through the years I have created five basic meditations to help my athletes discover grace in CV training. These meditations

---

Wholistic Fitness® CV Meditations

- Keep the spine out of the hips
- Lead with the heart
- Keep your eyes and shoulder girdle soft
- The hands drive the legs; think full-body tempo
- Breathe softly from the belly; concentrate like a mountain

---

are appropriate to all forms of CV training. Merge with them while training and see how quickly they shift you toward a higher level of performance.

KEEP THE SPINE OUT OF THE HIPS

The bodyworker Ida Rolf said, "Strength that has effort in it is not what you need, you need the strength that is the result of ease." By urging students to keep their spines out of their hips, I am coaching from a perspective of elongation instead of compaction. Most of us are quick to compact our spines downward into our pelvis, which in turn collapses both posture and performance. Concentrate on lifting the spine out of the hips. This complements all aspects of improved CV motion.

Try it right now. Stand up. Feel the heaviness of your spine and how it sits like an iron girder pressing into your sacrum. Now align your legs so they fall straight down from the pelvis and point your toes straight ahead. Pressing the feet into the earth, feel an energy rising from the feet up the legs. Tense the frontal thigh muscles and note how in doing so, elongation throughout the upper legs and hips occurs. Now stretch your spine up, opening the chest. Do not strain. Finally lift the head as though someone were pulling it from above. Feel the space between the cervical vertebrae expand. There should be a palatable sense of awakened energy radiating up and down the spine, tingling the feet and hands. A fresh awareness and acuity seem to occur and suddenly your breath is being delivered from the belly and feels deep, soft, and profound.

LEAD WITH THE HEART

This simple but profound meditation brings our spiritual and emotional energy right where it belongs—to the heart. The heart symbolizes love and compassionate power. However, many of us lead from what is known in the energetic sciences as the "fear line" in the body: the area of the waistline. We tend to push our hips forward in everyday life, an outer reflection of leading our lives from fear.

Shift your awareness so that your posture adjusts as your heart center remains in front of the hips. Performing CV activities while keeping the heart forward keeps the spine out of the hips and allows the seat of power to flow freely from the gluteal muscles. Go for a quick jog while invoking this meditation. You'll feel the difference, just like hundreds of other Wholistic Fitness students who have discovered remarkable mind/body benefits from this simple meditation!

KEEP YOUR EYES AND SHOULDER GIRDLE SOFT

Sensei Kishiyama, a martial arts teacher of mine, used to remind us during sparring and *kata* sessions, "Relax! Relax! Relax! Whenever you relax, you perform better!" This rings totally true in CV activity. The moment we tense up in response to the normal effort required in CV workouts, we take a major step in the wrong direction. When we tense, we turn effort into struggle, and soon struggle leads to suffering.

The Mount Evans Road Race is one of Colorado's premier bicycle races as well as the world's highest, topping out on a 14,264-foot summit. Mike Engleman was the winner of one race in the late '80s that I had also entered. My category had started about fifteen minutes before the pros category 1 and 2, of which Engleman was a part. After having finished in eighth place, I was trying to recover from my effort, standing over my bike and taking in the 360-degree view from the top. Suddenly Mike came charging up the final few meters toward the finish line, handlebars swinging side to side with almost violent power through the rarefied air. He won by a large margin over the rest of the pack. Seconds after crossing the line, Mike complained to reporters about how much pain he had been in during the last few miles. "It's not supposed to hurt this bad," he said. "If you're in shape, it doesn't hurt."

He was right. During those times in my own races or extreme performances when things just came together, nothing really hurt. Oh there is effort, but when we are in peak form, a certain sense of relaxed alertness seems to pervade the competition or event. On such days, one can "relax into" the effort and not really suffer that much. We reach transcendent experience when we relax.

I've used the "soft eyes, shoulder girdle soft" meditation as a way to stay relaxed during CV workouts and races. Too frequently, we look out at the world through "hard eyes." We squint and grimace. We contort our faces, necks, and shoulders. When you feel that happening, practice soft eyes. Allow the light of the day to flow *into* your eyes instead of looking *out* through rigid eyes. Allow your shoulder girdle to drop, releasing tension in the neck. Practice this meditation during your next CV workout, and you'll feel what I mean.

The hands drive the legs; think full-body tempo

Santa Monica's well-known San Vincente Boulevard is a tree-lined street with a large, grassy median. Each day hundreds of fitness athletes walk, jog, or run down this island of green sandwiched between a high-speed parade of Mercedes and stretch limos. Cyclists also use San Vincente, as it is a major artery to the Pacific Coast Highway. Whenever I cruise this street—on bike, foot, or car—the nonstop flow of athletes fascinates me.

I get the chance to observe an amazing variety of running forms. Most runners would do well to take a clinic. Many fitness runners swing their upper body from side to side in an attempt to transfer lower-body strength into the upper body. Unfortunately, the upper torso is no match for leg strength. So as the runners lose their upper-body stabilization strength and their postures collapse, an awkward struggle replaces fluid body mechanics. Instead, the arms should drive the legs. This gets the athlete into a full-body expression of fitness and provides support via the erector spinae muscles to transfer lower-body power throughout the whole body. During your next run, in-line skate, nordic ski, or snowshoe, exaggerate your hand and arm movement by really driving the hand up in front of your face in a clean, linear fashion. Keep the elbows high and close in toward the body. Notice that when arm drive increases, the legs follow suit. When you're hurting and your legs seem tired, don't try to make them go faster. Instead, focus on your arm drive.

Breathe softly from the belly; concentrate like a mountain

On a physical level, when we breathe from the belly (the diaphragmatic breath), we allow more oxygen to enter the bloodstream while expelling old breath and toxic irritants.

Mentally, mindful breathing reduces stress and anxiety while it enhances concentration and clear-minded focus. The meditation of "Breathe softly from the belly; concentrate like a mountain," helps to access and maintain even-mindedness during CV workouts or races. The even-mindedness is invaluable in a discipline that is bothersome to the ego due to its repetitiousness. The ego always wants to chatter away and fill our minds with such negatives as, "Aren't you getting tired yet? This is so boring, let's just stop. Three more miles? No way! It's too cold out. ..." Control the ego by using breath and a concentrated posture of mind and body. By returning to the belly breath and invoking the concentration of a mountain, we can experience conviction, serenity, and often joyfulness until the end of the workout. It helps to invoke the massive stillness of a mountain. To concentrate like a mountain means to stand firm against an onslaught of emotional weather. When you concentrate like a mountain, you maintain even-mindedness through outer obstacles like rain, snow, or wind, as well as inner obstacles such as self-doubt, fear, or pain.

One of my students, Dean Goodfellow, an ultra-cyclist from California, recently finished in the top twenty of a 750-mile bicycle race. During one portion of his eighty-five-hour ride, he encountered a 150-mile stretch of constant twelve to fifteen mile per hour headwinds. Dean wrote, "Breath and posture got me through this thing. Just focusing on breath and posture allowed me to somehow rise above the circumstance while others were just giving up, having been mentally rattled to the breaking point."

BODY FAT?
WHO SAID THAT?

According to Wholistic Fitness philosophy, too much body fat is too much stored molecular energy. Spiritually, a person who needs to lose significant body fat is someone who needs to release some fear. Most of the over-fat people I train try to use food to fill a spiritual void or an unfocused craving stemming from unresolved emotional issues. Significant amounts of stored body fat are usually not metabolically activated until about thirty minutes into a CV workout. Most research states that to metabolize stored body fat, the intensity of the CV workout should stay low—in Zones 1 and 2. Fat tissue is like a heavy log in a fireplace that needs plenty of oxygen to keep it burning. Thus if the intensity is too high, say advocates of this "go easy" theory, fat will no longer burn as the body switches to an anaerobic metabolism.

Of course, there is another school of thought (there always is), which says we need a high-intensity workout to burn fat. The more calories we burn, the theory goes, the greater the metabolic activity over a twenty-four-hour span, which is more effective to losing body fat in the long term.

Wholistic Fitness sides with both schools. I've had students lose body fat using either approach, but my greatest success with over fat students has come by using a combination of both approaches: frequent low-intensity CV workouts with regular bouts of high-intensity interval sessions. Wholistic Fitness also encourages strength training to lose body fat. Strength training increases the lean-tissue to fat-tissue ratio of the body, making us metabolically more active … even when we are at rest. At my peak of rock-climbing fitness, I healthfully carried only 2.3 percent body fat. I achieved that low level by following the programs and principles in this book. If I can do it, I know you can do it!

> It is when your practice is rather greedy that you become discouraged with it. So you should be grateful that you have a sign or warning signal to show you the weak point in your practice.
>
> —D.T. Suzuki

WARM-UP

A warm-up is as valuable as a cool-down. Some physiological changes that occur during a warm-up include the following:

• Increased blood and muscle temperature. A warm muscle contracts more powerfully and relaxes more quickly, while warmed-up blood carries more oxygen. This is especially important in winter sports, as a higher body-core temperature reduces the likelihood of overstretching muscles in the cold, which will cause injury.

• Improved range of motion (ROM). A warm-up increases ROM, again decreasing injury potential, especially in kinesthetic winter sports with high shear forces such as alpine skiing and snowboarding.

• Enhanced energy production. During a warm-up, we stimulate hormones that in turn make carbohydrates and fatty acids more accessible for energy production.

• Psychological preparedness. My worst performances have often followed inadequate warm-ups, especially in nordic ski racing and snowshoe racing. Arrive early for races and warm up well. That way, when they throw the hammer down, your mental and physical systems will have been primed, and the red-line intensity won't be such a shock to your system. Going into oxygen debt at the beginning of a race is not only an unpleasant experience, but it's also not the way to win.

The type and duration of a warm-up should relate to the specific needs of the event. It should include skill-specific motion. For example, if you are a snowshoe racer and know that when the gun goes off you'll have to "hammer it," then you should do a fifteen- to thirty-minute jog as a warm-up, including several thirty-second Zone 4 intervals. The effects of a warm-up normally last up to thirty minutes. It is best, though, to time your warm-up to dovetail with the start of the race or event, leaving several minutes before the start to take off warm-up clothing, drink some fluids, drain some fluids, and recover before the gun goes off.

The warm-up also serves as "crisis intervention." I cannot tell you how many races I've been in when during my warm-up I found some crisis requiring immediate attention: mountain-bike derailleurs in need of adjustment, ski waxes in need of tweaking, telemark bindings in need of modifications, etc. Once I was late getting to a snowshoe race in Leadville, Colorado. I was product testing some new snowshoes and grabbed a pair while rushing off to the start line, where others had already gathered. I transitioned quickly into the 'shoes, just making the start. Within one hundred meters, I realized that I had a broken frame on my right snowshoe! Had I gotten in an adequate warm-up, I could have switched snowshoes and saved my performance. As John Stamstad, multitime winner of the IditaSport, says, "I've never done a race yet in which crisis isn't a normal part of the racing."

COOL-DOWN

A cool-down offers physiological benefits equal to those of a warm-up. The cool-down is a period of easy intensity CV work done until the heart rate has reached 120 beats per minute. Some athletes include light stretching as part of their cool-down ritual. Perhaps the most valuable benefit of a cool-down is faster recovery since the light exercise rids lactate from the blood and muscles. Some sport researchers suggest that if CV activity is stopped too quickly, the blood has a pooling effect in the vascular system, particularly in the lower body. Heart rate then increases as the heart attempts to bring that lethargic blood back up the legs. If you've ever felt dizzy after a CV workout or endurance race, you probably have too much blood in the legs and not enough in the head! Lie down and put your legs up. Help the body help itself.

Here's one example of a very poor approach to cooling down. At the State Nordic Championships in Winter Park, Colorado, I was nearing the finish of a race on a bitterly cold morning. I had just topped out on a long climb during the classic-style event. My hat had slipped down on my forehead. For the past several kilometers I had wanted to push it higher, but the intensity of the race mandated that I keep skiing without a break in technique. Now, however, I could glide downhill and recover. Taking advantage of the opportunity to push my hat up, I raised my hand to do so. In nordic ski racing the ski poles are tightly lashed to the hand because good technique involves releasing the pole in the backstroke. As I brought my hand to my forehead, the long ski pole came up also. By this time I was skiing downhill at a fast speed. The sharp end of the pole, which had angled away from me, struck a tree right next to the ski track. The pole handle transferred the impact directly to my head, knocking me out of the ski track and into deep powder. I was out cold! So much blood was in my legs from the exertion of racing that I was out for what felt like minutes. Fellow competitors who witnessed the comical stunt reported that I was really out for only a few seconds. I managed to finish the race, but I was feeling distinctly loopy by the end.

CV SUMMATION

Fred Rohé, author of *The Zen of Running*, summarized the lush inner world that CV training can provide for the insightful athlete, saying that the CV experience "is a newly discovered form of meditation or one more way for you to discover you."

Meditation? Isn't that funny? Meditation is the next Wholistic Fitness discipline we will investigate!

7

Discipline 4: Meditation

"To train the mind is first to see directly how the mind works. ... Then you can use that understanding to tame the mind and work with it skillfully, to make it more and more pliable, so that you can become master of your own mind and employ it to its fullest and most beneficial end."

—Sogyal Rinpoche

The author leading a guided meditation with students in the Sierra Mountains near Mammoth Lakes, California. Photo by Anne Sasso.

THE SPIRITUAL HEART OF WHOLISTIC FITNESS®

If one thing has distanced Wholistic Fitness from other forms of personal fitness training for the past decade, it has been my emphasis on mental training, or meditation. Meditation is, in fact, the heart of Wholistic Fitness training. It is the glue that binds the Five Fitness Disciplines and the Four Lifestyle Principles into a synergistic body/mind training system. I use the Tibetan transliteration of the word meditation, which means, simply, "training the mind." The Latin origin of meditation has a different connotation, "to reflect upon." The training of a winter athlete pivots upon the resolute conditioning of the mind, to serve the athlete in times of low motivation, at high-risk moments, and in high-pressure situations. Far from being a sentimental rumination, meditation is a forceful fitness discipline that can transform ordinary training into transcendental experience. More important, however, is that knowing oneself through the practice of meditation results in individual freedom, because the athlete has control of the mind instead of being subservient to random thoughts.

Some students of Wholistic Fitness are not students at all. Many athletes accept my coaching and enjoy the immediate benefits of the creative strength training programs as well as the delightful blend of CV and kinesthetic routines. Through these "popular" disciplines my athletes lose body fat, gain strength, win trophies, and improve their body shapes and compositions. For most coaches or training methods, such apparent success would be a crowning glory. In the philosophy of Wholistic Fitness, however, trophies or personal records mean nothing if inner, spiritual growth has not accompanied such outward victory.

HARMONIOUS MIND AND BODY

Numerous studies document the physiological rewards of meditation (see sidebar). These include increased immune system

---

Some Physical Benefits of Meditation

- reduces heart rate
- reduces oxygen consumption
- body requires less sleep and is less stressed
- prolongs body's period of growth and cell production
- reduces the degenerative processes

Some Mental Benefits of Meditation

- new patterns of thinking develop, enhancing creativity and expression
- mind becomes steady; negative self-talk decreases or vanishes
- brings freedom from fear of death, essential for high-risk sports
- personality becomes more magnetic and energy levels increase

---

support, lower blood pressure, a more efficient respiratory rate, enhanced blood alkalinity, enriched brain wave function, and other parameters that counteract accumulated negative stress in the body and mind. For winter athletes, I use meditation to teach them how to direct attention and become more perceptive, which promotes efficient and harmonious movement. One would think that any athlete would be quick to follow a proven system of training that promises such performance-enhancing benefits. Yet even nominal meditation volumes that I craft into Wholistic Fitness training weeks are often ignored. The cherished intellect and savored ego, when faced with itself, rebels. The beginning Wholistic Fitness student soon finds it very difficult to be consistent with the simplest yet most demanding discipline of his or her training: meditation.

In this path, contrary to perhaps all other Western fitness methods, you either "sit" or get off the path! I have refused to continue training students who are not meditating. Why not just take their money and hold their hands and tell them, "That's okay, you don't *really* have to meditate"? Because they are not ready for this level of work. I am especially sincere about this matter when athletes come to me seeking an increase in their performance. At a certain level of athletics, the differences between winning and losing on any given day are infinitesimal. Usually, it's the mentally stronger one who wins. When I say "wins" I am not just referring to structured competitions, but also to noncompetitive winter sports. If a student is not willing to train his or her mind through meditation, the chances of injury greatly increase.

My emphasis on meditation acts as a natural sieve. It filters out athletes unable to accept that mental training is as important as physical training. Meditation separates the run-of-the-mill athletes from the inner-directed athletes, those who are ready to use their training as a source of personal growth. The sports world is full of athletes who, having reached the pinnacle of their sport, can only ask, "Now what?" This spiritual crux arrives because nowhere in these athletes' training was there a recognition and development of transpersonal fitness. Their coaches never taught them how to use their training to become balanced human beings. Instead, they were taught how to succeed and win in only one area of their lives.

My use of meditation was born from real need. I trained myself and numerous athletes for adventure sports, such as ice climbing, that have a high degree of risk. These sports demand rigorous mental capability and control. I have learned, through personal, poignant experience, that a coach must make sure his or her athletes put in the hours training their minds. I have often saved my life, and I have saved the lives of others through my insistence on mental training.

Why should a winter athlete sit still for even five minutes of his or her busy day? Why waste this "quiet time" when we could be, well, *training* for Pete's sake?!

The answer is not logical, because we cannot approach meditation with the logical mind. As a society, we have been conditioned to trust in and to protect the intellectual, logical mind. Meditation asks us to throw all that away and return to our natural mind, our genuine mind that is freed from the chains of ego forms and outer-directed illusions.

Scholars, drunk on words and obscure
   meanings,
Weave a tangled web of concordances.
Simple practice never occurs to them.
                    —from the *Tao Te Ching*

This chapter will provide you with proven meditation techniques that I've used to steady the mind of many winter athletes, from Grade V free-solo ice climbers to world champion hockey goalies.

FUN TIME

The "fun" occurs as the meditator plays along with the meditation, as long as it feels benign. As long as the ego is entertained, it is happy and satiated. Let's take a moment to understand the difference between mind and ego. The mind is that aspect of consciousness that originates in the brain and is manifested in thought, perception, emotion, will, memory, and imagination. All these things influence mental and physical behavior.

The ego is that aspect of mental energy that identifies itself as an independent self, distinct from the world and other selves. The ego thrives on a dualistic view of life: happy/unhappy, pleasant/unpleasant, fun/not fun. When the ego is forced to meditate upon nothingness, it gets bored. Fast. It then retaliates like a hungry child and is very difficult to control. The Hindu tradition likens this lack of control to a monkey, swinging from tree to tree, constantly grabbing for the next branch and seeking the

next entertainment fix. Hindis call such a mind a "monkey mind." American society is addicted to monkey mind. Compare:

Lao Tzu, *"The excited mind is the sick mind."*

Lee Iacocca, former chairman of the Chrysler Corporation, *"We build excitement."*

Should we wonder why our lack of sustained awareness and mindlessness results in injury and emotional highs and lows? The process of meditation permits the differentiation of natural mind and ego. This understanding is vital for optimal winter sport performance.

OUT ON A LIMB

Meditation soon becomes suffering when we do not allow this monkey mind to reach the next branch. The ego gets quickly disenchanted with meditation practice. After we sit regularly for a week, a month, a year, we quit. The ego goes back to craving the nonstop entertainment that the outer world provides in dramatic, easily accessible ways. Thus the nonmeditator lives a life of mental, egocentric slavery.

No athlete can ever be truly free without meditation. It is the only way to train the mind. Author and Buddhist nun Ayya Khemma wrote, "Meditation has one object only, namely to prepare the mind to get out of all suffering, to prepare it for liberation." As any top athlete realizes, our optimal performances come freely, almost effortlessly. If we don't train the mind to reach a liberated state of awareness, we cheat ourselves out of life. Winter athletes do not need to be Buddha to have a wholesome influence over their athletic pursuits. They just need to be awake enough to find the softness and the fun in the free, natural, fluid mind.

CONSCIOUSLY QUIET

One of the qualities most often associated with peak performance relates to what I term "conscious quietness." This feeling of well-being often visits athletes during moments of high-risk or tense situations. When Steve McKinney described his world-record speed skiing feat for *SKI* magazine he said, "I discovered the middle path of stillness within speed, calmness within fear, and I held it longer and quieter than ever before." During the peak of my ice-climbing career, it was during my most tenuous moments of free-soloing or dangerous leads that my mind was most quiet. I felt attuned to the ice, as though I belonged there. I moved deftly, without regard to the abyss that tugged like an angry cat at my back on less attuned days. Similarly, it was during crisis situations, when my partner was hurt or in white-out conditions high on a Canadian peak, that I moved most smoothly, without fear.

This sense of belonging or appropriateness has been noted by many winter athletes, particularly skiers and mountaineers. Arlene Blum, an alpinist, wrote that her climbing brought her, "to a place where I felt I belonged and to which I would return again and again." The qualities that ruin performance and invite disaster and/or injury are rigidity and tenseness. The quieter we are inside, the more appropriate and familiar high performance becomes. Soon, we are no longer daunted by crowds or dangerous situations or the knowledge of extreme effort. I tell my athletes that the way to overcome anxiety is to make the situation familiar. Make it known. Make it appropriate.

We can bring the mind to a place of quiet by returning to our first Lifestyle Principle, breath and posture. Being consciously quiet is a positive mental state that allows peak performances to be released through us, instead of us forcing the performance (which never works for long). This ability to be consciously quiet is a very trainable mental component that can be attained through the meditation techniques described in this book.

RECEIVING PRESENCE

For winter athletes, the ability to receive presence is like a mental worry stone. Recall any or all of the following situations you may have encountered:

- Your heart rate is plastered sky high in a snowshoe or nordic ski race. You question if you can keep up the pace or even finish the race.

• You are standing on the lip of the head-wall above your first black-diamond ski run. You try to summon the courage to push over the edge.

• You've just launched off the highest cliff in your life on your snowboard, and it's *way* bigger than you imagined.

• You are thirty feet above your last "snarg" on a Grade V ice climb, and your forearms are so pumped you can barely hold onto the ice axe, let alone extract it and place it repeatedly to finish the lead.

• You are on your tele skis, cranking the steepest couloir you've ever done, miles from nowhere. Suddenly your skis rip into a patch of ice, spinning you sideways down the mountain gully.

Each of the above situations can be dealt with by receiving presence. What does that mean, receiving presence? It implies a form of yoga, or union with the universe, in which we are not a separate entity "trying to" perform. Instead, we receive the presence of the trees, snow, birds, sky, and clouds, for example. Doing so can take us out of our dualistically conditioned mind and place us at the receiving end of nature's power. Here is where the meditation cushion pays off. For instead of freaking out during one of the above examples, the Wholistically-trained winter athlete will breathe into the fullness of the moment,

and by doing so will not contract his/her emotional state. Instead, they will receive the presence of the moment and respond to it with fluidity instead of rigidness and contraction; never separate, all one, softness.

Are we open enough to receive this power? Not usually. That is why athletes who push themselves into extraordinary experiences have sensed and have been able to tap into a higher power. They have fatigued their normal perceptions and ego noise. Their body/mind has adapted to the extraordinary effort by recruiting new levels of performance. Public records, my case files, and my personal diary are full of instances of such altered states, in which the presence of a higher power was felt and used.

In a 1983 issue of the *Journal of Humanistic Psychology*, James Lester, a psychologist on the 1963 Mount Everest expedition, reported, "As I climb I begin losing contact, in a physical sense, with the world below my feet, and begin to feel wafted into an ethereal 'space.' ... The real world becomes the world above and beyond what I touch, smell, taste, feel, and see. I feel an extremely intimate oneness with the universe and all physical aspects vanish. ... It seems that the world is all turned around and the most unreal is reality."

In Wholistic Fitness, students are encouraged to study and apply a variety of meditation techniques or at least be aware of the wide variety of energetic traditions available to the modern athlete. The ability to receive presence can come from within, such as knowing how to activate the chakra system along the spine. The ability to receive presence can also come from without, such as seeing a horse during a hard workout or race and feeling the "medicine" of the horse, which, according to many American Indian traditions, is physical and spiritual power. Shamans used to use "horse medicine" to fly from the physical world to the mystical world. So, if we are suffering in our workout or race, caught up in the ego, which is busy telling us negative things, seeing a horse may remind us of our spiritual power and enable us to "fly" to another level at that very moment!

Shambala training, which is the sacred path of the warrior tradition from Tibet, has a principle known as *drala*, or natural wisdom. In his book *Shambala*, Rinpoche Trungpa wrote that drala is "the self-existing wisdom and power of the cosmic mirror that are reflected both in us and in our world of perception." There is both external and internal drala. My example of the horse medicine is an instance of external drala, or invoking power from one's physical environment. Finding external drala is a good exercise for the winter athlete, for in doing so we discover a much needed harmony with the environment in which potentially dangerous sports are practiced. In my study of drala, I have found that magic is delivered to me during sport performances when I breathe into an attitude of sa-

credness toward my environment—even if I am suffering through a long nordic ski race and my back injury is killing me. Through drala we can receive presence from our environment in order to shut off the ego and return to a place of higher performance. It is another way to find oneness, the expression of individual creativity within the universal flow of nature.

Although these examples and principles may seem far out to conventionally trained athletes, they are really just the opposite. What could be more simple, more effective than gaining personal power from the world around us? Humans tend to complicate things, especially when it comes to mental performance.

RELAXED AWARENESS

Most people think of meditation as relaxation. As we have seen, there are many benefits of meditation, and relaxation is one of them. Contrary to popular opinion, it is not, however, a synonym for meditation. Meditation involves training the mind to attain a relaxed awareness. When my students begin a meditation session, their purpose is to train the mind. The relaxed awareness, a soft expansion of consciousness, occurs naturally and sometimes pleasantly. Often, it takes years of practice until the actual sitting of meditation could be termed pleasant. While meditating, we teach the mind to keep coming back to the object of the meditation when it begins to

Through a process of softness, relaxed awareness allows us to regain inner peace and attain high performance. Photo by Anne Sasso.

wander. There are many methods by which to anchor the mind for meditation, such as breath, posture, mantra, deity meditation, or visualization. Relaxation can also be an effective meditation tool; it is common among yogic traditions. Even wolves and lions must rest to regain their strength.

Relaxed awareness offers us the opportunity to regain inner peace and achieve high performance through a process of softness instead of hardness. We all seek relaxation in different ways. Often we do not even realize that we need it. When I teach group meditation, many people fall asleep. This is common among beginning meditators and is a symptom of finally beginning to calm what Krishnamurti termed "undigested thought." Winter sport performance often attracts a certain type of person, who has

not learned how to relax inwardly. Instead, they seek the elevated states of perception afforded by winter sports as a way to relax. Henry David Thoreau aptly expressed this tendency: "Many men spend their entire lives fishing, never realizing it's not fish they are after."

Look deeply into your motivation for doing winter sports. Is it not relaxation of mind that you are after? If so, the following mental skills will enhance your relaxation skills for both performance and in everyday life.

BEINGNESS

Perhaps most beneficial about meditation as a means toward relaxation is that we re-learn how to be a human *being* instead of a human *doing*. Our society places formidable emphasis on doing, accumulating, and attaining. We teach athletes in particular to value goals and results instead of presence and awareness. The popular advertising slogan "Just Do It" epitomizes our culture. According to Wholistic Fitness philosophy, however, we should not "Just Do It," we should "Just Be It."

Meditation practice should dissolve the doing, or dualistic entity, of our ego. Proper meditation teaches us to merge with our present action until there is no separation between, say, skier and snow, ice climber and ice, snowshoer and breath. Meditation may be the only time during our day (or week!) that we are quietly conscious and in the present. We are often so busy achieving and doing we never realize we are spiritually asleep!

I often use the example of brushing teeth. Did you brush your teeth this morning? Or was your mind already busying itself with nonstop thoughts about this and that? Be honest, now. Did you actually merge into the space where bristle met tooth? If you were not brushing your teeth, where were you?

The mind we cannot control when brushing teeth is also the mind that is not listening to loved ones, not honoring the sanctity of food; the same undisciplined mind that is easily rattled by the demands of sport performance. Through meditation practice, we can just as easily relax into a high-speed descent of a double black-diamond ski run as we can relax into the brushing of our teeth. What other fitness training method teaches you to train for elite sport performance by brushing your teeth?

BASIC WHOLISTIC FITNESS® MEDITATION METHODS

When athletes begin their study of Wholistic Fitness training, I introduce them to three basic meditation forms. Each of the forms is spaced throughout the training week to afford a comprehensive but easily attained mental training effect by the end of it. Not much time is needed to practice meditation in the early programs, just a few minutes per day.

Passive Meditation

This can be thought of as care-for-the-spirit time. We set aside several minutes to nourish our spirit instead of being immersed in the "thick of thin things."

Each of us requires an experience of eternity—something that nourishes one's soul—every day. When I prescribe a passive meditation in Wholistic Fitness, I ask that the athlete find a way to feed his or her spirit. Sample passive meditations include doing an artistic or leisure activity in deep appreciation of the act itself. Other examples include coloring, drawing, practicing calligraphy, preparing meals, writing letters to government agencies about various environmental/animal rights causes, and reading spiritual literature. It may just mean riding your bike to a pretty vista or walking through a garden and really taking in the flowers to feed your soul. Some students like to visit playgrounds or parks to allow the smiles of children to touch their souls. These timeless things are what feed our spirits and keep our minds healthy and whole.

Active Meditation

During this meditation form, the athlete performs physical work while keeping the mind on the act itself. This sustained attention during activity is similar to what we know as dharana in the yogic tradition. Examples include housework, other domestic duties, maintaining sports equipment, gardening, or performing recycling duties. An active body with a concentrated mind is the purpose of active meditation.

Zazen

This is the only formal style of meditation that beginning students of Wholistic Fitness practice. A zazen session should be done in solitude, during a time and in a place where you are not likely to be interrupted. It is a wise practice to return to this place for every session. Sit cross-legged on the floor with the spine straight. Begin counting the inhales and exhales, in cycles of ten, as they rise and fall from the belly. Concentrate the mind on the passage of air at the nostrils. Hold your body erect, but not stiff. Your hands are held near the

Racin' Jason demonstrates good zazen posture outside the Wholistic Fitness headquarters in Los Angeles. Note how Jason's feet are uncrossed. This "Burmese" style of leg position is a good alternative to the half-lotus for athletes. Photo by the author.

navel, left over the right, palms upward, thumbs touching. The moment a random thought interferes with your counting— which may happen almost instantly— begin counting the breaths again, restarting at one.

KEEP IT SIMPLE

In Wholistic Fitness we do not encourage students to jump into fancy visualizations, imagery, chanting, mantras, or affirmations as part of their meditation. I consider such techniques advanced, and I introduce them only after a mental training foundation has been created. It is my experience that visualization, imagery, and affirmation techniques can be a confusing disservice to the athlete. If we haven't developed a controllable, quiet mind as a foundation for such techniques, the mind/body is unprepared to adequately synthesize the meditation. Simple zazen practice is enough, especially for the first year or so of meditation.

Certain underpinnings must be established for the mind in order for mental training to take deep, productive hold. We first must display the willingness to sit and pay attention. We must also be able to create consistently the quiet time needed for meditation. Then we must practice being alone with our current mental chatter and neuroses in order to reach the clearer nature of our true mind. Until then, visualizations and complex meditative techniques are mere fluff and ego entertainment. Most of the mental sports-training literature I come across only adds more clutter to the athlete's mind!

Wholistic Fitness encourages simplicity and clarity of mind. Eventually advanced meditations are introduced. This initial process of what I term mental cleansing can and should take a long time, involving at least several months of inner study. This rather stark approach to meditation presents a high challenge for most people, who may have entered into this work with expectations of fancy mental-training techniques and electronic biofeedback. As the saying goes, "Blessed is he who has no expectations, for he shall never be disappointed." My genuine approach to purifying the mind first filters out "wannabe" meditators from the true spiritual athletes who want something deeper from their training experience.

INNER SPACIOUSNESS

We carry over the tenet of mental cleansing into other Wholistic Fitness training. As some of my athletes already—and somewhat begrudgingly—know, Wholistic Fitness does not encourage regular use of personal stereos or other forms of synthetic, external motivation when training. Wholistic Fitness tries to teach us our true nature. Whether we want to or not, we must know the degree to which our minds rattle on and on about the circumstances in our lives: how hard this is, how uncomfortable this is, how great I feel, how cool I am, etc. When externals entertain our ego, we experience no inner growth.

Perhaps you know someone who is so frightened by the aspect of silence or of being bored that he surrounds himself with nonstop music, gossip, computer games, work, or friends. Some people cannot workout without music piped into their ears or without a well-paid personal trainer at their side, cheerleading. This outward dependence on external motivation does not develop personal growth. Just as addictive behavior must become a spiritual work-shop for personal growth, so the athlete must not depend on external forms of mo-tivation or entertainment for the sake of the ego.

This discussion is not about behavior that is bad or good. Do not judge others that are running or lifting while wired up to a Walkman. It is just where their aware-ness is at. The occasional use of externals to help on a low-energy day or for novelty is no big deal. The Norwegian national nordic team often uses classical music to develop rhythm for ski technique. Never-theless, serious spiritual athletes should never use external aids during training more than a few times per month. It is usu-ally best to go by the spirit only. Listen to your inner music to begin the most color-ful part of transpersonal training ... know-ing who you really are!

ANCIENT WISDOM READY FOR USE

Western sports experts have largely ig-nored the amount of science known to the world for centuries regarding proper train-ing of the mind. Before 600 B.C.E., the his-torical Buddha (Shakyamuni Buddha) taught a complete method of mental train-ing. In the meditative absorptions, the first absorption is known as vitakka, or "initial application." It means the ability to fix one's mind on the meditation subject, be it the breath, our posture, or a mantra, for example. Practically, this might mean being able to brush our teeth without mental chatter. The Rig Veda of Hinduism con-tains recorded mental-training techniques from about 1550 B.C.E. Around 150 A.D. (or perhaps even much earlier) the sage Patanjali produced the yoga sutras, which contain such precise methods of training the mind that they remain the unques-tioned standard to this day. Patanjali's pratyahara is parallel to the Buddha's vi-takka. The Buddha's second meditative factor, vicara, which means "sustained ap-plication," describes a mind that no longer wanders from the meditation subject but remains concentrated. We can relate this second stage of Buddha's mental-training system to Patanjali's dharana stage. Just starting these first two steps from ancient meditation techniques could well catalyze great performances, enhancing our ability to concentrate all the way through a down-hill ski run, a nordic ski race, or a day at the office.

After the preliminary stages of mental training have been mastered, the ancient sciences describe the exact manner in which to attain higher meditative absorptions. De-tailing such science in this book is inappro-priate. I spend time on this matter only to let the winter athlete know that there is in place a scientific path of mental training that has enjoyed centuries of success. The meditation techniques used in this book are but a springboard for the spiritual athlete to leap into higher levels of performance.

Meditation is a way to realize that true happiness is found within. It is about achieving equanimity without regard to external situations or circumstances.

NEW VISION/ROCKY PATH

I am sure that you, like many of my students, will enjoy greater performance as you practice these meditation techniques. It is difficult at first, since most of us are so locked into accepting the ego as an authentic reality. It is not. The ego is actually an impostor, an intruder upon otherwise perfect awareness. There is a wonderful saying by Sujata in the book *Beginning to See:*

A saint is a very simple man:
when he walks, he walks
when he talks, he talks
and that's all.
He doesn't think while listening,
daydream while walking,
see while touching.
That is very hard.
That is why he is a saint.

The Wholistic Fitness path to meditation can be rocky. Beginning the practice of meditation is more like skiing a mogul run than fresh powder. The rockiness is vital, though; obstacles force us to stretch and grow stronger. Eventually, as our minds reach deeper levels of stability, the powder days will come more frequently.

At various stages of meditation practice, we may notice significant shifts in our awareness. These shifts may alter our life

and our relationships, sometimes into a more narrow, more directed flow. Masters such as Neem Karoli Baba advise seeking an outer environment that is conducive toward spiritual growth. That is one reason that I created this work (and this book); I wanted to surround myself with others who are trying to find their higher side through fitness and performance. When I am hanging out with my Master Students, our relationship is less teacher/student and more like friends helping friends. If I'm slouching over in my posture, they'll catch me. But not until they have adjusted their own! We both learn this way. Once we have established this conducive outer environment, life becomes a sangha, or community of like-spirited beings doing their best to move higher.

To discover our best winter performance, we must also use meditation as a way of severing those relationships that do not promote personal integrity. When I say relationships, I mean our rapport with all things. Our relationship with food must be examined, as must our career, our intimate associations, our relationship with the natural world. Use your Wholistic Fitness training to examine everything in order to arrive at a higher level of awareness. Often we must sever a relationship with outdated, destructive habitual behavior or patterns. There are times when new relationships or gifts or situations must not be allowed to grow. This is where Wholistic Fitness students must honor the warrior tradition. The student must use intuitive wisdom to realize when a situation is inappropriate to his or her personal growth and then sever it. This type of action must be as fast as a sword in full flight, so that the ego does not have time to start its clever rationalization process. But, oh, is this difficult! Paramahansa Yogananda taught, "Environment is stronger than will power." Meditation creates an inner environment that amplifies personal power. If personal power is increased, winter performance will come along for the ride.

AN EMPTINESS OFFERING

To train the mind for optimal sport performance we must nourish the natural mind. This mental training, according to Sujata, means working on yourself "every minute, every day, every year, from one life to another."

If we take up meditation thinking that it will help us, that we will gain something from it, we will never be satisfied. Such an approach is egocentric. True meditation means offering the body/mind to emptiness and having the courage to allow the universe to flow through us.

Meditation is not about divinity; it is about daily life and staying centered in the purest of human action. I mean really,

what good are all our efforts in winter performance if they do not impart a deepening appreciation for life? What good is increased sport performance if we do not gain from it a wider perspective of our place in the universe? What good is our fitness if we aren't flexible enough to bend with others and help them? Meditation practice keeps us calm, whether we are ice climbing and close to peeling or at home with loved ones in an emotionally turbulent situation. I want you to meditate because I want your inner joy to deepen.

I close this chapter with a few lines from Senri Ueno, an unjustly accused war criminal who was executed for trying to save the life of an American pilot:

In the morning the sun rises. I greet it.
I will do my best to live today.
In the evening, the sun sets.
Staring at the evening glow,
I want to sit still.

… Let's find happiness by ourselves.
Within silver tears like pearls
and laughter like the sun,
Let's keep walking ahead each day.
Certainly some day, as I look
back over my past,
I will quietly see my life with a smile.

(translated by Daixnin Katagiri)

8

Discipline 5: Nutrition

"Your body is a three-million-year-old healer. Over three million years of evolution on this planet it has developed many ways to protect and heal itself. You have all the knowledge, tools, materials, and energy necessary to keep yourself healthy."
—Mike Samuels and Hal Bennett

Nutrition begins at the cellular level. The human body consists of fifty trillion cells, more or less. Each cell has a unique function. Each tissue, each organ, and each organ system orchestrates specific tasks for the benefit of the body as a whole. Should something upset the cellular environment, other cells spring to restorative action. We, as a society, should be so devoted to harmony.

Take the liver as an example of the intricate harmony of the body. More than five hundred functions occur within it, including more than a thousand enzymes working to maintain digestion and metabolic health. The brain has ten million nerve cells. The lungs contain three hundred million air sacs, while the kidneys filter five hundred gallons of blood each day. When you go skiing, consider the volume of visual intake that the eye must process instantly so that you can react fast enough to avoid injury. The muscles that operate the lenses of the eyes move up to a hundred thousand times a day, and each optic nerve is composed of about 1.25 million individual fibers.

Our bodies are masters of regeneration, yet our society dwells on how quickly we age. Consider the following physiological facts. In less then a year, we replace 98 percent of our atoms. We regenerate:

- a new skin once a month;
- a new skeleton every month;
- a new stomach lining every five days;
- a new liver every six weeks.

All of this pivots upon regeneration. How we choose to nourish ourselves. How often do we appreciate the miracle of our bodies? Without this appreciation we overeat, for we have lost respect for the miracle of self. Without this appreciation, we consume substances that inhibit the natural regeneration of the body. Why is it that so few nutrition books and experts disregard appreciation of food as a form of nutrition? The first guideline in Wholistic Fitness nutrition is a simple one: "Appreciate your food. It is sacred."

BUILDING AND CLEANSING

Nutrition can be thought of in two categories. The first category is nourishment, that which promotes growth, also known as anabolism, or cell-building. Nourishment is what we hear and read about most: vitamins, minerals, carbohydrates, protein, fat, micronutrients, all of that stuff.

The second category is cleansing, or the detoxifying of cellular wastes and accumulations. We don't hear much about this aspect of nutrition because there are not many gimmicks related to it from which marketing people can make money. Cleansing nutrition can take a variety of forms: under-eating or fasting to preserve long-term cellular health; ingesting certain foods or teas that function as a biological wash; taking colonics; or even using an Ayurvedic tongue cleaner. It is a means of getting and

keeping those trillions of cells clear of toxic accumulations caused by incomplete digestive processes, chemical additives, pollutants, irritants, and other cell-clogging debris. Many popular food choices encourage gluey, thick mucus to arise within the body, causing internal pollution, especially in the digestive and respiratory organs. A lack of nutritional cleansing can cause our musculoskeletal systems to manifest ailments such as arthritis. Vascular health can suffer as well with hardened, inflexible veins and arteries. Allergies are another classic symptom of poor attention to nutritional cleansing.

SPIRITUAL NUTRITION

Wholistic Fitness also considers things like careers, relationships, sports, sun, wind, conversation, home, or friends as distinct and potent forms of nourishment. Breath work, yoga, energy work, meditation, training, and massage are all forms of nutrition that benefit the cleansing or building of mind/body. Like its physical foodstuff counterpart, each aspect of "spiritual nourishment" can be regenerative or degenerative. The choice is ours.

Under-appreciation of food, however, remains at the root of most dis-ease in this country. The people that I see in my private work are often several decades into their lives, yet still have not developed a simple sensitivity for the amazing gift of food. Brainwashed by popular media, most of us mindlessly cram foods down our throats that have little or no regenerative life force in them. Yet how we choose to nourish our mind/body/spirit is undoubtedly the most effective discipline available for self-knowledge.

To experience nutrition's transformative abilities, we could practice what is known in spiritual work as *tapasya*. Tapasya means "to straighten by fire." Perhaps you or someone you know is a coffee drinker, a smoker, or an alcoholic. This person may tell about trying to go cold turkey to get off the addiction. Going "cold turkey" is the Western counterpart to tapasya. It's very good spiritual practice. It throws us directly into the fire of self-confrontation, a place where highest learning lives.

Nutrition is a potent discipline along the path of Wholistic Fitness because it either straightens or twists us; it empowers or enfeebles us. The path of Wholistic Fitness encourages a principled and balanced approach to nutrition. The nutritional guidelines in this book impart a cellular clarity that allows the body—not the ego—to eat what is relevant. By regaining the body's natural attraction to wholesome foods, cellular clarity allows the wisdom of the body to speak more loudly. The act of eating then becomes sacred, and the sense of broad-spectrum nutrition begins to take on a multidimensional realm from which the advanced Wholistic Fitness student quenches both physical and spiritual thirst.

STAYING RELEVANT

Staying relevant with our nutrition leads to introspection, a magnificent quality one gains along the path of awakening. Introspection teaches us to respect the sacred cycle that continually nourishes the universe: birth, life, death, and rebirth. Can we see our genuine place in the cosmos, a cosmos so inextricably linked to everything but not elevated beyond anything else? Within the context of the universe, a human dying of cancer is no more dramatic than the death of a gazelle brought down by a lion or the slow death of an aspen leaf in autumn. As we learn to remember our true place in the cosmos, we become nourished by an elevated sense of gratitude for being alive right now. Wholistic Fitness encourages all serious athletes to contemplate the quality of death so that they may live each day fully and work out with full conviction!

WIDE PERSPECTIVE

A popular men's fitness magazine once asked me, "Are you satisfied with your level of fitness right now?" I replied, "Of course, I have two legs and two arms, I can breathe fresh air and move with the sun on my skin. Why be dissatisfied?"

I always strive to increase my sport performance, yet the core of my aspiration does not relate to podiums and peak performances. Simple breath and movement nourish the relevance of my fitness. Surprisingly, I was the only athlete polled who gave a positive answer to the interviewer's question. To think that so many athletes are training each day in an ocean of frustration is sad. It speaks poorly of our coaching and of our spiritual education.

All of this talk about relevance is true nutrition, though you will not read about it in nutrition or fitness books. Many of my students apologize for living in dirty cities, where they fill their lives with stress, pollution, and lazy-minded friends. They apologize for "having to live in the rat race" until the day when they can break free, when they make their million dollars or whatever. But if we are not happy right now, this instant, we will not be happy when (and if) the rainbow drops into our laps. Remember, even if we win the rat race … we are still rats.

VEGETARIANISM? NO "ISMS" OF ANY KIND

Eating mindfully is the second nutritional principle in Wholistic Fitness. Honor all foods. If we make our food choices mindfully, we will eventually arrive at the wisdom inherent to a vegetarian-based approach to nutrition. Note that I said "vegetarian-based," which is not necessarily "vegetarian."

From an academic perspective, vegetarian-based nutrition makes sense. For example, there are digestive benefits, since the anatomical structure of the human intestine seems to extract the most nutrients from a vegetarian, not a carnivorous, diet. Pollution is another consideration. Eating flesh foods means eating animals whose prey along the food chain contains high concentrations of pesticides, chemicals, and antibiotics. (Scientists know this effect as bio-amplification.) When studied from a fat, fiber, and cholesterol perspective, flesh foods again lose in a comparative analysis. Vegetarian foods contain nominal amounts of fat or cholesterol while maintaining a high fiber content. Animal products have virtually no fiber and are loaded with fat and cholesterol. Moreover, meat production is extremely wasteful and expensive. Nearly thirteen acres of land are required to supply the needs of one person on a meat-based diet; up to thirty vegetarians can be fed from the same 13 acres.

There are also ethical and ecological considerations for a vegetarian-based diet. Meat-based diets contribute to the destruction of huge amounts of rainforest (equivalent to the size of New York State each year) to create grazing land for slaughter animals. Finally, we must contemplate the simple respect for animals that we can show by not killing them. Studies reveal that an animal's pain and fear during the slaughtering process are transferred into our bodies when we consume their flesh. According to some yogis, this chronic ingestion of fear and pain is why each generation of humans finds it more difficult to control its emotions.

EMPOWERMENT THROUGH FOOD CHOICES

World hunger. Are you feeling guilty about it? Instead of just feeling guilty, *do* something, however small. Change your eating habits in a way that is relevant to the wasteful and unbalanced distribution of world food production, for example, eat less flesh foods. Conserve water in cooking and washing. Never eat so much that you are feeding your ego instead of your body. We can be part of a growing solution by simply taking our practice within.

As we go forth into the more familiar terrain of sport performance nutrition that involves physical foods and substances, do not forget spiritual nutrition. Ultimate sport performance is always a matter of spirit. I have coached every principle and fitness discipline discussed thus far from a spiritual transmission first, then physical teaching. With this understanding, let's explore the often wacky world of sport performance nutrition.

BASIC NUTRITION FOR WINTER SPORTS PERFORMANCE

I often get pleas from athletes seeking advice on 1) how to lose bodyfat; and 2) how to get stronger, faster, and/or have more endurance. Each of those two areas boils down to one nutritional goal: attaining optimal body mass. It is a tricky journey, and let me say from the start that there is no secret universal rule. Each athlete has a unique body constitution with ever-changing physiological currents. In fact, I refer some of my clients to a nutritionist who specializes in body composition alteration. I am an outdoor performance and transpersonal trainer. Even my method of Wholistic Fitness should not be considered a replacement for a competent nutritionist. Wholistic Fitness is about self-cultivation and general fitness. By traveling the journey of Wholistic Fitness, we may uncover certain areas of ourselves that require the work of a specialist, be it a particular sport, spiritual guidance, or nutritional counsel. Use Wholistic Fitness as your overall training method, but use expert specialists if and when needed.

Nutrition is the most uncoachable of my five fitness disciplines. Even if you were a private student of mine, and we trained together every day for two hours you would still have twenty-two hours each day to eat whatever you want in whatever volumes you choose. That's uncoachable. Wholistic Fitness provides a clear understanding of wise food choices, both spiritually and physically, but you must animate the path. As we explore performance nutrition, consider the following five observations that I've made while working privately with athletes and nutrition. Most of these observations have been supported by research findings.

1. Make dietary changes slowly. Western science has established sound nutritional advice, and many dietary traditions from other cultures also work very well for some of my clients. Engaging a dietary philosophy such as macrobiotics can help a person overcome a nutritional sticking point; other times an Ayurvedic approach may be better. Experimentation is wise, but make all changes slowly and steadfastly. It's hard to determine the true effect of a dietary change if we jump from one system to another.

2. Dietary changes must be accompanied by regular physical workouts. Do not expect the inclusion of a micronutrient to drop your 10K ski race time by three minutes. Similarly, do not count on a dietary change to drop five pounds of fat without expending the correct amount of calories through training. Nutrition + Exercise = Results.

3. Do not judge your progress by the progress made by another. Dietary testimonials are not the best gauge for how well a nutritional change will work for you. Sticking to what has been proven by science is usually a wiser approach than falling prey to some commercial product claims.

4. Be aware of the source of nutritional guidance. Even nutrition "experts" may not know what is best for you. I am saddened when I see personal trainers bloated by steroids advising real people on how to

eat! How would they know? They are nothing more than chemical processing plants! The same goes for skinny endurance athletes who claim to know all there is about performance nutrition. What good would their advice be to the ice climber when the skinny endurance expert can't even do one pull-up? Question nutritional experts. Ask about their qualifications: are they knowledgeable in *all* areas of fitness—flexibility, endurance, strength, power, and mental/emotional? If not, how do they know what good nutrition provides across the physiological spectrum? And keep in mind that bookstore shelves are filled with nutritional fad books authored by computer-tapping researchers with no competitive experience in athletics. They have not pushed any nutritional parameters within themselves. Instead, they rely on the clever sensationalism of study findings to fill the pages of their books. Don't be fooled by the testimonials of one or two athletes. Most genetically gifted athletes I know could eat dirt and twigs and still kick butt over the rest of the field. You and I, who have to truly work for our fitness, need real nutritional guidance, proven through both established science and long years in the field with hundreds of people.

5. Allow nutrition to be specific. An alpine ski racer eats differently than a nordic skier. An older athlete with an injury history must be fed differently than an adolescent athlete. Someone who needs to lose body

fat must eat differently than someone wishing to gain muscle weight. Though much of nutrition can be generalized, specific fitness goals require specific nutritional regimens. Dial in to the specifics of nutrition and allow the myths and fad diets to dissolve back from where they came—obscurity.

PROTEIN

I have been keen on protein intake since the early '80s, when I kept athletes in a positive nitrogen balance via full-spectrum amino acid supplementation. Once I had these athletes (and myself) in the cellular state most conducive to tissue regeneration, great things began to happen. Both endurance athletes and bodybuilders saw their performances skyrocket. Recovery times were cut in half. Training intensities became filled with inner fire. Training capacities increased. My case files are filled with reports of enhanced well-being, heightened immune response, stabilization of body composition, and the elimination of chronic injuries.

It's been that way ever since. The Wholistic Fitness nutritional philosophy predates many of the diet trends that were once popular, are currently popular, and will certainly come around again wearing yet another mask. During the '80s and early '90s, when the fitness media was going on about carbohydrate manipulation diets to "trick" fat off the body,

Wholistic Fitness athletes kept quietly centered on quality protein intake. We got all the body-fat loss results *plus* positive training effects.

ACID TRIP

Why does amino-acid awareness work so well for athletic performance? When I was an associate editor for a sport-science magazine, I came across much research on various aspects of performance nutrition. The following is an excerpt from a piece on protein and nitrogen balance by Peter Lemon, a Ph.D. from Kent State University:

Protein is essential for all living organisms. Found primarily in muscle, it makes up about 15% of bodyweight. Each of the many types of proteins is made up of small units called amino acids. The body can make proteins from amino acids, but it cannot produce all the required amino acids. Those that cannot be produced are called essential amino acids because they must be consumed in food. Therefore, our need for protein is really a need for amino acids. Some foods contain all the essential amino acids, whereas others do not. If insufficient complete protein foods are included in the diet, an athlete must eat an appropriate mixture of incomplete protein foods to obtain all the essential amino acids.

The amount of protein in the body is constantly changing because of changes in dietary protein and changes in the rates of protein synthesis and breakdown. To assess changes in protein metabolism, nutritionists traditionally measure nitrogen balance (nitrogen is a component of protein). These experiments require measures of all nitrogen consumed in food and all nitrogen excreted. When intake exceeds excretion, a positive nitrogen balance exists. A positive nitrogen balance is required for growth. When protein intake is insufficient, negative nitrogen balance occurs. In this situation, tissue protein (primarily muscle) is broken down to make amino acids available for other uses.

Protein is the most plentiful substance in the body next to water. It is the most significant source of building materials for muscles, blood, and internal organs (such as the heart and brain). It is also needed for hormonal function, which in turn controls metabolic activity and cellular growth. Athletic performance relies on protein's ability to prevent blood and tissues from becoming too acidic or too alkaline while regulating the body's water balance. Remember that I noted heightened immune response and enhanced well-being in my case files? These are tied to another function of protein: the formation of enzymes and antibodies.

Proteins, unlike carbohydrates and fats, cannot be stored in the body. Carbohydrates and fats can be stored within the organs and adipose (fatty) tissues, ready for use when the metabolic need arises. Proteins, however, become available only by an intracellular process wherein the body dis-

mantles its tissue proteins via molecular and structural pathways. The tissues of the liver are broken down first, then those of the muscles, and, lastly, the organs. Diets low or completely lacking in protein inevitably waste lean body tissue, which is particularly inadvisable for athletes.

DEANIMATE ME

People still get frightened when I prescribe a protein supplement. They have been informed that too much protein puts a strain on the liver and that excess protein turns to fat. While excess protein not used in cell building or energy can be converted into fatty acids and stored in adipose tissue, it can also be deanimated (which means the body jettisons the NH_2 radical from the amino compound) and excreted in the form of urine. What gets people into trouble is super-high protein intake, which forces the body to release calcium into the blood to buffer an acidic response from the protein conversion. Chronic elevated-calcium response could lead to osteoporosis stemming from a calcium deficiency. The amount of protein intake Wholistic Fitness endorses, however, is far below such radical intake levels. No coach or athlete is advised to take in an amount of protein beyond the physiological need created by exercise. Excessive protein intake does not increase skeletal muscle growth or fat loss.

The most profound test of whether or not we are in a positive nitrogen balance is to take note of our training. This is one reason I authored *The Outdoor Athlete's Training Journal*. Journaling is the best way to determine if a diet provides adequate nutrition to manifest training effects. An athlete needs to keep track of intuitive parameters, such as motivational levels, mood swings, mental fitness, joint and muscle flexibility, or immune response to determine effective nutrition. Lab tests are fantastic and fun for determining the physiological results of diets, but only through long-term daily awareness can nutritional be studied. Plateaus in progress, overtraining, chronically stiff and sore muscles and joints, and frequent illness are all symptoms of a negative nitrogen balance, the beacon that calls us toward a more wise amino-acid intake.

PROTEIN SUPPLEMENTS?

We need twenty-two amino acids in a specific pattern to formulate assorted body-tissue proteins. Eight of those twenty-two cannot be produced by the body and are thus termed "essential" amino acids. Although the nonessential amino acids can be manufactured by the body, they must still be present, in correct proportion to the essential amino acids, to attain and maintain normal metabolic function. Here is the kicker and the key factor for supplementation: If *one amino acid* (either essential or nonessential) is supplied in a smaller amount than required, protein synthesis

will be limited. But if one *essential* amino acid is completely absent, the other amino acids cannot be utilized and are wasted. (This doesn't hold true if a nonessential amino acid is completely absent.) I drill this into my athletes; protein synthesis is an all-or-nothing deal. Wholistic Fitness nutritional philosophy, therefore, encourages protein supplementation.

Protein supplementation is additionally valuable if we are trying to consume foods with an awareness of global sensitivity. Most dietary protein sources come from flesh foods. The vegetarian approach toward maintaining a positive nitrogen balance gets mucky as well: too much thinking about food combining, too many calories, too much digestive stress, etc. A simple amino-acid supplementation for daily protein needs is perhaps the best choice.

Athletes would likely benefit from more dietary protein than called for by the current RDA (recommended daily allowance). Additional proteins can prevent or minimize loss of blood proteins as well as provide exercise fuel and aid in muscle repair. Endurance athletes especially need adequate amino-acid intake for a source of exercise fuel. High-intensity or long-duration exercise leads to greater amino-acid oxidation, thus altering protein-synthesis rates. Moreover, as sport scientists have demonstrated, muscle damage occurs with any exercise (especially those with an eccentric component, like strength training, endurance training, or alpine skiing) and additional, high-quality amino-acid intake appears likely to ensure the repair of damaged fibers.

WHAT KIND OF SUPPLEMENTS?

I have used supplements from UniPro Performance Nutrition, Inc., (800-877-1704) personally and professionally for more than a decade. I attribute much of my success with athletes to the influence of these products. UniPro was one of the first research groups to conduct and document nitrogen balance studies in the early '60s, and they have continued to produce a select line of supplements that are—in my opinion—the best in the world. My athletes and I have tested them through thousands of demanding multisport performances.

In the upcoming discussions about other macro- and micronutrients, I'll occasionally refer to UniPro products. UniPro is not a multilevel company, nor do I receive any monetary compensation from it. I align myself with the company for a simple reason: its products are of high integrity, and they work. Following is a sample of UniPro products most often used in Wholistic Fitness nutritional counsel.

A Sample of Core Nutrition

Basic Plus: A strong nutritional base provides a straightforward and cost-effective multivitamin/mineral formula.

Amino 1,000: The trusted original for optimal insurance of a positive nitrogen balance; comes in caplets.

Perfect Protein: A powdered alternative to Amino 1,000, it contains the highest biological value of protein. Twenty-five percent of the protein is composed of branched chain amino acids (leucine, isoleucine, and valine), essential aminos as well as the only ones that are metabolized in muscle.

MyoSystem XL: A dietary supplement in powder form that provides superb amino-acid and broad-spectrum nutrition with low glycemic response.

Additions for Performance Nutrition

Muscl-Flex: For joint lubrication, muscle elasticity, and flexibility. This is not a vegetarian supplement since it is made from freeze-dried pure New Zealand green-lipped mussels.

Carboplex Orange: Medium and long-chain glucose polymer drink for recovery, and branched chain amino acids (BCAA), which are essential aminos, as well as being the only aminos that are metabolized in muscle.

Pro and Endura Optimizer: These metabolic optimizers reduce muscle catabolism during intense and prolonged training; scientifically proven to benefit performance; extremely absorbable source of protein and carbohydrate. Pro Optimizer is for strength athletes; Endura Optimizer is for endurance athletes. I affectionately call these Optimizers my anti-bonk insurance. Endura is perhaps UniPro's most recognizable product, and was the first fluid-replacement drink to contain full-spectrum electrolytes. It is the substance found most often in Wholistic Fitness students' water bottles.

VEGETARIAN PROTEIN

Yes, a veggie athlete can attain and maintain a positive nitrogen balance, but it requires considerable food-combining knowledge of complementary proteins that work synergistically to produce the appropriate cellular state. Essentially, the vegetarian athlete must combine two or more grains, legumes, seeds, nuts, and vegetables consistently throughout the day. This requires attention and time normally not available to most people. Such guidance is beyond the scope of this book, but there are numerous food-combining books available for vegetarians to study.

CALCULATING PROTEIN

The RDA for protein is 0.8 grams of protein per kilogram per day. This figure is based on the requirements of an average 154-pound male to repair and replace tissue proteins under normal conditions. This estimate delivers about 60 grams of protein per day to the average person. Most research I have come across recommends that athletes should use an intake formula

of 1.4 grams of protein per kilogram per day. Such an approach accounts for a possible increase in nitrogen losses due to training. Through my own studies, I suggest staying in this latter range.

To calculate your protein requirement, divide your weight in pounds by 2.2, which equals your weight in kilograms. Then take your kilogram weight and multiply it by 1.4 grams of protein per kilogram, which equals the grams of protein per day.

There are plenty of nutritional guides that provide the amount of protein and other nutrients in foods. Every athlete should have such a book and perform regular, informal dietary analysises to make sure that his or her diet provides an appropriate intake of protein and other nutrients.

CARBOHYDRATES

Carbohydrates (carbs) are the body's primary energy source. Muscular movement and physiological function increase carbohydrate metabolism. Even the digestion and utilization of proteins and fats depend on carbohydrates for regulation. This dependence leads to a quick depletion of both stored and circulating carbohydrates in the body. Most food cravings are carbohydrate based as a result.

Carbohydrate structure takes three primary forms: simple sugars, starches, and cellulose. These classifications are based on the length of the respective molecular chain.

For instance, high-fructose corn syrup (a simple sugar) has a simple molecular carbohydrate structure. Its bound energy is easily accessed by the body. Starches, such as pasta, require more systematic metabolism and are thus known as complex carbohydrates. Enzymes act upon complex carbs to break the molecular chain into simple sugars, such as glucose. Cellulose, found on the skins of fruits and vegetables, largely functions as a digestive aid; it is mostly indigestible by humans and possesses little energy value. But, like fiber, the indigestible remnants of carbohydrates, cellulose, aids digestion by binding with water to add weight, bulk, and softness to fecal matter. This allows for more regular and rapid elimination.

All sugars and starches are converted by the body into simple sugars like glucose or fructose. All sugars must become glucose before they can be used for energy. Some of the glucose is converted into glycogen, which is stored within the liver and muscles. Excess glycogen is, in turn, converted to stored body fat.

ATHLETES SHOULD DO WINDOWS

Athletes are interested in carbs because of their ability to provide energy and replenish muscle glycogen lost during exercise. During extended training sessions, an intake of a glucose polymer solution such as

UniPro's Endura can help delay fatigue while restoring vital fluids and nutrients.

After a training session of one hour or longer, we must acknowledge the "glycogen window." Studies have shown that athletes who consume a moderate to high amount of carbohydrates within one hour after an extended workout have more muscle glycogen twenty-four hours later than those who waited more than an hour to eat. A general guideline is to take in at least a hundred grams of carbs immediately after training. A pure carbohydrate drink, such as UniPro's Carboplex Orange, may be easier to consume directly after training than starchy foods. In addition, performance drinks replace fluids, contain concentrated amounts of carbohydrates, and may prevent the onset of an intense hunger bonk (hypoglycemia) several hours after training.

BELLY UP TO THE BARS

Energy bars, such as PowerBars™, are excellent alternative sources to meals in "crisis" situations, such as times when you need to eat but are simply too busy for a full meal or when you're trying to eat within the glycogen window. PowerBars™, for example, start their nutrient profile with a simple carb, go into a medium-chain carb, and finish with a superb amino-acid formula for both tissue repair and energy fuel. But don't mistake them for candy. They are sport-performance bars and require a lot of water to aid their ingestion and digestion. A high intake of these bars can tie up stomach fluids and impair elimination. Use the bars but do so with awareness.

THINGS ARE BEGINNING TO GEL

Carbohydrate gels provide another way in which to fill the glycogen window and provide energy on the run. I recommend HammerGels™. They have a not-too-sweet taste and the syrupy consistency is ideal for consumption while running a high heart rate. Besides containing pure carbohydrate gel for energy and glycogen replenishment, HammerGels contain branched-chain amino acids. Moreover, HammerGel is available in refillable pocket-sized flasks. PowerGel™, made by PowerBar, is also a very good carbohydrate gel and is widely available.

DIETARY INTAKE OF CARBS AND THE GLYCEMIC INDEX

I do not advise any diet composed of less than 50 percent carbohydrates, especially for winter athletes. A low intake of carbs can create an imbalance in cellular fluids and cause the metabolic rate to slow. Low carb intake can also cause the body to use protein for energy instead of for building and repairing muscle. Moreover, both personally and professionally, I have seen low-

Glycemic Index of Common Foods	
Percent	Food Type
20–29	Lentils, fructose, kidney beans, soybeans, grapefruit
30–39	Milk, ice cream, apples, oatmeal, peaches
40–49	Spaghetti, potatoes (sweet), oranges, yogurt
50–59	Sucrose, potato chips, All-Bran cereal
60–69	Rice (brown), white bread, shredded wheat, bananas, raisins
70–79	Rice (white), potato, millet, Weetabix cereal
80–90	Corn flakes, carrots, maltose, honey
100	Glucose

carb diets cause uncontrollable food cravings, which then lead to inappropriate food choices.

Any meal containing a high amount of refined or simple sugars and that is low in fiber, fat, or protein, is not a wise undertaking. Such an intake will drive blood-glucose levels so high that the pancreas will over-secrete insulin, pouring circulating glucose into the cells too fast. As a result, the blood-glucose level will crash, causing fatigue, lightheadedness, and dizziness (known as "bonking" in athletic lingo). This blood-glucose/insulin response is known as the *glycemic effect* to physiologists. Most people can handle occasional glycemic spikes, but it is not a healthy way to eat, nor is it conducive to athletic performance. Control your intake of refined or simple sugars. If you do eat them, make sure to consume them in the presence of other macronutrients such as fiber, fat, or protein.

The glycemic index on the previous page shows how various foods contribute to the body's ability to derive glucose from carbohydrates. The index is defined as the proportion of blood-serum glucose derived from particular foods compared to that derived from a solution of pure glucose. You should be aiming for the lower end of the scale.

It may surprise the athlete to realize that foods commonly thought of as sweet, such as fructose, the sugar found in fruits, causes virtually no insulin response. When choosing carbohydrate foods, the preferred choices are complex carbs like whole grains and vegetables. The only simple carbohydrates that I recommend are fruits, as they do not spike the blood sugar and contain an excellent source of fiber. Athletes need at least twenty-five grams of fiber per day to regulate their absorption of glucose.

Many of the athletes I see do not wisely regulate their carbohydrate intake. They eat foods that are too high on the glycemic index, which causes unpredictable food cravings and inconsistent blood-sugar levels. Many students are also misinformed about the relation of carbohydrates to body fat. They still think that a moderate to high intake of carbs will make them fat. Excess calories make us fat, not carbohydrate intake! After I have prescribed an increase in carbohydrates, students sometimes report a sudden increase in body fat. What they are actually noticing is weight gain due to the body retaining more water. Each part of glycogen stores 2.7 grams of water, which is needed to rehydrate the body and increase cellular efficiency. Once the body has been properly hydrated at the cellular level, the bloated feeling and the weight gain will pass.

FAT

Wholistic Fitness uses fat intake as a tool for developing mental toughness and spiritual tenacity. Most Americans eat too much fat. Yet, though they complain about how fat they are, they seldom do anything about it. Losing body fat is, as Richard Watson says in *The Philosopher's Diet,* "an activity requiring moral fiber." He goes on to say, "Dieting is a very serious business, but most dieters are not serious about maintaining the weight they reach after they've taken off a few pounds. They gain them back, and then lose again. 'Oh, here I go again,' they say."

Wholistic Fitness is adept at getting students to lose body fat. How? By encouraging them to honor foods and consider them sacred. If we eat with reverence and mindfulness, we eat less—the major component of losing body fat. The four other fitness disciplines as well as the lifestyle principles of Wholistic Fitness support the issues involved in fat loss. Body fat is fine in appropriate amounts. An excess of it can, however, symbolize inner greed, spiritual laziness, and insensitivity. Remember, it is the intake of excess calories—not just of fat—that contributes to being overly fat. Understanding the role of fat is very important for long-term health and sport performance.

ABSOLUTELY LIPID

Fats, or lipids, yield almost nine calories when oxidized, making fats far and away the most concentrated source of energy in the diet. Carbs and proteins yield only four calories per gram, by comparison. We must be very careful about our fat intake. Not all fats cause high cholesterol, and there is no sound reason to cut out all fat from your diet. We need dietary fat to transport fat-soluble vitamins and essential fatty acids within our system. In fact, our fat intake should constitute no less than 10 percent of our total caloric intake.

The role of fat in the body makes for fascinating study. Although Wholistic Fitness philosophy restricts dietary fat intake to nominal levels, it also acknowledges the value this nutrient provides. Our appreciation of fat should begin at the cellular level. Yes, *appreciation.* Some athletes regard fat as such a bad thing that they embark on foolish and even dangerous diets to avoid the very thing that could help them reach their fitness goals. By appreciating fat, we may invite a higher level of health and balance into our well-being.

All the cells in our body have membranes made of fatty acids. The membrane structure is extremely important. The properties of the membrane allow it to regulate the flow of nutrients into and out of the cells, acting like a traffic officer. Fat also surrounds, protects, and stabilizes important organs, such as the heart, liver, and kidneys. Historically, fat kept us alive long before such cold-weather outerwear as triple-laminated Gore-Tex™ parkas, insulating our bodies from environmental temperature changes and preserving body heat.

Take fat away from the diet, and eating behavior can assume unhealthy patterns. Why is this? Because it takes fat to metabolize fat! Barry Sears, Ph.D., author of the popular diet book *The Zone,* states that fat acts as "a control rod to slow the entry rate of carbohydrate into the bloodstream, thereby reducing the insulin response." Fat slows the absorption of nutrients, including sugars, into the bloodstream, thereby "balancing" blood sugar. According to the National Academy of Sports Medicine, blood-sugar regulation is the main way to accomplish satiety. Dietary fats also prolong the digestion process by slowing the stomach's secretions of hydrochloric acid, thus creating a longer lasting sensation of fullness after a meal.

CHOLESTEROL AND BIO-INDIVIDUALITY

Lipids come in a variety of forms. Cholesterol, for instance, is a normal component of most body tissues, particularly those of the brain and nervous system, liver, and blood. Cholesterol is required to form sex and adrenal hormones, and bile. Cholesterol receives a bad rap because it raises the level of low-density lipoproteins, or LDL. If the amount of lipid in a lipoprotein molecule is higher then the amount of protein, we say that the protein-to-lipid ratio is low, thus the term low density. The greater the amount of protein in the lipoprotein molecule, the higher the density. If the LDL concentration in our blood is too high, we are a more likely candidate for coronary disease. The current standards for desirable cholesterol levels for males and females over the age of twenty call for less than 200 milligrams per deciliter. Anything higher is considered borderline too high. Cholesterol levels can be lowered through the advice of your personal trainer or nutritionist. Regular exercise and refraining from smoking cigarettes are all it takes to bring down a high LDL count. Additionally, consuming monounsaturated fats (such as olive oil) and polyunsaturated fats (such as vegetable and fish oils) can also lower LDL levels.

Saturated fats, another lipid, need to be restricted. A high percentage of saturated fat in the diet stimulates the liver to make unhealthy amounts of LDL. The result is diminished circulatory fitness, damage to arterial walls, and coronary disease. The best way to avoid saturated fat is to restrict your intake of animal and dairy foods.

Bio-individuality means that we all convert food into energy differently. For instance, some people are genetically predisposed to metabolizing carbohydrates more rapidly than others. For this small percentage of the population, eating more Sara Lee desserts might be justified. Up to 30 percent of their total caloric intake may be fat, so that an overeating response stemming from an abnormal craving for carbohydrates can be offset.

MONITORING FAT INTAKE

You can monitor your intake of fat simply by educating yourself about how much fat is contained in what foods. Get one of those pocket-sized fat-counter books. Read labels. Keep track of your fat intake for three days. You'll be surprised to realize how much fat is sneaking into your meals. This self-study of dietary patterns is instrumental in maintaining a wise daily allotment of fat.

It's not food that is expanding America's waistline. Our natural food sources have not suddenly increased in caloric content. Instead it's our lack of will power to gather accurate information and execute firm eating decisions, as well as our sparse appreciation of food that are the causes. Currently, Americans consume 300 calories per day more than ten years ago and are less active physically. Meanwhile, technology continues to create calorically dense but nutrient-deficient foods. Our propensity for eating at fast-food establishments also contributes significantly to our fatness. In spite of our fear of getting fat, however, we continue to misunderstand its role during our travels along the way of fitness.

IS MORE FAT JUSTIFIED FOR WINTER ATHLETES?

The notion that a winter athlete needs to eat more fat than summer athletes in order to stay warm and/or perform better is a matter of individual constitution, not a rule of sport physiology. When I coach winter athletes involved in sports that require extended stays in cold temperatures, such as mountaineers, I rarely prescribe an increase in fat intake. The exception comes when the student is of a particular body type known in Ayurvedic tradition as pure or highly *vatta*. People with a vatta constitution have thin physiques and are often unusually tall or short. They also often have dry skin, dark complexions (compared to their relatives), and generally prefer warm climates, sunshine, and moisture. It is unusual for vattas to even be attracted to winter sports like mountaineering.

As an outdoor performance coach and a cold-weather athlete, I have not found that an increase in dietary fat will necessarily heighten winter performance. Individual constitutions must be acknowledged when manipulating fat intake. As a general rule,

any amount of weight on your body that is not functional is likely a hindrance to performance. Even 2 percent body fat is enough to fuel consecutive free-solo climbs up Mount Everest. My counsel? Stay lean year-round. This is especially true for athletes over thirty-five years old. The older we get, the less intense our metabolic fire. That means getting rid of unneeded body fat becomes more difficult as we age.

WATER

The importance of water for the winter athlete cannot be overemphasized. Given the potential for extreme loss of body fluid through evaporative cooling, staying hydrated is of primary concern particularly to backcountry winter athletes, such as mountaineers, ice climbers, and ski tourers. Studies show that fluid loss constituting as little as 2 percent of body weight will negatively affect performance by decreasing circulatory functions. Since the winter athletes most prone to dehydration are also the ones whose energy expenditure involves fat-burning metabolism, they must pay particular attention to consuming enough water to convert fat into energy.

How much water is enough? The winter athlete should consume about 3.5 quarts of water per day. Mountaineers and the like will require even more. My most intense memories from mountaineering revolve around the discipline needed to stop and melt snow for water during ascents.

Follow these general guidelines for fluid replacement:

- Cold fluids empty from the stomach faster than warm fluids and are thus used more quickly.
- If exercising longer than ninety minutes, use an electrolyte sports drink, such as Endura, that contains less than 7 percent carbohydrate to help replace depleted muscle glycogen.
- Cold-weather athletes involved in aerobic activity should drink six ounces of fluid every fifteen minutes. I often set a timer on my watch to go off every fifteen minutes as a reminder.

VITAMINS AND MINERALS

Vitamins are organic food substances that impart necessary stimuli for tissue growth and health maintenance. They work with enzymes to carry out specific and essential functions within the body. As vitamins cannot be created by the body, they must be supplied through food and/or supplementation. The only thing I want my athletes to know about vitamins is that without them, cells lose their efficiency due to lower enzyme levels. Over time, metabolic function becomes lethargic, and tissues and organs are negatively affected.

Minerals may be even more important to athletes. Existing within the body as well as in food, minerals help maintain physiological processes. They strengthen skeletal structures and preserve the in-tegrity of the nerve systems. Like vitamins, they also act as catalysts to aid muscle response, neural messaging, metabolism, and hormonal function.

I nearly always prescribe vitamin and mineral supplementation for my athletes. Relying on whole food sources too often falls flat in the face of daily obstacles. Even if we did take the time to mindfully prepare and eat several meals created from whole food sources, we may still come up short on the nutritional saturation. The primary reasons for this are poor environmental conditions, chemically altered foods, and nutrient-deficient soil.

GENERAL DIET CONSIDERATIONS

Physical food comes in one of two forms: whole foods or isolated nutrients. Whole food has both molecular and synergistic structure. Isolated nutrients have only molecular structure. The assimilation of whole foods is natural. The lost synergy of isolated nutrients is not. Therefore, the body must work and even fight to make isolated nutrients biologically valuable. This is why 50 percent of Americans digest and assimilate only 50 percent of their food. This is why we can be so overfed yet so malnourished. Because whole foods have *chi,* or life force, they assist the body naturally. The intake of whole foods brings us closer to the wonderful interaction of life feeding life. Within the study of yoga, it is more important to eat consciously and appreciatively than to line up various vitamins and minerals and take them thinking to gain something. Aivanhov states in *The Yoga of Nutrition*, "Eat whatever you want, but eat it mindfully and in reasonable amounts and you will stay well." Aivanhov speaks here of a highly attuned person, whose cellular clarity gives accurate clues on eating intuitively in complete accordance with the mind, not the ego.

Nutrition is the most individual path that one will encounter in the study of Wholistic Fitness. I teach all students to follow five nutritional principles. How deeply each student takes these principles into his or her heart depends on the level of consciousness and willingness to go higher.

THE FIVE WHOLISTIC FITNESS® NUTRITION PRINCIPLES

1. Honor all foods

Develop sensitivity to each food choice you make. Our choices reverberate around the world. Food is sacred, so treat it as such. If this first principle is truly meditated on and felt within, we would never overeat or become greedy.

2. Eat mindfully

Practice mindfulness during eating. Be aware of your posture while eating. The global/societal implications of our food choices, our eating environment, and our inner energetic awareness are all part of eating consciously.

3. Study books and teachings

Stay open to and study various teachings and philosophies, but do not attach yourself to any of them. Go within and experiment. Take from a teaching what feels appropriate and let go of what does not. Trust in the intuitive wisdom of the body; as long as you meditate, it will guide you.

4. Eat regenerative foods and emphasize a vegetarian-based diet

As stated earlier, foods come in two forms: molecular, and molecular/synergistic. The latter has life force in it. And life feeds life. Foods that are alive will feed other living beings. This is why whole foods are needed much more than isolated nutrients. The body/mind/spirit is regenerative by nature, and its nourishment should reflect that regenerative quality. Attending to this principle will eliminate from your diet the processed, overly refined foods that contribute to obesity. Restrict all dairy and flesh foods from your diet.

5. Stay aware of nitrogen balance and core nutrition

Most of us need to become aware of how influential amino acids (protein) are to cellular repair and growth. Wholistic Fitness encourages a daily working awareness of consistent amino acid intake and ingesting a simple broad-spectrum vitamin and mineral supplement to ensure improved training effects and long-term health.

SUPPLEMENTAL GUIDELINES

Wholistic Fitness endorses a diet of 60 percent carbohydrate, 30 percent protein, and 10 percent fat for most athletes. Winter athletes whose primary sports are cold-condition disciplines such as mountaineering, alpine skiing, and backcountry skiing or boarding might experiment with a more liberal fat intake, such as a ratio of 60 percent carbohydrate, 20 percent protein, and 20 percent fat.

In addition, athletes should drink a minimum of 3.5 quarts of water per day and eat approximately twenty-five grams of fiber daily.

THE BEAUTY OF UNDEREATING

The best exercise is to exercise discretion at the dining table. Undereating has long been a tenet of Wholistic Fitness practice. We should all feel gratitude for even having the option of undereating. Much of the world has no such choice. As a form of personal health care, however, undereating has a long-standing track record of success. The yogic tradition, for example, teaches practitioners to fill the stomach one-third with food, fill another third with fluid, and keep the final third empty. A slight sensation of hunger is not bad. It means you are eating lightly on the planet and maintaining an appropriate food allowance for optimal body composition. There is spiritual integrity, global responsibility, and athletic prowess in staying hungry.

Greedily stuffing our stomachs in an attempt to satisfy the ego has no place in the practice of Wholistic Fitness. Use nutritional discipline to become a committed person. That's why the five nutritional guidelines are principles to follow instead of recipes to mimic. If I or anyone else simply measures out food for you, where is the spiritual lesson? These guidelines will also help you balance intellect with body wisdom. I have also included some Wholistic Fitness mealtimes in the appendix for direct nutritional guidance.

NUTRITIONAL ERGOGENIC AIDS

Ergogenic means performance-enhancing, or work-producing. There are several types of ergogenic aids:

Nutritional—foods and isolated nutrients
Pharmocological—amphetamines, caffeine, anabolic steroids
Physiological—blood-doping, oxygen
Psychological—hypnosis, visualization, meditation
Mechanical—intrinsic: body position, postural alteration; extrinsic: clothing, equipment

In this chapter our discussion is limited to nutritional ergogenic aids, namely foods and food substances. These fall into three categories: traditional foods, or substances to be used everyday as a source of core nutrition; medicinal foods, or substances to be used infrequently in response to supportive cravings; toxic foods or substances to be avoided. A traditional food for me is rice, especially basmati rice. Its beauty and simplicity and gentle cleansing feel good to me. A personal example of a medicinal food that I use might be garlic. If I sense that I'm overtraining or that an illness is coming on, I increase my intake of garlic. Its antibiotic, antiseptic, and immune-support properties obviously work; I've yet to lose more than two days of training to illness in the past ten years, even at my notoriously crazy training intensities! A spiritual food choice that is also medicinal for me are the Ai Imawa postures, ancient Taoist healing poses that are performed like Tai Chi, but more slowly and with more emphasis on breathing. If I am feeling "off center," just practicing these ancient postures with special breathing techniques purges the imbalance, and my health is restored. Examples of toxic nutrition range from chronic coffee drinking to drugs to unhealthy relationships.

The choice to use nutritional ergogenic aids is as much a physiological as a philosophical one. Generally, due to the stress created by training, the body undergoes an adaptation response, which may require more nutrients. The wise athlete, however, eating in harmony with the basic guidelines above, rarely needs to rely upon ergogenic supplements. The following ergogenic nutrients are ones you've probably either used or heard mentioned. Their ergogenic effects are all debatable and certainly depend upon a variety of genetic and physical influences. For example, some athletics might respond shockingly well to Vanadyl Sulfate due to their particular cell receptors. Other factors influencing the efficaciousness of ergogenic supplements include:

genetic factors regarding nutrient absorption;

an improper or cheap formulation of the supplement;

low consumption of certain foods, creating a nutritional gap; and

consistent consumption of certain foods that nullify a supplement's effect.

I've given my impression of the following nutritional ergogenic aids based on my personal and professional observations of both winter and summer athletes over the course of many years. There are many other nutritional supplements. Rare is the day when I do not receive correspondence regarding the next great miracle micronutrient. Most nutritional ergogenic aids constitute what is known as "hocus-pocus" supplementation; they promise great results, but the validity of the product does not live up to the exaggerated claims. At least the products on the following list have demonstrated consistent results relative to manufacturers' claims.

Anti-Oxidants

This group contains vitamin C (ascorbic acid) and vitamin E (tocopherol). Studies have shown these anti-oxidants to reduce free-radical damage brought on by intense training. They do not increase sport performance per se, but may benefit long-term health, which of course, helps maintain training consistency. They also reduce post-exercise blood lactate levels, which could help many winter athletes, especially alpine skiers. Safe dosages range from 0.5 to 3 grams per day for vitamin C; and 400 to 800 IU per day for vitamin E.

Chromium Polynicotinate

All athletes are prone to exhaust chromium, which enhances insulin's activity in glucose metabolism. I've had several endurance athletes respond well to this supplement. A dose of 200 mcg per day is prudent.

B-Complex Vitamins

I've had significant success among endurance athletes with B_1 (thiamine) and pantothenic acid. B_1 improves lactate thresholds and heart-rate fitness while pantothenic acid has been shown to decrease blood-lactate levels and oxygen consumption. The dosages I prescribed were 800 milligrams per day for B_1 and 2 grams per day for pantothenic acid.

Amino Acids

Full-spectrum amino acids. I've spent enough time emphasizing my good rapport with full-spectrum amino acid supplementation. When using supplementation, such as the Amino 1,000 product, cycle on and

off. For example, most of my athletes use the product for five days, then take two or three days off.

Branched chain amino acids (BCAAs). What could be more refreshing after a hard workout than an intake of your favorite BCAAs? Taken within ninety minutes after a strength-training or cardiovascular session, these amino acids (leucine, isoleucine, and valine, in a 9:1:2 ratio, respectively) help me and my athletes recover more quickly.

L-glutamine. This amino acid is the one most vulnerable to stressed tissues. Increasing your intake of it may increase growth hormones so that you can keep your training intensity and recovery at high levels. I am frankly lost on what to recommend for dosage. Both low dosages (2 grams per day) and high dosages (30 grams per day) appear to have helped various athletes.

Caffeine

You were wondering when I'd get around to this one, right? Did you scan through this section until you saw this category? If so, you probably need to cut down on your caffeine.

There is no lack of studies documenting significant increases in exercise performance after caffeine ingestion. Generally, participants, who included nordic skiers, cyclists, and runners, ingested an amount of caffeine equivalent to two to three cups of strong, fresh-brewed coffee. They experienced an increase in the time before reaching exhaustion, total work performed, and a decrease in race times. Caffeine-loading works best for endurance athletes and is optimized by avoiding the substance until race day.

The downside to caffeine is that it causes addiction, depletes nutrients, dehydrates cells, and places the body's neural and hormonal systems on red-alert status for an emergency that never comes. This chronic overstimulation is very degenerative. Too much of my work involves weaning athletes from coffee addiction. Muscle pulls, sprains, and strains are also symptoms of too much coffee intake. If you are a coffee drinker and tend to cramp while racing or training, dump the coffee, as well as the colas and black tea.

One of my New Mexico training partners, 43-year-old Mike, was a devout coffee drinker. An exceptional cyclist in road racing, Mike suffered from chronic cramping and could never quite finish a whole season with good fitness. Then I moved to town, and out went his coffee. Mike filled the void with two state championship medals and a state road racing series champion's jersey, which goes to the racer who can hold podium-topping fitness all season long. So what do you value more in life: self-discipline and optimal performance or coffee?

Dr. Andrew Weil, in his best-selling book *Spontaneous Healing* suggests replacing coffee, cola, or black tea with green tea, which, he writes, is a relatively benign form of caffeine and "offers impressive benefits as a general tonic, as well as a powerful anti-oxidant." The Wholistic Fitness herbal arsenal includes a wonderful tealike food that I have used for years to dramatically erase addictions of all sorts, but particularly coffee addiction (see Calli Beverage).

Calli Beverage

In a cover feature that *Outside* magazine did about me, I introduced a mysterious Chinese herbal tea to the author of the article, whom I was training for a winter triathlon. The mysterious tea was Calli Beverage, which consists of special herbs formulated to produce a tea that is adaptogenic; that is, the tea helps the body support functions it needs to balance self-regulating mechanisms. These functions include elimination of toxic debris as well as the regeneration of organs and tissues. The Shao Lin priests developed this formula, according to Dr. Dean Black, an expert in herbs, to help them concentrate during long meditation sessions. Enhanced mental clarity is quite noticeable among Calli drinkers and is considered the tea's most alluring benefit. Calli's cell-cleansing effect can be gentle or dramatic as the body processes the cellular waste animated by the tea. Rash, headaches, and nausea are common symptoms of cleansing nutrition and an initial Calli experience can produce similar symptoms. But cleaner cells are worth the temporary discomfort as the body completes its shift to a higher level of functioning on all levels.

Dosage of Calli ranges from one cup per day initially to three cups per day as the body purifies. Athletes in particular need cleansing nutrition, but they don't need to eat or drink substances that are dehydrating or depleting to accomplish it. Fasting, a former practice of mine, can be sidestepped when drinking Calli, because it provides the beneficial effects of a fast while nourishing, instead of depleting, the body. Calli Beverage is only available through a direct-marketing company known as Sunrider International. (This, in my opinion, is a bit unfortunate since many people—myself included—tend to shy away from such companies even if the product is very good.)

Ginseng

There are many types of ginseng, and I've had good success with the following: Korean white ginseng for adaptogenic purposes (Russian athletes swear by it); Siberian ginseng for joint health, performance enhancement, and immune support; and panax ginseng *(P. quinquefolium)* as an adaptogenic. Ginseng is generally nontoxic, and moderate consumption of the herb appears to be quite safe and often very helpful.

Creatine Phosphate (monohydrate)

Designed to increase amounts of the phosphate responsible for muscle contraction, this supplement appears to work for a large number of athletes. I've personally experienced considerable strength gains plus retention of strength levels while using

it. Similar positive responses come from my athletes, both those in endurance and in strength sports. Key to the uptake of this supplement is the concept of loading and maintaining. I use UniPro's Creatine Phase I (to load) and Phase II (to maintain). This system suggests a load of thirty grams per day for three to five days, then a maintenance phase of one to three grams per day for up to six weeks. Stay off the supplement completely for two weeks, then repeat this triple-step cycle.

SPECIAL-USE SUPPLEMENTS

Through the years, I've found the following supplements indispensable for Wholistic Fitness athletes.

Muscl-Flex
(UniPro Performance Nutrition)

This mucopolysaccharide formula provides superb nutritional support for joints and muscles. (Vegans should note that the product is made of 100 percent lyophilized New Zealand mussels.) Use it whenever joint conditions flare up or muscular trauma has been incurred, such as with strains or sprains. The supplement lubricates joints and nourishes synovial fluid.

Garlic

Many experts use garlic as a daily tonic, and for good reason. Fresh garlic may well be the best overall food choice to keep the body's systems healthy. Garlic's numerous benefits include lower cholesterol, lower blood pressure, powerful antiseptic and antibiotic properties, and activation of the immune system, which increases anticancer activity. Garlic can also be taken in the form of deodorized capsules, oil, or tablets.

Traumeel

This analgesic/anti-inflammatory homeopathic remedy is worth its weight in gold among us holistic people. It is the first thing we reach for to relieve any type of soft-tissue or joint pain. Mountain bikers tend to buy it by the case. It comes in either cream or sublingual form; both types are effective. Let the mainstream have Motrin … we've got Traumeel!

Yin Chiao Chieh Tu

This Chinese herbal extract is a simple patent formula that provides unbelievable protection against colds, flus, and general illness stemming from stress, overwork, or seasonal change. As soon as you start to feel achy, chilly, or run down, pump down several vials of the tablets. Its effects are instantaneous as the herbs begin purging the illness from the system. Yin Chiao has been a most successful herbal "weapon" for keeping my athletes illness free.

Huang Lien

This herbal extract is similar to Yin Chiao but is for advanced conditions or a condition that has already settled deeper into your system.

SunBreeze

Available from the same source as Calli Beverage (Sunrider International), this super-potent healing balm is used by Wholistic Fitness athletes as a healing remedy for sore muscles, joint inflammations, and fatigue. Adaptogenic in nature, the balm restores *chi* throughout the afflicted area. It also cools inflamed sites or brings restorative heat to open up blocked restrictions in muscles or joints. It's great for low-back pain. As it's very potent, avoid contact with the eyes and keep it away from children.

Oral Absorption Sprays

A direct-marketing company, Karemor®, owns the international patents for an oral delivery system of nutrients in micro-droplet form. This company produces a fascinating and effective range of vitamin, mineral, amino acid, and herbal oral sprays called Vitamist®. Oral sprays are not new to physicians, who use them in hospitals due to their instant absorption. A nutrient taken in pill form requires between three and four hours for absorption, the amount of absorption is often low, around 15 percent. According to the *Physicians Desk Reference*, non-prescription intraoral sprays provide 85 to 95 percent absorption. But here is the kicker: This high absorption rate is accomplished within twenty-two to thirty seconds! This is because the sprays are absorbed via the cheek lining instead of the gastric lining of the stomach.

Part III

Preseason Training Activities

photo by Anne Sasso

"I went to the woods because I wished to live deliberately, to confront only the essential facts of life, and see if I could not learn what it had to teach, and not, when I die, discover that I had not lived."
—Henry David Thoreau

9

General Training Overview

*"The athlete who thinks he knows it all
has evidently stopped thinking."*
—unknown

This book assumes that you, the reader, understand the concept and importance of year-round training. Training for winter sports is no longer done a few weeks before the winter season arrives. Those of us who love winter sports are usually the ones who also approach training as a year-round activity. We do so, not because we fear not being in shape for the winter, but because training is fun! Training year-round is our source of physical and spiritual health.

I have introduced a relatively short training approach for this book, compared with most conventional sport-specific programs. The least stringent of those programs chart out at least six highly structured, finely detailed training phases of six weeks apiece. That's a minimum of thirty-six weeks of sport-specific training! You know what happens to most athletes who try to follow these programs? Burnout!

After fifteen years of athletic and coaching experience, I have arrived at a formula

of Wholistic Fitness sport performance that outperforms other training methods with a flair for fun and spiritual growth that is simply unmatched. Most athletes cannot maintain consistent training for more than three months. In fact, most exercise programs falter within three weeks.

My reason for a short training approach for winter sports performance is simple: People can do it because the training stimulus never gets old! Most of my students are actually sad when I change their program, because they feel as though they have finally just adapted to it! I much prefer to have my athletes saddened by enthusiasm for their training than to have them burnt out or overtrained from too much specificity before the season even begins!

THINK DIFFERENTLY, NOT SPECIFICALLY

You will start your training plan approximately fifteen weeks before you plan to be doing serious winter sports. This ensures four full weeks of two preparatory programs, with a week recovery between. It also allows for another five weeks of a sport-specific program so you can refine your fitness to your favorite winter sport. You will then follow your regular peak-season program during the winter.

The overall intensity of the mind/body/spirit transformation is very complete in the Wholistic Fitness system. My athletes have a mere four weeks to master their program. Thus, every workout is vital, and they know it. My athletes are consistent, and their motivation is not only full throttle, but it also comes from a deep, special, inner space. This is due to the Five Fitness Disciplines and Four Lifestyle Principles, which influence every aspect of their lives.

Since many winter athletes want their winter-sport fitness to be ready by Thanksgiving weekend, a sample periodic (cyclic) approach might look like this:

Sample Winter Sport Training Overview

Active Recovery: May to mid-August

Strength training: relaxed approach; begin training each body part two times per week by mid-July; three sets of ten to twelve reps.

Cardiovascular training: relaxed approach; no real structure. By mid-July, consistent CV workouts three times per week

for one hour each at Zones 1 to 2. No high-intensity training at this time.

Kinesthetic training: relaxed approach unless flexibility is a real weak point; by mid-July, consistent flexibility workouts should be done three times per week. General flexibility arts such as yoga or martial arts are encouraged during the early part of this phase.

Meditation: no structured sessions required.

Nutrition: relaxed approach unless body fat is an issue; prepare to crank down on diet/supplements by mid-August.

Recovery week: no strength training; reduce CV volumes by 50 percent; all other disciplines are discretionary.

The Green Tara Strength Phase: mid-August to mid-September

Strength training: focus on structural integrity; establish deep fiber strength for musculoskeletal system.

Cardiovascular training: establish base volume of 80–90 percent aerobic, 10–20 percent threshold training; emphasize cross-training; develop soft-tissue transmission.

Kinesthetic training: flexibility volumes should be moderate to high.

Meditation: begin consistency in formal sessions; begin quieting and controlling the mind; emphasis on zazen.

Nutrition: stabilize core nutrients; increase caloric intake.

Recovery week: no strength training; reduce CV volumes by 50 percent; all other disciplines are discretionary.

The Perfect Power Phase:
mid-September to late October

Strength training: increase intensity and focus on speed-strength movements; add some semi–sport specific movements.

Cardiovascular training: stabilize volume and increase specificity; workouts should be 75 percent aerobic, 25 percent threshold; make interval training a priority.

Kinesthetic training: flexibility volumes should be moderate to high; increase sport-specific activity; no new sports/disciplines.

Meditation: shift emphasis to breathing meditations, energy work, and some general visualization work.

Nutrition: make intuitive adjustments as needed; monitor caloric intake and energy expenditure; if excess body fat is still an issue, prioritize nutritional discipline immediately.

Recovery Week: no strength training; reduce CV volumes by 50 percent; all other disciplines are discretionary.

Specialization Phase: late October
to Thanksgiving

Strength training: engage in a sport-specific program to refine prior strength work; superhigh intensity; stabilized or slight decrease in volume.

Cardiovascular training: Sport-specific dryland or on-snow practice only; minimize cross-training.

Kinesthetic training: Stabilize practice to moderate volume.

Meditation: Balance zazen and visualization styles; transfer mental poise to sport-specific activity.

Nutrition: make intuitive adjustments as needed; monitor caloric intake and energy expenditure; if excess body fat is still an issue, prioritize nutritional discipline immediately.

Peak Season Phase: Thanksgiving
to March

Reduce all volumes and intensities in strength training; train one to two times per week.

Stabilize cardiovascular work; volumes and intensities contingent upon sport.

Stabilize all kinesthetic, meditation, and nutritional disciplines.

Keep general fitness training minimal, as the demands of the winter sport refine the fitness.

PRESEASON TRAINING PRINCIPLES: EXAGGERATION AND VISUALIZATION

Two inner training modalities are important to practice during preseason, or dryland, training. The first is exaggeration; exaggerate the correct technical form during training. No matter how closely a dryland training tool mimics the real thing, the minute essentials remain different. The best we can do in dryland training is mimic and exaggerate. For example, if you want to nordic ski with a deeper knee bend, then inline ski with a deeper-than-usual knee bend.

The other modality is visualization. Visualization during dryland training develops the "teacher within," who constantly checks your form for flaws. For example, do not think of the road when you are inline skiing. See and feel yourself skiing with a deep, powerful tempo on real nordic skis. Imagine that there is snow, not pavement, beneath you. Feel the adrenaline rush of whizzing by spectators. See those spectators dressed in winter clothes, ringing nordic bells as you V-1 skate up a hill like it is nothing. Imagine the steaming figure of a competitor thirty meters ahead of you. Make the bridge; close that gap!

> I focus on being quiet.
> The more I listen to the snow,
> the faster I go.

Visualization must be carried through whatever sport you are training for. The ice climber must visualize tool placements while doing pull-ups in the gym. The alpine skier or tele skier must visualize smooth descents on snowy slopes while ex-

aggerating movements on inline skates. The mountaineer must visualize his or her piston-like legs churning up the mountain through all forms of weather conditions while out doing hill intervals. The more accurate our visualization and the more exaggerated our dryland technique, the more sport-specific inner and outer power we will develop.

BUCKLE UP!

In the following chapters you will learn activities that are appropriate for use in the preseason cycles of the Strength and Power Phases. I also provide two ready-to-practice training prescriptions. After completing these two basic programs, you will be ready to follow the Specialization Training Programs located in the chapter covering your favorite winter sport.

When individualizing this book for your personal use, remember to allow four full weeks of training for each of the two preparatory cycles: the Green Tara and the Perfect Power Phase. Also allot one week of recovery between those phases, plus another week before engaging in your Specialization Training Program.

Buckle up! These programs will push ego buttons. If you are serious about winter performance, the practice begins right now!

10

Preseason Climbing

*"On a mountain-top a man feels himself to be an entity whose span
is timeless, whose scope is magnificent beyond conception,
whose birth, whose death are incidental milestones
on a splendid road without beginning or end."*
— mountaineer Frank Smythe

ROCKS AND METAPHORS

For a time, I lived in Pagosa Springs, Colorado. There was an ancient rock wall nearby that helped hold together an old building near an abandoned courtyard. I would visit this wall often and practice the art of buildering, or climbing on buildings. Buildering or bouldering (climbing on boulders) is one of several climbing arts that alpinists use to refine their craft. Climbing on this dilapidated wall held an athletic mysticism that was as beautiful a feeling as the one I receive in the high mountains. Upon this grizzled wall, which would hold no normal person's interest whatsoever, I found bliss. I danced upon the tiniest of sandstone aberrations in the wall. Over the span of two years, I created a very difficult climbing route that I called the Balloon Saloon Traverse. To this day,

The author on his infamous Balloon Saloon Traverse in 1990. "The dilapidated wall held no interest for most people. To me, it held an entire Universe." Photo by Lincoln Frye.

119

that traverse has never been repeated. The route, although requiring extraordinary finger strength and complex footwork sequences, is more about softness than it is about power. I learned metaphorical lessons upon that wall. Those lessons influence my sport performance to this day.

DISAPPOINTMENT GONE

Dr. Steve Samuelson, a neurosurgeon from Englewood, Colorado, is a climber and one of my students. Previous to our work together, Steve had tried a number of workouts from "celebrity" climbers but suffered only frustration and inflamed joints as a result. I recognized, however, that Steve's performance hinged not so much upon his physical conditioning but rather his mental fitness. During leads, Steve had developed a common symptom of inadequate mental fitness: hanging on his protection.

By choreographing his mental training through varied but structured volumes and intensities of meditation, Steve soon reported that, "My meditation has cured my disappointments of previous years. I've stopped hanging when the climbing gets tough! Now I just do it or fall. And I am looking forward to 'doing it' better this year!" Within two years of study, Steve went from being a hesitant, hang-dogging leader to one who is fluid, determined, and focused, climbing three grades higher in technical ability. I did not change his physical training disciplines that much. In fact,

I decreased his climbing-specific training. Instead, I focused more on his "softer" disciplines: meditation, kinesthetic training, and nutrition.

THE CENTERED CLIMBER

The process of climbing expands and eventually releases the habits of the smaller mind. The interconnectedness of all things—animate and inanimate—is not just pleasant fiction, but fact. To surrender into this world of expansion releases the conditioned tendency to view ourselves as something other than, or apart from, our actions and our environment. Once we learn this process of surrender, our ability to receive the presence of the moment is enhanced. Ridding ourselves of differentiation and separateness while *being* our movement is where genuine sport performance begins.

Climbing has many subcategories, two of which are discussed as dryland training activities for winter athletes: sport climbing and general mountaineering. Each of these climbing arts holds unique benefits for winter athletes. Explore them to feel for yourself their transpersonal teachings. Their lessons can only benefit your winter training.

SPORT CLIMBING

Here the climber uses balance, strength, and agility to safely ascend routes of varying difficulty and length on either natural rock formations or synthetic walls. Sport climbing grew of out "traditional" climbing, in which the aim is to gain the top of the route by starting from the ground upward. Any form of protection is placed as one climbs. The sport climber is not concerned about reaching the summit of a rock or a mountain. Many routes are protected by preset bolts and chains drilled into the rock or synthetic wall, but this equipment is employed only as a safety "net'" in case of falls, never for upward ascent. The emphasis is on gymnastic sequences of moves to gain the top of the route. The safety factor is as high in sport climbing as the kinesthetic difficulty. Nevertheless, beginners need expert instruction.

Bouldering and buildering are subcategories of sport climbing and are usually done without technical equipment such as ropes and hardware.

Sport climbing is superb muscular training for the upper body, profoundly imparting both muscular endurance as well as power to the upper body and midsection. It also enhances flexibility throughout the body while increasing mental focus and emotional equanimity. The lower body also benefits greatly from sport climbing. Enhanced neural service results in overall greater body control and coordination. Much sport climbing involves having the feet and legs in a splayed-out, or spread eagle, position. This movement opens up the muscle and tendon units of the hip, greatly increasing an athlete's range of motion throughout the body.

The most beautiful aspects of climbing are the friendships they create. Jennifer Heightley tapes up for another knuckle-eating climb in Vedauwoo, Wyoming. Photo by the author.

Sport climbing can be done outdoors at local climbing crags, which are usually already well protected with bolts and chains. It can also be done indoors. Indoor sport-climbing walls have experienced a huge explosion in popularity. I built one of the nation's first public sport-climbing walls at Farentinos Gym in Boulder, Colorado, in 1983. Today, nearly every city in America has at least one climbing gym. These modern climbing gyms provide quick, safe, and fun exercise. Sport climbing is one of the best forms of mind/body training that exists.

GENERAL MOUNTAINEERING

Less technical but usually more bucolic than sport climbing is general mountaineering. In this activity, attaining the summit of the mountain is the most important goal. As the lowlands unfurl beneath the mountaineer, heart, lungs, legs, and the inner spirit burn with desire for the summit. Mountaineering routes vary in difficulty, from an aggressive hike of two or three hours to the top of a nearby knoll, to multipitched, roped climbing up a couloir or steep rock walls.

For the purposes of this book, I've differentiated general mountaineering from advanced or extreme mountaineering. General mountaineering may necessitate occasional scrambling up and over rocky pitches but is not especially difficult in a gymnastic type of way. A rope may be used for protecting these occasional steeper pitches, but, for the most part, general mountaineering is considered aggressive hiking with some scrambling. Whereas the sport climber uses ballet-like shoes for dancing up vertical or overhanging walls, the general mountaineer uses hiking boots for locomotive progress up talus and/or snowy terrain. Ropes, backpacks, crampons, and ice axes are normal pieces of gear for the general mountaineer, though these items may only be used infrequently.

General mountaineering provides splendid cardiovascular and muscular endurance training, as well as the opportunity to be in some spectacular places. The consistent up-hill climbing provides a steady-state aerobic workout, while the unfaltering work of the legs develops a deep-fiber type of fitness that helps all winter athletes. Meanwhile, the long descents require eccentric fitness of the legs, ideal training for alpine skiers. And the perseverance required to reach the summit develops mental endurance and inner conviction. When weather moves in, the mountaineer is forced to reach even deeper within his or herself to foster resolute qualities. I know of no other more pleasant, more beautiful dryland training than general mountaineering.

PROTECT YOURSELF

This section functions as a specific safety-awareness tool.

Climbing has obvious injury potential. Beginners must receive basic instruction. When used as a form of dryland training by winter athletes, however, the level at which climbing is pursued does not invite anything particularly perilous. Regardless, a working knowledge of fundamental rope work, first aid, and backcountry skills is needed.

For the most part, climbing is easy on the joints. Sport climbers need to warm up well before attempting difficult routes, however, so that the elbow, wrist, and finger joints are well lubricated and prepared to withstand the forces created by vertical climbing.

General mountaineers often suffer callouses on the feet, usually a symptom of improper boot fit. Purchase your boots from a mountain-specialty shop and only invest in quality gear. Ankle injury is another common affliction. Wholistic Fitness training is the best protection, due to its emphasis on strength training, flexibility, nutrition, and meditation for awareness. Many hikers and mountaineers suffer sprained ankles during the final third of their excursion. Prefatigue of the neuromuscular system (when the larger muscle groups tire along with the depletion of neurochemicals) is a significant factor as well as simple loss of focus.

Backache is common among mountaineers who have yet to become accustomed to the dynamics of carrying a pack. Again, choosing a pack that fits you is vital. Proper strength training can help minimize backache.

SPORT CLIMBING BEAUTIFULLY: LOOK DOWN AND SOFT BREATH

This section offers two sport-specific meditations to practice. In order to find the harmony in any sport, one must be able to control individual body parts before they can merge into a unified whole.

Look Down

A common tendency among sport climbers is to lock the head upward, always looking with hard eyes for the next handhold. Doing so limits ocular and kinesthetic vision, which inhibits dancelike, open expression. Sport climbing is first and foremost a full-body, creative-mind exercise. Beautiful, fluid expert climbers often look down, not up, seemingly contradictory to their goal of attaining the top of the route. Yet elegant climbers know that the key to any climbing sequence lies in footwork. Handholds are secondary. It's the feet that dance with the rock.

When the climber looks down, peripheral and kinesthetic vision increases. Suddenly, a world of microedges and ripples emerges near the feet and hips. Look down as you climb. This oxymoronic hint will reward you with an emerging sense of resourcefulness and sensitivity on the wall.

Soft Breath

Another predictable pattern among sport climbers is keeping the breath too high in the chest, or even holding the breath! Hyperventilation, a natural response to fear, is a real dilemma for some beginning climbers. Once their skill level increases, the ensuing confidence usually quells any hyperventilation.

Keeping the breath high (chest breathing) leads to problems for sport climbers. High breathing is often a manifestation of a chaotic mind, the usual affect of anxiety. Soft breath is delivered from a calm mind. The best way to calm the mind while climbing is belly breathing. A soft breath from the belly softens the mind. Use a Cleansing Breath to restore calmness. Suddenly, anxiousness departs the body, and fluid, beautiful movement is more accessible. I suggest doing a lot of bouldering—especially traverses—to really practice climbing with soft, belly breathing. Yoga helps, too. You'll feel the difference immediately. Go with the breath, learning to perform dynamic moves on the exhale and inhaling deeply during stabilization poses.

MOUNTAINEERING BEAUTIFULLY: HEART SUMMIT AND ARM DRIVE

Through the years, I've been fortunate to set several speed ascent and descent records on various peaks in the Rocky Mountains. My mountaineering performance improved dramatically when I made two simple adjustments in technique, one energetic, the other physical. Although I am not nearly as fast as I once was, these two modifications remain my trusted allies. It is my hope that they will empower your mountaineering and illuminate your enjoyment.

Heart Summit

The first meditation is wonderful in its simplicity. Though it may sound trite, practice it with the mountain before judging. The technique works best for those athletes who already integrate formal meditation into their fitness training. As you begin ascending the mountain, go into your heart center and open it up. One way in which you can do this is by invoking the color green in the space where your heart is located. Once you open the heart center, you may feel a distinct sensation of appreciation or compassion. You may feel suddenly very thankful for the ability to enjoy being outside and doing such fun practice as mountaineering. You may feel sudden compassion for the earth, as it continues to give and give while we humans insist on abusing its resources in varied and often shortsighted ways. Just be present with these feelings for a few moments.

Working from your open heart space, imagine a line of energy extending from your heart to the summit of the mountain. Connect the two and materialize the connection with some sort of image, such as a rope binding your heart to the summit. The rope should be made of an unbreakable material. Now, with every step you take, feel the summit reeling in the rope, or line of energy. It is as if the summit of the mountain is pulling you toward it. The closer you get to the summit, the more powerful the pull. Things will get pretty intense toward the top!

Once you are at the summit, perform a personal ritual of appreciation for the mountain. This can be as simple as taking a restorative breath in tune with your appreciation for being in such a pretty place.

During the descent, keep the heart center open, but this time, imagine the summit offering a helping hand to push you down the slopes. If you stumble, its hand will catch you—you will not fall. At the bottom of the mountain, turn to the summit and know in your heart that you and the mountain have shared a gift together. Close your heart center with reverence.

This "hook-your-heart-to-the-summit" meditation creates an entirely different energetic paradigm than the conventional, ego-oriented mountaineering approach of man versus mountain. Wholistic Fitness does not see the mountain as something separate from us or something that must be conquered. Instead, the mountain has become you, and you have become the mountain. This teaching is powerful medicine.

Arm Drive

The second meditation is a body-oriented one involving awareness of arm drive. I also cover this technique in the chapter on running. Too many mountaineers have developed "lazy arms." To heighten mountaineering performance, focus on keeping both arms active, from elbow to fingertip—even if you have an ice ax in your hand.

Driving the arms activates a neural response favorable to knee drive, which results in more powerful self-propulsion. A lot of mountaineering at the general level is very simple, one-step-at-a-time, just-keep-going type of stuff. Within this simplicity is a lot of space for the ego to play and come up with complaints and rationalizations that ultimately degenerate performance. Repeating inwardly to yourself, "Arms drive the legs, arms drive the legs" will de-crease this ego chatter by anchoring the mind with a mantra-type focus.

CLIMBING BIOMECHANICS

This section offers informal sport-specific analysis for deeper understanding and practice.

Sport Climbing

Sport climbers experience horizontal abduction and inward rotation at the glenohumeral joint. Upward movement is gained by powerful pulling action generated by the teres complex and latissimus dorsi, with the prime mover being the biceps brachii. All the forearm, wrist, and finger joints are active throughout sport climbing, requiring trained responses from all the extensor and flexor muscles respective to those body parts. While the upper body pulls, the lower body pushes, helping to overcome the drag force of gravity. As the climber's legs and feet dance upward, hip flexion and adduction is continual, activating the iliopsoas, rectus femoris, and all the adductors. The weighting of the active leg is accomplished via hip extension by the gluteus maximus and associated musculature; hamstring involvement is also of prime consideration. The lower leg is particularly active, with strong endurance and stabilization plus powerful, smooth dorsi and plantar flexion. The gastrocnemius, soleus, tibialis, and the smaller muscles of the calf complex must be trained. Special attention should be given to the ankle joint and the peroneal group, as both are important in protecting against injury and in increasing power transfer to the rock.

General Mountaineering

The basic forward propulsion biomechanics of mountaineering are similar to those of running. The difference lies in the stabilization musculature required at the spine to accommodate the carrying of backpacks. Isometric contraction is constant when the spine is loaded, creating ligamentous strain throughout the body. The abdominal, oblique, lumbar, and erector spinae muscles are crucial for retarding intramuscular fatigue. As a mountaineer scrambles or climbs up rocky pitches, the upper-body movement pattern is similar to that in sport climbing but at a far less intense level.

CLIMBING HINTS

This section provides at-a-glance reminders and suggestions for daily practice.

Sport climbers should focus on the hips and hamstrings during flexibility practice. The Wholistic Fitness flexibility routine Medium Form (see Appendix) is ideal for climbers, as are hatha yoga classes.

Learn to rest on the skeleton, not the muscles, during sport climbing. One way you can accomplish this is by hanging at arms length once you've found good handholds. Do not flex the elbow; instead release muscular tension onto the bones so that your arms don't get "pumped" by unnecessary muscle contractions.

In general mountaineering, pay attention to your posture. Keep the spine upright. Refrain from collapsing the trunk forward, which is a less powerful posture. Place your hands on your hips, not your thighs. Note the difference in energetic flow.

Conditions change dramatically with weather fluctuations. It's a wise idea to always be prepared for the most inclement weather.

The best investment a climber can bring to the mountain is strong tendons and ligaments. Good lungs are also important, but I see far more injuries in both mountaineering and sport climbing that result from inadequate strength level and symmetry. The second best investment is mental tenacity.

When climbing in a group, you are only as strong as the weakest member. Do not allow the goal of reaching the summit to override your common sense, especially when the safety of others is involved. Know basic first aid.

RELATED ACTIVITIES

This section considers some other dryland activities that are in the same family as the sport described.

Trekking Poles

Some of you who are avid campers know Cascade Designs, Inc., by their hallmark product, the Therm-A-Rest® mattress. In 1990, Cascade purchased Tracks®, a line of walking staffs. The Trek'R3, a pair of twenty-one ounce, three-sectioned poles with tungsten carbide tips, is the flagship of this line. According to Cascade Designs, these poles can be used for "hiking, backpacking, skiing, roller blading, or just striding or walking for exercise." They come with interchangeable rubber feet and snow baskets. The push-button convenience of the telescopic staff adjusts to every one and a quarter inches.

The allure of the Trek'R3 is that the staff collapses down to a mere sixty-one centimeters! I can easily pack these poles into a fanny pack, ride my bike to a mountain peak, run the peak with the poles extended, and then stow them for the descent! This makes for fantastic, full-body CV workouts. The poles retail for $75 and are available from Cascade Designs, Inc. (800-531-9531)

Hiking

Hiking involves the same movements, often at similar intensities, as general mountaineering and offers the same physiological benefits. The primary difference lies in the goal. During a hike, attaining a summit is less of a concern. Usually the hiker has a more moderate destination, be it the completion of a loop trail or an out-and-back excursion to a secret waterfall. Hiking is a wonderful calorie burner. You can even use hiking/trekking poles (see sidebar) to increase your energy expenditure and speed. A winter athlete's fall training plan should include plenty of hiking. Local mountaineering shops can provide details on hikes in your area as well as contact numbers for local hiking clubs.

SPECIFIC EQUIPMENT

This section covers specific equipment needed for the sport described. See Part Five for general cold-weather clothing and gear.

Technical Climbing Gear

If you live in a city, it is best to begin your initial study of sport climbing at a climbing gym. There you can rent shoes and a harness and learn preliminary belaying and climbing techniques. If you get bit by the climbing bug, take out your wallet. Sport climbing is expensive to get into and you cannot skimp on quality equipment. Your first investment should be qualified outdoor instruction! The new-generation climbers who have grown up on indoor climbing walls are dropping like flies in the outdoors due to absurdly poor technical knowledge.

Your next investment should be climbing shoes and a harness. If you have friends who already have additional climbing gear and are looking for belay slaves, you can get away cheaply by going climbing with them! After a while, however, you'll need to buy all the toys yourself: a rope, carabiners, quick draws, and slings.

General Mountaineering Gear

The gear you'll need depends on the level at which you want to partake of this activity. If you're just into cranking off half-day or day-long excursions, quality footwear and a pack will be about all you'll need. The longer and more technical the ascent, however, the more gear you'll need. Multi-day excursions require backpacking tents, stoves, and utensils. Technical ascents require crampons, ice tools, ropes, and hardware. Befriend an expert at a mountaineering shop and ask for guidance. Most importantly, get qualified instruction in all the mountaineering fundamentals.

Sport-climbing Clothing

My old Boulder bro' Christian Griffith has calmed down considerably from his younger, more controversial days and now produces a wonderful line of sport climbing wear known as Verve™. It's available via catalog; 303-443-7010.

General Mountaineering Clothing

Part Five of this book covers the layering system vital to a mountaineer. Mountaineers require heavier jackets, with a nylon shell to keep warmth in and keep wind and wet out. A balaclava is the best protection for head, face, and neck. Eyewear is also important, as are winter gloves.

RESOURCES

REI (Recreational Equipment, Inc.). This chain has got it all for outdoor gear, clothing, resource literature, and local contacts. 800-426-4840.

Black Diamond Equipment, Ltd. This Salt Lake City – based company produces high-quality ice tools and other mountaineering gear. 801-278-5533.

American Avalanche Institute provides information on first aid and mountain safety. 307-733-3315.

Rock & Ice magazine. I helped get this publication off the ground back in the old days. It has grown into the ultimate source of information and inspiration for all the alpine arts. 303-499-8410.

11

Preseason Inline Skating and Skiing

"You cannot fly like an eagle with the wings of a wren."
—William Hudson

VAMOS A LA PLAYA

Before in-line skating became the province of the masses, off-season nordic skiers used prototype in-line skates for conditioning ski-specific muscles. I recall skating in the early '80s with Bob Farentinos, a 50K Masters Nordic Champion. We would drive from his house above Boulder, Colorado, to the Peak-to-Peak Highway near the town of Nederland. We'd go early in the day, because there was less chance of getting caught. Back then, there were no official laws regarding inline skating on public roads except for one: "You're not allowed to be doing that." You would have laughed if you saw us in those formidable prototype skates. They were unstable at speed and had no ventilation.

Within a few years, everything changed. Today, millions of people inline skate for recreation, racing, and fitness. Inline skating encompasses three categories: fitness skating, which emphasizes the cardiovascular aspect of recreational inline skating; inline racing, which focuses on the competitive disciplines of criterium, distance, and downhill racing; and aggressive street skating, which focuses on kinesthetic challenge and uses props such as curbs, handrails, vert walls, and halfpipes. Inline skating is without par among dryland training modalities for winter athletes. It stresses the same cardiovascular and muscular systems of winter sports and can be done without snow, lift tickets, ski patrol, or layers of clothing!

INLINE RACING

Inline racing is most appropriate for readers of this book. More attention is given to economical, fast technique and cardiovascular training than to recreational pleasure. Inline racing is essentially speed skating without the ice. The key to good inline race technique is, in fact, to mimic good speed-skating form: keeping the upper torso parallel to the earth; maintaining a quiet upper body; using a synchronized arm swing or keeping both arms on the back; and pushing the skates away from the center of the body, that is, pushing from the heel of the skate and keeping the knees bent and soft.

INLINE SKIING

Inline skiing is less known among fitness skaters, and I have no idea why. The skater becomes, in essence, an alpine and nordic skier combined! With the simple addition of pavement-adapted ski poles, the skater enjoys and practices all the techniques of alpine skiing (downhill, giant slalom, and slalom) as well as the nordic techniques of skate skiing (V-1, V-2, alternate V-2, flying V, marathon skate, etc.) and classic skiing (diagonal stride).

I've been inline skiing for more than fifteen years and still totally love it. I rarely see anybody else do this sport, which astounds me. Perhaps this book will change that. With the popularity of inline skating, plus all the cyclists, skiers, and snowshoers who need cross-training ideas, inline skiing is sure to follow. The only additional equipment needed is a pair of roller ski poles. To determine ski pole height, see Chapter 14 on Road Skiing.

Wholistic Fitness student Scott Dupuis during his inaugural inline ski near Rio Rancho, New Mexico. He "skied" nearly ten miles, never fell once, and learned nordic ski-skating skills as well as alpine-skiing technique. What's not to love? Photo by the author.

PROTECT YOURSELF

This section functions as a specific safety-awareness tool.

Unless you fall, inline skating is very easy on the joints. Studies indicate that skating produces less impact than running on the musculoskeletal system. Skating spreads its demands across a greater number of muscle groups than do running and cycling. Because of this, skating produces less trauma to the joints while burning more calories per unit of time than either running or cycling.

Falling is inevitable as you learn to inline skate, but if you use poles, your chances of falling are reduced considerably. When I clinic beginners in inline skating, very few of them fall. It is usually in the intermediate learning stage that potentially dangerous accidents occur. It pays to hire an inline skate coach for beginning and intermediate lessons. The first thing I coach an inline skater is how to stop. Fractured wrists from skaters trying to catch themselves during a fall is the leading injury among inline skaters. Again, why not use poles? If you don't use poles, four forms of protection are a must for beginners: helmet, wrist guards, elbow guards, and knee guards. And finding low-traffic terrain, with plenty of runout, is essential.

SKATING BEAUTIFULLY: LOW KNEE BEND AND HEEL PUSH

This section offers two sport-specific meditations to practice. In order to find the harmony in any sport, one must be able to control individual body parts before they can merge into a unified whole.

Endestad 101

Skating with a low knee bend and heel push was emphasized to me by Olympic nordic skier Audun Endestad. Audun's training intensity was legendary. Nearly all his physiological test results were off the chart at the Olympic Training Center in Colorado Springs. One story has it that scientists were testing Audun's frontal thigh physiology on a leg extension machine. Midway through this standardized test, Audun left the machine broken and literally smoking!

Audun drilled into me, on skis, skates, and a slideboard, the value of a deep knee bend and a heel push. Those two aspects remain my most effective coaching tools for inline and nordic skiers. Bending the knees until the top of the thighs are nearly parallel to the earth loads more weight onto the skate. That, in turn, means a greater stroke length. And more load plus a longer stroke equals increased speed.

Low Knee Bend

The winter athlete will not begin to soar on skates until he or she feels the dance of the movement. The challenge lies in accepting the dance where it exists, down *low*! At first, your knees will retaliate, then your lower back will hurt, then your energy demand will go up and you will say to yourself, "No way!"

Yes, way. In fact, the way, or the tao, of fast distance skating will present itself within a few minutes of practicing low knee bend. You will sense the speed coming from deep hip and gluteal muscles instead of the thigh muscles that propel most skaters. Then, you will find how a heel push generates terrific force, adding several feet to each glide.

The author practicing classic skiing on off-road skates above Santa Fe, New Mexico. Photo by Marc Romanelli.

Heel Push

Pushing from the heel means doing the exact opposite of what most skaters do. Most skaters push away from the earth with their toes. The big-toe push-off is great for running mechanics, but it is the last thing you want to do as a skater! Toe-ing-off will cause you to collapse forward, resulting in a backward push that eliminates the desired loading phase described above. Pushing from the heel means you will displace more force to the side instead of backward. This lateral power is what

propels a skater. You should experience a feeling of "sitting back" once you've mastered the heel push technique. So, bend the knees, sit back, and heel push to the side. Got it? Good, 'cause you'll be soaring when you do!

INLINE SKATING BIOMECHANICS

This section offers informal sport-specific analysis for deeper understanding and practice.

Upper Body

When distance skating, significant trunk extension must be maintained by the long back muscles of the erector spinae, illiopsoas to bend the hip, tensor fascia latae, and the antagonists to that musculature, the abdominals. During inline skiing, all the upper body muscles are engaged for production and/or stabilization of the poling strokes. Particular emphasis falls on the latissimus dorsi and deltoid complex. Abdominals assist in force production during poling as well as stabilization.

Lower Body

After a long skate, you KNOW what is working! The skating motion is a lot of abduction and adduction of the hip orchestrated by the adductor brevis, longus, and magnus while abduction is taken care of by the sartorius, tensor fascia latae, gluteus medius and minimus. Most of the power stroke is accomplished through the gluteal complex along with the vastus complex. The biceps femoris is active in hip extension and recovering the leg.

INLINE SKATING HINTS

This section provides at-a-glance reminders and suggestions for daily practice.

Fitness skaters should use bigger wheels and better bearings than street skaters.

Boot fit is critical. Your boots should be snug when you stand in them, but you should be able to slightly wiggle your toes.

Fitness skaters can tweak their wheel/hub combination. Heavier wheels and low-precision bearings result in a better workout (due to more resistance), while light wheels and high-precision bearings are less durable but way faster.

Inline skiers should accentuate their upper-arm drive and follow through to produce greater power production from the upper body. Contract the abdominals the moment the ski pole tips dig into the pavement.

Inline skiers should note that even union carbide ski pole tips will not stab into concrete. It's an asphalt sport.

Inline skating can produce significant blisters as you increase distance or time. Always build up your skate volumes gradually and wear "frictionless" socks, which are available at running specialty stores.

RELATED ACTIVITIES

This section considers some other dryland activities that are in the same family as the sport described.

Roller Hockey

Some weird rogue thing comes out of me when I get engaged in this totally fun sport. I once put one of my star students in the hospital during a pick-up game that got a little scrappy! Roller hockey is a superb form of cross-training, and the scars look cool. Contact your local snowboard/skate shop or USA Hockey Inline (see "Resources") for info.

Slideboard

A slideboard is a rectangular piece of plastic, usually about six feet long and three feet wide, upon which one can slide back-and-forth across, wearing socks over one's shoes. Audun Endestad helped us build a monster one of these in the early '80s at Farentinos Gym. Today, some facilities have entire classes devoted to slideboards. These commercial versions are lightweight, portable, and offer a good workout. They get a nod of approval for preseason training. You can find them at most large fitness stores.

Off-Road Skating

Inline skating still has a lot of potential, such as incorporating rougher, off-road terrain. The Coyote™ skate from Roller-

The author using a slideboard for preseason training. Photo by Jason Williams.

The Coyote™ Off-Road Skate by Rollerblade®. Photo by Kenneth D. Greer.

blade® has offered me some provocative moments on smooth dirt roads.

SPECIFIC EQUIPMENT

This section covers specific equipment needed for the sport described. See Part Five for cold-weather clothing and gear.

Skates

I've been with Rollerblade® since the early days, and I know of no other company that puts as much time and effort into product R&D. For fitness skating, the Quantum L3 or Synergy X models, both of which have APEC 5 high-precision bearings, are lightweight and responsive. Models change often, however, and it is best to contact the company directly for the latest upgrades

(see "Resources"). If you are into hardcore distance skating, consider investing in a pair of five-wheeled speed skates. These skates, when compared to a fitness skate, are not as comfortable or as maneuverable, but do they go fast! If you live in hilly or mountainous terrain, these five-wheeled monsters probably are not a wise investment. But if you are a flatlander, go for it!

Poles

For inline skiing, you'll need a pair of roller poles for jetlike propulsion. They are also excellent anti-dog devices as well as a safety net for beginners. You can order them from nordic catalogs such as Eagle River Nordic (800-423-9730) or Nordic Equipment, Inc. (800-321-1671) as well as Reliable Racing Supply (800-223-4448).

Protective Gear

Helmets, wrist guards, elbow guards, and knee guards are all important pieces of equipment for the inline skater, especially beginners and intermediates. This safety gear is available wherever inline skates are sold. Remember: don't skate naked!

RESOURCES

Rollerblade: 800-232-ROLL or www. rollerblade.com.

USA Hockey Inline: 719-599-5500 or www.usahockey.com.

USA Inline Racing: 215-564-0995.

Inline skating still has a lot of off-road potential. The author tests a pair of Rollerblade's off-road skates. Photo by Marc Romanelli.

12

Preseason Road Cycling

"The important thing is to not stop questioning."
—Albert Einstein, bicycle enthusiast

SELF-PROPELLED EFFICIENCY

There are few things on earth as efficient as a fit human being on a road bike. I came into competitive road cycling after a running career. Many other multisport athletes make a similar transition. Runners are astonished at the immense training distances and speeds at which a road cyclist (a roadie) trains. By the time I earned my upgrade to a Category 3 racer, I could scarcely believe the hours and miles I had logged on the bike. Though I've trained cyclists for years, and knew the hours and the miles on paper, it was not until I lived the sport that the map became the territory. And what awesome territory it is!

The sport of road cycling requires a high standard of fitness. If you are getting ready to compete at the beginning level (Category 5), be prepared! It's not like signing up for beginning tennis! Competitive road cycling can be a humbling sport. If you can't hang

The epitome of self-propelled efficiency. Forty-three-years young, Michael Secrest exhales into his first hour of effort as he attempts to set a new twenty-four-hour world record at the Olympic Velodrome, Dominguez Hills, California, August, 1996. After his long day and night in the saddle averaging twenty-one miles per hour, he covered 503.5 miles and broke not one but three world records. Note the catheter—Michael never got off his bike during the twenty-four hours. Photo by Chris Kostman.

onto the peleton (the main group of riders in a race or training ride), you will get "dropped" rather quickly. Then you're all alone, usually fighting a headwind, with many miles to go before the finish. It's not like mountain bike racing, where everybody and their grandmothers are getting flat tires, crashing, and bonking. DNF's (for "Did Not Finish") are common in mountain biking because of mechanical failures. But in the cosmopolitan sport of road racing, with its long European tradition, getting dropped is the ultimate embarrassment. DNF's are not a consideration. You are expected to hang with the peleton and then sprint for the finish in one form or another.

HIGH-SPEED FITNESS

Road cycling can be a grand builder of cardiovascular fitness. Research shows that outdoor cycling at speeds of less than ten miles per hour is not of great aerobic benefit. At a speed of fifteen miles per hour, however, all the cardiovascular aspects of fitness are significantly and positively stressed. Speeds over twenty miles per hour are considered racing speeds, and the energy expenditure is extraordinary. Pro cyclists competing in the Tour de France (a three-week stage race with average speeds of thirty miles per hour) consume between 3,500 and 7,000 calories per day to keep pace with their caloric output! At nonracing speeds, however, the bike is so efficient

that the average energy expenditure is less than that of swimming, walking, dancing, and even downhill skiing!

My counsel for winter athletes is to use outdoor cycling aggressively. Join a cycling club or team, enter some races, and have fun with it. If you often cycle alone, and your average speed is between fifteen and twenty miles per hour, supplement your cycling with hiking and running. You'll get a greater return on your aerobic fitness for the time input.

One of the best things cycling develops is explosive, fast-twitch power in the lower body as well as an insane level of muscular endurance, both of which create what may be the best general fitness base for a winter athlete. As a cross-training and dryland-training tool for winter athletes, recreational road cycling gets my full nod of approval. Competitive road racing is even better. It is easy on the joints, enhances skills quickly with practice, and establishes an off-the-chart level of fitness that is quickly transferred into any winter sport.

PROTECT YOURSELF

This section functions as a specific safety-awareness tool.

If running is the most concussive of cardiovascular disciplines, road cycling is one of the least. There really is no joint stress in road cycling. The knee joint may undergo some adaptation pains in the beginning, but with proper bike fit and good positioning, the knees quickly adapt. This is one reason why the masters category is so competitive in road racing. Many endurance athletes eventually turn to road racing as their last bastion of exercise after their joints have withered and frayed from running, triathloning, or whatever. Many physical therapists prescribe cycling as a prime rehabilitation choice for those recovering from surgery.

There is one exception, however, to the no-stress characterization. It's not a particularly thrilling area, and, in fact, is a little sobering. An unknown percentage of men may be getting impotent, due to chronic saddle pressure on the genitalia. Recent evidence suggests a compression of the penile arterial and vascular system. Researchers have also noted arterial scarring, which hampers blood flow to the penis. Chronic saddle pressure on the perineum muscle can apparently damage nerves and the blood supply to the penis. Currently, more research is being done on saddle design and in other areas to alleviate this disturbing finding. The good news is that individuals respond differently to the activity of cycling and male impotence is not likely to affect most recreational or fitness cyclists. The real concern may be for the sport-specific, higher-category bike racers. Don't let this news sway you from riding a bike, however; just be aware.

I encourage you to also read the "Protect Yourself" section in the chapter on mountain biking that follows, especially the information on road rash and saddle sores.

ROAD CYCLING BEAUTIFULLY: POSTURE AND PEDAL CADENCE

This section offers two sport-specific meditations to practice. In order to find the harmony in any sport, one must be able to control individual body parts before they can merge into a unified whole.

Posture

Two mechanical aspects of cycling should be the primary meditation for cyclists: posture and pedal cadence. I list posture first, because as you arrive at the right posture, pedal cadence will naturally mature. By posture, I mean how your body position fits with the bike. Not *to* the bike, *with* the bike. There is a difference. As in the rest of Wholistic Fitness study, we do not want to approach cycling from a separatist perspective. The sooner we merge with the bike—the sooner we and the bike become one—the better. If you study pro roadies (go to races and buy some videos), you'll notice it's as if there is no separation between them and their bikes. Their maneuverability, reaction, and agility are almost magical.

When I adjust a cyclist's posture, I look for the most aerodynamic and mechanical advantages. Each cyclist has a specific position that puts his or her joints at the optimal angle to engage the greatest muscular contractile force. Most cyclists get hurt because they are not connected with their bikes and are at a mechanical disadvantage. We must not ride like robots. Softly merging with our bikes and finding freedom and relaxed alertness invites high performance dividends. The more relaxed we are, the better our performance. This means that we will be faster if racing and safer when riding in traffic or with other cyclists. Stability is also essential, and the fastest way to stability is by way of serenity. Practice the following guidelines.

On-the-Bike Posture: Five Things to Practice

1) Get *low* in order to get maximum torque! When the upper torso is horizontal, the powerful hip extensors are engaged!

2) Keep your shoulder girdle dropped, your elbows low, flexed, and soft.

3) Keep your back flat, not rounded. Lengthen the lower spine away from the hips. A low, flat back decreases air resistance, which can account for up to 80 percent of the force acting to slow a rider!

4) Prioritize efficiency over comfort until you adapt to a low riding position.

5) Bring the knees in toward the top tube. This maximizes power, joint health, and aerodynamics.

Pedal Cadence

Pedal cadence refers to the aesthetic and athletic nature of how we make our bike pedals go around and around. Beginning cyclists often have a cadence that is too slow and too choppy. It takes several months of daily training to produce a smooth, fast, elegant pedal cadence. A cyclist's pedal cadence is like a ballerina's plié—it can never be perfect enough!

On-the-Bike Pedal Cadence: Five Things to Practice

1) Maintain a pedal cadence of at least eighty to ninety rpm's (revolutions per minute) on flat to rolling terrain. A high rpm is the signature quality of an experienced roadie. To determine rpm's, count the number of times your right knee reaches the top position during a twenty-second period. Multiply that number by three to get your rpm's.

2) Work the circle! Think of your pedal stroke as a clock: The top spot, when your foot is highest, is twelve o'clock. The bottom position is six o'clock. Learn to pedal through all the numbers on your clock instead of just mashing the pedal stroke down from twelve to six! Sweep or pull the foot across six o'clock, engage the hamstrings, and pull up on the pedal from six to twelve. Be aware of any "dead spots" in your pedal stroke and fill them in.

3) Snap the knees at the top of the stroke. It's easy to get lazy and just let the knee pass through the top position. Instead, snap the knee upward at the top to increase neural speed and efficiency.

4) Stay seated. The most efficient riding comes from staying seated and spinning the pedals at high rpm's. Listen to your chain. If your pedal cadence is choppy, chain tension will fluctuate.

5) Keep the ankles level, not low. Although some people have a naturally high ankle position, for most cyclists this creates less power transmission and faster onset of fatigue. Naturally, the heel elevates during the recovery phase (bringing the pedal up to the top position), which is fine in most cases.

TERMS OF EN-GEARMENT (AN ASPECT OF CADENCE)

With practice the cyclist learns to shift into the proper gears quickly and soundly. There is art in gearing; the art comes from anticipation and listening. Proper gearing stabilizes effort. It pays to have good components on your bike frame. I've lost podium spots in races due to poor components that misshifted during crucial moments. Road cycling is a sport of seconds. The ability to stay with a peleton means having the fitness and the gear selection to handle repetitive surges and attacks made by other riders. The moment the pack speed increases, you've got to jump up to speed or you will get dropped. The moment the pack resumes its average pace, another explosive surge will be launched. So it goes for hours and hours.

GRIN AND GEAR IT

Knowing what gear to be in at the appropriate time requires anticipating when the pack is going to surge, as well as uphills and downhills. Any geographic aberration will shatter the peleton into pieces. If you are in the wrong gear, you will lose a second or two on the jump. And a second or two is all it takes to lose the drafting effect. Soon you'll be all alone, left behind. Practice appropriate gearing whenever you ride. Where I live, in the mountains, I use a front chainring with a large ring of forty-two and an inner chainring of thirty-nine. My rear cluster is typically a twelve/twenty-two. For some races in flatter parts of the country, I use a fifty-two/forty-two up front and as low as an eleven/twenty-one on the rear. It is best to keep the gearing very close together, without leaving big gaps in between.

CYCLING BIOMECHANICS

This section offers informal sport-specific analysis for deeper understanding and practice.

More than any of the other dryland training activities covered in this book, cycling requires the presence of a licensed coach or cycling expert to help beginners with their bike fit. This book focuses on the trainable components of physical and spiritual fitness. The cyclist must assume the responsibility of attaining the correct mechanical adjustments to his or her bike. Measurements such as frame size, crank length, and stem dimensions should be fully explored, especially if an injury arises.

Unique Biomechanics

Since every cyclist fits differently on a bike, it is impossible for me to tell you where your maximum hip flexion or knee extension occurs. However, the basic movement pattern remains the same for all cyclists. The muscles to be trained are accurately targeted in a general program. The gluteus maximus and hamstrings (biceps femoris) drive the pedal down from the top position. As the pedal sweeps across the bottom position, knee extension occurs by the frontal thigh (rectus femoris and lateralis muscles) and is helped by the hamstrings. Knee flexion is very important to cyclists, and strength-training programs must serve this need in order to produce an even pedal cadence without glaring dead spots.

At the ankle, there is significant stabilization present in all the calf muscles (gastrocnemius, soleus, peroneus) during cycling. It is imperative to strengthen this complex to transfer the watts of energy generated from the primary muscles through the lower leg and into the pedal.

Upper-body posture is vital to the road cyclist. Maintaining a horizontal upper body while pumping the pedals requires great stabilization strength of all the upper-torso musculature. Of particular impor-tance are the lumbar (lower back) muscles, which are in an extended state of contraction to balance the flexion of the abdominals. The obliques, intercostals, and serratus groups should receive indirect strengthening in order to accommodate the dynamic balance of bike handling, drinking, eating, etc., while on the bike at high and/or sustained speed.

CYCLING HINTS

This section provides at-a-glance reminders and suggestions for daily practice.

Some training programs in this book contain low to moderate cycling volumes. Occasionally, cycling intervals are given. As you engage in cycling as part of your Wholistic Fitness journey, use the following hints to specifically enhance your performance. Refer to Chapter Six for general CV guidelines. Each pedal revolution can be meditation or mindless exercise. Keeping focused on elegant cycling mechanics will anchor the mind and enable you to use cycling as a spiritual workshop.

Go easy at first. Allow the body to raise its core temperature slowly. Spin for several minutes at a slow, easy pace (Zone 1) to allow physiological adjustments to occur before you undertake any higher intensity effort.

Position your foot so the ball of the foot is directly over the pedal axle. Clipless pedals will enhance pedal cadence and power.

Position your knee over the pedal spindle when the crank arms are parallel to the earth.

Your leg length determines the length of your seat tube (the tube that holds the seat on conventional, double-diamond–framed bikes). Generally, allow for one to two inches of space between your crotch and the top tube when standing barefoot over the bike. Four to five inches of seat post should be visible on a properly fitted bike.

Use long, gradual uphills to enhance strength and form. Go steady. Do not surge or spurt while training unless prescribed as intervals.

The saddle tilt should usually be level. Although both men and women may experiment with a slightly nose-down angle to prevent perineal pressure, men should not use a nose-up angle.

The stem height should either be level or no more than five centimeters below the top of the saddle. A higher stem is more comfortable but less aerodynamic. If the top of your thigh pounds against your chest when you ride, your stem is too low.

The length of the stem extension should allow your elbow to come within an inch of touching your kneecap when you ride with your hands in the drops (lowest section of the handlebars) and elbows bent at about a seventy-degree angle.

Alignment is important. Make sure your knee-over-toe alignment remains straight during the pedal stroke. If anything, bring your heels out, not in.

Always maintain a quiet upper body; your head should not bob, nor should your torso "swim" side to side.

Soften the neck musculature; don't compact the cervical vertebrae by jutting your jaw forward and upward. Ride with a relaxed face, neck, and shoulders.

Use seated downhills to increase your leg speed every now and then. Don't just stop pedaling on descents.

Occasionally try cycling for several minutes using only Filling Breaths (nasal inhales and exhales) during low aerobic workouts. This balances the energies of the left and right sides of the body as well as contributes to more efficient respiration.

Intervals

You will find cycling intervals prescribed throughout the programs in this book. They can be done at high intensities, with nominal joint stress resulting. Interval training develops both aerobic and anaerobic capacities. Once developed on the bike, this physiological training benefit can transfer into any winter sport. One word of caution: When using outdoor cycling for interval training, find a section of road that is low in traffic and without dogs or other things that may interfere with your session. Intervals require full body/mind focus, and the fatigue factor is high. It's easy to get sloppy with your awareness and reactions during or after intervals. Keeping this in mind, train safely!

I will use the following cycling interval

workouts in the programs outlined in this book. Always be sure to thoroughly warm up and cool down during the workouts.

In and Outs

Stand out of the saddle for fifteen seconds at a moderate cadence, in a moderate gear, then sit in the saddle and spin for fifteen seconds with fast (100-plus) rpm's. Repeat for five minutes, then recover for five minutes. Repeat this sequence for a total of two to three sets.

Sprints

While on the drops, jump and "run" on the pedals into a seated position, still building your speed and pedaling in circles, with your head up looking at the "finish line" about forty meters ahead and arms bent. Focus on high rpm's and smooth pedaling at a superhigh cadence (110-plus rpm's). The total distance you'll cover is about 150 meters.

Jumps

This involves a standing, explosive acceleration of twenty meters or so, usually building into a sprint or attack.

Pyramids

Perform a series of intervals in the following increments: one minute, two minutes, three minutes, four minutes, another at four minutes, then three minutes, two minutes, and back down to one minute. Begin doing these intervals at Zone 2, building to

Zone 4 by the end of each one. Each interval should be a gradual acceleration. Each recovery period should equal the length of the preceding interval. For instance, after cycling for twenty minutes at Zone 1, accelerate for a one-minute interval. Recover for one minute by easy spinning. Then go hard for two minutes and recover for another two minutes. Repeat this sequence up and down the "pyramid." The intervals can be done sitting, standing, or alternating.

Power Jumps

Find a hill with a 4 to 6 percent grade, if possible, then perform five jumps of fifteen pedal revolutions each. These should be explosive, standing bursts. Recover for forty-five seconds. Repeat. After five jumps recover for five minutes. Do a total of three sets. Your total number of jumps will be fifteen.

Wholistic Intervals

Perform nine work intervals of two minutes each, with a recovery interval of thirty seconds. Alternate between the low gear, big gear, and time trial gear. Increase the tempo during the last 30 seconds of each repeat. You should be in Zones 3–4.

15x15's

Stay seated during the entire session. Keeping your cadence high, go hard (Zone 4) for fifteen seconds. Recovery spin for fifteen seconds. Repeat this sequence for five minutes. Then recover for another five minutes. Repeat the whole set two to three times. This exercise will increase your aerobic capacity, pedaling efficiency, leg speed, and fast recovery as well as your ability to respond to peleton surges.

Minutes Are Forever

Go hard for one minute (Zones 3–4), then recovery spin for one minute. Keep doing this until you throw up or ten minutes has gone by. Recover for ten minutes, then repeat. These intervals can be done standing, sitting, or alternating.

RELATED ACTIVITIES

This section considers some other dryland activities that are in the same family as the sport described.

Indoor Cycling

I realize that many readers may have to perform their cycling intervals or workouts indoors. This is okay if you have either rollers or an indoor trainer. Rollers are preferred, since they demand the skill coordination specific to cycling. Indoor trainers are the second choice. Another alternative is studio cycling (popularly known as SPINNING™), which is done in a class environment. The instructor leads the class through a workout choreographed to music. The stationary bikes usually accept clipless, SPD, and toe-clip pedals. Most studio cycling classes are about 45 minutes in length and high intensity in nature. The heavy flywheel of a studio cycle is good for developing explosive power and high rpm's. The best classes I attend are usually taught by certified SPINNING™ instructors. The best indoor studio cycle I have tried is the Johnny G. SPINNER™, by Schwinn.

Cyclocross

To be honest, I've only worked with a few cyclocrossers, and I have not had much direct experience in this sport since the cyclocross season overlaps with the nordic ski season. I fully encourage winter athletes to explore this eccentric but traditional sport, which combines the best of road cycling, mountain biking, and cross-country running. Cyclocrossers use modified road bikes on a short (one to three mile) technical circuit. Most races last about one hour. The primary challenge of cyclocross racing involves the mandatory dismounting and running sections. This high-intensity sport is hugely popular in Europe, but relatively unknown in the U.S. If you are a nordic ski racer, however, I would use caution if doing cyclocross. It comes at a time of the year when your nordic training should be ski specific, and the intensity of cyclocross may throw a monkeywrench into the training. Other winter athletes, however, could certainly benefit from this fun, wacky, semi-winter sport. Your local bike shop can put you in contact with the cyclocross community in your area.

SPECIFIC EQUIPMENT

This section covers specific equipment needed for the sport described. See Part Five for general cold-weather clothing and gear.

Most of the following gear is available through bike shops or through catalogs such as Bike Nashbar (800-NASHBAR; www.nashbar.com/cat) or Performance (800-727-2453; www.performancebike.com).

Bike

It's important to research your bike purchase well. Work with a knowledgeable racer or coach. Speciality bike shops are usually staffed by bike racers who love cycling. Usually you'll get good attention, bike fit, and follow-up through such a shop. Purchasing a bike can get rather "techy," so narrow the choices down by deciding three things up front: How much are you going to ride? How much are you willing to spend? What type of frame material do you want? Answering these three questions will provide a good starting point.

Heart-Rate Monitor

Road cycling lends itself to heart-rate monitorization. Unlike many other cardiovascular sports, it can fool the athlete. You may feel like you are going too slow when actually you should be going even easier, and vice versa. I suggest using a heart-rate monitor, especially for easy or recovery days, such as after an interval day. Many cyclists go too hard on easy days and not hard enough on hard days. Monitoring heart rate will also help you determine full recovery during interval workouts. And monitors are valuable if you are gradually regaining lost fitness due to an injury or illness. I am a firm believer in monitoring the resting heart rate first thing in the morning. If your morning heart rate is ten beats higher than normal, it's a mandatory recovery day, whether you like it or not!

Helmets

Riding without a "brain bucket" risks your life. Helmets are mandatory in USCF races for good reason: Every cyclist crashes. In the 1995 Iron Horse Race in Durango, Colorado, I was up front in a huge peleton, soaring along at thirty-five miles per hour, when suddenly everybody went down hard. Human flesh and bones do not mix well with asphalt at such speeds! According to my friend and prolific cycling author Ed Burke in his book, *Serious Cycling*, "75% of the 1,400 annual deaths from bicycle accidents are due to head injury." I know that many cyclists still refuse to wear a helmet, and I am guilty of the occasional solo ride without one. Modern helmets are cool looking, so you won't look like a dork wearing one. This season I used a Bell® Evo Pro™, and because it was so light, I couldn't even tell I was wearing it. Some research has shown that the modern helmet maximizes airflow across the skull, ventilating and cooling the head up to four times faster than the traditional hairnet helmet. Get an American National Standards Institute (ANSI) approved helmet from your local bike shop. If you join a cycling club or team, you can often purchase a helmet very inexpensively through it.

Booties

Made from neoprene or a fabric such as Polartec four-way stretch, these overboots slide over cycling shoes to add protection against cold, wind, and wet. They work best in cold, dry weather. In wet conditions, they usually get saturated and become very heavy very fast.

Cyclocomputers

These are a wise investment. You probably do not need to invest in a fancy model, but accurately knowing your current, average, and max speeds as well as distances and time is very valuable. Cyclocomputers are notorious for being undependable. I've had the best luck in this fickle genre with the simple Avocet® Cyclometer 25 and 35 models.

Face Mask/Balaclava

This is a wise idea for cold-weather cycling. I prefer a balaclava, since it can be used as a neck gaiter, face mask, or hat. I use one made of Polartec 200PS power-stretch fleece—it's a great investment.

RESOURCES

United States Cycling Federation: One Olympic Plaza, Colorado Springs, CO 80909; Phone: 719-578-4581; Fax: 719-578-4628; e-mail:uscf@usacycling.org.

Bicycling magazine: 33 E. Minor, Emmaus, PA 18049; 610-967-5171.

VeloNews magazine: 1850 N. 55th Street, Boulder, CO 80301; 303-440-0601.

Visit your local bookstore for cycling-specific titles.

Visit the Web for cycling-specific sites. www.iBIKE.com is a good place to start, as is the USCF website, www.usacycling.org.

13

Preseason Mountain Biking

"Allow the beauty of what you love to be what you do.
There are a hundred ways to kneel and kiss the ground."
—Jalludin Rumi

ANGEL'S FIRE

I half-sit, half-stand over my mountain bike's top tube on a crisp August morning in Angel Fire, New Mexico. Dew, as if sent by a cherub's moist breath, glitters among pine needles. A lone raven, a totem animal of magic, stalls overhead in the early morning light. A throng of nervous cyclists, anticipating suffering, crowds the chalked start line. This race is an important one, the State MTB Championships. This championship has drawn New Mexico's finest mountain-bike athletes at their peak levels of fitness. Awaiting the start gun, some of the athletes pray. Some have their game faces on; they stare blankly, resolutely ahead. One fellow appears to be meditating. Most simply fidget. The guy next to me dissipates his nervousness by speaking in tongues. Worse, he didn't even have the common decency to shave his

legs! Maybe I have spent too much time racing on the roads this season ...

The first two hundred meters of a mountain-bike race are licensed insanity. Every one of the overly caffeinated, testosterone-amped cyclists sprint for the "hole-shot," the spot where the course suddenly bottlenecks into a singletrack, its space wide enough to accommodate but one bike at a time. The first one to the hole-shot dictates the race pace. The others must follow and eat the leader's dust (or mud, as the case may be).

Once, at a race in Telluride, Colorado, I was in the top ten approaching the hole-shot after a six-hundred-meter, anaerobic, high-speed catfight. There were approximately 125 racers in my group, and we were flying, our peleton kicking up a huge cloud of terra firma. We soon came to a river with a pedestrian bridge spanning it.

And just before the bridge stood two cement pillars. I rammed into one of those pillars so damn hard that I soared head first through the air for fifteen feet. I hate it when that happens.

This particular start, however, is ingratiating by comparison. As we establish ourselves past the hole-shot, I am in fifth spot, a good place to be. After a loamy traverse, the climbing begins. The course is Colorado-ish, about twelve miles per lap, with the first half up ski slopes and through thickets of pine forest, the second half a blistering downhill. We would do two laps.

The ascent lends itself to a rhythm. Around me swirls signs of autumn in the form of cool puddles, quaking aspen leaves, and thin clouds scampering across a cobalt sky. Frost, sure to arrive soon, will then slip over each twig and leaf like gloves of Asian silk. Then, when cold dawn emerges, sunlight will bounce off the morning frost, producing a mystic radiance, a gift known only to those who inhabit this valley. Native Americans witnessed this daily phenomenon and thought it to be a form of fire delivered from angels. They called this place the "Land of Angel Fire."

By midway up the climb, I have passed three of the five riders in front me. One of them, the state off-road series leader, has dropped back, gluing himself to my rear tire. On a steep pitch, he passes me and presses the pace. I jump onto his rear wheel, determined to stick to it like spots on dice. Then, pilot error. I have been climbing in

my middle chain ring, pushing a high gear, but now have to shift down to my inner chain ring. As I do, the chain leaps like Superman off the chain wheel and dangles limply beneath the bottom bracket. I have to dismount, reattach the chain, remount, regain my climbing rhythm. By the time I've recovered from my shifting error, "Almighty Todd" Jones, the series leader, is a hundred meters ahead.

After I remount my bike, I have great difficulty maintaining focus. Stopping on that uphill effectively severed my flow. My heart rate soars. Oxygen debt looms close. My legs fill with fatigue toxins that won't flush out. As my motivation to catch Almighty Todd dwindles, my lower-back injury rears its head. Soon my lumbar muscles are deep in spasm, and the all-too-familiar pain blinds me from sensing anything save for surviving the next moment, holding on for one more breath.

The guy who is in front of Almighty Todd and me blows up. He went out too hard, a common mistake in these Rocky Mountain races. I am in second place as I begin the descent. Approaching thirty miles per hour through a serpentine line, I dare not blink for fear that I should miss a hidden compression or overshoot the next line. Not having preridden the course, I must anaerobically grope my way down the steep, rock-studded descents. At one steep headwall, a gathered crowd adorned with cameras awaits my arrival. Entering a gnarly section, I scoot my butt off the saddle and hang it out over the rear wheel … just in time. My world drops away. A second later I'm at the bottom of the near-vertical headwall, still upright, still riding, and people are applauding. Evidently, some riders have chosen to dismount and walk down the section. Another lap still remains.

Mountain-bike racing is for me a transcendent experience. Certain elements in the sport give rise to a sublime mysticism. This field of spirituality requires the pain of racing to impart the deep sphere of inner power. I feel that many mountain bikers are drawn to this sport because they, too, have touched on this transcendent experience, which draws on their inner resources in ways they cannot summon in daily life. When we study Wholistic Fitness, we can come close to such an experience.

The author and "Almighty Todd" Jones (left) await the start gun at an MTB race at Sandia Peak Ski Area outside Albuquerque, New Mexico. Photo by Michael Dalfonso.

COSMIC SENSE

After finishing his first mountain-bike race in Keystone, Colorado, one of my students wrote in his Cycle Summation: "I have learned that bowling is overrated as a sport! Oh my God did this race hurt! I had no idea I could withstand that much pain." A week later he wrote: "During my meditation session yesterday, the thought came to me that we tend to place so much importance on what in a cosmic sense are the most meaningless. I mean, we take so seriously things that really don't matter."

This particular student is an alcoholic. Wholistic Fitness was his intervention. It is also his way to stay sober. Through his practice of Wholistic Fitness and through experiences like mountain-bike racing, he is owning the responsibilities he has created. He now approaches his inner dragons with nobility and a warrior's heart. He may never reach the top of a podium or be placed on a magazine cover, but like many of us, he is finding a higher way to know himself. I like to think that many mountain bikers do their dirt riding, mix it up with Mother Earth, for very simple reasons: to know their higher selves better and to chase their highest stars. There is a saying, "Two men look from behind the same bars. One sees mud, the other the stars." Mountain biking can help us see stars—sometimes literally!

PROTECT YOURSELF

This section functions as a specific safety-awareness tool.

Like road cycling, mountain biking offers a rich, diverse, and nonconcussive way to train the cardiovascular system. It affords significantly more involvement for muscles of the upper body and more neural activity than road cycling due to the numerous obstacles to overcome, terrain changes, and occasional hike-a-bike sections. About the only warning label comes from physicians advising against the activity for pregnant women. I would like you, however, to read the "Protect Yourself" section in the preceding chapter on road cycling. The counsel given there also holds true for mountain biking.

With that preface, let me say this: Mountain biking will likely leave you with scars. For those of us who think scars are sexy and cool, this is fine. For normal folk, this may be a consideration for staying on the road bike, where crashes are fortunately very rare. If you ride a mountain bike, you *will* go down. Those of us who push our limits on technical terrain go down quite often. More frequent than

crashing is something called "dabbing": putting a foot out to regain balance while riding through tricky terrain like rocky sections, roots, or loose uphills. It is a good idea for beginners to sign up for a clinic or a private session with a coach. There are also some good instructional videos out that cover technical aspects of the sport (see "Resources").

This book does not cover riding technique, just fitness. In other words, I'll give you a high degree of fitness so you can really crash well! Actually, the well-balanced approach of Wholistic Fitness is ideal for decreasing the likelihood of mountain-bike injury. My approach will create for you joints that are super strong but also supple. Appropriate nutrition and meditation help keep the cells of the body and mind soft and open. Meditation also sharpens awareness, making crashes less likely. Wholistic Fitness athletes are more likely than others to "relax" into crashes when they do happen. I've had some pretty extraordinary yard sales* during my cycling career, but I've never suffered anything more than advanced road/dirt rash. I attribute this solely to my practice of Wholistic Fitness.

Injury Treatment

Follow these procedures to treat common injuries you may incur from mountain biking.

---

*Yard Sale: MTB and Alpine Ski/Snowboarding lingo meaning "major crash."

Road Rash: This terms refers to cycling-induced wounds that have broken the skin. When the body's protective barrier (skin) has been opened, bacteria can penetrate.

1. Clean the wound. Use germ-killing hydrogen peroxide when available or otherwise soap and water. Make sure all visible foreign particles are scrubbed out.

2. Apply a topical antibiotic ointment such as Neosporin®.

3. Cover the wound with a nonadhering dressing such as Tefla®, then hold that in place with fishnet (gauze) material such as Surgiflex® or Bandnet® (available from medical-supply companies). The fishnet material is great. It will hold the dressing in place without causing heat buildup and while allowing full range of motion. It also shows the world that you are a warrior, not afraid of going down for the sake of personal growth!

Saddle Sores: This term refers to spots of severe chafing in the groin area. The key to preventing saddle sores is to minimize friction.

1. Make sure your bike fit is ideal. Consult your local bike shop about proper fit.

2. Wear clean, padded cycling shorts. Wash them after every use.

3. Use a product such as Chamois Butt'r™ (Paceline Products, 816-781-0287). I've had good luck and fun times applying it to the chamois of my cycling shorts, along with a little dab on my groin where it counts. I've never had a problem with chafing as a re-sult, even after three top-twenty finishes in the Leadville Trail 100-mile MTB race!

4. Get the heck out of those sweaty, gross shorts as soon as possible after rides or races! If you are away from home, take them off and swipe your crotch clean with moist, antiseptic towelettes such as Baby Wipes®. Shower as soon as possible.

Knee Pain: The reasons for cycling knee pain are compounded in mountain biking, due to its aggressive nature. Dr. Thomas Dickson, a cycling expert and orthopedic surgeon writes in *The Physician and Sportsmedicine:* "New riders often make two mistakes which cause knee problems. First, they set the saddle too low, and, secondly, recreational riders often use gears that are too high." The guidance given in this book, coupled with more specific coaching, should help you eliminate or avoid undue knee pain.

MOUNTAIN BIKING BEAUTIFULLY: POSTURE AND PEDAL CADENCE

This section offers two sport-specific meditations to practice. In order to find the harmony in any sport, one must be able to control individual body parts before they can merge into a unified whole.

That's right; it's the same gig as in the "Road Cycling Beautifully" section in the preceding chapter. If you have not read that section, do so now, then come back here.

Posture

Because of a higher handlebar, mountain biking requires a slightly more upright riding posture than road biking. Champion mountain bikers who come from a road-racing background, however, such as John Tomac, maintain a very low body position on their mountain bikes. In general, the mountain-bike setup requires that the rider place more body weight on the saddle and rear wheel, which is vital for traction. The more you ride on the road, the more road-like your mountain-bike setup will be.

The principle remains the same for the dirt as it does for the road: Get low! You'll need a slightly greater reach in order to whip the mountain bike around in technical terrain. There should be no overlap between your elbows and knees while riding.

Pedal Cadence

Pedal cadence in mountain biking undergoes many changes over the course of an excursion or race. Given the terrain, cadences can range from a low of fifty revolutions per minute to a high of 130 rpm's! It is the versatility required in pedaling technique that makes mountain biking so much fun. The sport requires constant cultivation of awareness to discover which gear is most appropriate. Each individual will approach each section of trail differently.

Pedal cadences change from day to day as well. I experimented at length with different pedal cadences on Animas Mountain in Durango, Colorado. I would ride the same uphill section (about three miles and 1,500 vertical feet) pushing a high gear (slow cadence), then do it using a moderate gear (faster cadence). My ascent times were always within sixty seconds of each other. If you are a racer, sixty seconds can mean a lot, and you should keep studying to determine your optimal pedal cadence. If you are a fitness cyclist, it's no big deal—pedal at whichever cadence feels best to you.

TERMS OF EN-GEARMENT (AN ASPECT OF CADENCE)

Mountain biking demands much more shifting than road cycling. The multitude of terrain changes means constant anticipation and fluid shifting. Small pilot errors, like the one I mentioned in this chapter's opening story, can have disastrous performance results in races. Invest in quality components! The modern mountain bike can handle a ton of abuse … if it's high quality. If not, you will be lost in the hellish situation of fluttering gears and mechanical breakdowns.

CYCLING BIOMECHANICS

This section offers informal, sport-specific analysis for deeper understanding and practice.

The biomechanics of mountain biking differ from those of road cycling because of the slightly higher upper-body position required as well as more upper-body muscular involvement. I train my elite mountain-bike racers primarily as roadies during the off-season and early preseason. Their late preseason and in-season programs are quite different, however. I both nonspecifically and specifically strength train my mountain bikers, with more attention given to the deltoid complex of the shoulder. The shoulder joint is active in all phases of mountain biking. The trapezius, teres major and minor, lattissimus dorsi, levator scapulae, and rhomboids are also trained to stabilize and prepare the shoulder girdle for the dynamics of mountain-bike handling. When descending on a mountain bike, a rider uses the serratus anterior and pectoralis to abduct the shoulder; thus, training the chest is valuable for mountain bikers. Descending also puts eccentric force on the elbow extensors, so strength training the triceps brachii is also wise.

I am also big on directly training the forearm musculature, particularly the brachioradialis as well as the wrist extensors: extensor carpi radialis and extensor carpi ulnaris. With some mountain-bike athletes, I prescribe direct finger training to improve strength, speed, and endurance to the gripping muscles of the hand, such as the flexor digitorum group.

Mike Longmire midway on the descent of Cinnamon Pass above Silverton, Colorado. Notice Mike's flat back and low body position. A state road race champion, Mike's MTB performances are also podium toppers. Photo by the author.

MOUNTAIN-BIKING HINTS

This section provides at-a-glance reminders and suggestions for daily practice.

Some training programs in this book contain low to moderate mountain-biking volumes. Occasionally, cycling intervals are given. As you engage in mountain biking as part of your Wholistic Fitness journey, read the cycling hints in the road cycling chapter. Then use the following hints to specifically enhance your mountain-biking performance. Refer to Chapter Six for general CV guidelines.

Safety is in your speed. Don't approach obstacles with timidity and at a slow speed. Generally, you'll "clean" more obstacles with momentum and balance than with slowness and balance.

Emphasize exhalation. Mountain biking bounces you around a lot, and it's easy to allow the breath to get high in the chest, which invites cramping, rigidity, and poor oxygenation. Use a "blowing breath," which prioritizes exhales instead of inhales to find softness and power. Try to hit obstacles on the exhale.

Work your skills! Refrain from just going out riding. Instead, have a purpose for each workout, especially if you are not working with a trainer. Practice no-hands riding, cornering, pace line (riding in close proximity to and harmonic flow with several other riders in a single-line formation that rotates), etc. Training is meant to increase awareness, not monotony.

Use a wristwatch timer with an alarm to remind yourself to drink every fifteen minutes until it becomes a ritual.

When the going gets tough, breathe deeper, not faster. Don't gasp. Flush the fingertips with softness. Feel your feet. Stay in the body.

To improve speed, meditate on faster leg speed, not necessarily pushing the pedals harder.

One half-hour before training, eat an energy bar and drink twelve ounces of fluid.

Intervals

See the road cycling chapter. Mountain bikers will use the same interval workouts described there.

RELATED ACTIVITIES

See this section in the road cycling chapter.

SPECIFIC EQUIPMENT

See this section in the road cycling chapter.

RESOURCES

United States Cycling Federation: One Olympic Plaza, Colorado Springs, CO 80909; Phone: 719-578-4581; Fax: 719-578-4628; e-mail: uscf@usacycling.org.

Mountain Bike magazine: 33 E. Minor, Emmaus, PA 18049; 610-967-5171.

VeloNews magazine: 1850 N. 55th Street, Boulder, CO 80301; 303-440-0601.

Ned Overend: Performance Mountain Biking video. 800-234-8356.

Visit the Web for cycling-specific sites. www. iBIKE.com is a good place to start, as is the USCF website, www.usacycling.org.

14

Preseason Roller Skiing

*"Talents are best nurtured in solitude; character is
best formed in the stormy billows of the world."*
—Johann Wolfgang von Goethe

PRESEASON SPIRITUALITY

I often tell my athletes, "You never get a
second chance at your preseason." By the
time snow falls, winter fitness must be at a
high level. On-snow training should refine
specific ski technique and fitness, but it is
during the preseason when dryland activities like roller skiing nurture your talent.
Early-season training also deepens reverence for winter. There is a seeming im-
plausibility about dryland training and its
spiritual connection with on-snow performance, but in my experience, no question exists. Spiritual tenacity is developed
in the preseason. Roller skiing during autumn is a kind of homage to winter that
provides eminent dividends when the
snows finally fall. This activity is not for
the impatient. It requires precision of
movement and endurance of mind. For
these reasons, roller skiing is a sterling ac-

You never get a second chance at your preseason. The author roller skiing near Chimayo,
New Mexico. Photo by Marc Romanelli.

tivity for all winter athletes, particularly the
nordic skier.

Road-ski technology has been surprisingly sluggish when compared with other
outdoor sports–equipment development.
In the early '80s, the Durango ski team used
wood contraptions called appropriately the

"road ski." It was designed and served adequately as a sport-specific training tool for kick-and-glide ski technique, also known as classic-style or diagonal-stride skiing. Everyone back then thought that these new road skis were the miracle preseason training secret. This imagined potential, however, has never quite been fulfilled. Still, roller skis have their benefits. For starters, they make you feel like you are skiing in August, which is pretty cool. They also increase awareness of form, and if used with exaggeration and visualization, they can develop ski-specific conditioning.

The shortcomings of roller skis keep them from being more popular. A roller ski is simply different than a snow ski, which can result in neural microflaws in poling and stroke technique that can hamper the subtleties of good skiing form. And roller skis are heavy and difficult to handle, which can result in a little too much intimacy with the asphalt. I've got a few good roller-ski stories, but I don't want to scare you away from what essentially is a good training aid.

PROTECT YOURSELF

This section functions as a specific safety-awareness tool.

Roller skiing has significant injury potential. Though normal, flat-terrain roller-ski speeds are fairly slow (four to eight miles per hour for classic-style roller skiing and five to twelve miles per hour on skate skis), brakeless road skis can pick up speed surprisingly fast. Along with that speed comes lack of control. For these reasons, protective gear such as helmets, wrist guards, elbow guards, and knee guards are all strongly recommended.

The good news? Joint concussion is small on roller skis. Poling, however, can result in minor elbow inflammation. Roller poles transfer the shock of asphalt to elbow and shoulder joints. Engage in roller skiing at low to moderate volumes only. Do not perform a lot of distance workouts on roller skis because it will invite micro-trauma to the elbow joint, and possibly the lower back. It's better to use roller skiing for *quality* workouts, not quantity workouts.

ROLLER SKIING BEAUTIFULLY: WEIGHT SHIFT AND REACH!

This section offers two sport-specific meditations to practice. In order to find the harmony in any sport, one must be able to control individual body parts before they can merge into a unified whole.

Weight Shift

Regardless of whether you roller ski in skate or classic style, two fundamental meditations contribute to powerful, elegant skiing form. If you use classical style, exaggerate the knee bend as you push down on the kick ski. And be sure to push *down*, not back! Visualize the wax (grip) pocket of your snow ski being pressed into the snow. Center the hips over the kick ski, then feel the weight shift begin as you keep your chest and hips forward. Begin shifting your weight to the glide ski and use your poling stroke to help complete the weight transfer. Imagine riding a flat ski by focusing a line of energy down the outside edge of the glide ski.

When skate skiing on the road, exaggerate weight shift by deepening the knee bend before coming onto the dominant ski (as in V-1 technique) and really feel your hip extend as the poles come forward and you shift weight onto the dominant ski.

Reach!

When working with classic poling technique, keep the hands very active. Always reach high with the "hang arm" to complete your weight shift to the dominant ski. Imagine reaching up to pick an apple from a limb located just above your head. "Pluck" the apple, then train your follow-through technique by tossing the apple into an imaginary bucket behind you. Release the pole at the end of each backswing. Line up the nose, knees, and toes in precise symmetry. Merge into a meditation with the dancing of the poles and skis and weight shift.

Practice on the asphalt and your snow performance will be more economical, faster, and more enjoyable than ever before!

ROLLER SKIING BIOMECHANICS

This section offers informal sport-specific analysis for deeper understanding and practice.

Classic Style

Movements to be trained in classic style (kick-and-glide) in the lower body are hip extension, flexion, and lumbar extension and flexion, with eccentric and isometric contraction within the adductors and abductors. Primary musculature to allow such articulation center on the illiopsoas, rectus femoris for hip flexors, the gluteals for hip extension, rectus abdominis, obliques, and erector spinae group for the midsection motion and stabilization of lumbar involvement.

In the upper body, poling movement must address the glenohumeral joint, since reaching is a very active motion in classic style. Flexion and extension at this joint is a primary area of focus, thus the latissimus dorsi and teres major should be trained not only to develop the power phase of the poling motion (shoulder extension) but also to stabilize the spine in order to eliminate excessive, energy-wasting movement. Shoulder flexion is taken care of by the deltoid and clavicular pectoralis.

The author off-road roller skiing near Coralles, New Mexico. Photo by Scott Dupuis.

Skate Style

In skate style, all the above musculature is called upon but with more emphasis in the adductor and abductors for the lower body by the adductor brevis, longus, and magnus, while abduction is taken care of by the sartorius, tensor fascia latae, and gluteus medius and minimus. Most of the power stroke is accomplished through the gluteal complex along with the vastus complex. The biceps femoris is active in hip extension and recovering the leg.

Upper-body poling movement places more emphasis on the rotary trunk muscles and greater priority to the power delivery of the poling stroke. I also train my skaters with emphasis in the abdominal region. In recognition of this, ski skaters should bring attention to not only the rectus abdominus

for strong trunk flexion during completion of the power stroke during poling, but also the internal and external obliques for powerful V-1 technique along with the erector spinae and rotatores/multifidus.

ROLLER SKIING HINTS

This section provides at-a-glance reminders and suggestions for daily practice.

When roller skiing uphill, focus on reaching up the hill with greater arm frequency.

While skating, exaggerate the motion of compressing the upper body while pushing down and behind you.

Keep your torso erect. In skate technique, rotate it so it faces the skating ski. This is the key to riding a fast, flat gliding ski before pushing off on the skating ski.

Ski racers should limit the time spent training on roller skis, since the neural system will get "grooved" with microflaws for snow-ski technique. Instead, do distance work using non specific dryland activities such as running or cycling. Even inline skating should not be relied on for distance work.

Pick your pavement wisely: the smoother, the better; the less traffic, the better; the wider the shoulder, the better.

Get aerodynamic when being passed by cars. The car-driving public is not used to the motion or the image of a road skier. Ski with the flow of traffic, but when you hear a car coming up behind you, break technique and bring in your arms, poles, and

Another Close Call

The afternoon sun flickered among the pine needles of Lefthand Canyon near Boulder, Colorado. Roller skiing up the narrow road, I was alert to oncoming cars behind me. Hearing what sounded like a big pickup truck, I immediately tucked into a narrow body position and glided to the absolute edge of the road, where paved shoulder met dirt. Something told me this would be a close call (seems to me, pickups are usually close calls). Sure enough, a thundering blast of noise whipped past my left ear. It was a pickup with extended side-view mirrors. The passenger mirror had missed my head by what felt like a fraction of an inch. Just another close call, I thought. I stepped out with my left leg to resume skiing when something caught my peripheral vision. In a flicker of an instant I retracted my left leg. A nanosecond later, a wide flat-bed trailer attached to the pickup truck with a long-nosed hitch came flying past the exact space where my left leg had been just a moment earlier.

I tell this particular story not to frighten roller skiers, but to increase their awareness. Just because a vehicle has passed you, don't assume it's not towing a trailer. Don't step out from the shoulder until you are certain the coast is clear!

legs toward the midline of the body. Only after the car has passed should you resume skiing. I know it sucks to break striding and gliding form, but it also sucks to get hit by a vehicle (see sidebar).

RELATED ACTIVITIES

This section considers some other dryland activities that are in the same family as the sport described.

Off-Road Roller Skiing

It's a great idea that hasn't quite worked out. I mean, we can send people to the moon and back, but we can't seem to be able to produce an off-road roller ski that really cranks. If you live in an area with a supply of smooth dirt roads, it might be fun to try out a pair of off-road roller skis (see photo on previous page). Off-road skis are usually intended for both classic and skate styles (see the dual-technique skis following). Some classic-style roller skiers even use off-road skis as their main ski. I have had my best off-road roller ski experiences on Elpex skis (see "Resources").

Dual-Technique Roller Skiing

This activity uses a roller ski designed for both skate and classic-style skiing. Generally speaking, I don't endorse hybrid types of outdoor sports gear because they compromise performance.

Hybrid roller skis are no exception, but they don't bother me as much as some other hybrid gear for a few reasons. First, roller skiing is not a performance sport as much as it is a low-volume, specific training tool. Second, the dual-technique roller skis go slower, which increases resistance and, in turn, ups the energy expenditure and overall training effect. Finally, the speed and action of the dual-technique skis may actually mimic the neural coordination of snow skiing even better than specific roller skis. See the "Resources" section for contact numbers for ordering dual-technique skis.

SPECIFIC EQUIPMENT

This section covers specific equipment needed for the sport described. See Part Five for general cold-weather clothing and gear.

Skis

Various types of roller skis are available; see the "Resources" section.

Poles

For classic technique, the handle of the pole should be at chin level when you are standing in the roller skis. For skating technique, the handle should reach "mustache" level. Various types of roller ski poles are available; refer to the "Resources" section.

Protective Gear

See "Specific Equipment" in Chapter Eleven (Inline Skating and Skiing).

RESOURCES

You won't find *Roller Ski Illustrated* at your local newsstand just yet. Sometimes, mountaineering shops that carry nordic skis will have a pair of roller skis in inventory. Trustworthy brand names include Jennex, Inc. (603-672-2600); and Elpex (518-793-5677, ext. 246).

Nordic Equipment, Inc.: 800-321-1671, P.O. Box 980259, Park City, Utah 80498.

Reliable Racing Supply: 800-223-4448, 643 Upper Glen Street, Queensbury, New York 12804.

15

Preseason Running

"It's easy to see farther than you can run.
But that doesn't mean you should stop running."
—The author

COMPLETE HUMAN AUTHENTICITY

Running is a precise and humbling art. Wholistic Fitness philosophy considers running the most noble of all cardiovascular activities because it is the most genuine. No article of equipment separates the runner from his or her movement. Unlike cycling, there is no coasting in running. Unlike nordic skiing, there is no gliding. Swimmers, paddle athletes, and snowshoers ... all have flotation. But when it comes to running, baby, you've got nothing but yourself! In the moment the foot feels the earth, there is complete human authenticity.

The very essence that attracts us to running is the same thing we reject about it: simplicity. There's nowhere for the ego to hide. If we are lucky, running can be meditation. Even then, running is part zazen mixed with escapism. To me, running encourages self-control and introspection. In

Wholistic Fitness philosophy considers running the most noble of all cardiovascular activities because it is the most genuine. The author training in Durango, Colorado. Photo by Denise Jackson.

sum, there is nothing like running, and all winter athletes would do well to embrace this vehicle of fitness and enlightenment.

Profound simplicity is also what makes running the most concussive of all cardiovascular training. Running requires careful monitoring and wise program design. Three-quarters of all sports injuries are running related. So although running is superb for imparting cardiovascular and transpersonal fitness, it must be approached with wisdom.

LAKE PEAK SPEAKS

Today, some training partners and I ran Lake Peak, a 12,409-foot mountain above Santa Fe, New Mexico. We ran directly up the ski slopes until we reached timberline. From there we traversed the windswept, talus-sloped crown. We then scrambled across a rocky arete with expansive voids opening on either side of the knife-edge ridge.

Once on the summit, we turned around and plunged down the steep slopes. What had taken me nearly an hour to run and hike up required but twenty minutes to descend. Nearing the end of my running descent, the tension within my leg muscles was emphatic. The nature of steep downhill running is such that muscle fibers are literally being pulled apart as they attempt to shorten. Within my fiber membranes and connective tissue, radical stretching, beyond what is normal for the human body, was being repeated as I bombed toward the bottom.

This same tearing and stretching occurs at all levels of running, just not as severely as on steep terrain. Some studies show that

intense running, such as peak running, road racing, or interval workouts, require up to thirty days before complete muscular and neural regeneration is complete! Fortunately, adaptation to such demands can be safely attained by the athlete.

MEASURED DOSAGES

Unfortunately, running can result in injuries. Its aftereffects are damaging enough that I only prescribe running as cross-training in carefully measured dosages. Winter athletes should run most of their miles on flat or gently rolling dirt trails to minimize joint concussion. Competitive road races should be entered only with a solid base of running; pavement produces too great a joint stress for a nonspecific runner. Even my nordic ski racers, the winter athletes for whom I prescribe the highest volumes of running, stick to low-intensity workouts on the roads. Intervals should be done on a cinder track or on smooth dirt roads. It's stupid for winter athletes to get injured in preseason training. Though running is one of the best cardiovascular activities a winter athlete can do, it's got to be done wisely.

PROTECT YOURSELF

This section functions as a specific safety-awareness tool.

The joint stress of running is one more reason why I push my athletes to strength train aggressively. The most common injury among runners, chondomalacia patellae, is often caused by muscle imbalance or compression at the knee, which pulls the kneecap out of alignment. The way around this injury? Don't get it in the first place! Strength train to ensure muscle balance and to alleviate overall joint compression. If you already have chondomalacia, consider doing structural bodywork in order to realign the muscle play and bring the knee back into alignment. Then strength train to balance the workload of running throughout the muscle system. Too much running too soon causes inflammation and injury.

Don't running shoes protect the winter athlete from running injuries? The quality and technology of running shoes is very high these days. Still, you should not look to shoes for injury prevention. That attitude is typical of the brainwashing so prevalent in our society. The warrior athlete never looks to externals first. The key is to always look within first. Wholistic Fitness runners are taught to strengthen ankle, knee, and hip ligaments and tendons. By maximizing the integrity of the connective tissue associated with running, we more fully prepare ourselves for the concussive nature of running. If we look to fancy running shoes to protect us, we subconsciously accept the notion that our inner belief is not within ourselves, but in things outside of us.

True Performance Comes from Within

Perhaps you are familiar with the humorous circumstances involving the Tarahumara In-dians and the Leadville 100 trail run in the high mountains of Colorado. This occurred several years ago. The Tarahumaras are native Mexicans who are are known for running ultra distances at great speeds, with absolutely none of the performance diets, fluids, shoes, or training plans advocated by our American sport physiologists.

Tarahumaras are also very confused by the idea of competition. Once, for marketing purposes, a well-known American running-shoe company sponsored several Tarahumaras to compete in the Leadville race. The company paid big bucks to fly the would-be competitors up to Leadville and outfitted each of them with its best racing shoes. After conducting their own brand of research with the high-performance shoes, the Tarahumaras sat on a rock, took off their new shoes, and ran to the town landfill. Finding some old tires, they slashed out some rubber and fashioned crude sandals from the tires. Content with this more refined high-performance "shoe," they happily outran the competition.

True performance always comes from within.

RUNNING BEAUTIFULLY: STRIDE LENGTH AND RATE

This section offers two sport-specific meditations to practice. In order to find the harmony in any sport, one must be able to control individual body parts before they can merge into a unified whole.

Even though winter athletes only use running as a cross-training activity, it is important to be as beautiful a runner as we can. This be-your-best approach is not only the lifestyle attitude of a Wholistic Fitness athlete, it is also the optimal way to stay injury free. In the art of self-cultivation, we strive for gracefulness and elegance in the face of difficulty. Running beautifully is a high-priority meditation. It increases the mystical fun and transcendent aspects of running. The best way to run beautifully is to pay attention to two biomechanical aspects: stride rate and stride length. When these two qualities are harmonized, beautiful running form emerges naturally.

Stride Length

Stride rate, or frequency of steps, and stride length, how long you sail between steps, are what dictate running speed. Of the two, stride rate is more important to practice. But stride length is where many runners need to make adjustments. There are two areas in which to work within stride length: understriding and overstriding.

Understriding: Things To Be Aware Of

- underswinging the arms
- droopy shoulder girdle, slouched upper body
- arms tending to crisscross the midline of the body too much
- upper body "swimming" back and forth; too much lateral movement
- chronic shin problems

Overstriding: Things To Be Aware Of

- overswinging the arms
- high shoulder-girdle elevation
- radically arched lower back
- sore hamstrings, due to exaggerated stride
- herky-jerky vertical motion in running gait

Stride Rate

Many runners think that to run better they need to increase the length of their stride. False! Stride rate is more important than stride length. For years now I've had the misfortune to study several Rocky Mountain athletes, such as Eric Black of Colorado, as they pass me on the running sections of winter multisport competitions or snowshoe races. When Eric passes me, I am struck by his short stride length. Yet his leg turnover is fantastic. Using his legs like pistons, he just pulls away from me. Exasperated, I start overstriding, trying to keep up. It doesn't work. Soon my heart rate soars because I am not running within my most efficient mechanics. I am not running beautifully. To improve, I must increase my stride *rate*, not length. Many runners are in the same predicament. Fortunately, stride rate is responsive to training. It just takes some practice. The interval drills and techniques described later in this chapter will increase a runner's stride rate.

Harmonic Flow

With time, the runner attempts to bring

three phases of running into harmony: drive phase, float phase, and compression phase. Once each of these areas is mindfully practiced, a smooth, fluid running form will emerge. Instead of analyzing each of the phases, I ask runners to be aware of "braking," an abrupt deceleration or acceleration that tends to jam the upper thigh bone into the pelvic bowl. This is not only fatiguing but also damaging to the joints. If you feel jerky while running, hire a personal trainer or coach for an hour's consultation. Stay out of those hips!

RUNNING BIOMECHANICS

This section offers informal, sport-specific analysis for deeper understanding and practice.

Lower Body

Running movement is not complicated. The two smaller gluteal muscles, the gluteus medius and minimus, plus a hamstring muscle, the semitendinosus, are the major players in forward propulsion. During steep uphills, the backward drive of the leg shifts more emphasis to the gluteus maximus. Many of the hip muscles are in a state of stabilization during running; while the foot is on the ground, they contract to stabilize the hip joint so the upper body does not fall to the opposite side. The gastrocnemius and soleus (the calf muscle) are also major contributors to running motion, as those muscles work together to produce

a powerful push-off. Hip movement is needed in running and, thus, the hip muscles should receive training. At an eight-minute-per-mile pace, the hip moves from 154 degrees to 188. At a six-minute-per-mile clip, the hip moves from 143 degrees to 196. One of the first things I look for in runners is hip contribution. Remember, the hips are more powerful than the legs!

Upper Body

I usually go nuts when I see my athletes not using their arms while running. Remember, one of our cardiovascular meditations is, "Arms Drive The Legs; Think Full Body Tempo!" The winter athlete, particularly snowshoers and nordic skiers, must prioritize strong arm carriage to achieve strong leg stride. The deltoid complex as well as the trapezius muscles of the upper back are important here. Maintaining brisk arm swing is a function of the biceps and brachialis. I'm also big on midsection training for runners; keeping good upper-body posture means more leg and hip drive. The lumbar, abdominals, and obliques are all body parts that need training attention by the runner.

RUNNING HINTS

This section provides at-a-glance reminders and suggestions for daily practice. ·

The training programs found in this book may contain low to moderate running volumes. Occasionally, run intervals are given. As you engage in running as part of your Wholistic Fitness journey, keep the its mechanical aspects at the forefront of your awareness. The following hints are specifically geared toward running; refer to Chapter Six for general CV guidelines. Remember, each step you run can be meditation or mindless exercise. Keeping focused on elegant running mechanics anchors the mind and enables you to use running as a spiritual workshop.

Go easy at first. Allow the body to raise its core temperature slowly. Jog for several minutes at a slow, easy pace (Zone 1) to allow physiological adjustments to occur before undertaking higher-intensity effort.

Shake out the arms every ten to fifteen minutes. Drop the shoulder girdle and release tension in the neck and shoulder area. Do exercises such as butt-kicks or knee-ups during easy runs to keep the neural stimulus high.

Use the "pistol mudra" (mudra means hand gesture) to keep from having "rigid" hands or fists. To activate this energy-enhancing mudra, make a pretend pistol in each hand by extending the two index fingers and thumb while folding the remaining fingers into the palm. This mudra activates meridian pulses and helps maintain good upper body running mechanics.

Use partners for paceline intervals and practicing passing, drafting, surging, and bridging. Use running like cycling; think peleton tactics! A paceline interval is when

Legs still shaky from a leg workout at *Powerhouse Gym* in Chatsworth, California, Racin' Jason performs "Knee Ups," a running drill to increase neural drive to the lower body. Note Jason's use of the "pistol mudra" hand posture to keep from having "rigid" hands. This mudra activates meridian pulses and helps maintain good upper body running mechanics. Photo by the author.

Illustration of "pistol mudra" by Anne Sasso.

a group of runners "play" follow-the-leader while in a single-line formation. The leader must break the wind, which requires more effort. After taking his or her "pull" at the front, the next person in line assumes the lead. The former leader drifts back to the end of the line to recover. The paceline continues to rotate in this manner.

Use long, gradual uphills to enhance strength and form. Go steady. Do not surge or spurt while training unless prescribed as intervals.

Think about foot placement: begin with an outward heel strike, roll onto the mid-foot, finish by pushing off from the big toe.

Big Toe Push Off: Concentrate on pushing off from the big toe. The big toe should be the last part of your foot to leave the earth.

Remember that the arms drive the legs. To increase stride rate, begin a more aggressive arm-pumping movement.

Focus on good knee drive and softening the hips. Don't tighten the hips; allow them some freedom. Focus the knees upward, especially on uphills. This maximizes the gluteal involvement and should increase postural form and hip/leg power.

Make sure knee-over-toe alignment remains straight during the recovery phase of your leg stride and that you're not swinging your feet wide.

Use puddles to check your foot mechanics and use your shadow as an upper-body posture coach—your head should not be bobbing up and down.

Hold your head up while running—don't look down.

Keep the spine out of the hips, with a slight forward lean, and keep your elbows back and close to the body.

Use downhills to increase leg speed every now and then.

Occasionally, try running for several minutes using only Filling Breaths (nasal inhales and exhales) during low aerobic runs. This balances the energies of the left and right sides of the body as well as contributes to more efficient respiration.

Intervals

Since the goal of interval run training is to develop running speed, you will not find a lot of running intervals prescribed in this book. Winter athletes who need to develop leg speed, such as nordic ski racers, should do the bulk of their speed training while skiing, not running. However, I will occasionally prescribe run intervals to raise an athlete's lactate threshold, or the ability to remove lactate from the muscles. I have found that running intervals in the preseason increases athletes' ability to tolerate higher levels of intensity during their winter sports. For example, an alpine skier who performs run intervals in the preseason is more likely to develop greater tolerance for handling the "burning-thigh" syndrome when the snow falls. Psychologically, run intervals impart the transpersonal aspects of inner power and mental tenacity.

I use the following run-interval workouts in the programs outlined in this book. Always be sure to thoroughly warm up and cool down.

Cruise Intervals

While on a Zone 1–2 run, perform four to six intervals of two minutes each, with a full recovery between. During the intervals, focus on smooth, powerful running mechanics. You should increase your intensity to Zone 3 as soon as possible and finish at Zone 4. Up the tempo during the last thirty seconds of each interval. After each interval, jog at Zone 1 until your heart rate lowers to Zone 2. Resume fluid running form, then pop off another interval.

Surges

While running, initiate an explosive acceleration of twenty to thirty meters. Regain your former pace for forty-five seconds or so, then surge again. Repeat for three to five minutes. Recover for ten minutes, then do another set of three to five minutes.

Pyramids

Perform a series of intervals in the following increments: one minute, two minutes, three minutes, four minutes, another at four minutes, then three minutes, two minutes, and back down to one minute. Begin doing these intervals at Zone 2, building to Zone 4 by the end of each one. Each interval should be a gradual acceleration. Each recovery period should equal the length of the preceding interval. For instance, after twenty minutes of Zone 1 running, accelerate for a one-minute interval. Recover for one minute by light jogging. Then go hard for two minutes and recover for another two minutes. Repeat this sequence up and down the "pyramid."

15 x 15's

Keeping your stride rate high, go hard (Zone 4) for fifteen seconds. Do a recovery jog for fifteen seconds. Repeat this sequence for five minutes. Then jog for ten minutes to recover. Then repeat. This exercise will increase your aerobic capacity, stride rate, recovery ability, and ability to respond to surges.

Minutes Are Forever

Run hard for one minute (Zones 3–4), then do a recovery jog for one minute (Zone 1). Keep doing this until a) you throw up; or b) ten minutes has gone by. Recover for ten minutes, then repeat. These intervals can be done on gradual uphills to increase lactate threshold, steep uphills to increase leg strength, and gradual downhills to work on stride rate.

Track Work

In this book, I have selected only two workouts that are to be done on the track.

Speedy Workout

A fifteen-minute warm-up jog into:

- Two sets of 400 meters with a one-and-a-half minute recovery into
- One set of 800 meters with a two-minute, forty-five second recovery into
- Two sets of 400 meters with a one-and-a-half minute recovery into
- One set of 800 meters with a two-minute, forty-five second recovery into
- Four laps, sprinting the straightaways and walking the corners
- Fifteen-minute cool down.

Speed-Enduro Workout

A fifteen-minute warm-up jog into:
- Two sets of 800 meters with a two-minute, forty-five second recovery into
- One set of 1,000 meters with a full recovery into
- Two sets of 800 meters with a two-minute, forty-five second recovery into
- One set of 1,000 meters with a full recovery into
- Fifteen-minute cool down.

RELATED ACTIVITIES

This section considers some other dryland activities that are in the same family as the sport described.

Pole Bounding

Pole bounding is a term I use to describe running with ski poles. Usually the poles are used when running uphill. It gets awkward and even dangerous to try to pole plant while running downhill. Pole bounding serves the specific needs of nordic skiers, but remains a super way for all winter athletes to increase energy expenditure and overall training effect. The poles should be classic-style height, which means the top of the pole grip should be around chin level. Don't use your fancy nordic poles. Get a beat-up pair, since you'll be using them while running up dry ski slopes and other rocky terrain. Unless you are a hard-core nordic skier, wearing gloves might also be wise.

SPECIFIC EQUIPMENT

This section covers specific equipment needed for the sport described. See Part Five for general cold-weather clothing and gear.

Most of the following gear is available through running specialty shops or through running catalogs such as Road Runner Sports (800-662-8896; www.roadrunner-sports.com)

Shoes

When I sold running shoes (one of my Boulder incarnations), I was taught about five categories of training shoes: 1) stability shoes; 2) trail shoes; 3) lightweight training shoes; 4) cushioned shoes; and 5) motion-control shoes. Each category addresses the needs of different foot types (normal, flat, high-arched), terrain (road, trail, or track), or injury history. You'll probably be best off in a trail shoe since most winter athletes need to spend running time on trails. The other option I'd advise is a motion-control shoe if you overpronate, need a deep heel counter, have flat feet, or are a heavyweight. I've reviewed dozens of shoes over the years, and each brand usually has a model or two that would work well for any individual. Take time to find a good shoe/model that fits. Unfortunately, the moment you finally find a shoe that fits like a glove, the manufacturer inevitably changes that model and you are back to square one. Finally, find the last that works best for you. Women and young adults require different lasts than men do. It pays to go to a running speciality store at least once to get dialed into what works best for you.

RESOURCES

Runner's World magazine: 33 E. Minor, Emmaus, PA 18049; 610-967-5171.

Running Times magazine: P.O. Box 6509, Syracuse, NY 13217; 800-668-0650.

Visit your local bookstore for running-specific titles. If you're into philosophical running, look for titles by the dearly beloved Dr. George Sheehan. He covers running inspiration from the heartspace.

16

Preseason Yoga

"A soft mind equals a steady posture.
A steady posture equals a soft mind."
—The author

BE A YOGI

Yoga is one the best activities any winter athlete could do for his or her off-season training. I was first introduced to yoga in the early '80s by a female climbing friend who was also a yoga teacher. What exactly is yoga and how does it differ from conventional stretching routines? How can it help a winter athlete?

The very dialogue that a yoga teacher uses to bring students to higher levels of practice reveals why yoga is good for winter athletes. When I teach yoga, I say the same things as when I give an on-snow clinic to skiers, snowshoers, or snowboarders; I use the same words in yoga as I do when working with an ice climber:

"Feel the tightness dissolving."

"Soften the hips."

"Allow the body and mind to become absorbed by the breath."

"Let the energy of the posture draw you deeper."

"Practice with preciseness."

Can you see how directly the practice of yoga can be transferred to winter performance? For example, how often do we immediately go tight when we perform on the snow? Yoga unites us with the mountain and with the environment by teaching specific techniques on how to release into the power of the moment. Yoga is about letting go and surrendering, two very important qualities along the way to higher levels of winter performance.

IT'S NOT A FAD

Most Americans associate the word yoga with a form of flexibility training. In truth, yoga is the original and oldest-known science of self-development. Although traditional yoga originated in India as a spiritual path, it is not a religion. The earliest recordings of yogic philosophy predate written history. Patanjali's Yoga Sutras are the first written synthesis of yogic teach-

Let the energy of the posture draw you deeper. The author takes a moment to explore Pasciomottanasana before some snowfield skiing. Photo by Deborah Ilg.

ings and have been traced to the second century B.C. Obviously, this stuff ain't a fad! Nothing hangs around for 2,000 years unless it works. Yoga works because of its unique fusion of science and art. The athletic aspect, contrary to popular belief, is not a significant factor to yoga. Living life appropriately is the most important thing to a yogi, or a practitioner of yoga. Therefore, yoga is a very practical discipline.

There are five primary forms of yoga. Each one is a vehicle through which the yogi attempts to unite mind with body. At more advanced levels, the yogi attempts to unite the separate self with the divine or the universal energy. Bhakti yoga is a form of devotional yoga using chanting, mantra, and prayer. Jnana yoga is a path of intellec-

tualism pivoting upon scripture study. Karma yoga is the "active path" by which the yogi releases ego attachments through selfless service to others. Raja yoga, or the "scientific path" is the path in which hatha yoga is found. Hatha yoga (Ha = Sun, Tha = Moon) is the form currently identified with physical exercise. It combines two of the eight steps along the Raja path: physical postures (asanas) and breath control (pranayama). The Raja Yoga steps are as follows: 1) Yamas or ethical guidelines, 2) Niyamas or moral observances, 3) Asanas or steady poses, 4) Pranayama or breath control, 5) Pratyahara or sense withdrawal, 6) Dharana or mental concentration, 7) Dhyana or meditation, and 8) Samadhi or bliss consciousness.

HATHA YOGA

Hatha yoga has multiplied into many styles, each reflecting the characteristics of its progenitor. It's a little crazy these days with so many teachers promoting their brand of "yoga," some of which bear little traditional connection. One should travel carefully along the yoga road. Following is a guide to the forms of hatha yoga that I most often recommend as part of Wholistic Fitness practice in the kinesthetic discipline. I usually suggest yoga only after my athletes have shown consistent practice and progress in the Wholistic Fitness Flexibility Forms, which are perfect preparatory forms for the more advanced flexibility practice of hatha yoga.

Iyengar Yoga

The most recognized name in yoga circles, B.K.S. Iyengar is the author of the yoga standard *Light on Yoga*, as well as many other books. Iyengar classes are precise and slow paced. Particular awareness is given to feet, hands, and hip placement. The emphasis is on standing balance postures. Iyengar has been nicknamed "the furniture yogi" due to his employment of various props, such as blocks, straps, and bolsters, to help beginning students adapt to the correct form of each posture. Highly certified Iyengar instructors are often very strict; some even make ballet teachers seem laid back! This form of yoga is a very good choice for winter athletes, especially those engaged in sports where form and alignment are crucial for success, such as nordic ski racing (learning how to balance and ride a flat ski) and ice climbing (learning how to conserve energy by relying on the skeletal system instead of pumping out using too much muscle energy).

Sivananda Yoga

A holistic, traditional approach to hatha yoga, sivananda is very much in alignment with several Wholistic Fitness principles. Five disciplines exist in this practice: exercise, breathing, vegetarianism, deep relaxation, and meditation. Although advanced variations will push even the most flexible of athletes beyond their limits, the standard basic practice remains fairly straightforward and consistent. Classes begin with pranayama, which leads to a fluid sequence of warm-up postures known as the Sun Salutation, then a series of twelve yoga postures, then deep relaxation. Often prayers or a chant begin and/or end a class. Sivananda is a good choice for the more recreational winter athlete looking for a nice lifestyle-oriented practice.

Bikram Yoga

This is one of my favorite and most often prescribed yoga styles. Bikram Choudhury was himself a multisport athlete. He was a marathon runner and a world record holder in Olympic weightlifting. That fact alone drew me to his Beverly Hills studio in the '80s.

Bikram was a yoga champion of India before coming to America. What he saw here must have appalled him: chronic low-back pain, rigid muscles, poor postures, and many forms of joint problems. He selected twenty-six postures to cure the Western body, emphasizing the lower back and hips. Bikram Yoga is also intense, another quality I like for athletes. The typical studio is intentionally heated to ninety degrees or more. This is done to open up the body and make it more conducive to expansion. The routine is simple but demanding: twelve standing postures, followed by fourteen floor postures. Each is repeated twice. Classes begin and end with deep breathing. There is not much talk about spirituality. Bikram yoga is physical stuff and does not make many adjustments for pre-existing ailments. Consistent practice pays off, however. Bikram's track record with curing all types of injuries is remarkable. His studios in Los Angeles are the preferred choice of celebrities, which has earned him the nickname of "yogi to the stars." Bikram yoga is an excellent choice for serious athletes and for those with a predisposition to lower back and joint pain.

Ashtanga Yoga

This is rightfully considered the most athletic form of yoga. Created by K. Pattabhi Jois of Mysore, India, this yoga is performed in vinyasa style, which means that a sequence of postures is performed fluidly and often dynamically. Theoretically, this continuous flow produces tapas, or heat, in the body, which is intended to purify the mind and body. The emphasis is first on strength and stamina, and then flexibility! This intense style provides a cardiovascular workout that should satisfy even the hard-core endurance athlete. Ashtanga has since been stylized into "power yoga," which is now the current "in" thing to do, especially in Los Angeles and New York. Ashtanga or power yoga is good for hard-core athletes who desire a no-fuss approach to their flexibility training.

Kundalini Yoga

I do not prescribe kundalini yoga for athletes very often. Kundalini is more appropriate for those spiritual seekers interested in developing their energy-work understanding. This form of yoga uses physical postures, but relies on breathing, chanting, and meditative exercises aimed at awakening and raising the kundalini (coiled energy at the root of the spine) and refining this energy by the help of chakras, or energy centers, located along the spine. It was created in 1969 by Yogi Bhajan, a Sikh who has headquarters in Los Angeles and New Mexico. This yoga may benefit the winter athlete who finds it difficult to find an energetic relationship with his or her sport. If you often find yourself scared and rigid while doing your winter sport, an off season of kundalini yoga might be of significant help.

FINDING A TEACHER

Finding good teachers or a yoga style that suits you may take awhile. My first years of researching yoga styles often produced attitude-ridden teachers who proselytized only yoga. If you admitted to doing any other fitness discipline or sport, you immediately received a scornful look. Remember, too much of any one discipline is not healthy. Some yogis have overstretched their connective tissue, creating too much joint laxity. Make sure your teacher is open to a more wholistic integration of yoga into an athletic lifestyle.

YOGA HINTS

This section provides at-a-glance reminders and suggestions for daily practice.

Make sure your teacher knows that you are not a yogi, but a winter athlete looking to improve your flexibility and mental focus.

Once you find the right class or method, persevere! Don't jump ship right away.

Focus on form and alignment before depth of posture. Yoga is not competitive, so stay tracked on what is happening inside of you, not the person next to you.

Work within yourself, not in the posture. Inwardly guide yourself toward a posture. Don't try to contort your body into an idealistic notion of what the posture is "supposed" to look like. Work with both the physical and the spiritual planes to guide toward, not force into, each posture.

Breathe. While doing yoga, the body needs oxygen. Breathe slowly and evenly, and from the belly as much as possible. Ask your yoga teacher for help if your breath remains high in the chest or is sporadic.

Learn the essence of the postures. Each yoga posture has traditional meaning. Study the history of the posture and its meanings in order to understand it better. Each posture has physiological ramifications, too; familiarizing yourself with what the posture is doing for you helps deepen yoga practice.

Listen. Every seven seconds, the body lets go a little more. It instinctively surrenders to a posture once its "red-flag alert status" recognizes the posture as beneficial instead of damaging. Listen for this letting go and make a microadjustment to deepen into the posture.

Love yourself for doing something like yoga, which is aimed at self-cultivation. We do very few things that nurture us in the way yoga practice does.

RELATED ACTIVITIES

This section considers some other dryland activities that are in the same family as the sport described.

Some of the Western-based stretching books and videos may provide flexibility benefits, but I don't personally or professionally endorse their rather mechanical approach to stretching for athletes. Use the Wholistic Fitness kinesthetic routines described in this book or contact Wholistic Fitness for one of our two kinesthetic videos.

SPECIFIC EQUIPMENT

This section covers specific equipment needed for the sport described. See Part Five for general cold-weather clothing and gear.

Yoga is a bit like running—it is very simple. In fact, not even shoes are worn. The only sport-specific equipment that a yogi might purchase is a "sticky mat." These roll-up mats are placed on hardwood yoga studio floors to provide a nonslip surface for standing postures and a cushioned surface for floor postures. I use a Tapas® mat from Hugger-Mugger™.

Other yoga props include blocks, bolsters, and straps. Most studios, especially Iyengar studios, have these props available for student use. If you practice alone, you may want to buy some to help you adapt to particular postures in better form and alignment. These props are available via mail-order sources (see "Resources").

RESOURCES

Yoga Journal magazine: 510-841-9200; www.yogajournal.com; P.O. Box 12008, Berkeley, California 94712.

Bheka Yoga Supplies; 800-366-4541, www.yogavoices.com/bheka/; e-mail: bheka@yogavoices.com.

Fish Crane (yoga equipment); P.O. Box 791029; New Orleans, Louisiana 70179; 800-959-6116.

Hugger-Mugger (yoga products); (800-473-4888).

Most yoga centers can be found in the phone book.

Local massage schools or bookstores often have leads on yoga classes in your area.

Part IV

Preseason Training Programs

photo by Roy Wilkinson

17

The Green Tara Strength Phase

"We are always stepping into the mystery of each and every moment, of who we are. We are reinventing ourselves hopefully every moment and rediscovering the mystery of who we really are."
—Lynn Swift, a body-centered psycho-therapist

The Green Tara strength program is to be followed for four consecutive weeks. This phase "reinvents" and prepares the physical body for more advanced training by placing a training priority on structural integrity and deep-fiber conditioning. Green Tara also serves as an introduction to transpersonal fitness practice.

THE GREEN TARA STRENGTH PHASE

In Tibetan Buddhism, Green Tara is the female aspect of enlightenment. Green Tara guides novice practitioners along the path of awakening. She encourages victory over inner obstacles and fear.

Length of cycle: four weeks.
Frequency: seven-day cycle.
Next cycle: recovery week into Perfect Power Phase.

Primary goals: structural integrity; practice of transpersonal fitness concepts.

GREEN TARA MASTER SHEET

All workouts are described in the next section, Wholistic Notes.

Wholistic Fitness® Training Precepts

1) Be prepared.
2) Be on time.
3) Give 110 percent.

Monday: Day One

Recovery day. No strength or CV training. All other disciplines are discretionary. Enjoy the day off!

Tuesday: Day Two

Strength training: Green Tara chest, shoulders, triceps workout.

CV training: None, or thirty minutes of a CV activity of your choice at Zone 1.

Kinesthetic training: Medium Form before or after strength training.

Meditation: Beeper Guru breath and posture assignment.

Wednesday: Day Three

Strength training: Green Tara lower-body workout.

CV training: None, or thirty to sixty minutes of a CV activity of your choice at Zone 1 after strength training (nonconcussive CV activity suggested).

Kinesthetic training: Medium Form after strength training.

Meditation: 3 x 30 assignment.

Thursday: Day Four

Strength training: Green Tara back, biceps workout.

CV training: None, or thirty minutes of a CV activity of your choice at Zone 1.

Kinesthetic training: Optimally, a yoga class. If not, Medium Form before or after strength training.

Meditation: Early-morning zazen session.

Friday: Day Five

CV training: Interval day—perform the following using any CV activity you wish: Twenty minutes at Zones 1–2; Five sets of one-minute intervals at Zones 3–4, with a one-minute recovery period; Twenty minutes at Zone 1.

Kinesthetic training: Medium Form quickly before and again slowly after CV training.

Meditation: Let your intervals be your meditation: Focus fully into the intensity, and do not let your mind wander. Concentrate!

Saturday: Day Six

Strength training: EEE-GAD full-body workout.

CV training: None.

Kinesthetic training: Take a yoga class if you didn't do so on Thursday.

Meditation: Let yoga be your meditation.

Sunday: Day Seven

CV training: Two to three hours at low-to-moderate aerobic pace; hike, run, cycle, whatever. Mix it up if desired.

Kinesthetic training: Medium Form Flexibility after CV training.

Meditation: Passive meditation; set aside ten to twenty minutes of leisurely quiet time. Use some of this time to plan your upcoming training week.

WHOLISTIC NOTES

This section provides the specific workouts prescribed in the Green Tara Master Sheet.

Strength-Training Workouts

For each of the following workouts, adhere to these three guidelines:

1) Limit the recovery phase to thirty seconds.

2) Perform all sets to momentary muscular failure or failure of elegance, unless otherwise noted.

3) Refer to the Appendix for instructions on all movements and techniques.

The Green Tara Chest, Shoulders, Triceps Workout

Dumbbell Flat-Bench Flyes into Dumbbell Bench Presses: Do ten reps of Dumbbell Flat-Bench Flyes to failure, then immediately dissolve into high-frequency Dumbbell Presses for fifteen reps. Do three sets.

Dips: Take three sets at body weight to failure. Accept *no* limits!

Bench Press: Five sets of ten reps. Nasal in-breathe on the yin (lowering) phase. Strict form is essential.

Seated Dumbbell Press: Two sets done with Three-Stage Technique®. No whining … this is a beginning program!

Seated Dumbbell Side Lateral Raises: Three sets of ten to twelve reps.

Lying Triceps Extension: Three sets of ten to twelve reps. Maintain an extremely controlled yin phase.

Two-Bench Triceps: Two sets of one-minute. I will grant you a one-minute recovery phase between sets, but don't expect any more favors! I want BEAUTIFUL form for one minute within four weeks!

The Green Tara Lower-Body Workout

Stiff Leg Deadlifts: Two sets of five reps. Do *not* go to momentary failure. Use a resistance that challenges you to keep your back flat, no more. This movement is for postural perfection. Think strong spine!

Leg Extensions: Two sets done with Staccato Technique®.

Leg Curls: Three sets of six to eight reps.

Alternate Weekly:

Week A: Superset for four times. Recovery between supersets can be one minute.

a) Squats = ten reps at 75 percent effort
b) Leg Press = one minute

Week B: Superset for four times. Recovery between supersets can be one minute.

a) Squats = ten reps at 75 percent effort
b) Jump Squats = thirty seconds … GO, GO, GO!

Standing or Seated Calves: Two sets done with Staccato Technique; then go into heavier resistances and do three more sets of eight to ten reps!

Superset—Oblique Twists into Abdominal Crunches: Do one minute of each, then take a thirty-second recovery. Do two supersets for Weeks One and Two, three for Weeks Three and Four.

The Green Tara Back, Biceps Workout

Pull-Ups: Take three sets at body weight to failure. Time your recovery! Do your best, and don't waver! You should do more reps each set with each workout.

Front Lat Pulldowns: Do two sets of ten to twelve reps, then get ready, baby, because then you enter the Ku! Immediately perform three more sets of eight to ten reps with a Ku Top Form recovery.

V-Handle Pulldowns: Do two sets of ten to twelve reps, then again get ready to enter the Ku. Immediately perform three more sets of eight to ten reps with a Ku Top Form recovery.

Hang Cleans: Four sets of eight reps. Be fluid and have fast feet! There's lots of technique, and you only have four weeks to master it.

Concentration Curls: Two sets of ten reps for each arm. Remember, elegance, always elegance.

Barbell Curls: Three sets of six to eight reps.

Barbell Curls: This time use the Envelope Technique®. I know, I love you, too! You'll thank me in the future. You may use a low pulley for these if desired.

Superset: Abdominal Crunches into Suspended Leg Raises. Do one minute of each, then take a thirty-second recovery. Do three supersets.

EEE-GAD Full-Body Workout

The name says it all. EEE-GAD comes in two versions, one for beginning students and another for more advanced students. The following is a hybrid of both. The EEE-GAD full-body workouts were finalized in 1986 and have been serving students well ever since. The real trick is to master the entire workout from start to finish with unwavering attention to posture and lifting tempo.

Pull-Ups: Two sets of however many you can do.

Front Lat Pulldowns: One set done with Staccato Technique; three sets of eight to ten reps.

Dumbbell Flat-Bench Flyes into Dumbbell Bench Presses: Flyes for ten reps to failure, then crank out high-frequency Dumbbell Bench Presses until you reach 20 reps or puke black blood. Do three sets.

Back Squats Superset with Leg Extensions: Do Squats for twelve reps to failure, then run over and perform Leg Extensions with Staccato Technique. Do two supersets.

Seated Dumbbell Presses: Two sets done with Three-Stage Technique. Commit to fluidity.

Two-Bench Triceps: Two sets of one minute each. See each rep in a "clean" top and bottom position. You should feel the contraction in the triceps up top. Bring chi to the triceps.

Barbell Curls: Three sets done with Shivaya Technique®. Be beautiful; be elegant.

Abdominal Crunches Directly into Leg Raises: Three sets of one minute each. Really stay concentrated in the abs!

CV Training

Follow the volumes and intensities prescribed in the Master Sheet. Your range should cover a low of three hours per week to a high of six hours per week. I suggest starting at the low end and increasing your weekly hours as you adapt to the program.

You may be surprised at how the amplitude of the multidisciplined Wholistic Fitness approach fatigues you even when low weekly hours are done in the CV discipline.

Kinesthetic Training

During this cycle, you are to learn Medium Form Flexibility and take at least one hatha yoga class per week. The Appendix describes Medium Form Flexibility. To heighten your study of this form, order the *Four Kinesthetic Teachings of Wholistic Fitness* video. Get bodywork at least twice during this cycle, preferably deep-tissue massage.

Meditation

Beeper Guru Breath and Posture Assignment. Set your watch alarm to go off every hour. Upon the beep, take note of where your breath, posture, and mind are. Make adjustments into alignment. Note how often the Beeper Guru catches you in random thought, out of posture, or with the breath high and shallow instead of low and deep.

3 x 30 Assignment. This is taken from a Theravada Buddhist mindfulness exercise. At each mealtime (assume three sit-down meals per day) chew your first bite of food thirty times. During this chewing, feel the significance of the food being eaten. Appreciate the fact that you are not different from the food you eat and that one day, you too will be "eaten" by the universe. Use this time to honor and revere your food and "tell" the food that you will do your best to use its life-giving energy to refine yourself in order to help others.

Early-Morning Zazen Session. Wake up, relieve yourself, then assume the zazen posture. Sit for five minutes. Perform Kin Hin (walking meditation); it should be performed with hands in a "gassho mudra," or prayer hand, position. The meditation is designed to mindfully place each step with awareness and not to let the mind wander from the walking. It is best done in an environment where you are not likely to be interrupted in any way. The walk can be as short as one minute to as long as several minutes in duration. Sit for another five minutes. End the session and take mindfulness with you.

Nutrition

Follow the nutritional principles described in Chapter Eight. Begin expanding your definition of nutrition to include more than physical or gross foods. Expand your nutritional base to include spiritual components, such as your workouts, conversations, driving, sunrises and sunsets, relationships, and books. Finally, read the following paragraph each Monday (your recovery day) for spiritual nutrition:

> My practice of the multidisciplined study of Wholistic Fitness is going to nourish every aspect of my body/mind/spirit. Yet like any form of personal growth, I must accept and trust in the process! As I follow the Way of Wholistic Fitness, I will gradu-

ally receive useful insight for my highest performance. Wholistic Fitness is creating the most healthful cellular state in my body, mind, and spirit. All I have to do is attend to my practice.

During this week of practice, I make an inner vow to really listen to my body. I choose to consciously study each choice I make, whether it be in food, voice, or ac-

tion. I will practice awareness. I choose to learn by self-observation, not trial and error. I will execute willpower as my body/mind shifts toward a higher level of health and awareness.

After you have completed four consecutive weeks of the Green Tara Strength Phase, complete the following summation.

Wholistic Fitness® Winter Performance Training *Green Tara Strength Cycle Summation*

Cycle's Dates: _____

Athlete's Name: _____

Please address each category as openly as possible.

STRENGTH TRAINING

1) Note any observations that stand out during this discipline. How was your consistency?

_____

_____

_____

_____

_____

2) Did any body part seem to respond faster/slower/more strangely than others? If so, describe.

_____

_____

_____

_____

_____

3) Which movements or workouts seemed more difficult? Why?

_____

_____

_____

_____

_____

4) The most important teaching of this strength-training discipline that I can use in my winter performance is:

_____

_____

_____

_____

_____

CV TRAINING

5) Did you have any standout reactions in this discipline?

_____

_____

_____

_____

_____

6) Record the average number of CV hours performed each week. Comment:

_____

_____

_____

_____

_____

7) Note the consistency of and reaction or response to the weekly interval workout:

_____

_____

_____

_____

8) The most important teaching of this CV-training discipline that I can use in my winter performance is:

_____
_____
_____
_____
_____
_____

KINESTHETIC TRAINING

9) Did you have any standout reactions in this discipline?

_____
_____
_____
_____
_____

10) Did you manage to do the weekly yoga class? Comment.

_____
_____
_____
_____
_____

11) The most important teaching of this kinesthetic-training discipline that I can use in my winter performance is:

_____
_____
_____
_____

MEDITATION

12) How did your once a week attempt at zazen go? Comment.

_____

_____

_____

_____

_____

13) What was your Largest Dragon in this cycle? How did you deal with this Dragon?

_____

_____

_____

_____

14) The most important teaching of this meditation discipline that I can use in my winter performance is:

_____

_____

_____

_____

_____

NUTRITION

15) Submit a few words on how you felt about your diet during this cycle:

_____

_____

_____

_____

16) Describe exactly what and how you ate yesterday. Include all supplements, fluids, drugs, etc.

_____

_____

_____

_____

_____

17) Overall, what did you learn from Green Tara?

_____

_____

_____

_____

_____

Congratulations on your practice of the Green Tara Strength Phase. Now take a well-earned recovery week. During the next seven days, do not do any strength training and reduce CV training by 50 percent of your weekly average during Green Tara. All other disciplines are discretionary.

Enjoy your week off! But get ready for four more exciting weeks of Wholistic Fitness training. After a few days, begin visualizing your performance of the Perfect Power program.

18

The Perfect Power Phase

*"The greatest battles of life that we ever fight are usually fought
in the silent chambers of our soul and usually everyday."*
—Stephen Covey

The Perfect Power program is to be followed for four consecutive weeks. This phase provides explosive power development to be transferred into and refined by sport-specific training. The Perfect Power Phase promotes physiological and transpersonal fitness concepts as they relate to inner power development for winter-sport performance.

THE PERFECT POWER PHASE

The Perfect Power Phase is classic Wholistic Fitness training. Attributes include unobscured personal growth and many hidden treasures as the student digs deep within to keep training volumes stable.

Length of cycle: four weeks.
Frequency: seven-day cycle.
Next cycle: recovery week into specialization training.

Primary goals: 1) explosive fiber development; 2) zero tolerance for emotional timidity; 3) Increased mental, physical, and spiritual tenacity.

PERFECT POWER MASTER SHEET

All workouts are described in the next section, Wholistic Notes.

Wholistic Fitness® Training Precepts

1) Be prepared.
2) Be on time.
3) Give 110 percent.

Monday: Day One

Recovery day. No strength or CV training. All other disciplines are discretionary. Enjoy the day off!

Tuesday: Day Two

CV training: Interval workout as prescribed in Wholistic Notes.

Kinesthetic training: Long Form after CV training.

Meditation: Early-morning zazen practice.

Wednesday: Day Three

Strength training: Perfect Power chest and back workout.

CV training: None, or thirty minutes of a CV activity of your choice at Zone 1.

Kinesthetic training: Medium Form before strength training.

Meditation: Beeper Guru breath and posture assignment.

Thursday: Day Four

Strength training: Perfect Power lower-body workout.

CV training: Mandatory thirty to sixty minutes of a CV activity of your choice at Zones 1 to 2 immediately following strength training.

Kinesthetic training: Medium Form after strength training.

Meditation: Early-morning zazen practice.

Friday: Day Five

Strength training: Perfect Power shoulders and arms workout.

CV training: None, or thirty minutes of a CV activity of your choice at Zone 1.

Kinesthetic Training: Optimally, a yoga class; if not, Medium Form before strength training.

Meditation: If yoga class, none. Otherwise, twenty minutes of active meditation.

Saturday: Day Six

CV training: One-and-a-half to two-and-a-half hours of your choice at Zones 1–2.

Kinesthetic training: Long Form Flexibility after CV training.

Meditation: Prepare one meal today with reverence and mindfulness.

Sunday: Day Seven

Strength training: Yang Day workout.

CV training: Cross-train from yesterday for at least one hour, maximum of three hours, at Zones 1 to 3, after strength training; no more than 20 percent of this workout should be spent at Zone 3.

Kinesthetic training: Optimally, Medium Form before strength training, Long Form after CV training; Mandatory: Medium Form whenever you can fit it in.

Meditation: 3 x 30 assignment; passive meditation for twenty minutes.

WHOLISTIC NOTES

This section provides the specific workouts prescribed in the Perfect Power Master Sheet.

Strength-Training Workouts

For each of the following workouts adhere to these three guidelines:

1) Limit the recovery phase to forty-five seconds.

2) Perform all sets to momentary muscular failure or failure of elegance, unless otherwise noted.

3) Refer to the Appendix for instructions on all movements and techniques.

The Perfect Power Chest and Back Workout

Weighted Pull-Ups: Four sets of six reps. Think power! Accelerate! Power! Watch your recovery time. If you can do any of the four sets at six reps at body weight, it is time to add weight.

Seated Rows: Four sets of a heavy but heavenly six to eight reps. Fill in that back musculature; this exercise is great for posture!

High Pulls with Ku Bottom Form Recovery: Four sets of eight reps using Ku Bottom Form for "recovery." Think speed! Sure the forearms are gonna scream ... so what?! Persevere and focus! These are Hang Cleans without the catch phase. Link your reps together and keep the elbows high and proud. The yin phase should be *slow.*

V-Handle Pull Downs with Ku Bottom Form Recovery: Four sets of six to eight reps. Accelerate on the yang phase. P.S.: The ego will retaliate—discipline it!

Two-minute water-break recovery.

Dips: Four sets of six reps. Think power! Accelerate! Power! Watch your recovery time. If you can do any of the four sets at six reps with bodyweight, it is time to add weight.

Bench Presses: Five sets total, consisting of one set of eight reps, three sets of three reps each, finishing with one set of eight reps. I want you to develop power ... get someone to spot if you have to!

Standing Cable Flyes: Three sets of fifteen reps. Be poetically strong and never let your mind wander from the chest. Squeeze the pecs!

Plyo Push Ups: Two sets of (as many as you can) reps. Hands must detach from the earth due to an explosive yang phase.

Now give yourself about five minutes of creative, intense ab work. Include Suspended Leg Raises, please.

Lower-Body Workout: Do an active warm-up for five to ten minutes before this workout, please!

Gunther Hops: Two sets of sixteen jumps. This is a plyometric movement just to get you cruising!

Superset for Four Times: Recovery between superset equals one minute.

a) Back Squats = eight to ten reps at 80 percent effort.

b) Jump Squats = forty-five seconds. Go ahead and look like a fool in the gym; if anybody heckles you, ask them to join you!

Beginning Wholistic Fitness Athletes = Split Jumps; Intermediate Wholistic Fitness Athletes = Scissor Jumps: Two sets of eight reps for each leg. Release inhibitions and GO!

Leg Curls: Five sets of six reps. This balances out all the frontal thigh work. Merge into the leg bicep; study from there!

Seated or Standing Calf Raises: Five sets of ten reps. Don't even *think* about not pinching the heck out of that top position.

Stiff Leg Deadlifts: Two sets of five reps. Keep a beautiful, clean, straight spine. Release tension from all the previous work.

Triset for Three Sets: 1) Crunches for one minute; 2) Leg Raises for one minute; 3) Ab Wheel or Inversion Sit-Ups for forty-five seconds.

Perfect Power Shoulders and Arms Workout

Repetition Jerks: Three sets of five reps. Go at 80 percent effort and be your speed. I want your arms to be a blur on the explosive phase!

Seated Barbell Presses: Give me three quality sets of six reps. Keep your spine strong and mind strong!

Seated Behind Neck Presses: I need another three quality sets of six reps. No mental fidgeting—fidget mentally, and you'll fidget during your winter performance.

Barbell Curls: Five sets of six to eight reps. Use the Entré Nous recovery technique.

Concentration Curls: Three sets of eight to ten reps for each arm. Strict form = bicep power.

Lying Triceps Extension: Five sets of five reps. Use the Entré Nous recovery technique.

Triceps Press Downs: Three sets of eight to ten reps. Stay present every second.

Superset:
a) Dumbbell Arm Swings for fifteen seconds into
b) Dumbbell Horizontal Swings for fifteen seconds

Recover for fifteen seconds, then repeat superset once or twice more.

Yang Day: Full-Body Strength-Training Workout

In the East, the balance of all that exists is represented by yin/yang. Yin is the female, the dark, the yielding. Yang is the masculine, the light, the forceful.

Yang day sessions are special. They develop what is known as samu in Asiatic traditions or ekagrata in the yogic traditions. Both describe the performance of physical effort with maximum mental concentration. During this workout, note how quickly your mind will want to wander. Use these sessions to develop mental focus.

Recovery Phase: One minute.

Bench Presses: Five sets of five reps. Use regulation power lifting form—bar to the chest, no hip movement.

Squats: Five sets of five reps. Use regulation power lifting form—thighs must go parallel to the ground.

Hang Cleans: Five sets of five reps. There is no substitute for inspiration. Go!

Dips: Two sets of as many as you can perform at body weight.

Pull-Ups: Two sets of as many as you can perform at body weight.

Congratulations. Thanks for playing!

> *The best way out, is always through.*—Robert Frost

CV Training

Yes, CV training does have its power development side. But back off if little aches or inflammations arise. This is a subtle phase, and many cellular things are happening, so practice patience. Speed is instrumental in learning this power phase.

Perform the following interval workout using any activity you wish; however, competitive winter athletes should do this workout as sport-specifically as possible.

- Ten-minute warm-up at Zone 1
- Three minutes at Zones 3–4
- Two minutes at Zone 1
- Four sets of one minute each at Zone 4, with one-minute recovery intervals
- Three sets of two minutes each at Zones 3–4, with one-minute recovery intervals
- Ten minutes cool-down at Zone 1

For your other CV training, follow the volumes and intensities prescribed in the Master Sheet. Your range should cover a low of four hours per week to a high of eight-and-a-half hours per week. As with the Green Tara program, start training at the low end and increase your weekly hours as you adapt to the program. Competitive winter athletes, however, such as nordic ski racers and snowshoe racers, need to crack down here and train at the high end of this range.

Kinesthetic Training

Wholistic Fitness excels at helping us discover what our "weak" points are. Genuine sport performance means cultivating the ability to receive the presence of the universe in our training. Your awareness should be increasing during this phase; always know that the entire wisdom, beauty, and power of the universe works through our practice, not from it. Your ability to channel that power will come as long as you practice the Perfect Power program to your utmost.

During this cycle, you are to learn Long Form Flexibility and take at least one hatha yoga class per week. The Appendix describes Long Form Flexibility. To heighten your study of this form, order the *Four Kinesthetic Teachings of Wholistic Fitness*® video.

Get bodywork at least twice during this cycle, preferably deep-tissue massage.

Meditation

Early-Morning Zazen Session. Wake up, relieve yourself, then assume the zazen posture. Sit for five minutes. Perform Kin Hin (walking meditation); it should be performed with hands in a "gassho mudra," or prayer hand, position. The meditation is designed to mindfully place each step with awareness and not to let the mind wander from the walking. It is best done in an environment where you are not likely to be interrupted in any way. The walk can be as short as one minute to as long as several minutes in duration. Sit for another five minutes. End the session and take mindfulness with you.

Beeper Guru Breath and Posture Assignment. Set your watch alarm to go off every hour. Upon the beep, take note of where your breath, posture, and mind are. Make adjustments into alignment. Note how often the Beeper Guru catches you in random thought, out of posture, or with the breath high and shallow instead of low and deep.

3 x 30 Assignment. This is taken from a Theravada Buddhist mindfulness exercise. At each mealtime (assume three sit-down meals per day) I want you to chew your first bite of food thirty times. During this chewing, feel the significance of the food being eaten. Appreciate the fact that you are not different from the food you eat and that one day, you too will be "eaten" by the universe. Use this time to honor and revere your food and "tell" the food that you will do your best to use its life-giving energy to refine yourself in order to help others.

Nutrition

During this phase, take a moment of silence before each mealtime. Appreciate and honor. Visualize how you will use the food to help others and yourself. Visualize how the food will contribute to your sport performance. Wholistic Fitness cultivates mindfulness, so make sure you are on the Path. You are going higher and deeper, so get focused and stay that way until it becomes your nature. That is the nature of the warrior. Everyday is your chance to be noble. Lead from the heart and feed yourself wisely from the spiritual and physical planes.

By this point in your study, you should be dropping off or decreasing all mutative or degenerative foods and substances, such as coffee, alcohol, junk foods, and refined sugars. You should be opening up and feeling attracted to whole foods and healthy eating as described in Chapter Eight. All your performance supplements should be in stock and a routine of your daily life. No nutritional gaps should be present as you enter into the upcoming sport-specific phases!

Read the following paragraph each Monday (your recovery day) for spiritual nutrition:

I accept everyone and every circumstance as my guru. I will do my best to see what each person or situation is trying to teach me in terms of sensitivity and mindfulness. My practice of Wholistic Fitness means using my exercise as a vehicle for spiritual growth.

After you have completed four consecutive weeks of the Perfect Power Phase, complete the following summation.

Wholistic Fitness® Winter Performance Training
Perfect Power Cycle Summation

Cycle's Dates: _____

Athlete's Name: _____

Please address each category as openly as possible.

STRENGTH TRAINING

1) Describe the differences you felt between the Green Tara and Perfect Power strength-training programs.

_____

_____

_____

_____

_____

2) Which movements or workouts seemed more difficult? Why?

_____

_____

_____

_____

_____

3) The most important teaching of this strength-training discipline that I can use in my winter performance is:

_____

_____

_____

_____

_____

CV TRAINING

4) Did you have any standout reactions in this discipline?

_____

_____

_____

5) Record the total number of CV hours performed this cycle.

_____

6) What did you notice about about your interval workouts?

_____

7) The most important teaching of this CV-training discipline that I can use in my winter performance is:

_____

KINESTHETIC TRAINING

8) Comment on your Long Form Flexibility practice. What insights have you learned from this form?

_____

9) Did you manage to do the weekly yoga class? Comment.

_____

_____
_____
_____

10) The most important teaching of this kinesthetic-training discipline that I can use in my winter performance is:

_____
_____
_____
_____
_____

MEDITATION

11) Provide an insight from your meditation practice.

_____
_____
_____
_____
_____

12) Do you feel as though you are carrying your awareness better these days?

_____
_____
_____
_____
_____

13) How did your Beeper Guru Breath and Posture assignments go? What did you learn from them?

_____
_____
_____
_____
_____

14) The most important teaching of this meditation discipline that I can use in my winter performance is:

_____
_____

_____

_____

_____

NUTRITION

15) What were your initial reactions in this discipline?

_____

_____

_____

_____

_____

16) Yesterday, exactly what and how did you eat? Include all supplements, fluids, and any drugs or medications.

_____

_____

_____

_____

_____

17) Overall, what did you learn from the Perfect Power Phase?

_____

_____

_____

_____

_____

Congratulations on your practice of the Perfect Power Phase. Now take a recovery week. You've earned it! During the next seven days, do not do any strength training and reduce CV training by 50 percent of your weekly average during Perfect Power. All other disciplines are discretionary.

Enjoy your week off. But get ready for and start to visualize your specialization phase and five weeks of Wholistic Fitness training refined for your ultimate winter performance.

Part V

Winter Sports Wisdom

photo by Roy Wilkinson

19

Cold Weather Fabrics and Gear

"The more challenging or threatening the situation or context to be assimilated and affirmed, the greater the stature of the person who can achieve it. The demon that you can swallow gives you its power, and the greater life's pain, the greater life's reply."
—Joseph Campbell

This chapter provides philosophy, clothing, and gear that I feel is of worthwhile consideration for winter athletes. This is just a basic list; standard stuff. Fabric technology changes constantly. What may be great this season may be outdated by next season. I've included only those things that have worked for me, proven their worth, and withstood the test of Ilgonian time (which, by the way, roughly approximates dog years).

LAYERS OF WISDOM

Rule numero uno: Always layer cold-weather clothing. I cannot stress the point enough. The modern world of cold-weather fabrics is sensational. In the retail business, high-tech outdoor fabrics revolve around something called "microclimate management." Clothing made of these fabrics insulates the exercising body without creating a saunalike environment that would first soak, then freeze you. Besides providing insulation, the clothes must not restrict movement. Finally, they must furnish a bombproof defense from wind, cold, and wetness. Quality cold-weather clothing is expensive because of the technology that has gone into its development.

Enter the concept of layering. Flexibility is the grand charm of layering. As your exercising body moves through different temperature ranges, it creates a variety of microclimatic shifts. With layering, regulating your body temperature is simple. Take things off, put things back on. Without layering, the body suffocates in sweat. Sooner or later, the cold air gets to you and presto change-o!—you're hypothermic!

BASE-LAYER CLOTHING: THE STUFF NEXT TO YOUR SKIN

This layer needs to cover your entire body with a comfortable, form-fitting yet unrestrictive wicking fabric. Go for the newer synthetic blends like Capilene® or Polar Fleece® or Nike's Dri-F.I.T.™ Polypropylene, once the saving grace of winter athletes, is obsolete. Basically, polypropylene stinks. Literally. The new-generation synthetics don't lock in perspiration smells nearly as much as the old polypro duds.

Never wear cotton as a base layer unless you are into chattering teeth and possible missing digits. Synthetic fabrics like Capilene come in lightweight, midweight, and expedition weight. The thicker the fabric, the colder the temperature for which it's suitable. Midweight is a wise choice for stop-and-go excursions, while lightweight is better for sustained exercise. Expedition weight comes in handy for climbing Mount Everest or deluxe chilling in the crib.

Socks

The new generation of moisture-wicking socks is fantastic. Some brands even have friction- and abrasion-reduction designs. My favorite pair, called The Air-E-Ator™, are made by de-Feet® (800-688-2067). I wear these in hot weather as well as cold. I wear them for running, cycling, skiing, snowshoeing, whatever! They're a really wise investment. Buy several pairs. You'll love them.

For really cold conditions I've had good success with something called a Short-Cut Sock made by Traverse Bay Manufacturing, Inc. (800-521-0549). This is a low-cut sock made from Polartec 2000® napped fleece with a thermal stretch shell. The shell provides a high-tech barrier against wind, water, and wear while the four-way lining provides wicking and siphoning qualities. This sock is an excellent alternative to neoprene. The new generation of wool and wool/synthetic socks are good, too. Look for a combo of 35 percent polypropylene, 35 percent nylon, and 30 percent wool.

For wet and cold-weather conditions, like in snowshoeing, where moisture accumulation is unavoidable, I like wearing an Air-E-Ator sock as a base layer, then slipping a neoprene sock over it. Many cold-weather cyclists and climbers prefer a neoprene sock with a Gore-Tex oversock.

SportBras

Research demonstrates the need for sport bras. Unrestricted "bobbing" of breast tissue is not healthy. Sport bras limit the motion of the breast relative to the body, which helps prevent bruising, and soreness. Also, endocrine hormone balance has a tendency to make breasts sag and sports bras help prevent this. Sport bras are readily available from running or cycling catalogs or in sports stores. Some bras are made with Capilene for moisture-wicking properties, and some have nylon wind protection on the exterior of the cup.

Turtlenecks

Make sure this garment, worn next to the skin, is lightweight, with superior wicking capabilities. All-polyester fabric is lightweight and quick drying. My all-time favorites in the turtleneck category are a half-zip, microfleece number by Marmot® (707-544-4590) and Nike's Therma-F.I.T™. Micro Half-Zip. I wear these luxuriant garments as a base layer for supercold conditions and alone during less extreme excursions. They are also great, comfortable pieces to kick around the house in.

Windproof Briefs

To be worn under tights on cold, windy days, windproof briefs have a nylon shell that protects genitalia from wind. Patagonia (800-638-6464) makes an excellent windproof brief out of Capilene. They also make wind briefs for women, although I cannot speak directly for their benefits.

INSULATION LAYER: THE FEEL-GOOD PLY

Along with a base layer, you need an insulation layer, which traps warm air while also wicking away moisture. Materials such as synthetic fleece and pile are good at doing this, but they are not good at blocking out wind or shielding from water. Use this middle layer to dissipate moisture and provide a warm, fluffy feeling during cold conditions. During warmer days, this layer can even be the outer layer.

Microfleece Jerseys, Turtlenecks, and Vests

The Malden Mills 100 series of microfleece is great, as is Nike's Therma-F.I.T. fleece. Microfleece cycling jerseys are nice even for noncyclists. I use mine for running, in-line skating, and snowshoeing. The jersey pockets are also convenient for all sports. (See the sidebar on Melanzana outdoor wear for a great multisport fleece jersey).

Heavier Insulation

For some winter sports a goose-down sweater or jacket may be appropriate. Although such a garment is is virtually impenetrable to cold, the trade-off is restricted movement. And though down can block out wind, it also is hydrophilic, or moisture-loving, and can get wet and heavy. Therefore it's not appropriate for sustained activity. There are quick-drying synthetic alternatives to down, including PrimaLoft®, MicroLoft®, Polarguard®, and LiteLoft®, that are good in wet and, especially, humid climates.

Tights

Depending on the temperature and your cold tolerance, you can choose tights ranging from lightweight Lycra to heavier fleece to something like a Polartec stretch tight. The latter gets the thumbs up from me. Remember, this layer needs to breathe, insulate, wick, and dry quickly. For cyclists, a tight with more protective fabric

My Favorite Piece of Clothing

I want to clue you in on my a secret weapon for outdoor performance, the DriClime Windshirt made by Marmot Mountain Works. This beautifully sculptured shirt is highly effective as both a jacket and a base layer. The secret lies in the DriClime lining. This "second-skin" lining creates a stable microclimate that allows the wonder fabric to keep moisture away from the skin, even during high-expenditure sports such as nordic skiing. At first I was skeptical; my logical mind kept saying, "There's no way you can be out in such cold, windy weather wearing only this little thirteen-ounce shirt." Well, for several winters, this little shirt has been my faithful companion through all types of conditions. In fact, it has easily replaced several articles of cold-weather clothing.

The Windshirt has elastic cuffs, a high collar, mesh underarm inserts, and a shirt-tail split hem that makes it ideal for biking, skiing, and running in inclement weather. It's an amazing outdoor garment that will save you closet space and money by eliminating the need for multiple polypro base layers, pile insulation, and shells. I'm really pushing the limits of what this Windshirt can do, and I haven't found its limit yet! To find out where you can buy your own miracle shirt, contact Marmot (707-544-4590).

over the frontal thigh and knee areas is wise. Rapid cooling of the thigh muscles and the connective tissue of the knees, due to the high speeds and wind chill factor from cycling, can cause unprotected knees to become strained more easily. Cycling tights can be bought padded or unpadded.

Windshirts, Windvests, and Windpants

These nifty garments block wind, rain, and snow by means of a tough, lightweight nylon shell, while an inner membrane manages body moisture very effectively. They can be worn either over a base layer or by themselves. Microfleece windpants should have elasticized waists, zippered pockets, and Spandex binding at the cuffs to help keep out wind.

THE OUTER LAYER: THE DEFENSIVE LINE

The outer layer is your frontline of protection against intense elements. It can range from a wispy windbreaker to a triple-laminated Gore-Tex® parka. Like each of the other layers, this layer should be made of a breathable fabric. That very quality, the ability to breathe while being waterproof, is what made Gore-Tex fabric a revolution in outdoor-performance clothing. Up to nine billion microscopic holes per square inch in a Teflon-treated, laminated

Gore-Tex fabric permit perspiration to escape, yet these openings are too small to let in rain and wet snow. There are some spin-off fabrics that mimic Gore-Tex, but if moisture is a real factor where you train and perform, go Gore-Tex.

You can do a lot of outdoor training without a shell. In fact, I've logged more skiing and mountaineering hours in my base layer alone than with full layering. However, it is plain stupid to do winter training and performance without at least carrying a shell.

Lightweight Shells

Runners, nordic skiers, and cyclists do well with a light material like 100 percent polyester microfiber taffeta as their shell layer. Look for ventilated and mesh backing, high collars, and elasticized waists and cuffs. A Teflon finish is best to repel water. Nike offers some good upper- and lower-torso outfits in their A.C.G., or All Conditions Gear, line.

Heavyweight Shells

Climbers and alpine skiers need something heavier. Visit a mountaineering shop and look for labels such as Patagonia and Marmot. In my mountaineering career, I used and relied upon Marmot gear almost exclusively. And I've still got ten toes and nine-and-a-half fingers (due to a rock-climbing fall—no fault of Marmot!).

Eyewear

Eye protection is vital for the outdoor athlete. Invest in quality eyewear. The amount of dinero paid for high-end eyewear goes for lighter weights. My Briko Stinger model (800-GO-BRIKO) weighs less than twenty-one grams. Your money also buys you a quality frame material and quality lenses. A quality lens sharpens vision in flat-light yet brings calming relief in bright light, decreasing eye fatigue. Make sure you have a variety of lenses on hand for use in different forms of light. Total UV protection increases with quality eyewear, including blocking of UVA, UVB, and blue light. Plan on spending at least $100 for a good pair of shades, and please try not to sit on them or leave them at the espresso cafe. Mountaineers and skiers require goggles for added wind, cold, snow glare, and windswept-particulate protection.

Gaiters

Lunging through deep snow, or postholing, makes snow accumulate at the junction of boot top and leg. Even cuffed windpants don't prevent this, as they tend to get pushed upward in the snow. Gaiters or overboots solve the problem. Buy the sturdiest ones you can find if you are a backcountry athlete. If you are a snowshoe racer or area telemarker, find a lighter-weight version. Regardless, the gaiter should be made of a waterproof nylon blend and have a full zipper. Backcountry athletes need

Melanzana Outdoor Wear: A Unique Company

Several years ago, school teacher Fritz Howard said, "Mmm ... b'bye," to his high-school students in Washington, D.C. After that farewell he said hello again to home, which was one of the small mountain towns where he had lived before the ill-fated journey back East. This time it would be Leadville, Colorado, the highest incorporated city in the U.S. at something like a million thousand feet in elevation. When asked why, Howard answers in the vague fashion typical of those who cannot let mountains leave their sight, let alone their heart, "Well, I moved here cuz', well, you know all kinds of reasons. The mountains, the races, the people. Leadville rules! It's just the perfect place to start my business."

That business is Melanzana Outdoor Wear, founded in 1992. The word Melanzana, according to Howard, means eggplant in Italian. He pauses, then sheepishly admits, "I think. I'm not sure. I had to change the name from Eggplant, the original name, because some skatewear business trademarked it already."

While up in Leadville for the 100-mile MTB race, I met Howard in his indubitably austere shop on Harrison Avenue. His demeanor was laid back and gregarious. I liked him instantly and wanted him to succeed. In an age when clothing corporations hire pencil-necked physicists to synthetically breed the Next New Thing in outdoor wear, Howard retains his individualism. He has produced a line of superb clothing fashioned by his zealous participation in outdoor sports. Each garment is handmade by him and his assistants. And you won't find them on fancy retail store shelves. That's how he keeps his prices affordable. With conviction in his voice, Howard states that the big clothing corporations put out too many overspecialized and overpriced items. Howard is very much the common man's best friend. His guarantee is as simple and effective as his character; he will repair defective stitching in any of his products, at no charge.

I tested two items from the Melanzana Fleece line, the Shortsleeve and the Tights. The Shortsleeve is a wonderful piece. Howard calls it "the poor man's fleece vest." Crafted from either 100- or 200-weight Malden polyester fleece (the same quality fleece all the big clothing corporations use), this sporty number is extremely comfortable. Airy lightness sifts through the fleece, which is known for its insulation, even when wet. The Shortsleeve is brave enough to take on a Leadville winter trip as an underlayer, then shifts into a great looking T-shirt during other seasons. The color I tested was a beautiful maroon. When I asked Howard to specify the color for this review, he answered, "Oh, that would be our maroonish color." Works for me. So does the price: $25 for the 100 weight, and $28 for the 200 weight!

Next up were the tights, recently redesigned. This time I tested the lightweight version, made of Malden's 100 Powerstretch LT, an "advanced material with a slick nylon/Lycra outer surface" and a cushy inner fleece. The outer surface wicks moisture from the thin inner fleece, really crucial in this genre of outdoor wear. Due to the polyester fleece, a Melanzana garment can be wrung nearly dry, since the poly fibers do not absorb water. I have run, cycled, and hung out in my Tights with only positive, contented adjectives to describe their performance. They now also come in 200 Powerstretch, a midweight, double-sided Lycra fleece. I doubt if you can beat the price: $32 for the 100 PS and $34 for the 200S.

These items were just two of twelve products that Melanzana manufactures, including sweats, cycling jerseys, overmitts, River Shorts, Recycled Shorts, and a Windshirt. For more information, give Fritz Howard a call at 719-486-3245. Most orders are shipped within twenty-four hours.

high gaiters, which come up to the knee, while the more cosmopolitan winter athletes can get by with a short gaiter.

Hats/Headbands/Balaclavas

At least half of our body-heat percentage is lost through the head. Your mother told you this, and it's true. It is always wise to keep the head, or at least the temples, covered while doing winter sports. This increases sport performance. If you start to overheat, take off your hat and the body will regulate itself. Headbands are fantastic, offering good protection but allowing you to feel the wind through your hair. Balaclavas, which are a combination of hat, face mask, and neck gaiter, are superb for extremely cold conditions. Popular versions of each of these items are made of storm (wind-blocking) fleece with a wicking fiber or of lighter-weight fabrics such as Spandex, Lycra, or a polyester combination.

Winter Gloves

Make sure your gloves have an interior construction that includes a synthetic insulative fabric and a liner. The two-finger, or "lobster-claw" style is wise for many winter sports where hand dexterity is not a priority, such as snowshoeing, alpine skiing, or backcountry touring. The exterior should have a terry-cloth backing so you can wipe the ol' schnoz and storm fleece for lightweight wind protection. Winter cycling gloves work great. Peruse the cycling catalogs for ideas.

Sunscreen/Lip Balm

I used to have a macho attitude toward sunscreen and lip balm: "That stuff is for wimps; I don't need it." This attitude has caused premature aging of my skin due to its prolonged exposure to outdoor weather.

Most skin experts suggest a sunscreen rated SPF 15 or higher. You should anoint the bridge of the nose, back of the neck, ears, and under the chin before and during every winter excursion. Lip balm prevents windburn, chapping, and peeling. In recent years, I've wised up and now regularly apply Ironman Triathlon™ sunblock and lip balm. These products are waterproof for up to eight hours and are used by pro athletes on five continents. It will not sweat off, has not been tested on animals, and has an SPF of 35 for the sunscreen, 30 for the lip balm. Both are available through Sports Pharmaceuticals of America (800-728-7873).

GEAR: TOOLS OF THE TRADE

Heart-Rate Monitors

Many winter training activities can fool the athlete. While cycling, for instance, you may intuitively think you are going too slow during your ride when actually you should be going even easier. A heart-rate monitor allows you to keep track of how hard you are actually working. A heart-rate monitor is especially good for recovery days, such as after an interval day. Many athletes go too hard on easy days and not hard enough on hard days. A heart-rate monitor will assist you in training within your most effective zone.

Monitoring your heart rate allows you to determine full recovery during interval workouts. It is also valuable when you are gradually regaining fitness lost to an injury or illness. And I am a firm believer in monitoring the morning heart rate during hard training and race phases. If your morning heart rate is ten or more beats higher than normal, it's a mandatory recovery day, whether you like it or not! Monitors are available through cycling catalogs or local running stores.

Hydration Systems

There are two ways to go: water bottles or hands-free systems. Traditional water bottles can be carried in bottle cages on a bike frame or holster style by noncycling athletics. Ultimate Direction, Inc., (800-426-7229) is the most innovative pioneer. This company began with a single water-bottle carrier sewn onto a waist belt and has subsequently introduced an awesome line of hydration systems.

Hands-free systems have made a significant impact upon athletic hydration. These systems, first pioneered by Camelbak (800-767-8725), are usually worn backpack style, although around-the-waist models are available as well. They consist of bladders with a drinking tube attached. My winter favorite is the amazing Artica SportVest. The Artica is ideal for full-day winter activities such as backcountry skiing or snowshoeing. It includes a Polartec fleece vest as well as pockets galore to hold energy bars, a camera, and spare clothes. A unique internal drinktube routing helps ensure fluid does not freeze, a potential drawback of these systems in the winter. Best of all, the Artica holds up to ninety fluid ounces!

Personally, I'm mostly a water-bottle guy, although I do use a Camelbak during sports such as mountain biking and nordic skiing, where my hands may not be free. I also love my Ultimate Artica for day-long speed ski tours and general mountaineering exploits.

Performance Watches

Having a watch with a stopwatch, lap counter, countdown timer, and alarm is a wise investment. Many Wholistic Fitness strength-training techniques are timed, as well as interval workouts in cardiovascular training. The Timex Ironman Triathlon watches have pretty much cornered the market, although spin-off brands are readily available and also quite dependable.

Avalanche Beacons

Plan on going into the backcountry with at least one other person during the winter? Bring an avalanche beacon. Your local mountaineering shop can show you various models. Before heading out with a group into the backcountry, make sure everyone has beacons that work on the same frequency. When skiing or climbing, the beacon should be in transmit mode. When crossing an avalanche path or questionable slope, the leader should leave his or her beacon on transmit, while the others in the group set their beacons to receive. What's not to love?

20

Cold Weather Safety

"Men die of fright and live of confidence."
—Henry David Thoreau

DOG COLLARS

I know that right now some of my old climbing and backcountry partners are rolling on the ground laughing. "What is *Ilg* doing writing about *safety?* (More laughter ensues.) He was the most dangerous dude I *ever* hung out with!"

All right, fair enough. So maybe I was *once* a little marginal in my interpretation of what constituted safe and what did not. I'll never forget the look on the face of one of my earliest climbing partners, Brook Blair, when I proudly pulled out a collection of dog collars at the base of an ice climb up Boulder Canyon in Colorado.

"What the hell are those?" Brook asked.

"Nylon webbed dog collars, man. Got 'em at McGuckin Hardware the other day—they're cheap! Check out these cool colors! And look, they've already got these bitchin' metal rings on the ends!" I stated enthusiastically.

"I see that, but what exactly are you doing with them here?" My poor friend was very confused. I had figured their use was obvious.

"Quickdraws, duh! We can clip these directly to the ice screws and the metal ring will allow way more rope freedom!" I was pumped to share my insight. Why hadn't other climbers thought of this, I wondered.

Brook went understandably berserk. He could not *believe* that I would have actually used dog collars as protection during ice climbing. Heck, I was going to use them for rock climbing as well!

I realize now, of course, that if I would have taken any one of my numerous climbing falls onto a dog collar, that little metal ring would have ripped out of the webbing faster than I could have thought, "Oh shi@#$!" It has been said that slow learners make the best teachers, and when it comes to safety, my education has been *slow*. I've learned through trial and error, somehow surviving long enough to write this chapter. Take it from me, do *not* mess around with winter safety. The absolute

213

best thing any winter athlete could do for his or her outdoor performance is to take a winter safety course such as those offered through the American Avalanche Institute (307-733-3315) or the Wilderness Medical Associates (800-742-2931). If you spend any time in the backcountry, you should also be CPR and first-aid literate. Contact the American Red Cross National Headquarters (202-737-8300) for local chapter information. The following words are not to be taken as a replacement for such courses but rather to inspire awareness of key winter safety issues.

HYPOTHERMIA

The day dawned soft and warm in Boulder, Colorado. I had my heart set on a new running record up and down Mount Audubon in the Indian Peaks Wilderness. To save time, I jumped on my motorcycle wearing only running shorts, shoes, and a tank top. Careening up the canyon toward Nederland, I was exhilarated. What a gorgeous day! Certainly today I will break the record, I thought. My fitness was as high as my spirits as I leaned my bike bold and deep up the winding road. Skidding into the trailhead at about 10,000 feet of elevation, I jumped off the bike, set my chronograph, and took off for the sunlit peak.

Nearing timberline, my footfalls were crisp and leg speed sincere. On target for the record! I pushed harder, driving each knee a little higher, a little faster. I ignored

the gathering clouds. Within thirty minutes, the sky was as dark as German lager. Thunder. Lightning. Rain. Then snow. It required another fifteen minutes of ego overcoming good sense before admitting to myself that this was insane and the record would not be mine today. Shivering, I turned around. I ran into a headwind of diagonal snow and sleet. I did not want to be here. Miles above my bike, sopping wet and already experiencing microconvulsions, I squatted near the first dwarf pine I came to after returning to timberline.

Getting from that pine tree to Boulder is a vague, dreamlike memory. Snippets come back to me. I recall summoning all my mental focus to reach my bike. I did not even want to sit on the cold, wet seat, let alone drive the machine downhill for twenty-five miles. The pelting rain felt like daggers of ice being driven into my half-naked body. Halfway down Boulder Canyon, the convulsions grew so violent, they forced my bike into involuntary lane changes back and forth across the highway. My overworked guardian angels once again did their jobs and delivered me home. Peeling white knuckles from my handlebars, I lay down on my front lawn. In seventy-degree heat, I convulsed for the next three hours.

Warning Signs

Hypothermia is a lowering of the body's core temperature to dangerous levels. It means your guts are too cold, and metabolism is slowing down. The winter athletes that generate the highest body temperatures, such as nordic skiers and snowshoers, are particularly vulnerable to hypothermia. The moment you stop exercising is the moment you need to put on some more layers (see Chapter Nineteen). Warning signs of hypothermia are:

- chattering teeth
- uncontrolled shivering
- spontaneous convulsions
- dizziness
- slurred speech
- confusion or disorientation
- lowered pulse rate

Treatment

A gradual warming of the body is needed. Do not try to get a hypothermic person too warm too fast. In fact, the old rule of body-to-body warming is no longer suggested. Hypothermia is an acidic state, and if the blood is warmed too fast, the acid is rushed to the heart, where it can cause cardiac arrest. Get the person (or yourself) out of the elements and into a warm, dry environment as quickly as possible. Remove any wet clothes. Do not administer drinks containing caffeine or alcohol, which pull heat from the body and dehydrate the cells. Hot but drinkable beverages or soups are wise. An energy bar with a good concentration of carbohydrates is also great. Even candy bars will work wonders. Don't let a hypothermic person go to sleep. Be forceful in your authority. Hypothermia screws up judgment. Even if the athlete says he or she is fine and wants to continue, don't allow it. Get the person warm and dry, and provide warm fluids. Then contact medical help.

ALTITUDE SICKNESS

I've lived at high elevations my whole life. Flying home sometimes, I've seen people drop to the ground with nausea right after landing. Even athletes who are totally fit at 5,000 feet have been suddenly hunched over, hands on knees and sick as a dog at 12,000 feet. Why is this? The decreased concentration of oxygenated blood sets up a whole physiological stage of trouble. Nausea, lethargy, intense headaches, dizziness, and feeling winded are all common complaints of those with altitude sickness.

Preventing altitude sickness lies in proper hydration and a gradual ascent to altitude. How do you know if you are adequately hydrated? If you are not urinating at least once every two hours, you are underhydrated. And the urine should be clear, not yellow. Other preventive tricks include using a humidifier at night to combat the dryness associated with sucking in cold air and using alternate nostril breathing, a yogic technique in which nasal breathing alternates from one nostril to the other. Western medicine prescribes Advil® or Tylenol® for relief from headaches, and Diamox® is commonly given to lowland travelers forty-eight hours before their high-altitude journeys.

There is no cure for altitude sickness save for living at high altitudes.

ACUTE MOUNTAIN SICKNESS (AMS)

This version of altitude sickness strikes during ascents to high altitude. Taking time to acclimate is the best way to avoid AMS. Don't attempt ascending more than 3,000 feet per day. For low-land skiers accustomed to fast travel and short weekends, such a rule is absurd and usually ignored. AMS is a much more serious consideration for mountaineers. If acclimatization is not done wisely, AMS can jeopardize a climber's health and most certainly his or her performance.

FROSTBITE

The winter athlete should always be aware of the potential for frostbite. Frostbite occurs when adequate blood supply to soft tissue is reduced. The most common sites for it are the fingers and toes, although ears and nose are frequently bitten as well. Early signs of frostbite are numbness and light discoloration of the skin. Skin turned a purplish shade is a sign of advanced frostbite, which requires medical assistance. Prevention is the best ally here, which is why I recommend only the highest quality coldweather clothing and gear.

I have used Korean White Ginseng and Siberian Ginseng as well as niacin to stim-

ulate circulation during cold-weather excursions with great success. Buying boots that allow enough room for you to wiggle your toes is also vital. Carrying a chemically activated heat pack is a grand idea for elite-level backcountry athletes who are pushing the envelope.

If you do succumb to frostbite, get warm and dry and inside shelter as soon as possible. Warming the affected area is a priority, but never rub damaged tissue. Instead, dunk the bitten area in warm water and wiggle it as best as possible. Otherwise, hold, tuck, or press the bitten area to something warm, be it your breath, hands, another person's body, or a heat pack.

AVALANCHES

Fear of frostbite and avalanches keep people away from winter sports more than anything else. The best friend a winter athlete has in the backcountry is education. Recognizing the potential for, preventing, and avoiding avalanches used to take up a considerable amount of my backcountry winter sports career.

The cause of avalanches lies in snow crystallization. The faster snow accumulates, the more slide potential it holds. The moisture content of snow can often be a factor. Wet snow falling atop a lighter snowpack results in fragility. Wind also changes the structure of snow crystals, inviting failure of the snowpack integrity. Open glades are often avalanche runways, so be superaware and stick to forested areas as much as possible. Listen to weather reports. If you are new to an area, inquire at the local Forest Service office to learn the locality of common avalanche areas. And all backcountry athletes should wear avalanche beacons (see Chapter Nineteen).

Avoiding avalanches means circumventing them. If you must cross a questionable slope or avalanche zone, use a slope meter to gauge the angle or poke-test the snow for stability. Take a ski pole and punch it downward into the snowpack. Feel for softness. Firm is good, soft is bad. Obvious layers are not a good sign, since slab avalanches (the most dangerous kind) tend to take off atop a multilayered snow pack. The general rule of nonfrostbitten thumb is: If the slope angle is between thirty and fifty degrees, find a way to cross above the zone, if possible. If not, you can risk crossing below it, but if that baby lets go above you, there's not a lot you'll have going in your favor. When avalanche danger factors are high—for example, lots of fresh snow— stay out of hazard areas in the backcountry.

If you must cross an avalanche zone, make sure the others in your party have set their avalanche beacons to receive while you (or whoever will be going first) have put yours on transmit. Button up your clothing, take your wrists out of ski pole straps, and disengage your backpack waist belt. Say your prayers to the avalanche gods, point your skis or self slightly downhill, and cross. Think "light." If the snow-

The general rule of nonfrostbitten thumb is: If the slope angle is between thirty and fifty degrees, find a way to cross above the zone, if possible. Little Cottonwood Canyon, Utah. Photo by Anne Sasso.

pack starts "speaking" to you (i.e., making "whoomph" sounds) or feels sketchy, turn the hell around and look for a safer crossing.

If you do get caught in a slide, try to get to its lateral edge. If you can't out-ski it, eighty-six your poles and starting "swimming." Stay as close to the top of the snow as you can. It may sound funny, but relax into the situation. Some of my most calm moments have been while swimming through avalanches, believe it or not. Staying calm in crisis situations is a trainable component, one that is advanced through the principles and techniques given in this book.

FIRST AID

Although knowing how to administer first aid is important, having a first-aid kit is even more important! Several premade first-aid kits are available at mountaineering shops. You can also fashion such a kit specifically for winter sports by taking the following list down to your local drugstore:

- Ace bandage
- antibiotic ointment (such as Neosporin or Bacitracin)

- adhesive bandages and butterfly types of closures
- blister aids (Second Skin, moleskin, a sewing needle)
- chemically activated heat pack
- gauze and gauze pads
- hydrogen peroxide
- identification of self, family, and friends, and a list of any contraindications
- medicines: personal prescription drugs, aspirin, ibuprofen, cold medicine, throat lozenges, an antibiotic (requires prescription), antihistamines
- painkillers
- rubber gloves
- tweezers and scissors

21

Questions and Answers from Students

"We must learn to love the question, not the answer."
—Rilke

The following questions from readers and students of mine reflect a wide spectrum of training and sport-performance topics. Many have been gleaned from my column in *Bicycling* Magazine. Some are directly related to winter sports, but most deal with common challenges associated with the athletic life. I like using ones with spiritual themes to them, since they are the most fun and most meaningful. Names have been changed, but letter content has not been edited.

SUBJ: BROKEN BONES
FROM: CRIS

Coach Ilg,

HELP! I love reading your totally unique training answers to people's problems but never thought I'd write you! Today I broke my shoulder and a couple of ribs, managing to get both sides of my body. I will have surgery on Friday. I am a

Cat 3, 38 year old woman and I have been training seriously since October. I was working towards a peak in June for Master's Nationals. I have between 10–15 hours a week for cycling. Any suggestions for time best spent during these next weeks of bone knitting? Nutritional Advice? Thank you so much for your help.

Dear Cris,

Currently, you are out of my field of expertise. After surgery, it's best to work with a sports-knowledgeable physical therapist. I usually begin my work *after* athletes are released from physical therapy. However, a couple of things might help you in your healing.

First and foremost, use the injury to learn. The only thing that hurts worse and is more expensive than an injury is repeating it in the future! Contemplate the "accident" to discover clues about which factors led to the situation. Without emotional attachment, ask yourself if your training was lacking any quality that could have prevented or minimized the injury: strength training? flexibility? bike handling? cornering? descending? Cat 3's have a lot of accidents. Fitness levels are high, but bike-handling skills may not be up to dealing with the aggressive nature of the peleton (I'm assuming you are a road racer).

Instrumental to your healing is the realization that bones are not hard by nature. They represent the most concentrated energetic structure in the body. A broken bone can often represent a conflict in our spiritual energy. If meditation is not part of your training program, this injury might indeed be a beacon alerting you to address some matters within. I know to conventionally trained athletes, this sounds odd. I just want you to be aware that this injury means more than just seeing a surgeon and having a fix-the-broken-part attitude. It means using a higher vision and cultivating a wholistic perspective to your training.

Healing visualizations are of utmost importance right now. Give your mind an accurate image of how you want the body/mind/spirit to heal, feel, and perform as you take responsibility to regenerate the injured area. Although this forum is not the appropriate vehicle for me to prescribe a series of healing meditations for you, contact me privately or find another expert in this field to assist you in this area.

Regarding nutrition, a couple of imperatives will help optimize cellular regeneration specific to the bone tissue. Although I cannot prescribe amounts since you are not a formal student, I suggest calling Metagenics/UniPro (800-621-6070) and asking for specific information on the following supplements and how they relate to the healing of your injury: Microcrystalline Hydroxyapatite, Mucopolysaccharide formula, Amino 1,000, and Basics Plus. Your body will need a combination of these supplements over the next few weeks.

Good luck in your journey. This situation will make you a stronger person in the long term. Let me know if I can be of further help.

SUBJ: NOT-QUITE-SORE KNEE
FROM: SANDA

Dear Coach Ilg,

I'm a triathlete and snowshoe enthusiast. For the last few weeks I've had a tender right knee after training runs. It started after 6 miles (on a 7 mile run) four weeks ago, pain on the outside of my right knee (more toward the lower leg than the upper). It responded to ice and a couple days later actually got better after a 70 mile bike ride. I've gone easy on it. But it gets a little tender when I run on it—especially downhill.

And it isn't swollen, it isn't enough to cause a limp or for me to favor it, but it keeps wanting to get tender. Any advise?

26 year old female

Dear Sanda,

Thanks for writing. Patellar tendon distress is common among all kinds of endurance athletes, regardless of sport. My office is flooded this time of year with cases similar to yours. The connective tissue of the athletic body is often worn and vulnerable to aches, inflammations, or worse. Factors that compound this affliction appear related to two main avenues: inadequate nutrition and poor periodizational structure.

Inadequate nutrition. According to Wholistic Fitness tenets, nutrition is one discipline that must be maintained full throttle all year long, seven days per week. This is why nutrition is called the most noble out of the five disciplines of Wholistic Fitness. Most cases like yours that I see stem from a negative nitrogen balance, which results from inadequate quality and/or quantity of protein. Also, I've had good success with introducing supplement glucosamine sulfate and chrondroitin. I especially like the oral-spray delivery form of glucosamine and chondroitin to deal with joint inflammation and the prevention thereof.

Poor periodizational structure. The first thing I do as a coach is provide my students with a year-long structure that pivots upon a balance of intense training stimulus with profound and properly timed restoration/regeneration phases. Examine your training structure to make certain your connective tissue is thoroughly strength trained in the off and transitional phases. Many joint inflammations can be traced to inadequate strength training and kinesthetic (flexibility and postural alignment) volumes. Thus the connective tissue cannot withstand the long months of endurance-specific work necessary for peak performances.

Finally, do not disregard the energetic lesson behind the physical manifestation. When the knees begin to act up or weaken, it sometimes reflects an inner fear of moving forward in some important area of our personal life. In other cases it means a certain type of inner arrogance or stubbornness. Take genuine quiet time to consider in depth why this injury has come into your experience. Learn from it. Awareness is the biggest issue here, not sport performance.

I hope this helps. Good luck with your journey.

FIRST CORRESPONDENCE FROM PAUL SUBJ: LOST FITNESS

HELP Steve,

I have spent WAY too much time at work the last couple weeks ... (months) and am getting hammered on training rides (road), much less races. I love the sport, but trying to work back into fitness training by myself is also burning me out. I love your style of coaching, wholistic, and feel that this issue needs a wholistic approach ... simply going out and hammering by myself is not what cycling enjoyment is all about. Do you have any suggestions as to an efficient way to regain fitness without losing my mind?? (I know, I am asking for a lot)

Dear Paul,

You ask for very little. You ask to regain what you always have had: balance.

The Buddha taught, "All know the Way. Few actually walk It." Many people sense their life is out of balance. Everything seems to be meaningless. In today's world, it has become increasingly difficult to even recall—let alone live—a life of balance, inner serenity, and inspired self-discipline. Zen teacher Thich Nhat Hanh says, "We have become so busy that we barely look into the eyes of those we love."

Cut the crap, Paul. Jettison the spiritual clutter. If you truly want better athletics, a more balanced life, and a higher way of seeing, you will do whatever it takes to practice it. That might mean studying Wholistic Fitness; it might mean quitting your job and doing something you love; it might mean reading a book; it might mean just sitting on a meditation cushion and starting to pay attention; or it might mean just doing what needs to be done. Cultivate actions, word choices, and thoughts that are appropriate to your higher self. Your intuitive wisdom will guide you flawlessly if you simply listen.

Practice this mantra: "Is what I am about to do/say/think appropriate to my dreams?"

Say it again right now, "Is what I am about to do/say/think appropriate to my dreams?"

Start here. It *is* this simple! Practice this mantra for thirty days, then write again. Let me know how your practice is going.

SECOND CORRESPONDENCE FROM PAUL
SUBJ: SPIRITUAL ATHLETICS

Steve ... the GURU!!

Took a less intense, more relaxed approach to riding (life). What is great is that I went from a tight screw to a much more relaxed rider, feeling better, doing better. I basically applied that which you said with my own religious/spiritual beliefs ... and bango. Thank you thank you thank you. What is so truly incredible is that my enjoyment (and performance) has almost directly paralleled my feelings of spiritual evolvement.

Thanks again!

Dear Paul,

Congratulations on the spiritual shift! The parallel you have discovered is not uncommon to those who seek and engage a higher way to their fitness. A fact of transpersonal fitness: If we work on ourselves as human beings, our athletic performance will naturally elevate. A tenet of transpersonal fitness: Whenever we relax, we perform better.

Keep up the inner study, and, again, what you've accomplished is far more valuable than standing atop podiums.

SUBJ: BACK PAIN
FROM: JIM

Dear Coach: Last summer you gave me some excellent advice about a back injury. One thing you advised was to ditch a back support belt, and I must confess, that was absolutely the correct thing to do. Almost immediately, some secondary symptoms disappeared. You also advised me to pay attention to my personal relationships, as the injury was in the pelvic region. Again, excellent advice as I was able to heal both.

SUBJ: LOWER BACK PAIN
FROM: TIM

I was recently diagnosed by orthopedics with an inflammation or, possibly a degradation, of the SI5 (Sacroiliac) joint near my right hip. I've had back problems for 11 years and cycling has never seemed to bring them on. Now my doc wants me to give up my road bike for something more upright like a mountain bike or hybrid to prevent long periods of time spent down in the drops. I live in Hawaii where wind is constantly 15 MPH or higher so riding low is common. Any recommendations on a pre-bike stretch routine or something else that might help. Have been riding a Lifecycle recumbent for the past 4 weeks to try and stay in some semblance of shape and my back still hurts.
Tim (Desperate in Pearl Harbor)

Dear Tim,

Conventional medical training insists that doctors treat the symptom. It comes as no surprise that your doctor wants you off the bike. That's the easy answer, but it's not the cure. Neither is switching to a recumbent, a hybrid, or an MTB. That's just shuffling. The true healing lies within, not on something external.

Lower-back musculature and skeletal tissue are prone to injury in sport-specific athletes. It's possible that a lack of structural balance has predisposed this area to your current injury. A couple of immediate notes: Make certain your training year includes at least three months of noncycling-specific strength training. Those three months should also include hatha yoga or wholistic stretching to help realign structural, spiritual, and biochemical imbalances.

The more cycling specific we become, the more the psoas musculature and associated connective tissue tends to harden, causing rotation of the pelvis and actuating physical conflict. A lot of my work with cyclists necessitates structural bodywork and energy work to open and soften this stockpiled rigidity. Look at your training: Do your training volumes reflect significant imbalances between contractive training, like cycling, and expansive training, like flexibility, regenerative nutrition, bodywork, and meditation? If so, this injury is a signal to get you onto a higher level of awareness. Giving up your road bike is *not* the way to learn from this injury!

Prioritize the following disciplines immediately:

1) Nutrition. Core nutrients must include amino acids, vitamins, and mineral supplements plus joint-specific nourishment.

2) Kinesthetic work. This should be in two areas: structural bodywork (not massage; you need to shift the pelvic fascia into alignment, not pamper imbalanced muscles) and flexibility. The flexibility routines that I created are designed specifically for the lower back and hips. These routines are available on video.

3) Meditation. Use energy-work techniques to reduce the inflammation and clear the blockage of energy at the pelvis. These techniques are available on audio tapes. Also, use this discipline to contemplate the spiritual teaching beyond the injury: What was out of balance in your physical and/or emotional life that gave rise to this manifestation?

4) Off-Season strength training. A precise choreography of movements and cycles should be followed to strengthen the spinal and midsection muscles. The new fiber development will alleviate the stress on the SI joint.

The real way to healing is to view this as the universe giving you a great opportunity to go deeper into your training with greater awareness and wholeness. To follow through on the specifics as to what was discussed above, e-mail me. Until then, use the energy in your desperation to self-heal. I know you can do it.

SUBJ: TOO TIRED?
FROM: PETER

Hi Steve,

I have enjoyed reading your column and books and I now have a question of my own. I seem to get too tired after a workout, be it a 1 or 2 hour ride, or some weights followed by a run. I get lots of energy during the workout but after I eat (maybe too much) I'm often tired the rest of the day. I'm not vegetarian but low meat intake, low fat and high carbs are not a problem but total calories maybe. Anyway I love to exercise and the peaceful feelings afterwards but I find it difficult to get work done.
Thanks for all your responses.

Dear Peter,

I appreciate the kind words.

Make nutrition your most valuable ally in figuring out (and learning from) these feelings of overtiredness. There are two categorically different forms of nutrition. One is physical, the basis of metabolizing foodstuffs into assimilative energy. That's the stuff most trainers are familiar with, and you can easily find volumes of information on the role of physical nutrition and how it can help your symptoms of lethargy, staleness, and overtraining.

But there is another form of nutrition overlooked by conventional coaching: spiritual. Blake said, "Man has no body distinct from his Soul: for that called Body is a portion of Soul discern'd by the five senses, the chief inlets of Soul in this age." Peter, do you meditate? Do you know how to recognize, develop, and influence your inner power? Do you work your energy pathways while you train? Don't feel bad if you answer no to the above. For some reason, in this country we are simply not educated in using our sport or fitness training as transformative practice.

Vitamins, minerals, amino acids, carbohydrates, and coenzymes are valuable to long-term health and performance. Yet our spiritual nutrition is even more important! Our relationships can either drain or empower us. The same is true for our occupations. We must also consider the geomantic influence of where we choose to live and how our constitutions relate to the sports we pursue.

If it would make you feel better, go ahead and do the traditional route: Get a blood test. Most probably, you'll learn nothing conclusive, but at least you would know that your tiredness is not something physical. Where would that leave you? At the beautiful threshold of transpersonal fitness!

You could then begin the journey toward athletic enlightenment in any number of ways, perhaps by a spiritual book or yoga class, a Wholistic Fitness training prescription, a course in somatic education, or meditation. It boils down to this: awareness. Dial in the physical nutrition but keep an open mind to what really matters (and which is way more fun) in the long run, *spiritual nutrition.* Let me know if you would like further guidance, and good luck in your journey!

SUBJ: BODY FAT AND EXERCISE
FROM: JILL

Dear Coach, I have read The Outdoor Athlete *(it is my bible!) and follow your prescriptions for training for cycling and skiing and maintenance and I would like to ask your opinion/advice on body fat & exercise.*

I am a 25 year old female, 5'3" and 132 pounds. In the summer I ride my mt bike recreationally and also jog and hike and weight train. Since moving to Breckenridge 3 years ago, my fitness level has increased tremendously and my diet has improved. But I have always carried extra body fat in my upper thighs and particularly my butt. I have become more firm, but have not had the significant muscle building and fat loss I expected. I do do weight training for all six body parts and focus on my legs for skiing and biking.

There have been two times when my body composition did change significantly. Last spring I did the PR Nutrition program. Cutting out sweets for six weeks and increasing protein intake had instant effects on my performance, recovery, and appearance. But I have no intention of buying $30 boxes of their bars or not eating any sweets for the rest of my life. (I did incorporate the increase in protein in my diet after I finished the program.) The second instance was last week when I completed Ride The Rockies. I normally mountain bike 50 miles a week, but training for and participating in it, I was road riding up to 410 miles in one week. This is the most exercise I have ever done at one time (and I didn't enjoy road riding enough to decide to buy a road bike) but it was fun and challenging. When I got home, my butt had shrunk enough for my boyfriend to notice! I have no documentation, but I suspect a large amt of fat had been burned or converted to muscle. But (again) I have no intention of riding 410 miles per week for this effect.

My question is: what activities and in what amounts would you recommend that would have the effect that both of these instances did? I would like to eliminate some of the extra fat so that I can do activities more efficiently and improve my health and appearance. I work a desk job 40 hours a week and have to contend with the chilly mornings and rainy afternoons of Summit County. I have a trainer

(rollers) which I used this spring but, even while watching TV, two hours is the most I can take of that. Any advice you have would be appreciated. Thanks in advance.

My second question is: how do you pronounce your last name? (smile)

Jill,

Thanks for writing. First, if you are twenty-five and have only been training for three years, practice some more patience! If you grew up with those fatty areas, three years is a pretty short time in which to reverse a couple of decades worth of body fat! Appreciate your body for doing as well as it is without injury.

I have addressed this culprit in this column previously. It's a definite dragon, especially for females. Just this week, I was working with one of my female students from Canada, a national-level rower. She had been training for many years but still had fat in the same areas you mentioned. When she began working with me, I took her out of her comfort zone, and she immediately began dropping body fat from those problem areas. Let me explain.

You are an efficient cyclist. Too efficient. You must begin doing other CV activities at which you are not as efficient. We have all met cyclists (especially roadies) who can crank with the best of them but are still fat. That's because they have learned how to spin without using a lot of energy. For the same reason they are so fast, they are also fat—too damn efficient on the bike! Unlike cycling, running does not support the body weight. Cross-training is a good place for you to start.

Additionally, you are doing the right things about increasing protein. I also suggest high-intensity training in the gym, using movements specifically targeting the glutes and thighs. I highly suggest strength-training movements such as lunges. Also, I've had great success incorporating plyometric movements in the jump family to stimulate fresh neural service that increases metabolic fire to the area. Stadium stair running is *really* good, although you'd be hard pressed to find a stadium in Breckenridge. Don't worry though, just substitute running up those ski runs instead of running stadium stairs!

Use your off-season to compete in snowshoe races; that's major glute/thigh work, as is running up ski slopes during dryland training. Inline skating is okay, but involves too much glide most of the time. Prioritize classic nordic skiing this winter as well. Enough to go on? As with any CV training, you'll need to vary volumes and intensities throughout the seasons. Proper choreography includes sessions of high intensity plus low intensity. I cannot prescribe anything for you casually, however, since you are not a formal student and that's beyond the intent of this forum.

Re: how I pronounce my last name. Well, I pronounce it, uh ... let me think here. I can't really write it out phonetically! Let's try this: Rhymes with ... geez, that

doesn't work either! Oh well, I guess it will remain a mystery!

SUBJ: MOTIVATION
FROM: LEFTSIDE

Dear Coach,

Having a little bit of a motivational problem with the training. I have kept up with all the volumes and items but am still filling stuck in the mud.

Have done some extra zazen to try and calm my racing mind. Have had many questions with the book by Sogyan The Tibetan book of living and dying. The whole idea of every thing we say, do will have repercussions on future 'lives'. Thus leading to a global responsibility for all beings ... man that is big! The idea of getting free from our minds and realizing our own trap ... to really see what is important, to not be a slave to our thoughts. I just have not been capable to do these things as of yet. I have done a pathetic job in the Tapasaya day (saying "no" to desired, but unneeded actions), really not that great. I am just falling back into similar patterns of wants and desires ...

Student Leftside,

Be patient in your spiritual seeking of the answers to the big questions. Just keep practicing, through boring weeks and through exciting weeks. Keep as even minded and as steadfast as you can with your Master Sheet (prescribed daily practices). Suzuki taught, "If you lose the spirit of repetition, your practice will become quite difficult." Work on forgetting yourself more. Merge into your awareness and leave the self behind. Your letter had several misspellings. Worry less about the big questions and more about being mindful when you are writing letters.

And what do you mean you have been "pathetic" in your Tapasaya? To what are you comparing your Tapasaya? There are no rights and no wrongs in the spiritual journey, just consequences of your practice. Don't overthink. Don't compare. The spiritual journey is a long, long, long trek. Be careful not to be too greedy for results in this journey. Everything drops away on the spiritual journey, so place no emphasis on big gains.

Yes, the idea that *every* thought, word choice, and action influences our next life and has global and even universal implications is a tremendous responsibility. Does it *all* count? Yes, every little bit counts. I remember a phrase that came to me shortly after I had my root chakra awakened by a facilitator in Denver: "Nothing matters, but everything counts."

Just practice.

SUBJ: THIS ISN'T FUN
FROM: CG

Hi Coach,

I have a few questions about my "reactions" to Wholistic Fitness training. They have not all been joyous times of bliss, in fact, I am starting to feel a little down. It seems to be getting more difficult to maintain any kind of mindfulness for each day. I feel myself becoming detached during my recovery weeks. A feeling of almost floating in space.

My new awareness is telling many things about myself that I do not like, in fact perhaps even afraid to admit. The real truth still is something I do not under stand in myself and about myself. Have I spent so long on this earth without noticing? Why? Is this grogginess I feel normal? Am I finally noticing my Dragons? Why am I confused about these reactions?

Dear Student CG,

The work of Wholistic Fitness is about waking up. Far from being a "cure" to life's perceived "problems," Wholistic Fitness—like other all spiritual training—is designed for self-understanding and wisdom. Magical solutions do not exist in spiritual training. What matters is to find tools such as mindfulness, meditation, and self-discipline and use them wisely to chart our own journey. Hopefully, the tools that work (such as Wholistic Fitness training) will reinforce our commitment to using our life to move higher while we have the chance. Wise tools are those that help us grow as human beings.

Depression, confusion, and lethargy are common dragons as we begin the arduous trek up the path of self-cultivation. Every now and then, we may stumble upon moments of outright beauty, onefulness, and joy. Some lead difficult, joyless lives. Others seem blessed by prosperity even though they are jerks. It doesn't matter. Everyone has their own unique karma to work out.

As inner work becomes transformative, the act of mindful living imparts inner peace, a type of sacred happiness far more profound than the Western model of linear success and material wealth. Your immediate work is to be as even minded as possible through the highs and lows of everyday life. Work on equanimity. Work within the present moment.

Explore the underpinnings of your recent awakenings. This cannot be done through the intellect. That is why we may feel so naked in this journey. The spiritual path is one that always is unfolding, contingent upon every thought, word, and action that we choose to do. That is big responsibility. There is not a moment to waste. Waking up is something each of us must do for ourselves. No one but you can choose to move out of ignorance and awaken. That is why the Buddha taught his disciples to "Be a light unto yourself."

Be patient and persevere. This awakening will constantly challenge you in ways never imagined. The efforts of this personal growth make athletic training pale by comparison. But you know what? En-lightenment happens, and you will become a more refined human being, with genuine human qualities of compassion, unconditional love, and deep sensitivity.

Keep practicing.

SUBJ: FANTASY OR VISUALIZATION
FROM: SS

Dear Teacher, I have a question that has arisen from my practice. What's the difference between visualizing something and fantasizing or wishful thinking? I suspect that attachment has something to do with it but I'm having trouble discerning the subtleties.

Dear SS,

The act of visualization is a specific mental training technique.

To visualize something involves a distinct step-by-step process having an origin, a middle, and a conclusion. Fantasies or wishful thinking lack this detailed, structured process. Visualization normally requires formal meditation whereas fantasies (at least the best ones!) are more spontaneous.

SUBJ: Q-ANGLE AND LACTATE THRESHOLD
FROM: LAURA

Dear Steve, I have two questions. Could you clarify what exactly the Q-angle is and how it influences sport performance?

And also, clarify the Lactate Threshold and how to train it. Thanks!

Dear Laura,

The Q-Angle (a.k.a. the femoral angle) is the natural angle between the upper leg and lower leg. Females generally have less than a 125-degree angle between the neck of the femur and the shaft of the bone. The smaller this angle, the more "knock-kneed" the physique. Contrary to popular belief, this knock-kneed stance results in *less* injury, due to a wider articulating surface between the femur and the tibia. Elite-level cyclists tend toward a knock-kneed position because it is more stable for the knee. And where there is more stability, there is also more power. Trying to pedal with the knees out or even straight forward "like headlights" results in soft-tissue transmission stress at the knee joint, especially in females, due to their wider pelvis. So the more "knock-kneed," the better in terms of injury prevention and power development.

This increased stability at the pelvis explains how elite women athletes, like snowshoer/runner Danelle Ballengee, can often kick many men's butts in snowshoeing and running downhill. They are more stable and may produce faster leg speed than most men running downhill.

Re: lactate threshold (a.k.a. anaerobic threshold). A cyclist can perform up to a certain intensity without building up too much lactic acid in the blood. When this intensity is exceeded, the acid in the muscles rises, and the muscles fatigue quickly. The point at which the muscles' contractile mechanism begins to shut down due to acidosis is called the lactate threshold (LT).

Training the LT is very important because all other things being equal, the higher your LT, the faster the speed you can hold over long distances or steep climbs. LT training takes two basic forms: long intervals and tempo training. Recovery is vital in LT training and no one should do more than two training sessions per week! You can increase the intensity and length of your LT sessions, but not the frequency.

Long intervals should be five to twelve minutes each. Gradually build the heart rate to your LT level and maintain it to the end of the interval. Recovery between intervals should range from two to five minutes. In tempo training gradually build your heart rate to your LT level with a group of riders and maintain a steady LT pace for five to ten miles. The group is needed for pace—solo riding builds strength and endurance, but not tempo … speed, rhythm, pace! The emphasis is on pace.

SUBJ: TRAINING
FROM: SAMUEL

Dear Coach Ilg,

Your insightful and unique approach to fitness and personal growth is awesome! I have something to ask you. My achilles tendon in my right legs hurts—my right ankle even swole last wk to the point that I couldn't even stand up on itt for about 3 hrs after waking up. Since then I have been off my bike but would like to resume ASAP. Now it's just the achilees. I was given Ibuprofen which I have been taking, I haven't iced it though. HELP, Please

Dear Samuel,

Well, you can help yourself by following through on that icing! Any swollen ankle should be immersed immediately in a bucket of ice water or iced with a cold pack. Given your degree of inflammation (not even being able to stand on it for several hours) may indicate a medical situation. Do not take this injury lightly. You did not inform me of the nature of the injury, but your first aid remains the same: RICE, as in

Rest,

Ice,

Compression, and

Elevation.

I suggest consulting a physician. A bursa (fluid-filled sac located beneath the tendon) may be inflamed. If this is the case, you've got several weeks of R&R ahead of you. I'm not trying to sound pessimistic, but I want you to hark to it and take care of this thing immediately.

If it is the bursa, consider yourself lucky. It's the better alternative to a rupture of the Achilles tendon. You don't want this to escalate into a chronic Achilles condition, because then the chances of a rupture will increase. The only cure for an Achilles rupture is surgery. Test your uric acid level. If it is high, you are predisposed to Achilles ailments. If that is the case, warm up and cool down very seriously and rethink your participation in lateral, explosive sports like basketball and tennis.

Much of my success with athletes comes from injury prevention. My prevention method is well known: intense strength training. I train my athletes hard in the gym so they each develop ligaments and tendons with the strength of aircraft cable. That's the only way to prevent conditions like yours. Perhaps this injury is a blessing in disguise. So listen to the lesson: Take care of this injury, get in the gym and strengthen your joint health, and eat good nutrition.

Finally, pay more attention to your spelling. Lack of awareness in writing a letter invites lack of awareness in sport performance. And lack of awareness is never a quality to be cultivated by any athlete!

Let me know how it goes; I hope this helps.

Part VI

Specialization Training Programs for Endurance Sports

photo by Roy Wilkinson

22

Nordic Skiing: Track Skiing (Classic and Skate Style)

"Life without discipline means death without honor."
—Norwegian proverb

The author stretches into classic ski technique while nordic skiing near Los Alamos, New Mexico. Photo by Marc Romanelli.

The following program is to be engaged immediately after the Perfect Power phase recovery week. This program is appropriate for all recreational and competitive nordic skiers who use a groomed (prepared) track preset with classic (kick-and-glide or diagonal striding) tracks and/or a skating lane.

This program does not cover specific track-skiing techniques but prepares the body, mind, and spirit for the pursuit of nordic track skiing. See Chapter Fourteen (on roller skiing) for basic movement analysis. Technique should be studied with a certified instructor or the guidance of an expert. Qualified instruction is available via the organizations, magazines, books, and videos listed in the resources section that concludes this chapter.

Now, let's get to training!

THE NORDIC MANIAC PROGRAM

The Nordic Maniac program is to be followed for five consecutive weeks. This phase produces muscular and cardiovascular fitness specific to nordic skiing. Appropriate transpersonal power development is also designed into the program.

Length of cycle: five weeks.
Frequency: seven-day cycle.
Next cycle: in season.
Primary goals: refine all prior mental, physical, and spiritual fitness gained from previous training cycles into nordic-specific conditioning.

Wholistic Fitness® Training Precepts

1) Be prepared.
2) Be on time.
3) Give 110 percent.

NORDIC MANIAC MASTER SHEET

All workouts are described in the next section, Wholistic Notes.

Get-a-Massage Monday: Day One

Recovery day. No strength or CV training. All other disciplines are discretionary. Get bodywork/massage if possible.

Torbjorn Tuesday: Day Two

Strength training: Nordic Maniac chest, shoulders, and triceps workout.

CV training: Run, inline ski, or roller ski for thirty to sixty minutes at Zones 1–2.
Kinesthetic training: Medium Form before strength training.
Meditation: Beeper Guru breath and posture assignment.

World Cup Wednesday: Day Three

Strength training: Nordic Maniac lower-body workout.
CV training: Cross-train from Tuesday: run, pole run, inline ski, or roller ski for thirty to sixty minutes at Zones 2–3.
Kinesthetic: Medium Form quickly after both strength and CV training.
Meditation: Early-morning zazen practice.

Ulvang Thursday: Day Four

Strength training: Nordic Maniac back and biceps workout.
Kinesthetic training: Yoga class or Long Form Flexibility after strength training.
Meditation: Beeper Guru breath and posture assignment.

Cera-F Friday: Day Five

CV training: Cross-train from Tuesday: run, inline ski, or roller ski for one to two hours at Zones 1–2 with cruise intervals.
Kinesthetic training: If no yoga class was done Thursday, do it today or Long Form Flexibility after CV training.
Meditation: Early-morning zazen practice.

Scandinavian Saturday: Day Six

CV training: In the A.M., cycle (road or

mountain) for two to three hours at Zones 1–2. If you can get to snow, ski for the same amount of time, with 80 percent of the time spent classic skiing. In the P.M., optimally run for forty-five minutes at Zones 1–2.

Kinesthetic training: Discretionary. Also, get or schedule bodywork (massage) for Sunday or Monday.

Meditation: 3 x 30 assignment; passive meditation for twenty minutes.

Sami Sunday: Day Seven

CV training: Snow ski if possible; otherwise, cycle for one hour at Zones 1–2, then perform Pyramid Interval workout. You can also run for one hour, then do the pyramids on a bike, roller skis, or skates.

Kinesthetic training: Discretionary. Also, get bodywork or schedule it for Monday.

Meditation: discretionary.

WHOLISTIC NOTES

This section provides the specific workouts prescribed in the Nordic Maniac Master Sheet.

Strength-Training Workouts

I think you'll find a pleasant, *almost* refreshing flow to these workouts, gleaned from the Wholistic Fitness nordic development department. I have modified them for this book, but you may still notice a slight competitive flavor. Whether or not you race any nordic events, you will notice an immediate transfer into your ski fitness. Note that we are only strength training each body part once per week in order to allot more time for the more important discipline of cardiovascular training. Still, believe me, you'll get a huge ski-specific strength gain from these workouts if you practice fully. Really use the gym time to visualize how this strength-training program will make you stronger on skis; to visualize new muscle fibers developing; and to visualize more muscle fibers exploding in powerful contractions during skiing! Use your mind and visualize!

For each of the following workouts adhere to these three guidelines:

1) Limit the recovery phase to thirty seconds.

2) Perform all sets to momentary muscular failure or failure of elegance, unless otherwise noted.

3) Refer to the Appendix for instructions on all movements and techniques.

Nordic Maniac Chest, Shoulders, and Triceps Workout

Dips: Three sets of as many reps as possible. Use a twenty-second recovery only.

Bench Presses: Use Envelope Technique.

High Pulls: Four sets of eight reps. Use Ku Bottom Form recovery.

Seated Dumbbell Front Raises: Two sets done with the Swan Medicine Technique®. Burn 'em!

Seated Dumbbell Side Lateral Raises: Three sets of twelve reps. Polish 'em up *now!*

Seated Presses: Two sets done with the Three-Stage Technique. Polish 'em *off* now!

Dumbbell Kickbacks: Four sets of eight reps for each arm, no recovery between arms.

Two-Bench Triceps: Two sets at one minute each. Pace yourself; I want the final fifteen seconds at tempo!

Plyometric Superset for Upper-Body Nordic Power:

1) Dumbbell Arm Swings for fifteen seconds.
2) Double Pole Plyos for fifteen seconds.
3) Recover for fifteen seconds.

Repeat two more times.

Nordic Maniac Lower-Body Workout

Seated Good Mornings: One set of ten reps. Keep a strong lower back.

Squats: Three sets of six reps. Establish the only core that counts.

Leg Curls: Three sets of six reps. Develops leg bicep strength.

Leg Extensions: Four sets of eight to ten reps. Develops connective-tissue health.

Gunther Hops: Two sets of sixteen reps. Focus on gluteal power!

Jump Squats: Three sets of ten reps. Keep the heart high and *power* in the legs!

Knee Tuck Jumps: Two sets of ten reps. Want leg speed?

Scissor Jumps: Two sets of eight reps for each leg.

Standing Calf Raises: Four sets of fifteen reps. Stay deep and strong.

Seated Calf Presses: Two sets done with Staccato Technique.

Nordic Maniac Back and Biceps and Ab Workout

Pull-Ups: Four sets of as many reps as possible. Use a twenty-second recovery only.

V-Handle Pull-Ups: Four sets of as many reps as possible. Use a twenty-second recovery only.

Seated Rows: Use Envelope Technique.

Bent Arm Dumbbell Pullovers: Four sets of ten reps with Ku Top or Bottom Form recovery—your choice!

Barbell Curls: Use Envelope Technique. You can also use a Low Pulley if desired.

Deadman Curls: Three sets of six reps for each arm.

Concentration Curls: Three sets of eight reps for each arm.

Superset for Three Times:

a) Wrist Curls for forty-five seconds.
b) Reverse Wrist Curls for thirty seconds.
c) Recover for thirty seconds.

Repeat!

Abdominal Workout

Tri-set the following for two to three circuits (tri-set meaning there are three different movements to be done per set, thus it is called tri-set):

1) Suspended Leg Raises for one minute.
2) Abdominal Crunches for one minute.
3) Abdominal Pulldowns or Ab Wheel for one minute.

CV Training

Minimum weekly times range from five hours, forty-five minutes to eleven hours, twelve minutes, so there's a lot of wholistic spice in this program. I suggest recreational fitness skiers stay at the low end and work up gradually, while the competitive monsters, who should be in pretty good shape by now, can start with seven weekly hours and increase one hour per week or as they feel appropriate. Be careful, however; Nordic Maniac is total training, and the effect upon the body is significant. It is better to start with low volumes, and finish at higher volumes.

Cruise Intervals

While on a Zone 1–2 workout, perform four to six intervals of two minutes each, with a full recovery between. During the intervals, focus on smooth, powerful mechanics. Bring your intervals to Zone 3 as soon as possible and finish at Zone 4. During the last thirty seconds of each interval increase the tempo. After each interval, go at Zone 1 until your heart rate drops down to Zone 2. Resume fluid form, then pop off another interval. Classic skiers should ski classic style during these intervals, while skate skiers should skate. If you do both, alternate weekly.

Pyramids

Perform a series of intervals in the following increments: one minute, two minutes, three minutes, four minutes, another at four minutes, then back down to three minutes, two minutes, and one minute. Begin the intervals at Zone 2, building to Zone 4 by the end of each one. Each interval should be a gradual acceleration. The recovery period after each one should equal the length of the preceding interval. For instance, after twenty minutes of going at Zone 1, then begin the pyramids by accelerating to high Zone 3 and hold that pace for one minute. Then recover for one minute by light effort. Then go hard for two minutes and recover for another two minutes. Repeat this sequence up and down the "pyramid." Classic skiers should ski classic style during these intervals, while skate skiers should skate. If you do both, alternate weekly.

Kinesthetic Training

The key is stabilization. Follow the Master Sheet for optimal injury prevention and ski performance. Do one hatha yoga class per week and get a massage or bodywork session at least three times during this cycle.

Meditation

Early-Morning Zazen Session. Wake up, relieve yourself, then assume the zazen posture. Sit for five minutes. Perform Kin Hin (walking meditation); it should be performed with hands in a "gassho mudra," or prayer hand, position. The meditation is designed to mindfully place each step with awareness and not to let the mind wander from the walking. It is best done in an environment where you are not likely to be interrupted in any way. The walk can be as short as one minute to as long as several minutes in duration. Sit for another five minutes. End the session and take mindfulness with you.

Beeper Guru Breath and Posture Assignment. Set your watch alarm to go off every hour. Upon the beep, take note of where your breath, posture, and mind are. Make adjustments in alignment. Note how often the Beeper Guru catches you in random thought, out of posture, or with the breath high and shallow instead of low and deep.

3 x 30 Assignment. This is taken from a Theravada Buddhist mindfulness exercise. At each mealtime (assume three sit-down meals per day) I want you to chew your first bite of food thirty times. During this chewing, feel the significance of the food being eaten. Appreciate the fact that you are not different from the food you eat and that one day, you too will be "eaten" by the universe. Use this time to honor and revere your food and "tell" the food that you will do your best to use its life-giving energy to refine yourself in order to help others.

Nutrition

Keep in mind the following six guidelines:

1) You simply will not survive Nordic Maniac if you do not eat according to the principles outlined in this book. You could get injured or suffer from overtraining if you have not gotten your nutritional act together by now. At this point, you are either on the path, or you've dropped off.

2) Use your active meditations and/or your recovery days to nourish yourself by attending to your training equipment and gear. This might mean waxing skis, getting new gear, shopping for good food and supplements, or getting race equipment dialed in. Remember our training principle: Be prepared! This is very important nutrition.

3) Make certain you are taking in a high-quality amino acid supplement consistently throughout the day. See Chapter 8 on Nutrition.

4) Also make certain you are taking in a high-quality vitamin/mineral supplement consistently throughout the day. See Chapter 8 on Nutrition.

5) If you'd like to experiment with a creatine load/maintain, now is the cycle to do so.

6) Sever all refined, junk, and fatty foods from your diet right now if you have not already done so. Remember, once the season gets here, you will not be able to make up for this vital preseason phase! How well you perform this winter depends on your actions now!

RESOURCES

Contact the following associations for qualified instruction in nordic ski technique.

Bill Koch Youth Ski League: P.O. Box 100, Park City, UT 84060; 801-649-9090.

Professional Ski Instructors of America (PSIA): 133 South Van Gordon Street, Suite 101, Lakewood, CO 80228; 303-987-9390; fax: 303-988-3005.

Magazines

Cross Country Skier: 1823 Fremont Ave. South, Minneapolis, MN 55403; 612-377-0312.

Skitrax: 2 Pardee Avenue, Suite 204, Toronto, ONT, Canada, M6K 3H5; 416-530-1350; fax: 416-530-4155.

Books

Cross-Country Skiing: A Complete Guide (Trailside Series), Brian Cazeneuve. 1995. $17.95. W.W. Norton & Company.

Good Glide: The Science of Ski Waxing, Leif Torgersen. 1985. $9.95. Human Kinetics Publishers.

Skating for Cross-Country Skiers, Audun Endestad and John Teaford. 1987. $15.95. Human Kinetics Publishers.

Videos

Reliable Racing Supply, Inc.: 800-223-4448; www.reliableracing.com; e-mail: nordic@reliableracing.com.

Video Action Sports, Inc.: 800-727-6689/805-543-4812; fax: 805-541-8544.

Equipment

Reliable Racing Supply, Inc. (see above).

Eagle River Nordic: P.O. Box 936, Eagle River, WI 54521; 800-423-9730.

New Moon Ski Shop: P.O. Box 591XC, Hayward, WI 54843; 715-634-8685.

Wholistic Fitness® Winter Performance Training Nordic Maniac Cycle Summation

---

Cycle's Dates: _____

Athlete's Name: _____

Please address each category as openly as possible.

STRENGTH TRAINING

1) Note your consistency during this discipline. How were your energy levels?

_____

_____

_____

_____

_____

2) What were your strengths? What were your weaknesses? Identify them and describe how you will deal with them this in-season.

_____

_____

_____

_____

3) The most important teaching of this strength-training discipline that I can use in my nordic ski performance is:

_____

_____

_____

_____

CV TRAINING

4) Did you have any standout reactions in this discipline? Were you able to do the volumes as prescribed?

_____

_____

_____

_____

5) Which dryland training activities did you do the most? How will this help you this season?

_____

_____

_____

_____

6) The most important teaching of this CV-training discipline that I can use in my nordic ski performance is:

_____

_____

_____

_____

_____

KINESTHETIC TRAINING

7) Did you have any standout reactions in this discipline?

_____

_____

_____

_____

_____

8) Comment on how the past fifteen weeks of intense study in this discipline has shifted your awareness compared to previous years.

_____

_____

_____

_____

_____

9) The most important teaching of this kinesthetic-training discipline that I can use in my nordic ski performance is:

_____

_____

_____

_____

_____

MEDITATION

10) What truth did you find in this cycle?

_____

_____

11) What are you suffering from the most?

_____

12) What are you doing to resolve this suffering?

_____

13) The most important teaching of this meditation discipline that I can use in my nordic ski performance is:

_____

NUTRITION

14) How did this cycle's workload affect you nutritionally?

_____

15) Describe exactly what you ate and drank yesterday and the manner in which you ate it. Note any cravings.

_____

_____

_____

_____

_____

16) What could you have done to better nourish yourself? Why didn't you? How will you make the adjustment over this in-season?

_____

_____

_____

_____

_____

17) Overall, what did you learn from your Nordic Maniac training cycle?

_____

_____

_____

_____

_____

23

Nordic Skiing:
Ski Touring

*"You don't get to decide how you're going to die, or when.
You can only decide how you're going to live. Now."*
—Joan Baez

THE RIGHT FIT

For the purposes of this book, ski touring contains several categories easily defined by the type of ski used. If your skiing fits into one of these categories, then the following training program is for you!

• *Backcountry touring or ski mountaineering.* The skier in this category uses a beefy, metal-edged ski not dissimilar to an alpine ski. The ski can have a big sidecut or very little. The former is good for telemark bums seeking the open glades and bowls while the latter is more apropos in a hut-to-hut situation. The boot/binding system is bombproof and designed for long, consecutive days of skiing in backcountry conditions, including couloir descents and long switchback ascents. Comfort and stability are key.

What's not to love? Wholistic Fitness student Scott Dupuis captures a moment's rest while on a backcountry ski workout near Santa Fe, New Mexico. Photo by the author.

• *Touring.* Touring skis are slightly longer and narrower than a backcountry touring ski but still have metal edges and a wide base, allowing self-made trails to be broken through virgin fields of snow. The added surface area of the touring ski offers better edge control as well as flotation in powder and multilayered crust snow.

• *Light touring.* Skis used in this category are lighter in weight than touring skis and narrower. Some have metal edges, others do not. The increased camber of these skis gives them a more sprightly feel, which results in good performance at the nordic center track. These skis can also handle snowmobile tracks or those made by other skiers but flounder in untracked powder.

The following program is to be engaged immediately after the Perfect Power phase recovery week. This program is appropriate for all recreational and elite-level cross-country skiers who use classic nordic form and usually ski in the backcountry, not at nordic centers.

This program does not cover specific backcountry and other off-track skiing technique but prepares the body, mind, and spirit for the pursuit of ski touring. Technique should be studied with a certified instructor or the guidance of an expert. Qualified instruction is available via the organizations, magazines, books, and videos listed in the resources section at the end of this chapter.

Now, let's get to training!

THE BACKCOUNTRY BOMBSHELL PROGRAM

The Backcountry Bombshell program is to be followed for five consecutive weeks. This phase produces muscular and cardiovascular fitness specific to nordic skiing. Appropriate transpersonal power development is also designed into the program.

Length of cycle: five weeks.
Frequency: seven-day cycle.
Next cycle: in season.
Primary goals: Refine all prior mental, physical, and spiritual fitness gained from previous training cycles into ski-touring conditioning.

Wholistic Fitness® Training Precepts

1) Be prepared.
2) Be on time.
3) Give 110 percent.

BACKCOUNTRY BOMBSHELL MASTER SHEET

All workouts are described in the next section, Wholistic Notes.

Mountain Hut Monday: Day One

Recovery day. No strength or CV training. All other disciplines are discretionary. Get bodywork/massage if possible.

P-tex Tuesday: Day Two

Strength training: Backcountry Bombshell upper-body workout.

CV training: None, or thirty to sixty minutes of a CV activity of your choice at Zones 1–2.

Kinesthetic training: Medium Form Flexibility before strength training.

Meditation: Beeper Guru breath and posture assignment.

Wasatch Wednesday: Day Three

Strength training: Backcountry Bombshell lower-body workout.

CV training: Thirty minutes of a CV activity of your choice at Zones 1–2.

Kinesthetic training: Medium Form Flexibility before strength training.

Meditation: Early-morning zazen practice.

Think Snow Thursday: Day Four

CV training: Run, hike, or cycle for one to two hours at Zones 1–2 with cruise intervals.

Kinesthetic training: Yoga class or Long Form Flexibility after CV training.

Meditation: Beeper Guru breath and posture assignment.

Holmenkollen Festival Friday: Day Five

CV training: None, or inline ski, inline skate, or roller ski for one to one and a half hours at Zones 1–2.

Kinesthetic training: If no yoga class was done on Thursday, do it today or do Long Form Flexibility after CV training.

Meditation: Active meditation for twenty minutes.

Sastrugi Saturday: Day Six

Strength training: EEE-GAD full-body workout.

CV training: Hike with a moderately loaded backpack for one to three hours at Zones 1–2.

Kinesthetic training: Discretionary; Also get or schedule bodywork (massage) for Sunday or Monday.

Meditation: 3 x 30 assignment; passive meditation for twenty minutes.

Sidecut Sunday: Day Seven

CV training: Run for one hour at Zones 1–2. Perform Minutes Are Forever workout.

Kinesthetic training: Discretionary. Also get bodywork or schedule it for Monday.

Meditation: Discretionary.

WHOLISTIC NOTES

This section provides the specific workouts prescribed in the Backcountry Bombshell Master Sheet.

Strength-Training Workouts

Not nearly as intense as the Nordic Maniac program for trackies, this strength program emphasizes a healthy degree of back training to prepare the spinal muscles for skiing with a backpack without postural fatigue.

For each of the following workouts adhere to these three guidelines:

1) Limit the recovery phase to thirty seconds.
2) Perform all sets to momentary muscular failure or failure of elegance, unless otherwise noted.
3) Refer to the Appendix for instructions on all movements and techniques.

Backcountry Bombshell Upper-Body Workout

Bench Presses: Use Envelope Technique.

Seated Rows: Use Envelope Technique.

Bent Arm Dumbbell Pullovers: Four sets of ten reps using Ku Top or Bottom Form recovery: your choice!

Dumbbell Seated Presses: Use Three-Stage Technique.

Dumbbell Side Lateral Raises: Three sets of twelve reps.

Barbell Curls: Four sets of fifteen reps.

Two-Bench Triceps: Two sets at one minute each. Pace yourself; I want the final fifteen seconds at tempo!

Plyometric Superset for Upper-Body Nordic Power:
1) Dumbbell Arm Swings for fifteen seconds.
2) Dumbbell Horizontal Swings for fifteen seconds.
3) Recover for fifteen seconds.
Repeat twice.

Superset for Two Times:
a) Wrist Curls for forty-five seconds.

b) Reverse Wrist Curls for thirty seconds.
c) Recover for thirty seconds.
Repeat!

Backcountry Bombshell Lower-Body Workout

Stiff Leg Deadlifts: Two sets of five reps. Develops a strong spine for ski touring.

Superset for Three Times:
a) Squats: Six.
b) Leg Extensions: Use Staccato Technique.

Superset for Three Times:
a) Leg Curls: Eight.
b) Split Jumps: Twelve each leg.

Gunther Hops: Two sets of sixteen reps. Focus on gluteal power!

Standing Calf Raises: Four sets of fifteen reps. Stay deep and strong.

Superset for Three Times:
a) Crunches for one minute.
b) Ab Wheel or Abdominal Pulldowns for one minute.

EEE-GAD Full-Body Workout

The name says it all. EEE-GAD comes in two versions, one for beginning students and another for more advanced students. The following is a hybrid of both. The EEE-GAD full-body workouts were finalized in 1986 and have been serving students well ever since. The real trick is to master the entire workout from start to finish with unwavering attention to posture and lifting tempo.

Pull-Ups: Two sets of however many you can do.

Front Lat Pulldowns: One set done with Staccato Technique; three sets of eight to ten reps.

Dumbbell Flat-Bench Flyes into Dumbbell Bench Presses: Flyes for ten reps to failure, then crank out high-frequency Dumbbell Bench Presses until you puke black blood. Do three sets.

Back Squats Superset with Leg Extensions: Do Squats for twelve reps to failure, then run over and perform Leg Extensions with Staccato Technique. Do two supersets.

Seated Dumbbell Presses: Two sets done with Three-Stage Technique. Commit to fluidity.

Two-Bench Triceps: Two sets of one minute each. See each rep in a "clean" top and bottom position. You should feel the contraction in the triceps up top. Bring chi to the triceps.

Barbell Curls: Three sets done with Shivaya Technique. Be beautiful; be elegant.

Abdominal Crunches Directly into Leg Raises: Three sets of one minute each. Really stay concentrated in the abs!

CV Training

Minimum weekly hours range from four and a half to twelve. The higher your skiing skill level and the more ambitious your winter touring plans, the higher those weekly hours should be! One of the most dangerous situations in the backcountry is a lack of fitness. If you are a track skier, the worst thing that can happen is losing a race. In the backcountry, it's losing your life!

Minutes Are Forever Workout

Run hard for one minute (at Zones 3–4), then do a recovery jog for one minute at Zone 1. Keep doing this until you throw up or ten minutes have gone by. Recover for ten minutes, then repeat. These intervals can be done on gradual uphills to increase lactate threshold, steep uphills to increase leg strength, and gradual downhills to improve stride rate.

Cruise Intervals

While on a Zone 1–2 workout, perform four to six intervals of two minutes each, with a full recovery between. During the intervals, focus on smooth, powerful mechanics. Bring your intervals to Zone 3 as soon as possible and finish at Zone 4. During the last thirty seconds of each interval increase the tempo. After each interval, go at Zone 1 until your heart rate drops down to Zone 2. Resume fluid form, then pop off another interval.

Kinesthetic Training

Stabilization is the key. Follow the Master Sheet for optimal injury prevention and ski performance. Take one hatha yoga class per week and get a massage or bodywork session at least twice during this cycle.

Meditation

Early-Morning Zazen Session. Wake up, relieve yourself, then assume the zazen posture. Sit for five minutes. Perform Kin Hin (walking meditation); it should be performed with hands in a "gassho mudra," or prayer hand, position. The meditation is designed to mindfully place each step with awareness and not to let the mind wander from the walking. It is best done in an environment where you are not likely to be interrupted in any way. The walk can be as short as one minute to as long as several minutes in duration. Sit for another five minutes. End the session and take mindfulness with you.

Beeper Guru Breath and Posture Assignment. Set your watch alarm to go off every hour. Upon the beep, take note of where your breath, posture, and mind are. Make adjustments in alignment. Note how often the Beeper Guru catches you in random thought, out of posture, or with the breath high and shallow instead of low and deep.

3 x 30 Assignment. This is taken from a Theravada Buddhist mindfulness exercise. At each mealtime (assume three sit-down meals per day) I want you to chew your first bite of food thirty times. During this chewing, feel the significance of the food being eaten. Appreciate the fact that you are not different from the food you eat and that one day, you too will be "eaten" by the universe. Use this time to honor and revere your food and "tell" the food that you will do your best to use its life-giving energy to refine yourself in order to help others.

Nutrition

Although ski tourers can afford to be a little more laid-back in their nutrition than track racers, you should still follow the nutritional guidelines outlined in this book and make certain to take a high-quality amino acid and vitamin/mineral supplement each day. If you are still carrying some unwanted body fat, this is the time to jettison it by keeping fat intake to 15 percent of total daily calories and following the Backcountry Bombshell Master Sheet to the letter! Remember, you want only functional body weight in the backcountry!

RESOURCES

Contact the following associations for qualified instruction in backcountry ski technique and winter travel.

Hurricane Island Outward Bound: P.O. Box 429, Rockland, ME 04841; 800-341-1744; fax: 207-594-9425.

National Outdoor Leadership School (NOLS): 288 Main Street, Dept. R, Lander, WY 82520; 307-332-6873; fax: 307-988-3005.

Contact the following association for qualified instruction in winter safety.

American Avalanche Institute: P.O. Box 308, Wilson, WY 83014; 307-733-3315.

Magazines

Back Country: 7065 Dover Way, Arvada, CO 80004; 303-424-5858.

Cross Country Skier: 1823 Fremont Ave. South, Minneapolis, MN 55403; 612-377-0312.

Outside: 400 Market Street, Santa Fe, NM 87501, 800-678-1131.

Books

The ABC's of Avalanche Safety, Edward R. LaChapelle. 1985. $6.95. Mountaineers Books.

Cold Comfort: Keeping Warm in the Outdoors, Glenn Randall. 1987. $10.95. Lyons & Burford Publishers.

Cross-Country Skiing: A Complete Guide (Trailside Series), Brian Cazeneuve. 1995. $17.95. W.W. Norton & Company.

Good Glide: The Science of Ski Waxing, Leif Torgersen. 1985. $9.95. Human Kinetics Publishers.

Wilderness Skiing and Winter Camping, Chris Townsend. 1993. $17.95. Ragged Mountain Press.

Videos

Reliable Racing Supply, Inc.: 800-223-4448; www.reliableracing.com; e-mail: nordic@reliableracing.com.

Video Action Sports, Inc.: 800-727-6689/805-543-4812; fax: 805-541-8544.

Equipment

Black Diamond Equipment, Ltd.: 2084 East 3900 South, Salt Lake City, UT 84214; 801-278-5533.

Eagle River Nordic: P.O. Box 936, Eagle River, WI 54521; 800-423-9730.

Fischer Skis: Geneva Road, Brewster, NY 10509; 800-525-0153.

New Moon Ski Shop: P.O. Box 591XC, Hayward, WI 54843; 715-634-8685.

Reliable Racing Supply, Inc. (see above).

Wholistic Fitness® Winter Performance Training
Backcountry Bombshell Cycle Summation

Cycle's Dates: _____

Athlete's Name: _____

Please address each category as openly as possible.

STRENGTH TRAINING

1) Note your consistency during this discipline. How were your energy levels?

_____

_____

_____

_____

_____

2) What were your strengths? What were your weaknesses? Identify them and describe how you will deal with them this in-season.

_____

_____

_____

_____

_____

3) The most important teaching of this strength-training discipline that I can use in my nordic ski performance is:

_____

_____

_____

_____

CV TRAINING

4) Did you have any standout reactions in this discipline? Were you able to do the volumes as prescribed?

_____

_____

_____

_____

_____

5) Which dryland training activities did you do the most? How will this help you this season?

_____

_____

_____

_____

_____

6) The most important teaching of this CV-training discipline that I can use in my nordic ski performance is:

_____

_____

_____

_____

_____

KINESTHETIC TRAINING

7) Did you have any standout reactions in this discipline?

_____

_____

_____

_____

8) Comment on how the past fifteen weeks of intense study in this discipline has shifted your awareness compared to previous years:

_____

_____

_____

_____

9) The more important teaching of this kinesthetic-training discipline that I can use in my nordic ski performance is:

_____

_____

_____

_____

MEDITATION

10) What truth did you find in this cycle?

_____

_____

_____

_____

11) What are you suffering from the most?

_____

_____

_____

_____

12) What are you doing to resolve this suffering?

_____

_____

_____

_____

13) The most important teaching of this meditation discipline that I can use in my nordic ski performance is:

_____

_____

_____

_____

_____

NUTRITION

14) How did this cycle's workload affect you nutritionally?

_____

_____

_____

_____

_____

15) Describe *exactly* what you ate and drank yesterday and the manner in which you ate it. Note any cravings.

_____

_____

_____

_____

_____

16) What could you have done better to nourish yourself? Why didn't you? How will you make the adjustment over this inseason?

_____

_____

_____

_____

_____

17) Overall, what did you learn from your Backcountry Bombshell training cycle?

_____

_____

_____

_____

_____

24

Polar Paddling

*"Through our skin and muscle and bone, we have to realize why
we don't come back to silence and the vastness of existence.
In the vastness of existence there are many sources of spring water."*
—Dainin Katagiri

SPLASHING ABOUT

Although I've trained paddle athletes to reach the podium at national levels, I approach most water sports from an academic and vicarious distance. As a child of the mountains, the non-frozen water element is the least known to me, though I absolutely adore it. I can think of fewer more memorable moments than those inspired near oceans, lakes, and rivers. Most of my childhood hours were spent splashing about to no discernible purpose in mountain creeks, ponds, and rivers. My wolf, Apache, and I would hang out for long mornings, immensely interested in studying a waterlogged leaf or a trout dancing among shadowy river stones. Delighted I was by the intricate details of riparian life, whose existence seemed to cause a calm excitedness within me. During spring runoff, I would take my inner tube and ride the crashing whitewater of the San Juan

Winter is a magical time of year to paddle.
Photo by Rick Donahue.

mountain rivers. Yet my swimming proficiency remains at the level of a rock. The water sports may be saving themselves for me, perhaps to surface at a time when the mountains have lost their hold on my soul.

MEET ERIC

I now introduce one of my star students, Eric Stiller. Eric is a water sports person—a good one. His unpublished manuscript, "Keep Australia on Your Left," is a must-read for us transcendentalist athletes who draw energy from reading literature written by those with courage enough to chase their dreams. Eric, who is the adventure sports program director at Chelsea Piers Sports Center in New York City, also owns and operates his own school of paddling, Manhattan Kayak Company in Montvale, New Jersey. It is my honor to have Mr. Stiller, a true Wholistic Fitness warrior, invite you into the world of polar paddling …

"Winter—or polar—paddling takes place during a magical time of year. Crowded summer haunts are now deserted, and are yours alone. It is clearer, crisper. As coldness returns, previously absent wildlife does also. This is the domain of the well-prepared paddler.

"It is a time when selection of equipment, partners, and conditions becomes more than an exercise in comfort and convenience. It is an issue of renewing your passport to participate in the first place. It is a matter of respect.

"All decisions should err on the side of safety. Choose a boat that fills you with absolute confidence. Capsizing is not an option. The same goes for your paddle and its spare. A well-fitted, fully functional spray cover is required, as are a paddle float, pump, signaling devices, drybag with food, extra clothing, communication device, compass, chart, headlamp, waterproof lighter, spare batteries, space blanket, energy bars, and a first-aid kit.

"Paddle with well-outfitted, competent partners. Good partners radically reduce risk, while bad or ill-equipped partners radically increase it. Always tell somebody where you are going and your anticipated return time. Bring reliable, fully charged, water-protected communication equipment.

"Paddling generates body heat. Winter generates a lot of cold air. Sweat and cold often add up to hypothermia. Therefore, proper clothing, especially external "skins" that shed water instantly, is mandatory. Use the layering philosophy that Steve puts forth in this book. Put an emphasis on vapor barriers—even plastic baggies will work for the feet. Fleece-lined neoprene socks and flexible neoprene gloves come next. The insulation layer is very important; follow the suggestions in this book. Nevertheless, the final shell layer is the most important in polar paddling. A Gore-tex drysuit with relief zippers and flaps is what I recommend. Make sure you have good seals at your ankles and wrists. Finally, you'll need a pair of well-fitted, waterproof shoes and possibly a set of sea mitts (sometimes known as pogies) to put over your paddles. These act as shrouds for your hands.

"The last piece of clothing is vital: your lifejacket. It must fit over your now-swollen physique. Make sure it has a couple of good-sized pockets to fit food, a knife, and signaling items that will be otherwise more difficult to reach. Winter paddling does not lend itself to extended lunch breaks. If you plan such breaks, bring a windproof layer, a dry hat, and gloves. A thermos with your favorite warm, nonalcoholic beverage or soup is fantastic. Drink plenty of water steadily throughout your excursion.

"Polar paddling is about knowing yourself, your area, the weather, and time constraints. Winter on the water in the dark is an alien environment for modern Homo sapiens. That is precisely why we choose to explore it!

"By following these suggestions and practicing Coach Ilg's Wholistic Fitness training programs, your body, mind, and spirit will be ready for an experience perhaps unequaled in all of winter sport. I wish you the best of transpersonal paddling in nature's most profound and beautiful season!"

—Eric Stiller

BIOMECHANICS

Since I did not cover paddling in any of my dryland training activities, let's take a moment and cover some of the fundamental movement patterns inherent to paddling.

Economical body position is critical to a paddler. Even a hasty kinesiological glance at flatwater kayak stroke mechanics reveals a formidable amount of athleticism. Torso stabilization and assistive musculature is continuously relied upon just to keep the craft in balance, let alone propel it! I specifically train my paddle athletes based on a four-stroke analysis: 1) the catch, 2) the pull, 3) the exit, 4) the pull.

The Catch: this phase begins with a horizontal blade position and ends with the blade submerged in the water. If our left blade is the submerged one, it got there thanks to anterior rotation of the thoracic vertebrae. That means oblique and erector spinae are at work as well as deep rotators of the back, especially the left side. The shoulders are also busy. While the rhomboids and pectoralis minor rotate the left shoulder girdle downward, the glenohumeral joint extends by the latissimus dorsi, teres major, and some sternal pectoralis. Of course, the forearm muscles are engaged mostly via isometric contraction, especially the digit flexors. This holds true for all four phases. Down below, the hamstring, hip and ankle are flexed, ready to extend for driving the hip backward. In this preparation posture, all these muscles are in an isometric contraction.

The Pull: Here the blade starts being fully submerged, passes through vertical where most of the force application and boat acceleration occurs, and ends when the blade is removed from the water. The

Photo by Jonathan Waterman.

pulling power is the result of a summation of muscular force being generated from both large and small muscles of the legs, back, and shoulders. The most exciting part is the force applied by the torso rotators, making the obliques (internal and external) and to a smaller degree, the serratus anterior, the paddlers' best friends.

The Exit: This is the phase in which the blade is taken out of the water. The scapula has to laterally rotate to do this and that means the trapezius and serratus anterior springs into action. Helping this action are the medial deltoid, supraspinatus, infraspinatus and teres minor to provide abduction and lateral rotation of the arm. The influence of the triceps depends to a degree on the amount of elbow extension favored by the paddlers' Catch mechanics.

The Recovery: As the Exit Phase ends, the paddle is held horizontally, thus establishing the Recovery. This phase ends as the athlete prepares to make the next Catch on the right side. This is the gliding phase for the craft and offers a respite for

the paddler, however fleeting it may seem! Often, the characteristic pause which identifies this phase lasts less than a second! Since the body position is held upright in an anticipatory posture, there are no dramatic biomechanical changes occuring during this phase that would make it stand apart from the Catch Phase.

THE WICKED BLADE PROGRAM

The following program is to be engaged immediately after the Perfect Power phase recovery week. This program is appropriate for all recreational and competitive paddlers whose love of their sport keeps them paddling throughout the winter.

This program does not cover specific paddling techniques but prepares the body, mind, and spirit for the pursuit of polar paddling. Specific paddling technique should be studied with a certified instructor or the guidance of an expert. Qualified instruction is available via the resource section near the end of this chapter.

Now, let's get to training!

The Wicked Blade program is to be followed for five consecutive weeks. This phase produces muscular and cardiovascular fitness specific to paddling. Appropriate transpersonal power development is also designed into the program.

Length of cycle: five weeks.
Frequency: seven-day cycle.
Next cycle: in season.

Primary goals: refine all prior mental, physical, and spiritual fitness gained from previous training cycles into paddle-specific conditioning.

Wholistic Fitness® Training Precepts

1) Be prepared.
2) Be on time.
3) Give 110 percent.

WICKED BLADE MASTER SHEET

All workouts are described in the next section, Wholistic Notes.

Get-a-Massage Monday: Day One

Recovery day. No strength or CV training (or Zone 1 for up to one hour of CV). All other disciplines are discretionary.

High-Speed Tuesday: Day Two

CV training: One-and-a-quarter hour paddle with two sets of 15 x 15's with ten RI.

Kinesthetic training: Medium Form before and after CV training.

Meditation: Make your CV workout your meditation. Focus on technique during intervals.

Wicked-Blade Wednesday: Day Three

Strength training: Wicked Blade upper-body workout.

CV training: None, or cycle, run, use an indoor rowing apparatus, or inline skate for one hour after strength training.

Kinesthetic training: Medium Form done fluidly after both strength and CV training.

Meditation: Prepare one meal with reverence and mindfulness as your active meditation.

Jump-Start Thursday: Day Four

CV training: Paddle indoors or out for one and a half hours. Do the first hour at Zones 1–2. If you are stuck indoors, you may spend up to forty-five minutes of the first hour doing a nonrowing or non-paddling CV activity. Start the second hour with six Jump Start Drills.

Kinesthetic training: Medium Form after CV training.

Meditation: Make your CV workout your meditation. Focus on technique during Jump Starts.

Fast-Twitch Friday: Day Five

Strength training: Wicked Blade lower-body workout.

CV training: None, or cycle or use the row machine for 30 minutes at Zones 1–2 after strength training.

Kinesthetic training: Medium Form after CV training.

Meditation: Early-morning zazen practice.

Winter Warrior Weekend: Days Six and Seven

Saturday: Get out and paddle! If you can't paddle, then cycle, run, and/or inline skate for one and a half to two hours. Keep the first hour within Zone 2, then increase your intensity to low Zone 3 for the majority of the second hour. Do a good cool down.

Sunday: Repeat Saturday at same volume but with lower intensity. Stay within Zone 2 for the entire workout. If you can't paddle, cross-train with an alternate CV activity from Saturday.

Both days: Prioritize kinesthetic training. Optimal training would include a yoga class on one or both days. If not, perform both Short and Medium Forms on both days. And on one of these days perform a pre-event meditation. On the other day do the Beeper Guru breath and posture assignment.

WHOLISTIC NOTES

This section provides the specific workouts prescribed in the Wicked Blade Master Sheet.

Strength-Training Workouts

The Wicked Blade upper-body workout is one of the most difficult in this book, so be prepared. It involves high volume coupled with high intensity. Note that we are only strength training each body part once per week in order to allot more time for cardiovascular training. Use your gym time to visualize how this strength-training program will make you stronger and smoother in the boat; to visualize new muscle fibers; and to visualize more muscle fibers ex-

ploding in powerful contractions! Use your mind and visualize!

For each of the following workouts adhere to these three guidelines:

1) Limit the recovery phase to thirty seconds.
2) Perform all sets to momentary muscular failure or failure of elegance, unless otherwise noted.
3) Refer to the Appendix for instructions on all movements and techniques.

Wicked Blade Upper-Body Workout

Dips: Three sets of as many as you can do. Use a twenty-second recovery only.

Standing Cable Flyes: Three sets of fifteen reps. Be as smooth as a placid bay at midnight.

Hang Cleans: Three sets of six reps. Use big weight and big full-body speed!

High Pulls: Two sets of ten reps using Ku Bottom Form recovery. Blast those traps!

Repetition Jerks: Two sets of eight reps. Fast-twitch shoulders—go!

Seated Dumbbell Front Raises: Two done with Swan Medicine Technique. Burn 'em!

Seated Dumbbell Side Lateral Raises: Two sets of twelve reps. Polish 'em up *now!*

Seated Presses: Two sets done with Three-Stage Technique. Polish 'em *off* now!

Barbell Curls: Four sets of fifteen reps. This is biceptual burn time—you gotta love it!

Dumbbell Kickbacks: Two sets of eight reps for each arm, no recovery between arms, just a prefatigue for the next exercise.

Two-Bench Triceps: Two sets at one minute. Pace yourself; I want the final fifteen seconds at tempo!

Superset for Three Times:
   a) Wrist Curls for forty-five seconds.
   b) Reverse Wrist Curls for thirty seconds.
   c) Recover for thirty seconds.
Repeat!

Wicked Blade Lower-Body Workout

Plyometric Superset for Wicked Blading Power:
   1) Dumbbell Horizontal Swings for fifteen seconds.
   2) Double Pole Plyos for fifteen seconds.
   3) Recover for fifteen seconds.
Repeat three more times.

Seated Good Mornings: One set of ten reps. Keep a strong lower back.

Superset for Three Times:
   a) Back Squats: Ten.
   b) Leg Presses: One minute. Use a narrow foot stance.

Leg Curls: Three sets of eight reps. Develops leg bicep strength.
   Leg Extensions: Two sets done with Staccato Technique.
   Jump Squats: Three sets of forty-five seconds. Keep the heart high and power in the legs!
   Standing Calf Raises: Four sets of fifteen reps. Stay deep and strong.

Abdominal Workout

Tri-set the following for two to three circuits:
   1) Suspended Leg Raises for one minute.
   2) Abdominal Crunches for minute.
   3) Abdominal Pulldowns or Ab Wheel for one minute.

CV Training

Minimum weekly times range from five hours, forty-five minutes to eight hours, fifteen minutes, so there's a lot of wholistic spice in this program. Recreational paddlers should stay at the low end, while competitive or advanced paddlers should work at the top of the CV range. Be careful, however; Wicked Blade is total training, and the effect upon the body is significant. It is better to start with low volumes and finish at higher volumes.

15x15's

Keeping your stroke rate high, go hard (Zone 4) for fifteen seconds. Recovery paddle for another fifteen seconds. Repeat this sequence for five minutes. Recover while you easy paddle for another ten minutes. Then repeat. This workout increases your aerobic capacity, stride rate, recovery ability, and ability to respond to surges. It can also be done using in indoor row machine.

Jump Start Drills

In your boat (or on an indoor row machine) hold a stall. Then perform four starts, beginning with a twenty-second sprint and increasing each subsequent sprint by five seconds. Make a full recovery between jumps. Finish the workout with eight sprints of no more than ten seconds, with full recovery between them. All sprints should be in Zones 4 to 5.

Kinesthetic Training

Stabilization is the key. Follow the Master Sheet without flaw for optimal injury prevention and paddling performance. Take at least one hatha yoga class per week and get a massage or bodywork session at least three times during this cycle.

Meditation

Early-Morning Zazen Session. Wake up, relieve yourself, then assume the zazen posture. Sit for five minutes. Perform Kin Hin (walking meditation); it should be performed with hands in a "gassho mudra," or prayer hand, position. The meditation is designed to mindfully place each step with awareness and not to let the mind wander from the walking. It is best done in an environment where you are not likely to be interrupted in any way. The walk can be as short as one minute to as long as several minutes in duration. Sit for another five minutes. End the session and take mindfulness with you.

Beeper Guru Breath and Posture Assignment. Set your watch alarm to go off every hour. Upon the beep, take note of where your breath, posture, and mind are. Make adjustments in alignment. Note how often the Beeper Guru catches you in random thought, out of posture, or with the breath high and shallow instead of low and deep.

Wholistic Fitness®
Pre-Event Meditation

Assume zazen posture;
perform ten cleansing breaths;
perform ten filling breaths.
Recite the following:

As I release my breath, I release my body.

As I release my breath, I let go of any physical, mental, or emotional tensions.

Relaxing into my breath, I realize no separation between myself and the world around me. Nor am I separate from the easy or difficult circumstances in my life. They are all me. I am all them. And it's all appropriate.

As I breathe, I realize that Joy is my natural state.

As long as I breathe, I know that nothing can interfere with this Joy.

Upon my inbreath, I sense a rush of beautiful, comfortable energy. This is my Divine Source. I allow this energy to flow into and out from my body. Relaxing ... feeling empty ...

When I relax, I perform better. When I am empty, I perform better. I will use my breath in my upcoming event in order to relax. In order to empty. I will surrender into the Universe. I trust completely that the Universe will power me into my best effort. Everything that I will go through during my event, will be precisely what I need to learn most.

I can already sense how powerfully I will compete because I will have the Universe charging through my emptiness ... all I need to do is breathe and relax into my effort.

As long as I breathe, my performance will be an elegant and strong expression of the Universe.

Recite three times. Go into a visualization of your event for three to five minutes; perform five cleansing breaths; perform five filling breaths; end the session.

Nutrition

Keep in mind the following six guidelines:

1) You simply will not survive Wicked Blade if you do not eat according to the principles outlined in this book. You could get injured or suffer from overtraining if you have not gotten your nutritional act together by now. At this point, you are either on the path, or you've dropped off.

2) Use your recovery days to nourish yourself by attending to your training equipment and gear. This might mean attending to your craft, getting new gear, shopping for good food and supplements, or getting race equipment dialed in. Remember our training principle: Be prepared! This is very important nutrition.

3) Take a high-quality amino acid supplement consistently throughout the day.

4) Make certain you are taking in a high-quality vitamin/mineral supplement consistently throughout the day. See Chapter 8 on Nutrition.

5) If you'd like to experiment with a creatine load/maintain, now is the cycle to do so.

6) Sever all refined, junk, and fatty foods from your diet right now if you have not already done so. Remember, once the season gets here, you will not be able to make up for this vital preseason phase! How well you perform this winter depends on your actions now!

RESOURCES

Contact the following associations for qualified instruction in winter paddling.

American Canoe Association (ACA): 7432 Alban Station Blvd., Suite B-226, Springfield, VA 22150-2311; 703-451-0141; fax: 703-451-2245; e-mail: ACADIRECT@aol.com.

Eric Stiller/Manhattan Kayak Company: c/o Chelsea Piers Sports Center, 23rd Street & the Hudson River, Pier 60, New York, NY 10011; 212-336-6068.

Trade Association of Sea Kayaking (TASK): 12455 North Wauwatosa Rd., Mequon, WI 52097; 414-242-5228.

Magazines

Canoe & Kayak: 10526 NE 68th, Suite 3, Kirkland, WA 98033; 425-827-6363.

Paddler: P.O. Box 775450, Steamboat Springs, CO 80477; 970-878-1450.

Sea Kayaker: 7001 Seaview Ave. NW, Suite 135, Seattle, WA 98117-6059; 206-789-1326.

Books

The Complete Book of Sea Kayaking, Derek Hutchinson. New Edition 1995. $19.95. Globe Pequot Press.

The Essential Sea Kayaker, David Seidman. 1997. $12.95. Ragged Mountain Press.

Whitewater and Sea Kayaking, Kent Ford. 1995. $14.95. Human Kinetics Publishers.

Video

Performance Sea Kayaking. Distributed by Performance Video, Durango, Colorado; 970-259-1361.

Paddle Gear

Kokatat: 5350 Ericson Way, Arcata, CA 95521; 800-225-9749; www.kokatat.com.

Stohlquist Waterwear: 800-535-3565; www.stohlquistwaterwear.com.

Wholistic Fitness® Winter Performance Training Wicked Blade Cycle Summation

---

Cycle's Dates: _____

Athlete's Name: _____

Please address each category as openly as possible.

STRENGTH TRAINING

1) Note your consistency during this discipline. How were your energy levels?

_____

_____

_____

_____

2) What were your strengths? What were your weaknesses? Identify them and describe how you will deal with them this in-season.

_____

_____

_____

_____

_____

3) The most important teaching of this strength-training discipline that I can use in my paddling performance is:

_____

_____

_____

_____

_____

CV TRAINING

4) Did you have any standout reactions in this discipline? Were you able to do the volumes as prescribed?

_____

_____

_____

_____

_____

5) Which dryland training activities did you do the most? How will this help you this season?

_____

_____

_____

_____

_____

6) The most important teaching of this CV-training discipline that I can use in my paddling performance is:

_____

_____

_____

_____

_____

KINESTHETIC TRAINING

7) Did you have any standout reactions in this discipline?

_____

_____

_____

_____

_____

8) Comment on how the past fifteen weeks of intense study in this discipline has shifted your awareness compared to previous years.

_____

_____

_____

_____

_____

9) The most important teaching of this kinesthetic-training discipline that I can use in my paddling performance is:

_____

_____

_____

_____

_____

MEDITATION

10) What truth did you find in this cycle?

_____

_____

_____

_____

_____

11) What are you suffering from the most?

_____

_____

_____

_____

_____

12) What are you doing to resolve this suffering?

_____

_____

_____

_____

_____

13) The most important teaching of this meditation discipline that I can use in my paddling performance is:

_____

_____

_____

_____

_____

NUTRITION

14) How did this cycle's workload affect you nutritionally?

_____

_____

_____

_____

_____

15) Describe *exactly* what you ate and drank yesterday and the manner in which you ate it. Note any cravings.

_____

_____

_____

_____

_____

16) What could you have done to better nourish yourself? Why didn't you? How will you make the adjustment over this in-season?

_____

_____

_____

_____

_____

17) Overall, what did you learn from your Wicked Blade training cycle?

_____

_____

_____

_____

_____

25

Sport Snowshoeing

"Our deepest fears are like dragons guarding our deepest treasures."
—Rilke

SPORTSTERS ONLY

Since this is a performance-oriented book, only sport snowshoeing is considered. Sport snowshoeing is, as the name implies, snowshoeing performed primarily for fitness, be it off-track noncompetitive or on tracked or marked areas for racing. I have elected not to design disparate training programs for the pure backcountry shoer, for two reasons: 1) The structural, biomechanical, and physiological differences between a backcountry shoer and fitness shoer are not great enough to warrant disparate training plans. 2) The number of backcountry shoers pales in comparison to that of fitness snowshoers, as most serious winter backcountry athletes use skis, not shoes, for their exploits. Backcountry shoers should use the following program, but train at the lower end of the prescribed exercise volumes.

The following clarifies the distinction between backcountry and fitness shoers:

• *Backcountry shoer.* The shoer in this category uses a larger snowshoe, with dimensions in the nine-inch by twenty-nine-inch (width by length) range. These shoes weigh around five pounds per pair, with more expensive models weighing slightly less. The binding systems on a backcountry or mountaineering snowshoe expand enough to fit around winter boots. The primary terrain of the backcountry shoer is off-track wilderness, often on steep terrain where ski touring is no longer efficient. Many backcountry ski tourers and mountaineers pack snowshoes for use in such extreme terrain. A rear heel cleat is strongly suggested for backcountry snowshoes. The backcountry shoer never runs; his or her usual mode of travel is walking through deep or crusted snow.

• *Fitness shoer.* This type of shoer can often be found flitting about on snow-covered roads or trails like a winter bird full of energy. The snowshoes used rarely weigh more than three pounds per pair, and are often closer to two pounds. The frame size has been knocked down also, compared to backcountry shoes. In fact, for most snowshoe races the dimensions of the shoe can be no larger than eight inches by twenty-two inches. Fitness shoes often have a sleek, tapered, or otherwise ergonomic frame shape to reduce drag and heighten flotation qualities. These smaller shoes can still manage off-track conditions quite well, and many snowshoe races incorporate at least some off-track powder sections. Fitness shoers do it all: walking, hiking, or running.

THE BENEFITS OF SPORT SNOWSHOEING

A sport does not hang around for six thousand years for no reason. Snowshoeing has had a rich and vital significance in our history. Using snowshoes measuring more than seven feet in length, humans were able to successfully inhabit northern continents. According to the Atlas Snowshoe website (www.atlasworld.com), by about 1900, snowshoeing had successfully completed its transition from a mode of transportation to sport.

> Not only did friends and families take to the woods, but large sporting organizations were formed to advance and celebrate the sport. Some legendary snowshoeing clubs of Canada's Quebec province had more than 200 members who wore flamboyant costumes on their outings. Snowshoe clubs often had their own drum and bugle corps, flags and banners, officers, scouts, and even mascots. Beyond arranging racing meets, these clubs organized purely social outings where members would gather for an evening, and snowshoe by moonlight to an outlying inn or tavern.

Today's latest winter rage is hardly something new! The sport's attractions are obvious from a physical fitness perspective: Snowshoeing builds endurance levels and strengthens lower-body musculature, especially the quadriceps. Climbing in snowshoes brings the hip flexors and extensors into play and often spikes the heart rate commensurately. According to Tubbs Snowshoe (800-882-2748): "Snowshoeing has been estimated to use 45% more energy than at a walking pace. In a packed trail condition, calories burned per hour approximate 450–550. Going uphill in unpacked snow conditions easily burns 1,000 calories per hour."

The learning curve on snowshoes takes all of about fifty meters. The kinesiology of snowshoeing is simply an enhanced version of running. Snowshoeing is an excellent form of rehabilitation for people recovering from lower-body joint injuries; there is little impact due to the snow's cushioning effect on the stride. One is, after all, walking on water. If used as physical rehabilitation, walking or hiking—not running—is suggested. The higher the intensity, the higher the concussion on the joints, even in such a low-impact sport as snowshoeing.

Snowshoeing's most meaningful benefits, however, may lie in its ethereal component. From a logical standpoint, running around on snowshoes through cold conditions may not sound very fun. Do it, however, and a definite magic arises that cannot be deciphered by the intellect. Each snowshoe session seems to hold spiritually evocative elements. At times when I am out snowshoeing, surrounded by Mother Earth adorned in her splendid winter plumage, the magnificence of mere breath and being seems to me beyond normal conception. Transcendent experiences come easily with each floating footfall awash in a wave of white beneath me. Or perhaps it is the hypnotic rhythm and tempo of the sport that lulls the analytical mind and releases natural flow and joy. If others share a similar experience from this simple, beautiful sport, is it any wonder why sport snowshoeing calls to us?

Each snowshoe session seems to hold spiritually evocative elements. The author at Santa Fe Ski Basin, New Mexico. Photo by Marc Romanelli.

TO POLE OR NOT TO POLE

Many people feel that using ski or backcountry poles during fitness snowshoeing contributes to better balance and stability. I have not found this true. I feel that poles subtract from the development of true balance and stability. Thus, I do not coach my snowshoers to use poles for racing. At the elite level of competitive snowshoeing, few athletes use poles. However, having said that, there are circumstances in which poles are appropriate. In backcountry situations where a snowshoer is carrying a pack during long, fatiguing ascents, poles lend stability to the weighted climbing stride in variable terrain. And for fitness shoers whose goals are overall body toning and conditioning, poles help develop arm, shoulder, and back muscles while increasing overall caloric expenditure.

When running moderate climbs, press more weight onto the front cleat for traction and accentuate arm drive. The author nearing the summit of Tesuque Peak, New Mexico. Photo by Scott Dupuis.

SELECTING SNOWSHOES

Your goal when selecting snowshoes should be to get the smallest, most comfortable shoe that will satisfy your needs. Also keep in mind the following key qualities during the selection process:

1. Flotation. Created by the snowshoe's decking, the main fabric or material found between the frame of a snowshoe, flotation keeps the surface area of the shoe from sinking into the snow. Be aware that some decking is more efficient than others. Traditional snowshoes use a webbed or laced system of rawhide, which is not as efficient as the solid deck of more modern snowshoes.

2. Traction. Snowshoes usually have some type of traction device. Most are sold with a cleat, though some manufacturers provide them only as an accessory (you will want to clarify this when buying). Cleats will quickly become invaluable to you. They offer traction on icy or steep terrain and allow you to maneuver with confidence in a range of conditions.

3. Harness and binding. This is a critical area that connects your foot to the snowshoe itself. Look for comfort and durability. To check durability, inspect the materials and craftsmanship. Look for strong materials that will stand up to a lot of abuse.

SNOWSHOE TRAINING TECHNIQUES

If you plan on racing or getting the most fitness out of your snowshoeing, you'll use three primary techniques: climbing, descending, and traversing.

Climbing

On moderate climbs, while running or walking, shift your weight forward, putting more pressure onto the front cleat for traction. On steep climbs, kick the front cleat into the snow like a mountaineer cramponing up steep snow or ice. Also accentuate arm drive.

Descending

Think tail to tip. Press the tail of the shoe into the slope and roll forward as your femur passes under the hip. Try not to compact the hip too much if you're running. Heighten the knee lift to clear the

Dance of the Snow Serpent

Our story takes place on March 2, 1996, at the World Mountain
Snowshoe Championships near Twin Lakes, Colorado.

The dimming of my day began as a wind-whipped sun struggled over the Mosquito Range. When I speak of dimming, I speak of psychological gloom, for physically the day was radiant. By 8 A.M., a large group of snowshoe racers huddled around Race Director Bill Perkins. Tethered to a cell phone, Bill was speaking to the leader of the summit aid station crew. These experienced mountaineers were supposed to be atop our turn-around pylon, the 14,433-foot summit of Mount Elbert. They lay instead like sardines in their tent at timberline. Two-thousand feet remained between them and the cap of the mighty peak. They wouldn't go up. Nor would the racers. Too much wind.

"I'm a two-time finisher of this race." As Bill began his prerace speech, his pensive expression was evident. "And I now must enforce a decision that's breaking my heart. We can't race to the summit. Our primary responsibility in this race is safety. Based on the summit crew's opinion, you'd die up there racing to the summit. We'll use the alternate course, which is longer but stays below timberline. See you all on the start line in half an hour and good luck."

That was that. My year-long preparation for racing to the top of Colorado's highest peak on snowshoes was wiped away in a flicker of a moment. Like a Presta tire valve gone bad, my race psychology deflated. Suddenly, the skittish charm of suffering for four hours through deep snow was no longer appealing.

Mere minutes remained before the start of one of the biggest races of my life, and I was psychologically flatter than a cheese omelet at high noon. This loss of psyche was unexplored spiritual territory. Hauling myself to the start line, I wondered if I had enough psyche to complete—let alone race—the grueling eighteen miles of high-altitude, world-class singletrack. I had come face to face with a big ole nasty dragon, lickin' his chops and ready to chew me up and spit me out. It would've been so easy not to toe that start line.

So I did what I teach my students to do when they meet their dragons:

I returned to my breath and posture. I began paying attention to the moment. As the start gun fractured the morning air, I began to run. My immediate goal? Nothing more glamorous than to attend to my running. Let futurity shift for itself. The universe had arranged another great opportunity to practice a principle that I preach: Remain present with what is happening instead of wasting energy on what you'd prefer to have happen.

Two hours later ... the wind was gentle, almost balmy. I've already been to timberline, the substitute turnaround point. On my snowshoes, I was skiing, lunging, and leaping down a powdery flank of Mount Elbert. The track through the fir trees was sinuous, as though left by an inebriated snow serpent. Far below, the thin brilliance of the Arkansas River headwaters cloaked in winter apparel helped sustain my pace. Ahead of me were twenty racers. Behind me, fifty more. As one endless mile bled slowly into the next, my fight for the top twenty began. Endurance athletes willingly place themselves into a world where security is fleeting. As the finish line draws near, our performance exists, as Irving Townsend said, "within a fragile circle, easily and often breached. Unable to accept its awful gaps, we still would live no other way. We cherish memory as the only certain immortality, never fully understanding the necessary plan."

At the finish line, Mount Elbert seemed to smile without disdain upon my blistered, beaten body. The summit would have to wait for another day. And wait, I'm sure, it would. Today however, I met my dragon. And not only did I calm him, I took the sucker for a run through the deep, seductive snow.

Paceline Technique: Mike Longmire has been breaking trail up a long section of "Heart Rate Hill" near Placitas, New Mexico.

Descending: When descending at speed, think tail to tip. Press the tail of the shoe into the slope. Advanced shoers can actually ski or glide as they ride the tail plant. The author training at Santa Fe Ski Basin, New Mexico. Photo by Scott Dupuis.

As Mike pulls to the side, Kevin Beshlian assumes the pulling position. This rotating paceline technique is continued for the duration of the workout.

cleats from snow and draw the heart center backward to lift your spine away from the hips. Advanced shoers can actually ski or glide as they ride the tail plant. Other advanced descending techniques include bounding and leaping.

Traversing

If your snowshoes do not have a rear heel cleat, you may notice that they "swim" as the tail pivots downslope. To compensate, evert your foot position toward the uphill if you're climbing. On downhills, however, it's always better to point the cleats straight down the slope and "stomp" the shoe for utmost traction.

BREAKING TRAIL

Use paceline techniques such as in road cycling: Run, hike, walk, or crawl (depending upon the steepness of the terrain and amount of powder) in a single line behind the leader, being careful not to "clip" the tails of the leader's shoes. The second person should step in such a way as to break down or collapse the little bridges of snow left between the leader's tracks. The leader, when fatigued to the point where his or her pace slows, signals for the second to take over by simply pulling off to the side. The leader than becomes the last person in line, and the process is repeated sequentially. My training buddies and I get to the point where the intensity and speed is so great that we each just collapse into the snow at the end of a pull. When we step back in at the end of the line, the broken trail is like a wonderful gift.

Each of the above techniques require subtle art. It is a joy to discover the nuances and then feel them radiate through your snowshoe performance. The following program maximizes fitness for each of these techniques.

THE SPORTIN', SNORTIN' 'SHOEING PROGRAM

The following program is to be engaged immediately after the Perfect Power phase recovery week. This program is appropriate for all recreational and competitive snowshoers. It is a real podium-topper for serious snowshoe racers and has consistently produced personal records from my students who have lived its teachings.

This program does not cover specific snowshoeing techniques but prepares the body, mind, and spirit for the pursuit of snowshoeing. Specific snowshoe technique should be studied under the guidance of an expert. The resources section that concludes this chapter lists sources of information and inspiration to deepen your enjoyment of this fantastic winter sport.

Now, let's get to training!

The Sportin', Snortin' 'Shoeing program is to be followed for five consecutive weeks. This phase produces muscular and cardiovascular fitness specific to snowshoe racing. Appropriate transpersonal power development is also designed into the program.

Length of cycle: five weeks.
Frequency: seven-day cycle.
Next cycle: in season.
Primary goals: refine all prior mental, physical, and spiritual fitness gained from previous training cycles into snowshoe conditioning.

Wholistic Fitness® Training Precepts

1) Be prepared.
2) Be on time.
3) Give 110 percent.

SPORTIN', SNORTIN' 'SHOEING MASTER SHEET

All workouts are described in the next section, Wholistic Notes.

Rest-the-Muscles Monday: Day One

Recovery day. No strength or CV training.
  All other disciplines are discretionary.
  Get bodywork/massage if possible.

On-Track Tuesday: Day Two

Strength training: Sportin', Snortin' 'Shoeing upper-body workout.

CV training: None, or thirty to sixty minutes of a CV activity of your choice at Zones 1–2.

Kinesthetic training: Medium Form Flexibility before strength training.

Meditation: Beeper Guru breath and posture assignment.

What-a-Workout Wednesday: Day Three

Strength training: Sportin', Snortin' 'Shoeing lower-body workout.

CV training: Thirty minutes of a CV activity of your choice at Zones 1–2.

Kinesthetic training: Medium Form Flexibility before strength training.

Meditation: Early-morning zazen practice.

Thigh Burn Thursday: Day Four

CV training: Run sixty to ninety minutes at Zones 1–2 with cruise intervals.

Kinesthetic training: Yoga class or Long Form Flexibility after CV training.

Meditation: Beeper Guru breath and posture assignment.

Fit Friday: Day Five

CV training: Pole bounding with hill intervals using 15 x 15's workout for one hour at Zones 1–2. If you do not live in an area with hills, perform speed enduro intervals.

Kinesthetic training: If no yoga class was done Thursday, do it today or Long Form Flexibility after CV training.

Meditation: Active meditation for twenty minutes.

So Sorry Saturday: Day Six

Strength training: IWT-IWCT workout (sorry about this, but it's got to be done!)

CV training: Hike with a moderately loaded backpack for one to three hours at Zones 1–2.

Kinesthetic training: Discretionary. Also get or schedule bodywork (massage) for Sunday or Monday.

Meditation: 3 x 30 assignment; passive meditation for twenty minutes.

Something Else Sunday: Day Seven

CV training: Pick a favorite nonrunning or nonhiking CV activity and do it for one to two and a half hours hours at Zones 1–2.

Kinesthetic training: Discretionary. Also get bodywork or schedule it for Monday.

Meditation: Discretionary.

WHOLISTIC NOTES

This section provides the specific workouts prescribed in the Sportin', Snortin' 'Shoeing Master Sheet.

Strength-Training Workouts

This strength program promises to deliver a state of upper-body muscular endurance that is immune to postural fatigue and that will impart driving power to the legs while maximizing stride rate.

For each of the following workouts adhere to these three guidelines:

1) Limit the recovery phase to thirty seconds.
2) Perform all sets to momentary muscular failure or failure of elegance, unless otherwise noted.
3) Refer to the Appendix for instructions on all movements and techniques.

Sportin', Snortin' 'Shoeing Upper-Body Workout

Bent Arm Dumbbell Pullovers: Four sets of ten reps. Use Ku Bottom Form recovery. You think this is stretching your rib cage? Wait until your first 'shoe race! Expand that diaphragm!

Bench Presses: Use Envelope Technique.

Seated Rows: Use Envelope Technique.

Seated Dumbbell Presses: Use Three-Stage Technique.

Repetition Jerks: Three sets of six reps. Helps neural development for speed; remember, arms drive the legs!

Barbell Curls: Four sets of fifteen reps.

Two-Bench Triceps: Two sets of one minute each. Pace yourself; I want the final fifteen seconds at tempo!

Plyometric Superset for Explosive Snowshoeing Power:

1) Dumbbell Arm Swings for fifteen seconds.

2) Dumbbell Horizontal Swings for fifteen seconds.
3) Recover fifteen seconds.

Repeat twice.

Sportin', Snortin' 'Shoeing Lower-Body Workout

Stiff Leg Deadlifts: Two sets of five reps. A strong spine equals fast legs.

Superset for Three Times:

a) Squats: Six. These are the core of all sport performance.
b) Leg Extensions: Use Staccato Technique.

Superset for Three Times:

a) Leg Curls: Eight. Develops balanced power.
b) Split Jumps: Twelve for each leg. Thigh drive! No, make that thigh overdrive!

Superset for Three Times:

a) Scissor Jumps: Sixteen. Think stride rate!
b) Knee Tuck Jumps: Twelve. Focus on gluteal power.

Superset for Three Times:

a) Standing Calf Raises: Fifteen. Injury prevention starts right here!
b) Seated Calf Raises: Use Staccato Technique.

Superset for Three Times:

a) Abdominal Crunches for one minute.
b) Ab Wheel or Abdominal Pulldowns for one minute.

The Sportin', Snortin' 'Shoeing IWT/ICWT Program

This two-part workout prepares the mind/body/spirit for the intensities that competitive endurance athletes confront during racing. This workout offers exceptional biochemical training besides the obvious spiritual benefits of tenacity and confidence. Your enriched inner power will bring on the training effect necessary for complete physiological and spiritual transfer. Good luck and remember: There is nothing like Wholistic Fitness strength training!

Part One: The IWT (Interval Weight Training) Program

Squats (Full or Back Squat preferred): Fifteen reps.

Stationary Cycle (or Versa-Climber or Elliptical Trainer): Two minutes at Zones 3–4.

Squats: Five reps.

Stationary Cycle: Two minutes at Zones 3–4.

Squats: Fifteen reps.

Stationary Cycle: Two minutes at Zones 3–4.

Pull-Ups: As many as you can do.

Gunther Hops: One minute.

Dips: As many as you can do.

Split Jumps: Twelve reps each leg.

Part Two: ICWT (Interval Circuit Weight Training) Program

V-Handle Pulldowns: Fifteen reps.

Bench Presses: Fifteen reps.

Seated Rowing: Fifteen reps.

Speed Cleans: Fifteen reps.

Seated Barbell Presses: Fifteen reps.

Barbell Curls: Fifteen reps.

Stationary Cycle: Two minutes at Zones 3–4.

Recover for one minute, then repeat: two times for recreational shoers; three times for serious snowshoe racers; four times for serious snowshoe racers who want the top of the podium.

CV Training

Minimum weekly hours range from five to a max of nine and a half. The higher level of shoer you are and the more ambitious your snowshoeing goals, the higher those weekly hours should be! Warning: This program is one of the most advanced in this book. Unless your nutrition and other disciplines are right on track, don't even try it! Go back to conventional training, because this program will kick your wholistic butt unless you have your act together for a solid five weeks of training!

Also, if your job or habitat is not conducive to workouts on hilly terrain or in snowy conditions, check out the new indoor cardio machines. I am particularly impressed with the elliptical trainer by Precor®. This new machine, widely available at good gyms, was originally designed to combine the best biomechanics of a treadmill, stairclimber, stationary bike, and nordic ski machine. What they actually invented was a snowshoe-specific trainer! The movement pattern mimics snowshoeing surprisingly well, and the resistance and ramp can be adjusted to cover a fair range of intensities. Of course, like any machine it is a distant second to the real thing and does little to aid neural development of the stabilizing muscles needed for snowshoeing. But for an indoor option, it gets the Wholistic Fitness nod of acceptance.

15x15's

Keeping your stride rate high, go hard (Zone 4) for fifteen seconds. Then recovery jog for fifteen seconds. Repeat this sequence for five minutes. Recover while you jog for another ten minutes. Then repeat. This workout increases your aerobic capacity, stride rate, recovery ability, and the ability to respond to surges.

Speed Enduro Workout

This workout should be done running on a track.
- Fifteen-minute warm-up into:
- Two sets of 800 meters with a two minute, forty-five second recovery into:
- One set of 1000 meters with a full recovery into:
- Two sets of 800 meters with a two minute, forty-five second recovery into:
- One set of 1000 meters with a full recovery into:
- Fifteen-minute cool down.

Cruise Intervals

While on a Zone 1–2 workout, perform four to six intervals of two minutes each, with a full recovery between. During the intervals, focus on smooth, powerful mechanics. Bring your intervals to Zone 3 as soon as possible and finish at Zone 4. During the last thirty seconds of each interval increase the tempo. After each interval, go at Zone 1 until your heart rate drops down to Zone 2. Resume fluid form, then pop off another interval.

Kinesthetic Training

Stabilization is the key. Follow the Master Sheet without flaw, and you will not get injured and your shoeing performance will crank. Take one hatha yoga class per week and get a massage or bodywork session at least twice during this cycle.

Meditation

Early-Morning Zazen Session. Wake up, relieve yourself, then assume the zazen posture. Sit for five minutes. Perform Kin Hin (walking meditation); it should be performed with hands in a "gassho mudra," or prayer hand, position. The meditation is designed to mindfully place each step with awareness and not to let the mind wander from the walking. It is best done in an environment where you are not likely to be interrupted in any way. The walk can be as short as one minute to as long as several minutes in duration. Sit for another five minutes. End the session and take mindfulness with you.

Beeper Guru Breath and Posture Assignment. Set your watch alarm to go off every hour. Upon the beep, take note of where your breath, posture, and mind are. Make adjustments in alignment. Note how often the Beeper Guru catches you in random thought, out of posture, or with the breath high and shallow instead of low and deep.

3 x 30 Assignment. This is taken from a Theravada Buddhist mindfulness exercise. At each mealtime (assume three sit-down meals per day) I want you to chew your first bite of food thirty times. During this chewing, feel the significance of the food being eaten. Appreciate the fact that you are not different from the food you eat and that one day, you too will be "eaten" by the universe. Use this time to honor and revere your food and "tell" the food that you will do your best to use its life-giving energy to refine yourself in order to help others.

Nutrition

Keep in mind the following six guidelines:

1) You simply will not survive the Sportin', Snortin' 'Shoeing cycle if you do not eat according to the principles outlined in this book. You could get injured or suffer from overtraining if you have not gotten your nutritional act together by now. At this point, you are either on the path, or you've dropped off.

2) Use your active meditations and/or your recovery days to nourish yourself by attending to your training equipment and gear. This might mean shopping for good food and supplements or getting race equipment dialed in. Remember our training principle: Be prepared! This is very important nutrition.

3) Make certain you are taking in a high-quality amino acid supplement consistently throughout the day. This consistent intake can be in the form of dietary protein foods or by amino acid supplementation. This intake should be consumed three times per day, in accordance with WF nutrition principles discussed in Chapter 8.

4) Also make certain you are taking in a high-quality vitamin/mineral supplement consistently throughout the day, usually two to three times.

5) If you'd like to experiment with a creatine load/maintain, now is the cycle to do so.

6) Sever all refined, junk, and fatty foods from your diet right now if you have not already done so. Remember, once the season gets here, you will not be able to make up for this vital preseason phase! How well you perform this winter depends on your actions now!

RESOURCES

Contact the following associations for qualified instruction in snowshoeing technique.

Hurricane Island Outward Bound: P.O. Box 429, Rockland, ME 04841: 800-341-1744; fax: 207-594-9425.

National Outdoor Leadership School (NOLS): 288 Main Street, Dept. R, Lander, WY 82520; 307-332-6873; fax: 307-988-3005.

Contact the following associations for qualified instruction in winter safety.

American Avalanche Institute: P.O. Box 308, Wilson, WY 83014; 307-733-3315.

Magazines

Back Country: 7065 Dover Way, Arvada, CO 80004; 303-424-5858.

Backpacker: 33 E. Minor Street, Emmaus, PA 18098; 610-967-5171.

Outside: 400 Market Street, Santa Fe, NM 87501; 800-678-1131.

Books

The ABC's of Avalanche Safety, Edward R. LaChapelle. 1985. $6.95. Mountaineers Books.

Cold Comfort: Keeping Warm in the Outdoors, Glenn Randall. 1987. $10.95. Lyons & Burford Publishers.

The Essential Snowshoer: A Step-By-Step Guide, Marianne Zwosta. 1998. $15.95. Ragged Mountain Press.

Snowshoe Manufacturers

Atlas Snowshoes: 1830 Harrison Street, San Francisco, CA 94103; 800-645-SHOE; www.atlasworld.com.

Redfeather Snowshoes: 4955 Peoria Street, Denver, CO 80239; 800-525-0081.

Sherpa Snowshoes: 444 South Pine Street, Burlington, WI 53105; 800-621-2277.

Tubbs Snowshoe Company: 52 River Road, P.O. Box 207, Stowe, VT 05672; 800-882-2748.

Wholistic Fitness® Winter Performance Training
Sportin', Snortin' 'Shoeing Cycle Summation

Cycle's Dates: _____

Athlete's Name: _____

Please address each category as openly as possible.

STRENGTH TRAINING

1) Note your consistency during this discipline. How were your energy levels?

_____

_____

_____

_____

_____

2) What were your strengths? What were your weaknesses? Identify them and describe how you will deal with them this in-season:

_____

_____

_____

_____

_____

3) The most important teaching of this strength-training discipline that I can use in my snowshoeing performance is:

_____

_____

_____

_____

_____

CV TRAINING

4) Did you have any standout reactions in this discipline? Were you able to do the volumes as prescribed?

_____

_____

_____

_____

_____

5) Which dryland training activities did you do the most? How will this help you this season?

_____

_____

_____

_____

_____

6) The most important teaching of this CV-training discipline that I can use in my snowshoeing performance is:

_____

_____

_____

_____

_____

KINESTHETIC TRAINING

7) Did you have any standout reactions in this discipline?

_____

_____

_____

_____

8) Comment on how the past fifteen weeks of intense study in this discipline has shifted your awareness compared to previous years.

_____

_____

_____

_____

_____

9) The most important teaching of this kinesthetic-training discipline that I can use in my snowshoeing performance is:

_____

_____

_____

_____

_____

MEDITATION

10) What truth did you find in this cycle?

_____

_____

_____

_____

11) What did you find out about yourself from meditation?

_____

_____

_____

_____

12) How will this discovery affect your snowshoe performance?

_____

_____

_____

_____

_____

13) The most important teaching of this meditation discipline that I can use in my snowshoeing performance is:

_____

_____

_____

_____

_____

NUTRITION

14) How did this cycle's workload affect you nutritionally?

_____

_____

_____

_____

15) Describe exactly what you ate and drank yesterday and the manner in which you ate
   it. Note any cravings.

_____

_____

_____

_____

16) What could you have done to better nourish yourself? Why didn't you? How will
   you make the adjustment over this in-season?

_____

_____

_____

_____

17) Overall, what did you learn from your Sportin', Snortin' 'Shoeing training cycle?

_____

_____

_____

_____

_____

26

Winter Mountain Biking

*"To move out of fear requires one thing; serious practice.
Don't give up the pain, give up the struggle."*
—Marianne Williamson

UNCOMMON TEXTURE

No longer do bikes hang off rafters during the winter. Ever since mountain bikes became popular, cyclists have discovered the quaint and challenging charm of winter mountain biking. Although ESPN's telecast of the Winter X-Games popularized the dynamic flash of slalom and downhill bike events, winter mountain biking doesn't depend on snow. Just the cold is enough to transform that local summer ride into a whole new adventure. Trails that were choked by users in the warmer weather are now yours alone. There is uncommon texture to the air, and the cold invites intensity of experience.

CREATING SUPPLE PEDAL STROKES

Cycling with snow beneath one's tires throws an entirely new set of kinesthetics into the game. Winter mountain biking is superb for improving bike-handling skills. When I lived in Pagosa Springs, Colorado, I commuted across fields of snow, sometimes crusty, at other times as hard and fast as concrete, and at still other times, slush. By winter's end, I had discovered and developed a new set of neurocircuitry that I deeply appreciated during the Colorado Off-Road Points Series the following summer.

Pedaling finesse is greatly enhanced by winter mountain biking. This is because you must listen to the pedaling action with greater attention when riding in snow. The dance of yin and yang energies within each pedal stroke are much closer to the surface in winter mountain biking. John Stamstad, multitime winner of Alaska's Iditabike, is renowned for being able to ride his bike through all snow conditions, from slush to powder. Often Stamstad will be the only

Think strategic layering. Photo courtesy Cannondale Bicycle Corporation.

rider in the field not pushing his bike as course conditions deteriorate. Somehow, he is able to find the delicate dance, enabling him to continue riding as others slowly and painfully splash through endless miles of cold slush or post-hole through powder bogs.

STAYING WARM

One thing that cannot be stressed enough for winter cycling is adequate clothing. I asked my friends at bike maker Cannondale (203-544-9800) to tell me what the pros use during winter mountain biking. Patty Davidson, Cannondale's clothing product manager, offered the following insights into keeping the pace up when the mercury drops:

Think "strategic layering." To fully get the most from your athletic experience in the cold, layering garments is essential. Not

only do they serve specific functions, but also together they complement and enhance each other's functions. From the base layer out, keep the moisture moving away. Use knit polyester fabrics that push sweat quickly and evenly away from the skin for fast evaporation. Our C-Tech Innertops are excellent for this.

Depending on temperature, intermediate layers will vary, but fleece is a good way to go up top. As an insulator, it's quick drying and breathable. Cannondale makes a variety of wind-resistant microfleece garments, as well as looser knit, insulating nylon fleece tops. Fleece is engineered for layering and is one of the best wicking materials around. For the legs, lightweight nylon/Lycra tights protected by windpants are an excellent choice when it's really cold. When it's not so chilly, Loftek tights are ideal. Loftek is slightly heavier, but is still very much vapor permeable.

Repelling the wind and elements while allowing moisture to escape is key to an outer layer's performance. We use Versatech® in many of our shells, which is windproof, water resistant, and breathable. For total protection against the rain, our Tempest Ultrex® jacket with sealed seams or our Vapex thermal jacket (a.k.a. Flame Thrower) will keep you covered.

How many times do you get out there to ride, and while you've successfully protected the majority of your body, your arms, fingers, and toes are still freezing? Covering your noggin is vital to your comfort and longevity behind the bars, and there are a variety of ways to protect it. A balaclava is standard for any winter cyclist. Not only does it cover the ears, but also the neck, which all too often goes unguarded. Our Polar Beak and headbands are good options, too, allowing you to fit a helmet over them.

For the hands, full-finger gloves are windproof and waterproof, yet breathable, and feature a longer cuff. There are many material choices; we use Loftek® and neoprene, as well as Pittards leather.

Finally, down to the feet. An intermediate layer between the sock and shoe is one option. We use a superthin, totally windproof material called Triad®. This lightweight membrane allows the feet to breathe, while protecting them from wind and rain. Another option is our shoe-covering booties. These are made of Lycra and power-stretch fleece with Vapex and fit over the shoes, offering total protection. If you've spent your cash on outfitting every other part of your body, and your foot budget is down to a shoestring, use plastic bags from the supermarket veggie section. They'll work for one ride, at least.

Stay warm, good luck and don't forget the lip balm!

EQUIPMENT ESSENTIALS

When I asked ultraendurance athlete Chris Kostman for a good person to contact about technical questions regarding winter riding, he answered instantly, "Call Simon. He's up in Fairbanks, Alaska. Has this to-tally awesome business, All Weather Sports. He's the best cold-weather tech guy in the world." Since Kostman has done Iditasport several times and operates his own adventure sport service (310-312-1841), I trusted his suggestion. And after speaking with Simon, I realized I had contacted the omnipotent source of winter-riding knowledge. If anyone on the planet knows how to winterize himself and his bike for winter riding, it's Simon Rakoor.

Simon's business, All Weather Sports, is like a one-stop learning place for winter riding, race information, and lots of other very cool stuff. Following are five tips by Simon on a few winter-riding topics. Visit his website, at www.mosquitonet.com/~aws, to find about a hundred more.

Tires

1) Wide tires with widely separated knobs work best on snow.

2) Panaracer Dart 2.2 (for the front) and Continental Pro-2 (for the rear) are the best tires for soft snow.

3) Use low pressure. Start with fifteen to twenty psi and experiment for yourself. Sometimes five psi feels great.

4) Glue the tires to the rims. Use tubular tire glue or any strong contact cement in about six six-inch strips. Only glue one side. If you always glue the right side, for example, you won't have to try to figure it out in the dark.

5) Snow Cat rims improve flotation, traction, and stability on snow or ice.

Lubrication

1) Bicycles don't need to be "winterized" the way cars do. The loads on bicycle bearings are so slight that just about any grease will protect them.

2) Some bicycles have grease in their freewheels, which can cause problems when it gets very cold. If you use grease that is good year round, you won't have to change it for the summer. So if your bike works in the cold, it's already "winterized."

3) Bicycles that are used regularly end up with more dirt and water than grease in their bearings. Yearly repacking will make them last a lot longer. Repack your bearings in the fall with low-temperature grease and call it winterizing.

4) Simon tests greases for winter bike use by putting them outside when it's minus-forty degrees Fahrenheit or colder. Some "low-temperature" greases get a lot stiffer than others at those temperatures. The best he's found so far is Lubriplate Mag-1.

5) A lubricant for cables that stays liquid at minus-forty degrees Fahrenheit can help your bike shift better in winter. Goretex RideOn cables require no lubrication, so they work well no matter how cold they are.

Lighting

1) Most states require bicycles to have a white light in front and a red light in back, both visible at five hundred feet, as well as side reflectors and a red rear reflector. Red flashers that meet this requirement are available for about $16.

2) Clear (white) reflectors return twice as much light as amber ones and more than three times as much as red ones.

3) Headlights that meet most state requirements also start at about $16. You'll get a basic, nonrechargeable light that will make you legal, let you be seen, and help you see under some conditions. This is often enough. However, those who ride longer distances and in all conditions usually use more powerful lights. One popular high-power system uses dual beams, produces thirty-five watts, and costs $300. There are many systems available between these extremes.

4) Winter trail riding requires surprisingly little light; four to five watts is plenty. The snow reflects well, and since there are no other light sources, your eyes can adapt to low light. If the moon is bright or the clouds are reflecting light from the city, try turning your light off.

5) Systems that power the taillight and headlight from the same battery may leave you invisible from the rear if a wire breaks without your knowing it. Independent rear flashers are very reliable and can run for at least a year on two AA batteries.

Miscellaneous

1) When your bike starts going sideways, make small corrections rather than oversteering and weaving down the trail. Practice riding in a straight line when the

trail is good so it'll be easier under bad conditions.

2) On some soft trails, higher speeds take less effort than lower speeds because your tires sink into the snow less. When riding in a group on soft trails, have the weaker, less skilled, or badly equipped riders lead so they can use the trail before the better riders cut it up.

3) Power grips are a type of oversized toe strap used in place of toeclips. They work well summer or winter, and they're available in an extra-long version to accommodate winter footgear. Because they're made of fabric and don't compress your toes, they're warmer than toeclips. Bike pogies are oversized mittens that fit over the handlebars. They let you ride barehanded when you'd normally wear gloves and let you wear gloves when you'd usually need heavy mittens. This improves your control of the bike and makes eating, drinking, clothes adjusting, and nose wiping easier.

4) Snow machines leave the center of the trail soft. The best tracks are left by their skis, if you can ride straight enough to use them. Dogsleds leave harder, smoother trails than snow machines. Road ice can provide lots of traction or very little. Learn how the different types of ice look and sound. Try not to brake hard on the slippery sort; if you must, use only your rear brake. Watch for dry patches where you can do your braking or turning.

5) Cover your tools with tape so you won't have to touch cold metal directly when doing emergency repairs. Few mechanical things work well when it gets very cold (say minus-thirty degrees Fahrenheit). Even a well-prepared bicycle isn't at its best then. Aluminum shrinks more than steel as it cools; on a bike with a steel fork and aluminum frame, the headset will get loose in very cold conditions.

THE ROLLING THUNDER CYCLISTS PROGRAM

The following program is to be engaged immediately after the Perfect Power phase recovery week. This program is appropriate for all recreational and competitive winter mountain bikers, including winter downhillers. It can also be used as early-season training for other winter sports or as cyclecross training.

This program does not cover specific winter-riding techniques but prepares the body, mind, and spirit for the pursuit of winter riding. See Chapters Twelve and Thirteen for basic movement analysis. Specific winter-riding technique should be studied under the guidance of an expert. The resources section that concludes this chapter lists sources of information and inspiration to deepen your enjoyment of this fantastic winter sport.

Now, let's get to training!

The Rolling Thunder Cyclists program is to be followed for five consecutive weeks. This phase produces muscular and cardiovascular fitness specific to winter riding, both competitive and recreational. Appropriate transpersonal power development is also designed into the program.

Length of cycle: five weeks.
Frequency: seven-day cycle.
Next cycle: in season.
Primary goals: refine all prior mental, physical, and spiritual fitness gained from previous training cycles into winter-riding conditioning.

Wholistic Fitness® Training Precepts

1) Be prepared.
2) Be on time.
3) Give 110 percent.

THE ROLLING THUNDER CYCLISTS MASTER SHEET

All workouts are described in the next section, Wholistic Notes.

Thank Goodness It's Monday: Day One

Recovery day. No strength or CV training. All other disciplines are discretionary.

Power Tuesday: Day Two

CV training: Do a CV activity of your choice for one to one and a half hours, including the 15 x 15 workout. Stay within high Zone 2 for most of the workout.
Kinesthetic training: Medium Form Flexibility before CV training.

Meditation: Passive or active meditation for twenty minutes.

Wholly Heaven Wednesday: Day Three

Strength training: EEE-GAD workout or IWT/IWCT workout (alternate weekly).
CV training: Road or MTB bike at Zone 2 for one to two hours. Every thirty minutes perform two sets of out of the saddle biggest gear intervals for three minutes each. Recovery interval for three minutes but stay within Zone 2 throughout.
Kinesthetic training: Medium Form plus schedule massage/bodywork for Monday if possible.
Meditation: Beeper Guru breath and posture assignment.

Rolling Thunder Thursday: Day Four

CV training: Do a CV activity of your choice one to one and a half hours at Zones 1–2.
Kinesthetic training: Yoga class if possible; otherwise do Short and Medium Form back-to-back.
Meditation: If you take a yoga class, allow that to be your meditation; if no yoga do early-morning zazen practice.

No Fear Friday: Day Five

CV training: Road or MTB bike at Zone 2 for one to two hours. After thirty minutes perform cruise intervals.

Kinesthetic training: Yoga class if possible; otherwise do Short and Medium Form back-to-back.

Meditation: If you take a yoga class, allow that to be your meditation; if no yoga do early-morning zazen practice.

Super Saturday: Day Six

Strength training: None, or (if you desire more strength and power before the season) do Yang Day full-body workout.

CV training: Road or MTB bike at Zone 2 for one to two hours.

Kinesthetic training: Still haven't done yoga this week? Do it today; otherwise, Medium Form before CV training.

Meditation: Discretionary.

Spin-it-Out Sunday: Day Seven

CV training: Cross-train from yesterday at Zone 2 for one to three hours.

Kinesthetic training: Still haven't done yoga this week? Do it today; otherwise, Medium Form before CV training.

Meditation: Passive or active meditation for twenty minutes.

WHOLISTIC NOTES

This section provides the specific workouts prescribed in the Rolling Thunder Master Sheet.

Strength-Training Workouts

This strength program packs a wallop of cycling-specific training into just one day per week! An optional Yang Day workout on the weekend is offered for those cyclists who can't make a ride on a weekend day or who need to prioritize more strength and power in the preseason.

The Rolling Thunder IWT/ICWT Program

This two-part workout prepares the mind/body/spirit for the intensities that competitive endurance athletes confront during training and racing. This workout offers exceptional biochemical training besides the obvious spiritual benefits of tenacity and confidence. Your enriched inner power will bring on the training effect necessary for complete physiological and spiritual transfer. Good luck and remember: There is nothing like Wholistic Fitness strength training!

Part One: The IWT (Interval Weight Training) Program

Squats (Full or Back Squat preferred): Fifteen reps.

Stationary Cycle (or Versa-Climber or Elliptical Trainer): Two minutes at Zones 3–4.

Squats: Fifteen reps.

Stationary Cycle (or Versa-Climber or Elliptical Trainer): Two minutes at Zones 3–4.

Pull-Ups: Go to muscle failure.

Jump Squats: Forty-five seconds.

Dips: Go to muscle failure.

Split Jumps: Thirty seconds each leg.

Part Two: The ICWT (Interval Circuit Weight Training) Program
   Bench Presses: Fifteen reps.
   Speed Cleans: Fifteen reps.
   Seated Barbell Presses: Fifteen reps.
   Barbell Curls: Fifteen reps.
   Dumbbell Horizontal Swings: Thirty seconds.
   Dumbbell Arm Swings: Thirty seconds.
   Recover for one minute, then repeat: two times for recreational cyclists dumb enough to be doing this workout; three times for serious cyclists; four times for racers who want to visit the top of the podium.

Yang Day Full-Body Workout

In the East, the balance of all that exists is represented by yin/yang. Yin is the female, the dark, the yielding. Yang is the masculine, the light, the forceful.

Yang day sessions are special. They develop what is known as samu in Asiatic traditions or ekagrata in the yogic traditions. Both describe the performance of physical effort with maximum mental concentration. During this workout, note how quickly your mind will want to wander. Use these sessions to develop mental focus in life.

Recovery Phase: One minute.

Bench Press: Five sets of five reps. Use regulation power lifting form—bar to the chest, no hip movement.

Squats: Five sets of five reps. Use regulation power lifting form—thighs must go parallel to the ground.

Hang Cleans: Five sets of five reps. There is no substitute for inspiration. Go.

Dips: Two sets of as many as you can perform at body weight.

Pull Ups: Two sets of as many as you can perform at body weight.

Congratulations. Thanks for playing!

> *The best way out, is always through.*—Robert Frost

CV Training

Minimum weekly hours range from six to a max of twelve. The higher your skill level as a cyclist and the more ambitious your winter-riding goals, the higher those weekly hours should be!

15x15's (for cycling or noncycling activities)

Keeping your stride or spin rate high, go hard (Zone 4) for fifteen seconds. Recovery jog or spin for fifteen seconds. Repeat this sequence for five minutes. Recover while you jog or easy spin for another ten minutes. Then repeat. This workout increases your aerobic capacity, stride or rpm rate, recovery ability, and the ability to respond to surges.

Cruise Intervals

While on a Zone 1–2 workout, perform four to six intervals of two minutes each, with a full recovery between. During the intervals, focus on smooth, powerful mechanics. Bring your intervals to Zone 3 as soon as possible and finish at Zone 4. During the last thirty seconds of each interval increase the tempo. After each interval, go at Zone 1 until your heart rate drops down to Zone 2. Resume fluid form, then pop off another interval.

Kinesthetic Training

Follow the Master Sheet for optimal injury prevention and cycling performance. Take one hatha yoga class per week and get a massage or bodywork session at least twice during this cycle. Always work on good, aerodynamic form while on the bike.

Meditation

Early-Morning Zazen Session. Wake up, relieve yourself, then assume the zazen posture. Sit for five minutes. Perform Kin Hin (walking meditation); it should be performed with hands in a "gassho mudra," or prayer hand, position. The meditation is designed to mindfully place each step with awareness and not to let the mind wander from the walking. It is best done in an environment where you are not likely to be interrupted in any way. The walk can be as short as one minute to as long as several minutes in duration. Sit for another five minutes. End the session and take mindfulness with you.

Beeper Guru Breath and Posture Assignment. Set your watch alarm to go off every hour. Upon the beep, take note of where your breath, posture, and mind are. Make adjustments in alignment. Note how often the Beeper Guru catches you in random thought, out of posture, or with the breath high and shallow instead of low and deep.

3 x 30 Assignment. This is taken from a Theravada Buddhist mindfulness exercise. At each mealtime (assume three sit-down meals per day) I want you to chew your first bite of food thirty times. During this chewing, feel the significance of the food being eaten. Appreciate the fact that you are not different from the food you eat and that one day, you too will be "eaten" by the universe. Use this time to honor and revere your food and "tell" the food that you will do your best to use its life-giving energy to refine yourself in order to help others.

Nutrition

Follow the nutritional guidelines outlined in this book and make certain to take a high-quality amino acid and vitamin/mineral supplement each day. If you are still carrying some unwanted body fat, this is the time to jettison it by keeping fat intake to 15 percent of total calories per day and to run instead of cycle when the Master Sheet offers a CV-training option.

RESOURCES

United States Cycling Federation: One Olympic Plaza, Colorado Springs, CO 80909; 719-578-4581; fax: 719-578-4628; e-mail: uscf@usacycling.org.

Magazines

Mt. Bike: 33 E. Minor, Emmaus, PA 18049; 610-967-5171.

Outside: 400 Market Street, Santa Fe, NM 87501; 800-678-1131.

VeloNews: 1850 N. 55th Street, Boulder, CO 80301; 303-440-0601.

Websites

www.iBIKE.com

www.iditasport.com

www.mosquitonet.com/~aws

www.usacycling.org

Wholistic Fitness® Winter Performance Training Rolling Thunder Cycle Summation

---

Cycle's Dates: _____

Athlete's Name: _____

Please address each category as openly as possible.

STRENGTH TRAINING

1) Note your consistency during this discipline. How were your energy levels?

_____

_____

_____

_____

_____

2) What were your strengths? What were your weaknesses? Identify them and describe how you will deal with them this in-season:

_____

_____

_____

_____

_____

3) The most important teaching of this strength-training discipline that I can use in my winter-riding performance is:

_____

_____

_____

_____

CV TRAINING

4) Did you have any standout reactions in this discipline? Were you able to do the volumes as prescribed?

_____

_____

_____

_____

_____

5) Which CV workout seemed most difficult? Which was the easiest? What does this tell you?

_____

_____

_____

_____

_____

6) The most important teaching of this CV-training discipline that I can use in my winter-riding performance is:

_____

_____

_____

_____

KINESTHETIC TRAINING

7) Did you have any standout reactions in this discipline?

_____

_____

_____

_____

_____

8) Comment on how the past fifteen weeks of intense study in this discipline has shifted your awareness compared to previous years.

_____

_____

_____

_____

_____

9) The most important teaching of this kinesthetic-training discipline that I can use in my winter-riding performance is:

_____

_____

_____

_____

_____

MEDITATION

10) What truth did you find in this cycle?

_____

_____

_____

_____

11) What did you find out about yourself from meditation?

_____

_____

_____
_____
_____

12) How will this discovery affect your winter-riding performance?

_____
_____
_____
_____
_____

13) The most important teaching of this meditation discipline that I can use in my winter-riding performance is:

_____
_____
_____
_____
_____

NUTRITION

14) How did this cycle's workload affect you nutritionally?

_____
_____
_____
_____
_____

15) Describe *exactly* what you ate and drank yesterday and the manner in which you ate it. Note any cravings.

_____
_____
_____
_____
_____

16) What could you have done to better nourish yourself? Why didn't you? How will you make the adjustment over this in-season?

_____

_____

_____

_____

17) Overall, what did you learn from your Rolling Thunder training cycle?

_____

_____

_____

_____

_____

27

Winter Mountaineering
(and Winter Camping)

*"I long for immediacy of contact to brighten my senses again, to
bring me nearly the world once more; in my security,
I have forgotten how to dance."*
—Yvon Chouinard quoted by
Michael Bane in his book, "Over the Edge"

The following program is to be engaged immediately after the Perfect Power phase recovery week. This program is appropriate for all recreational and elite-level winter campers and mountaineers. This is not a program for technical ice climbers, whose training program is provided in Chapter Thirty-one.

This program does not cover specific winter camping or mountaineering techniques but prepares the body, mind, and spirit for the pursuit of ski touring. See Chapter Ten for basic movement analysis. Specific mountaineering technique should be studied with a certified instructor or the guidance of an expert. Qualified instruction is available via organizations, maga-

zines, and books listed in the resources section that concludes this chapter.

Now, let's get to training!

THE COSMIC MOUNTAIN PROGRAM

The Cosmic Mountain program is to be followed for five consecutive weeks. This phase produces muscular and cardiovascular fitness specific to winter mountaineering. Appropriate transpersonal power development is also designed into the program.

Length of cycle: five weeks.
Frequency: seven-day cycle.
Next cycle: in season.

Primary goals: refine all prior mental, physical, and spiritual fitness gained from previous training cycles into mountaineering fitness.

Wholistic Fitness® Training Precepts

1) Be prepared.
2) Be on time.
3) Give 110 percent.

COSMIC MOUNTAIN MASTER SHEET

All workouts are described in the next section, Wholistic Notes.

McKinley Monday: Day One

Recovery day. No strength or CV training. All other disciplines are discretionary. Get bodywork/massage if possible.

Elbert Tuesday: Day Two

Strength training: Cosmic Mountain upper-body workout.

CV training: None, or thirty to sixty minutes of a CV activity of your choice at Zones 1–2.

Kinesthetic training: Medium Form Flexibility before strength training.

Meditation: Beeper Guru breath and posture assignment.

Washington Wednesday: Day Three

Strength training: Cosmic Mountain lower-body workout.

CV training: Thirty minutes of a CV activity of your choice at Zones 1–2.

Kinesthetic training: Medium Form Flexibility before strength training.

Meditation: Early-morning zazen practice.

Aconcagua Thursday: Day Four

CV training: Run, hike, or cycle for one to two hours at Zones 1–2 with cruise intervals.

Kinesthetic training: Yoga class or Long Form Flexibility after CV training.

Meditation: Beeper Guru breath and posture assignment.

Grand Teton Friday: Day Five

CV training: Cross-train from Thursday for one to one and a half hours at Zone 2.

Kinesthetic training: If no yoga class was done on Thursday, do it today, or do Medium Form Flexibility after CV training.

Meditation: Active meditation for twenty minutes.

Assiniboine Saturday: Day Six

Strength training: EEE-GAD or IWT/IWCT full-body workout (alternate weekly).

CV training: Hike with a moderately loaded backpack for one to three hours at Zones 1–2.

Kinesthetic training: Discretionary. Also get or schedule bodywork (massage) for Sunday or Monday.

As close to heaven as it's going to get ... the author in −30 degree temperatures and 50 mph winds atop 12,622′ Santa Fe Baldy in New Mexico. Photo by Scott Dupuis.

Meditation: 3 x 30 assignment; passive meditation for twenty minutes.

Super Couloir Sunday: Day Seven

CV training: Run or hike for 1 hour at Zones 1–2. Perform Minutes Are Forever workout; the intervals should be done on uphill terrain.

Kinesthetic training: Discretionary. Also get bodywork or schedule it for Monday.

Meditation: Discretionary.

WHOLISTIC NOTES

This section provides the specific workouts prescribed in the Cosmic Mountain Master Sheet.

Strength-Training Workouts

This strength program emphasizes significant back training to prepare the spinal muscles for moving dynamically with a backpack. It also puts a priority on lower-torso muscle endurance and power.

For each of the following workouts adhere to these three guidelines:

1) Limit the recovery phase to thirty seconds.
2) Perform all sets to momentary muscular failure or failure of elegance, unless otherwise noted.
3) Refer to the Appendix for instructions on all movements and techniques.

Cosmic Mountain Upper-Body Workout

Bench Presses: Use Envelope Technique.

Dips: Three sets at body weight to failure.

Seated Rows: Use Envelope Technique.

High Pulls: Three sets of twelve reps. Develops a strong trapezius for packing without postural fatigue.

Bent Arm Dumbbell Pullovers: Four sets of ten reps with Ku Top or Bottom Form recovery—your choice. Your choice!

Dumbbell Seated Presses: Use Three-Stage Technique.

Dumbbell Side Lateral Raises: Three sets of twelve reps.

Barbell Curls: Four sets of fifteen reps.

Two-Bench Triceps: Two sets at one minute each. Pace yourself; I want the final fifteen seconds at tempo!

Plyometric Superset for Upper-Body Mountaineering Power:

1) Dumbbell Arm Swings for fifteen seconds.
2) Dumbbell Horizontal Swings for fifteen seconds.
3) Recover for fifteen seconds.
   Repeat twice.

Cosmic Mountain Lower-Body Workout

Stiff Leg Deadlifts: Two sets of five reps. A strong spine is a mountaineer's best ally!

Superset for Three Times:

a) Squats: Six. Do big reps, deep reps; think inner power development.
b) Leg Extensions: Use Staccato Technique. Be elegant here!

Superset for Three Times:

a) Leg Curls: Eight.
b) Split Jumps: Twelve each leg!

Jump Squats: Two sets at one minute each. Hey, Wholistic Fitness is about performance—go!

Standing Calf Raises: Four sets of fifteen reps. Stay deep and strong.

Superset for Three Times:

a) Abdominal Crunches for one minute.
b) Abdominal Pulldowns or Ab Wheel for one minute.

EEE-GAD Full-Body Workout

Pull-Ups: Two sets of however many you can do.

Front Lat Pulldowns: One set done with Staccato Technique; three sets of eight to ten reps.

Dumbbell Flat-Bench Flyes into Dumbbell Bench Presses: Flyes for ten reps to failure, then crank out high-frequency Dumbbell Bench Presses until you puke black blood. Do three sets.

Back Squats Superset with Leg Extensions: Do Squats for twelve reps to failure, then run over and perform Leg Extensions with Staccato Technique. Do two supersets.

Seated Dumbbell Presses: Two sets done with Three-Stage Technique. Commit to fluidity.

Two-Bench Triceps: Two sets of one minute each. See each rep in a "clean" top and bottom position. You should feel the contraction in the triceps up top. Bring chi to the triceps.

Barbell Curls: Three sets done with Shivaya Technique. Be beautiful; be elegant.

Abdominal Crunches Directly into Leg Raises: Three sets of one minute each. Really stay concentrated in the abs!

Cosmic Mountain IWT/ICWT Full-Body Workout

This two-part workout prepares the mind/body/spirit for the intensities that confront mountaineers during alpine conditions. This workout provides exceptional biochemical training besides the obvious spiritual benefits of tenacity and confidence. Your enriched inner power will bring on the training effect necessary for complete physiological and spiritual transfer. Good luck and remember: There is nothing like Wholistic Fitness strength training!

Part One: The IWT (Interval Weight Training) Program

  Squats (Full or Back Squat preferred): Fifteen reps.

  Versa-Climber, Treadmill, or Elliptical Trainer: Two minutes at Zones 3–4.

  Squats: Fifteen reps.

  Versa-Climber, Treadmill, or Elliptical Trainer: Two minutes at Zones 3–4.

  Squats: Fifteen reps.

  Versa-Climber, Treadmill, or Elliptical Trainer: Two minutes at Zones 3–4.

  Pull-Ups: Go to muscle failure.

  Jump Squats: Forty-five seconds.

  Dips: Go to muscle failure.

  Split Jumps: Thirty seconds each leg.

Part Two: The ICWT (Interval Circuit Weight Training) Program

  Bench Presses: Fifteen reps.

  Speed Cleans: Fifteen reps.

  Seated Barbell Presses: Fifteen reps.

  Barbell Curls: Fifteen reps.

  Dumbbell Horizontal Swings: Thirty seconds.

  Dumbbell Arm Swings: Thirty seconds.

  Recover for one minute, then repeat: Two times for recreational winter campers; Three times for serious winter mountaineers; Four times for serious winter mountaineers who live by the "Summit or Plummet" philosophy!

CV Training

Minimum weekly hours range from five to a max of ten. The higher your skill level as a mountaineer and the more ambitious your winter goals, the higher those weekly hours should be! One of the most dangerous situations in the backcountry is a lack of fitness. You could lose your life or those of others if you are not mentally, physically, and spiritually prepared. My athletes have always been the strongest members of a mountaineering group, and I expect the same kind of fitness from you. Be a leader. It starts with this program!

Minutes Are Forever Workout

Run or hike hard for one minute (at Zones 3–4), then do a recovery walk for one minute at Zone 1. Keep doing this until you throw up or ten minutes has gone by. Recover for ten minutes, then repeat the sequence. Do these intervals on steep uphills to increase lactate threshold and leg stamina.

Cruise Intervals

While on a Zone 1–2 workout, perform four to six intervals of two minutes each, with a full recovery between. During the intervals, focus on smooth, powerful mechanics. Bring your intervals to Zone 3 as soon as possible and finish at Zone 4. During the last thirty seconds of each interval increase the tempo. After each interval, go at Zone 1 until your heart rate drops down to Zone 2. Resume fluid form, then pop off another interval.

Kinesthetic Training

The key is stabilization. Follow the Master Sheet without flaw, and you will not get injured. There will be more summits in your life than you ever expected. Take one hatha yoga class per week and get a massage or bodywork session at least twice during this cycle.

Meditation

Early-Morning Zazen Session. Wake up, relieve yourself, then assume the zazen posture. Sit for eight minutes. Perform Kin Hin (walking meditation); it should be performed with hands in a "gassho mudra," or prayer hand, position. The meditation is designed to mindfully place each step with awareness and not to let the mind wander from the walking. It is best done in an environment where you are not likely to be interrupted in any way. The walk can be as short as one minute to as long as several minutes in duration. Sit for another eight minutes. End the session and take mindfulness with you.

Beeper Guru Breath and Posture Assignment. Set your watch alarm to go off every hour. Upon the beep, take note of where your breath, posture, and mind are. Make adjustments in alignment. Note how often the Beeper Guru catches you in random thought, out of posture, or with the breath high and shallow instead of low and deep.

3 x 30 Assignment. This is taken from a Theravada Buddhist mindfulness exercise. At each mealtime (assume three sit-down meals per day) I want you to chew your first bite of food thirty times. During this chewing, feel the significance of the food being eaten. Appreciate the fact that you are not different from the food you eat and that one day, you too will be "eaten" by the universe. Use this time to honor and revere your food and "tell" the food that you will do your best to use its life-giving energy to refine yourself in order to help others.

Nutrition

Although mountaineers can afford to be a little more laid-back in their nutrition than competitive athletes, the stress upon their system is tremendous. You should still follow the nutritional guidelines outlined in this book and make certain to take a high-quality amino acid and vitamin/mineral supplement each day. If you are still carrying some unwanted body fat, this is the time to jettison it by keeping fat intake to 15 percent of total calories per day and following the Cosmic Mountain Master Sheet to the letter! Remember, you want only functional body weight on the mountain! If your mountaineering involves extended trekking, you may increase fat intake to 25 percent of total calories per day.

RESOURCES

Contact the following associations for qualified instruction in mountaineering and winter safety.

The American Alpine Institute: 1212 24th Street, Bellingham, WA 98225; 206-671-1505.

American Avalanche Institute: P.O. Box 308, Wilson, WY 83014; 307-733-3315.

National Outdoor Leadership School (NOLS): 288 Main Street, Dept. R, Lander, WY 82520; 307-332-6873; fax: 307-988-3005.

Magazines

Back Country: 7065 Dover Way, Arvada, CO 80004; 303-424-5858.

Outside: 400 Market Street, Santa Fe, NM 87501; 800-678-1131.

Rock & Ice: 603A S. Broadway, Boulder, CO 80303; 303-499-8410.

Books

The ABC's of Avalanche Safety, Edward R. LaChapelle. 1985. $6.95. Mountaineers Books.

Cold Comfort: Keeping Warm in the Outdoors, Glenn Randall. 1987. $10.95. Lyons & Burford Publishers.

Over the Edge: A Regular Guy's Odyssey in Extreme Sports, Michael Bane. 1996. $21.95. Macmillan.

Wilderness Skiing and Winter Camping, Chris Townsend. 1993. $17.95. Ragged Mountain Press.

Equipment

Black Diamond Equipment, Ltd.: 2084 East 3900 South, Salt Lake City, UT 84214; 801-278-5533.

Mountain Tools: 140 Calle Del Oaks, Monterey, CA 93940; 408-393-1011.

Patagonia: 8550 White Fir Street, Reno, Nevada 89523; 800-638-6464.

Wholistic Fitness® Winter Performance Training
Cosmic Mountain Cycle Summation

Cycle's Dates: _____

Athlete's Name: _____

Please address each category as openly as possible.

STRENGTH TRAINING

1) Note your consistency during this discipline. How were your energy levels?

_____

_____

_____

_____

_____

2) What were your strengths? What were your weaknesses? Identify them and describe how you will deal with them this in-season.

_____

_____

_____

_____

_____

3) The most important teaching of this strength-training discipline that I can use in my winter mountaineering is:

_____

_____

_____

_____

_____

CARDIOVASCULAR TRAINING

4) Did you have any standout reactions in this discipline? Were you able to do the volumes as prescribed?

_____

_____

_____

_____

_____

5) Which dryland training activities did you do the most? How will this help you this season?

_____

_____

_____

_____

_____

6) The most important teaching of this CV-training discipline that I can use in my winter mountaineering is:

_____

_____

_____

_____

_____

KINESTHETIC TRAINING

7) Did you have any standout reactions in this discipline?

_____

_____

_____

_____

_____

8) Comment on how the past fifteen weeks of intense study in this discipline has shifted your awareness compared to previous years.

_____

_____

_____

_____

_____

9) The most important teaching of this kinesthetic-training discipline that I can use in my winter mountaineering is:

_____

_____

_____

_____

_____

MEDITATION

10) What truth did you find in this cycle?

_____

_____

_____

_____

_____

11) On a scale of one to ten, with ten being the highest, judge your mental focus during training:

_____

_____

_____

_____

_____

During everyday life:

_____

_____

_____

_____

_____

12) What are you doing to resolve this difference?

_____

_____

_____

_____

13) The most important teaching of this meditation discipline that I can use in my winter mountaineering is:

_____

_____

_____

_____

NUTRITION

14) How did this cycle's workload affect you nutritionally?

_____

_____

_____

_____

15) Describe exactly what you ate and drank yesterday and the manner in which you ate it. Note any cravings.

_____

_____

_____

_____

16) What could you have done to better nourish yourself? Why didn't you? How will you make the adjustment over this in-season?

_____

_____

_____

_____

_____

17) Overall, what did you learn from your Cosmic Mountain training cycle?

_____

_____

_____

_____

_____

28

Winter Multisport Competition

"The arrow had best not be loosely shot."
—Henry David Thoreau

ADRENALINE FIX

The popularity of winter multisport competitions is on the rise. Perhaps it's because the need for an off-season adrenaline fix became too great for summer multisport athletes. Competitions such as the IceMan Triathlon and the opprobrious Mt. Taylor Winter Quadrathlon now attract high-caliber athletes and large volumes of competitors. It used to just be us winter weirdos out there.

Generally, winter multisport events are varied and quite creative. I've done some great winter duathlons and triathlons over the years. I recall a nordic ski race into a winter MTB race in Crested Butte, Colorado. Over in Telluride, the San Juan Winter Quadrathlon is a total kick. It starts atop the mountain with a nordic ski race, goes directly into an all-out alpine downhill, segues into a winter MTB race, and finishes with a run. Great stuff! Per-

sonally, I've always found winter multisport competitions to be way more fun than the summer ones. But then again, I've got some Scandinavian blood in me.

MT. TAYLOR

Perhaps the most notorious of all relatively "sane" winter multisport competitions is the Mt. Taylor Winter Quadrathlon in Grants, New Mexico (800-748-2142). This premier winter multisport event, begun in 1983, covers forty-four miles and 5,000 vertical feet. It begins with a bike race, which starts on the sagebrush desert in Grants and goes thirteen miles and 1,800 feet up to the run transition, which in turn climbs 1,200 feet in five miles, bringing the athletes to snow line. The runners then become uphill nordic skiers and climb a memorable 1,200 feet in two miles before exchanging skis for snowshoes. The

The author being checked out by EMT's during a particularly cold version of the Mt. Taylor Winter Quadrathlon. Photo by Deborah Ilg.

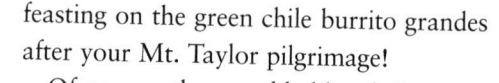

feasting on the green chile burrito grandes after your Mt. Taylor pilgrimage!

Of course, the granddaddy of all winter multisport competitions is the one-hundred-mile remote Iditasport, held near Big Lake, Alaska (907-346-3910). Few people—and I mean *very* few—actually "race" this event. Most people (and I have trained several for this event) merely try to finish it.

HEART, NOT EGO

From a professional coaching standpoint, I've turned down a number of athletes who wanted me to train them for this event and others like it. Too many people in this day and age see an event like Iditasport on TV and want to do it immediately. I don't like that approach. It is too egocentric. Remember, a tour is one thing; a race is something else. I want my ultra-athletes to earn their respect for Iditasport by living the multisport way of life. Raise your level of fitness high enough to race ultras instead of just surviving them. As far as Wholistic Fitness is concerned, competition must come from the heart, not the ego. Live the way. Love the way. And most of all, respect the way.

The following program has helped dozens of multisport athletes achieve personal records. Your practice of it will produce a higher way for you as well!

The following program is to be engaged immediately after the Perfect Power phase recovery week. This program is appropri-

snowshoe section starts near timberline and climbs another 600 feet in one mile to the 11,301-foot summit of Mt. Taylor, a sacred peak to the Native Americans who still live here. You can see for about a hundred miles from the summit (if you are still able to stand up). It provides a bit of a moment for most people. After the summit medical crew nods you past, you realize something—the race is only half over! You must then reverse all the sports until you are back in Grants. Your legs and lungs do not soon release a Mt. Taylor effort. Your spirit never does. Just take it easy while ate for all recreational and elite-level winter multisport athletes.

This program does not cover specific racing technique but prepares the body, mind, and spirit for the pursuit of winter multisport competition. Specific racing technique should be studied under the guidance of an expert. Recommended instruction is available via the organizations and magazines listed in the resources section that concludes this chapter.

Now, let's get to training!

THE MT. TAYLOR SPECIAL PROGRAM

The Mt. Taylor Special program is to be followed for five consecutive weeks. This phase produces muscular and cardiovascular fitness specific to winter multisport performance. Appropriate transpersonal power development is also designed into the program.

Length of cycle: five weeks.

Frequency: seven-day cycle.

Next cycle: in season.

Primary goals: refine all prior mental, physical, and spiritual fitness gained from previous training cycles into winter multisport fitness.

Wholistic Fitness® Training Precepts

1) Be prepared.
2) Be on time.
3) Give 110 percent.

MT. TAYLOR SPECIAL MASTER SHEET

All workouts are described in the next section, Wholistic Notes.

Thank God It's Monday, Monday: Day One

Off day on all disciplines. Get massage/ bodywork if possible.

In The Temple Tuesday: Day Two

Strength training: Mt. Taylor Special Workout One.

CV training: One to one-and-a-half hours of a CV activity of your choice at Zones 1–2.

Kinesthetic training: Medium Form Flexibility before strength training.

Meditation: Early-morning zazen practice.

Working It Wednesday: Day Three

CV training: Run for one hour at Zone 2 with cruise intervals.

Kinesthetic training: Medium Form Flexibility before CV training.

Meditation: 3 x 30 assignment.

Big Day Thursday: Day Four

Strength training: Mt. Taylor Special Workout Two.

CV training: None, or sixty minutes of a CV activity of your choice at Zones 1–2.

Kinesthetic training: Yoga class or Short into Medium Form Flexibility.

Meditation: Let your kinesthetic training be your meditation.

Fit Friday: Day Five

CV training: Cycle, inline ski, or skate for one hour at Zones 1–2.

Kinesthetic training: Yoga class or Short into Medium Form Flexibility.

Meditation: Early-morning zazen practice.

Dual Day Saturday: Day Six

CV training: Pick one or a combo of running/cycling/inline skiing and do it at Zones 1–2 for one and a half to two and a half hours. Perform Minutes Are Forever workout. The intervals should be done on moderate (5–7 percent grade) uphill terrain.

Kinesthetic training: Yoga class or Short into Medium Form Flexibility.

Meditation: Let your kinesthetic training and your intervals be your meditation.

Super Sunday: Day Seven

CV training: Cross-train from yesterday, but no intervals and go for two to three hours.

Kinesthetic training: Medium Form before and after CV training.

Meditation: Pre-event meditation; passive meditation for ten to twenty minutes; visualize your upcoming week of training. Schedule bodywork and yoga, plan mealtimes, etc.

WHOLISTIC NOTES

This section provides the specific workouts prescribed in the Mt. Taylor Special Master Sheet.

Strength-Training Workouts

This strength program functions as a catalyst to ignite the variety of cardiovascular efficiencies required by winter multisport competition.

For each of the following workouts adhere to these three guidelines:

1) Limit the recovery phase to thirty seconds.

2) Perform all sets to momentary muscular failure or failure of elegance, unless otherwise noted.

3) Refer to the Appendix for instructions on all movements and techniques.

Mt. Taylor Special Workout One

Pull-Ups: Three sets at bodyweight to failure. Get cranking and watch your recovery time.

V-Handle Pulldowns: Four sets of eight reps with Ku Bottom Form recovery on all sets!

Bent Arm Dumbbell Pullovers: Three sets of eight reps with Ku Bottom Form recovery on *all* sets!

Dips: Three sets at bodyweight to failure. Get cranking and watch your recovery time.

Bench Presses: Three sets of ten. Vary the angle; be creative with each workout.

High Pulls: Three sets of eight to ten reps. Use Ku Bottom Form and emphasize yin.

Seated Barbell Presses: Two sets of eight to ten reps. Visualize strong shoulders to drive the arms!

Seated Dumbbell Side Lateral Raises: Two sets of ten reps. Pump 'em baby!

Superset for Three Times:
a) Abdominal Crunches for one minute into
b) Suspended Leg Raises for one minute.

Mt. Taylor Special Workout Two

Superset for Three Times:
a) Dumbbell Arm Swings for twenty seconds into
b) Double Pole Plyos for twenty seconds into
c) Recovery for twenty seconds.
Repeat.

Barbell Curls: Three sets of fifteen reps. Stay smooth and fluid as in good CV form!

Concentration Curls: Three sets of ten reps each arm.

Overhead DB Tricep Extensions: Four sets of ten.

Two-Bench Triceps: Two sets of one minute each. Be a champion and crank 'em!

Leg Extensions: Two sets done with Staccato Technique.

Split Jumps: Two sets of ten jumps. Make a 100 percent effort with each leg.

Stiff Leg Deadlifts: One set of ten reps. Each leg should make 50 percent of the effort; prioritize depth and posture.

Oblique Twists: Three sets of one minute each. Twist and shout, scissor 'em—whatever!

Abdominal Pulldowns: Three sets of one minute each. Goodbye abs, goodbye workout.

CV Training

Minimum weekly hours range from six and a half to a max of ten. The higher the level of multisport athlete you are and the more ambitious your winter goals, the higher those weekly hours should be!

Minutes Are Forever Workout

Run or hike hard for one minute (at Zones 3–4), then do a recovery walk for one minute at Zone 1. Keep doing this until you throw up or ten minutes have gone by. Recover for ten minutes, then repeat the sequence. Do these intervals on steep uphills to increase lactate threshold and leg stamina.

Cruise Intervals

While on a Zone 1–2 workout, perform four to six intervals of two minutes each, with a full recovery between. During the intervals, focus on smooth, powerful mechanics. Bring your intervals to Zone 3 as soon as possible and finish at Zone 4. During the last thirty seconds of each interval increase the tempo. After each interval, go at Zone 1 until your heart rate drops down to Zone 2. Resume fluid form, then pop off another interval. Repeat.

Kinesthetic Training

Notice the high priority put on yoga and flexibility training. It will come back to you a hundred times over in the form of injury prevention, mental focus, and spiritual development. Stay consistent with the Master Sheet in this discipline and you will fly like an eagle come race day!

Meditation

Early-Morning Zazen Session. Wake up, relieve yourself, then assume the zazen posture. Sit for eight minutes. Perform Kin Hin (walking meditation); it should be performed with hands in a "gassho mudra," or prayer hand, position. The meditation is designed to mindfully place each step with awareness and not to let the mind wander from the walking. It is best done in an environment where you are not likely to be interrupted in any way. The walk can be as short as one minute to as long as several minutes in duration. Sit for another eight minutes. End the session and take mindfulness with you.

Beeper Guru Breath and Posture Assignment. Set your watch alarm to go off every hour. Upon the beep, take note of where your breath, posture, and mind are. Make adjustments in alignment. Note how often the Beeper Guru catches you in random thought, out of posture, or with the breath high and shallow instead of low and deep.

3 x 30 Assignment. This is taken from a Theravada Buddhist mindfulness exercise. At each mealtime (assume three sit-down meals per day) I want you to chew your first bite of food thirty times. During this chewing, feel the significance of the food being eaten. Appreciate the fact that you are not different from the food you eat and that one day, you too will be "eaten" by the universe. Use this time to honor and revere your food and "tell" the food that you will do your best to use its life-giving energy to refine yourself in order to help others.

Wholistic Fitness®
Pre-Event Meditation

Assume zazen posture;
perform ten cleansing breaths;
perform ten filling breaths.
Recite the following:

As I release my breath, I release my body.

As I release my breath, I let go of any physical, mental, or emotional tensions.

Relaxing into my breath, I realize no separation between myself and the world around me. Nor am I separate from the easy or difficult circumstances in my life. They are all me. I am all them. And it's all appropriate.

As I breathe, I realize that Joy is my natural state.

As long as I breathe, I know that nothing can interfere with this Joy.

Upon my inbreath, I sense a rush of beautiful, comfortable energy. This is my Divine Source. I allow this energy to flow into and out from my body. Relaxing ... feeling empty ...

When I relax, I perform better. When I am empty, I perform better. I will use my breath in my upcoming event in order to relax. In order to empty. I will surrender into the Universe. I trust completely that the Universe will power me into my best effort. Everything that I will go through during my event will be precisely what I need to learn most.

I can already sense how powerfully I will compete because I will have the Universe charging through my emptiness ... all I need to do is breathe and relax into my effort.

As long as I breathe, my performance will be an elegant and strong expression of the Universe.

Recite three times. Go into a visualization of your event for three to five minutes; perform five cleansing breaths; perform five filling breaths; end the session.

Nutrition

Keep in mind the following six guidelines:

1) You simply will not survive the Mt. Taylor Special if you do not eat according to the principles outlined in this book. You could get injured or suffer from overtraining if you have not gotten your nutritional act together by now. At this point, you are either on the path, or you've dropped off.

2) Use your active mediations and/or your recovery days to nourish yourself by attending to your training equipment and gear. This might mean getting new gear, shopping for good food and supplements, or getting race equipment dialed in. Remember our training principle: Be prepared! This is very important nutrition.

3) Make certain you are taking in a high-quality amino acid supplement consistently throughout the day. This consistent intake can be in the form of dietary protein foods or by amino acid supplementation. This intake should be consumed three times per day, in accordance with WF nutrition principles discussed in Chapter 8.

4) Also make certain you are taking in a high-quality vitamin/mineral supplement consistently throughout the day, usually two to three times per day.

5) If you'd like to experiment with a creatine load/maintain, now is the cycle to do so.

6) Sever all refined, junk, and fatty foods from your diet right now if you have not already done so. Remember, once the season gets here, you will not be able to make up for this vital preseason phase! How well you perform this winter depends on your actions now!

RESOURCES

Magazines

Inside Triathlon: 1830 N. 55th Street, Boulder, CO 80301; 303-440-0601; e-mail: insidetri@aol.com.

Multisport: 475 Gate Five Road, Suite 210-A, Sausalito, CA 94965; 415-289-1710; e-mail: mssportmag@aol.com.

Outside: 400 Market Street, Santa Fe, NM 87501; 800-678-1131.

Websites

www.iditasport.com

www.mosquitonet.com/~aws

Wholistic Fitness® Winter Performance Training Mt. Taylor Special Cycle Summation

---

Cycle's Dates: _____

Athlete's Name: _____

Please address each category as openly as possible.

STRENGTH TRAINING

1) Note your consistency during this discipline. How were your energy levels?

_____

_____

_____

_____

2) What were your strengths? What were your weaknesses? Identify them and describe how you will deal with them this in-season:

_____

_____

_____

_____

3) The most important teaching of this strength-training discipline that I can use in my winter multisport performance is:

_____

_____

_____

_____

_____

CV TRAINING

4) Did you have any standout reactions in this discipline? Were you able to do the volumes as prescribed?

_____

_____

_____

_____

_____

5) Which dryland training activities did you do the most? How will this help you this season?

_____

_____

_____

_____

_____

6) The most important teaching of this CV-training discipline that I can use in my winter multisport performance is:

_____

_____

_____

_____

_____

KINESTHETIC TRAINING

7) Did you have any standout reactions in this discipline?

_____

_____

_____
_____
_____

8) Comment on how the past fifteen weeks of intense study in this discipline has shifted your awareness compared to previous years:

_____
_____
_____
_____
_____

9) The most important teaching of this kinesthetic-training discipline that I can use in my winter multisport performance is:

_____
_____
_____
_____
_____

MEDITATION

10) What truth did you find in this cycle?

_____
_____
_____
_____
_____

11) On a scale of one to ten, with ten being the highest, judge your mental focus during training:

_____
_____
_____
_____
_____

During everyday life:

_____
_____
_____
_____
_____

12) What are you doing to resolve this difference?

_____
_____
_____
_____
_____

13) The most important teaching of this meditation discipline that I can use in my winter multisport performance is:

_____
_____
_____
_____
_____

NUTRITION

14) How did this cycle's workload affect you nutritionally?

_____
_____
_____
_____
_____

15) Describe exactly what you ate and drank yesterday and the manner in which you ate it. Note any cravings.

_____
_____
_____

_____

_____

_____

16) What could you have done to better nourish yourself? Why didn't you? How will you make the adjustment over this in-season?

_____

_____

_____

_____

17) Overall, what did you learn from your Mt. Taylor Special training cycle?

_____

_____

_____

_____

Part VII

Specialization Training Programs for Skill Sports

photo by Roy Wilkinson

29

Alpine Skiing

*"Be careful lest in casting out the devils
you cast out the best thing that's in you."*
—Nietzsche

FINDING THE DANCE

From a Wholistic Fitness perspective, high-performance alpine skiing is a wonderful dance of yin and yang, of soft and hard, of female and male energies. In each of the three primary aspects of performance skiing—technical, physical, and mental—there is a fantastic oscillation of energy and attitude. Sometimes the dance is floating and modern (bottomless powder in an open bowl); other times it's hip-hop (taking a ragin' fall line in the moguls); at still other times it's a ballet of precise structure and timing (racing). Regardless, the elegant skier is a highly intuitive and adaptable creature. Performance skiing is untethered by the intellect, yet maintains a strict standard of inner discipline. Since alpine skiing was not covered in Part Three, let's take a moment and do a little dancing.

TECHNICAL SKILLS

Our prior discussion of Feldenkrais' notion of *differentiation* is of forceful merit. The high-level skier knows how to independently control his or her limbs in both the slightest and most dynamic of ways to affect balance and speed control. Cultivating a soft sensitivity to the snow is absolutely vital to finding the edge-to-edge expression of the skis. Some ski instructors term this subtle kinesthetic capacity *ski feel*. The program in this book heightens neural recruitment patterns and expands neuromuscular ability in order to develop ski feel.

PHYSICAL SKILLS

The program in this book targets the primary kinesiology of alpine skiing, which involves a neutral ski position (the skier is

The ability to relax and ski from a centered mental and physical core is paramount to performance skiing. Wholistic Fitness student Dr. Josh Kleinman of Vancouver, British Columbia, spends yet another day at the office. Photo courtesy Josh Kleinman archives.

balanced in a semiflexed stance with equal weight on both legs); a lateral stepping motion (movement to the side initiated by a downward pole plant), and angulation and pressure control (the skier angulates and imparts pressure to the inside edge of the outside ski). The following major muscles need to be trained:

- Neutral position: quadriceps, anterior tibialis, gastrocnemius, and peroneals. The gluteals as well as the abdominals stabilize this ski position, while some upper-body musculature, such as the deltoids and forearm flexors, assist in balance and proper pole position.
- Lateral stepping motion: More emphasis falls onto the forearm flexors and triceps for proper pole planting, while a lateral

thrust is accomplished by the abductors of the upper leg. The erector spinae muscles, rectus abdominus, obliques, and gluteals all produce a smooth lateral movement while helping the skier maintain ski feel.

- Angulation and pressure control: Powerful extension of the quadriceps and tensor fascia latae is immediate. Throughout this phase, the illipsoas flexes the hip and the rectus abdominus flex the midtorso. Once again, the trusty gluteals and lower-back muscles act as stabilizers.

MENTAL SKILLS

The ability to relax and ski from a centered mental and physical core is paramount to performance skiing. Real mental fortitude comes from the confidence gained through experiencing a wide variety of skiing conditions: slush, cold, moguls, powder, crud, steeps, and trees, for example. The most graceful skiers seem to handle all conditions with poise and effortless control. Such high-speed artistry comes not so much from physical conditioning but from constant mental training in the forms of awareness, acceptance, and faith in oneself.

Alpine skiing is not a very difficult sport for which to train, compared to all the fun you get in return. Compared to nordic ski racing, for instance, training for alpine skiing is a piece of cake. My alpine race experience, combined with my nordic background, has enabled me to produce several training programs for the alpine skier that have always produced exceptional fitness among my students. It is almost as if Wholistic Fitness was custom designed for the alpine skier. This isn't surprising. Alpine skiing demands holism from an athletic perspective. It requires every aspect of athletic ability and conditioning: agility, balance, coordination, flexibility, strength, power, and cardiovascular fitness.

Unlike endurance sports, however, no one aspect of alpine skiing is prioritized over the others. My nordic teammates and I used to make fun of the alpine racers because their sport was so much easier to train for than nordic racing. In retrospect, my alpine ski racing days were a lot more fun than nordic racing. What's not to love about exploding from the start booth, running gates at high speed, and skidding to a cool stop after about eighty seconds of effort? And then you get to ride a chairlift back up the hill! Compared to two snot-blowing, lung-searing hours at threshold effort around and around a nordic ski track, is it any wonder alpine skiing is more popular among the mainstream? Having said that, however, my nordic racing experience is more meaningful to me than the days of flashy alpine racing. The point is, though, that alpine skiing is a tremendous sport for general fitness. The program I've designed will help you attain a fantastic level of alpine ski fitness. Have fun with it!

The following program is to be engaged immediately after the Perfect Power phase recovery week. This program is appropriate for all recreational and expert level alpine skiers, including bumps, steeps, powder, and performance racing.

This program does not cover specific skiing techniques but prepares the body, mind, and spirit for the pursuit of alpine skiing. Specific ski technique should be studied under the guidance of a qualified instructor. Recommended instruction is available via the organizations, books, and magazines listed in the resources section that concludes this chapter.

Now, let's get to training!

THE QUANTUM TAO ALPINE SKI PROGRAM

The Quantum Tao program is to be followed for five consecutive weeks. This phase enhances alpine ski performance while decreasing injury potential. Appropriate transpersonal power development is also designed into the program.

Length of cycle: five weeks.
Frequency: seven-day cycle.
Next cycle: in season.
Primary goals: refine all prior mental, physical, and spiritual fitness gained from previous training cycles for alpine skiing performance.

Wholistic Fitness® Training Precepts

1) Be prepared.
2) Be on time.
3) Give 110 percent.

QUANTUM TAO MASTER SHEET

All workouts are described in the next section, Wholistic Notes.

Mammoth Mountain Monday: Day One

Off-day on *all* disciplines. Get massage/bodywork if possible.

T-Ride Tuesday: Day Two

Strength training: Quantum Tao Workout One.

CV training: None, or sixty minutes of a CV activity of your choice at Zones 1–2.

Kinesthetic training: Medium Form Flexibility before strength training.

Meditation: Early-morning zazen practice.

Whistler Wednesday: Day Three

CV training: Run or cycle for one hour at Zone 2 with cruise intervals

Kinesthetic training: Medium Form Flexibility before CV training.

Meditation: 3 x 30 assignment.

Stowe It Thursday: Day Four

Strength training: Quantum Tao Workout Two.

CV training: None, or sixty minutes of a CV activity of your choice at Zones 1–2.

Kinesthetic training: Yoga class or Short into Medium Form Flexibility.

Meditation: Let your kinesthetic training be your meditation.

Lake Tahoe Friday: Day Five

CV training: Inline ski or skate for one hour at Zones 1–2. Focus on downhill ski technique during all descents. Option: Set up a street slalom or GS course and run "gates."

Kinesthetic training: Yoga class or Short into Medium Form Flexibility.

Meditation: Early-morning zazen practice.

Snow Summit Saturday: Day Six

CV training: Pick one or a combo of running, cycling, hiking, or inline skiing and do it at Zones 1–2 for one and a half to two and a half hours. Perform Minutes Are Forever workout. The intervals should be done on moderate (5–7 percent grade) uphill terrain.

Kinesthetic Training: Yoga class or Short into Medium Form Flexibility.

Meditation: Let your kinesthetic training and your intervals be your meditation.

Summit County Sunday: Day Seven

Strength training: Quantum Tao IWT/IWCT full-body workout.

CV training: Cross-train from yesterday, but keep it real easy: Zone 1 for one hour. This workout *must* follow strength training.

Kinesthetic Training: Medium Form either before strength training or after CV training.

Meditation: Pre-event meditation; passive meditation for ten to twenty minutes;

visualize your upcoming week of training. Schedule bodywork and yoga, plan mealtimes, etc.

WHOLISTIC NOTES

This section provides the specific workouts prescribed in the Quantum Tao Master Sheet.

Strength-Training Workouts

Survive these workouts, and you will experience unprecedented ski performance and injury prevention. Master these workouts, and you will experience enlightenment!

For each of the following workouts adhere to these three guidelines:

1) Limit the recovery phase to thirty seconds.
2) Perform all sets to momentary muscular failure or failure of elegance, unless otherwise noted.
3) Refer to the Appendix for instructions on all movements and techniques.

Quantum Tao Upper-Body Workout

Bench Presses: Use Envelope Technique.

Bent Arm Dumbbell Pullovers: Four sets of ten reps with Ku Top or Bottom Form recovery—your choice!

Seated Rows: Use Envelope Technique.

High Pulls: Three sets of ten reps with Ku Bottom Form.

Dumbbell Seated Presses: Two sets done with Three-Stage Technique.

Seated Dumbbell Side Lateral Raises: Three sets of twelve reps with Ku Bottom Form recovery.

Barbell Curls: Four sets of fifteen reps.

Two-Bench Triceps: Two sets of one minute each. Pace yourself; I want the final fifteen seconds at tempo!

Upper-Body Plyometric Superset:

1) Dumbbell Arm Swings for 15 seconds.
2) Dumbbell Horizontal Swings for 15 seconds.
3) Recover for 15 seconds.

Repeat twice.

Superset for Two Times:

a) Wrist Curls for forty-five seconds.
b) Reverse Wrist Curls for thirty seconds.
c) Recover for thirty seconds.

Repeat.

Quantum Tao Lower-Body Workout

Stiff Leg Deadlifts: Two sets of five reps. A strong spine is an absolute must for alpine conditioning!

Superset for Three Times:

a) Squats: Six. I want these to be deep! Think scuba squats!
b) Leg Extensions: Use Staccato Technique.

Superset for Three Times:

a) Leg Curls: Eight.
b) Squat Jumps: Sixty seconds, baby! No whining—strive for elegance through difficulty!

Gunther Hops: Two sets done with Staccato Technique. Go!

Expert Skiers Only—Add this Superset for Two Times:

a) Side Hops for twenty seconds.

b) Knee Tuck Jumps for twenty seconds.

Standing Calf Raises: Four sets of fifteen reps. Stay deep and strong.

Superset for Three Times:

a) Suspended Leg Raises for one minute.

b) Oblique Twists for one minute.

The Quantum Tao IWT/ICWT Full-Body Workout

This two-part workout prepares the mind/body/spirit for performance alpine skiing. This workout provides exceptional biochemical training besides the obvious spiritual benefits of tenacity and confidence. Your enriched inner power will bring on the training effect necessary for complete physiological and spiritual transfer. Good luck and remember: There is nothing like Wholistic Fitness strength training!

Part One: The IWT (Interval Weight Training) Program
Squats (Full or Back Squat preferred): Fifteen reps.
Stationary Cycle (or Versa-Climber or Elliptical Trainer): Two minutes at Zones 3–4.
Squats: Five reps.
Stationary Cycle: Two minutes at Zones 3–4.

Squats: Fifteen reps.
Stationary Cycle: Two minutes at Zones 3–4.
Pull-Ups: Go to muscle failure.
Side Hops: Thirty seconds
Dips: Go to muscle failure.
Jump Squats: Forty-five seconds.

Part Two: The ICWT (Interval Circuit Weight Training) Program
V-Handle Pulldowns: Fifteen reps.
Bench Presses: Fifteen reps.
Seated Rowing: Fifteen reps.
Speed Cleans: Fifteen reps.
Seated Barbell Presses: Fifteen reps.
Barbell Curls: Fifteen reps.
Gunther Hops: Twenty jumps.
Recover for one minute, then repeat: two times for recreational alpine skiers; three times for competitive alpine skiers; four times for competitive alpine skiers who want the top of the podium.

CV Training

Minimum weekly hours range from four and a half to a max of seven and a half. The higher your skill level as a skier and the more ambitious your winter goals, the higher those weekly hours should be!

Minutes Are Forever Workout

Run or hike hard for one minute (at Zones 3–4), then do a recovery walk for one minute at Zone 1. Keep doing this until you throw up or ten minutes have gone by. Recover for ten minutes, then repeat the sequence. Do these intervals on steep uphills to increase lactate threshold and leg stamina.

Cruise Intervals

While on a Zone 1–2 workout, perform four to six intervals of two minutes each, with a full recovery between. During the intervals, focus on smooth, powerful mechanics. Bring your intervals to Zone 3 as soon as possible and finish at Zone 4. During the last thirty seconds of each interval increase the tempo. After each interval, go at Zone 1 until your heart rate drops down to Zone 2. Resume fluid form, then pop off another interval.

Kinesthetic Training

Notice the high priority given to yoga and flexibility training. It will come back to you a hundred times over in the form of injury prevention, mental focus, and spiritual development. Stay consistent with the Master Sheet in this discipline, and you will be astounded at your ski performance. Note: This strength-training program has significant kinesthetic transfer for your skiing. Work with pure devotion on each strength-training session for optimal ski performance.

Meditation

Early-Morning Zazen Session. Wake up, relieve yourself, then assume the zazen posture. Sit for eight minutes. Perform Kin Hin (walking meditation); it should be per-formed with hands in a "gassho mudra," or prayer hand, position. The meditation is designed to mindfully place each step with awareness and not to let the mind wander from the walking. It is best done in an environment where you are not likely to be interrupted in any way. The walk can be as short as one minute to as long as several minutes in duration. Sit for another eight minutes. End the session and take mindfulness with you.

Beeper Guru Breath and Posture Assignment. Set your watch alarm to go off every hour. Upon the beep, take note of where your breath, posture, and mind are. Make adjustments in alignment. Note how often the Beeper Guru catches you in random thought, out of posture, or with the breath high and shallow instead of low and deep.

3 x 30 Assignment. This is taken from a Theravada Buddhist mindfulness exercise. At each mealtime (assume three sit-down meals per day) I want you to chew your first bite of food thirty times. During this chewing, feel the significance of the food being eaten. Appreciate the fact that you are not different from the food you eat and that one day, you too will be "eaten" by the universe. Use this time to honor and revere your food and "tell" the food that you will do your best to use its life-giving energy to refine yourself in order to help others.

Wholistic Fitness®
Pre-Event Meditation

Assume zazen posture;

perform ten cleansing breaths;
perform ten filling breaths.
Recite the following:

As I release my breath, I release my body.

As I release my breath, I let go of any physical, mental, or emotional tensions.

Relaxing into my breath, I realize no separation between myself and the world around me. Nor am I separate from the easy or difficult circumstances in my life. They are all me. I am all them. And it's all appropriate.

As I breathe, I realize that Joy is my natural state.

As long as I breathe, I know that nothing can interfere with this Joy.

Upon my inbreath, I sense a rush of beautiful, comfortable energy. This is my Divine Source. I allow this energy to flow into and out from my body. Relaxing ... feeling empty ...

When I relax, I perform better. When I am empty, I perform better. I will use my breath in my upcoming event in order to relax. In order to empty. I will surrender into the Universe. I trust completely that the Universe will power me into my best effort. Everything that I will go through during my event will be precisely what I need to learn most.

I can already sense how powerfully I will compete because I will have the Universe charging through my emptiness ... all

I need to do is breathe and relax into my effort.

As long as I breathe, my performance will be an elegant and strong expression of the Universe.

Recite three times. Go into a visualization of your event for three to five minutes; perform five cleansing breaths; perform five filling breaths; end the session.

Nutrition

Although alpine skiers are notorious for their poor nutrition and quality partying skills, they can ill afford to be mindless in the feeding of their body as they strive toward higher levels of ski performance. Especially at elite levels in extreme situations, one second of a poor neural service resulting from sloppy nutrition can mean a misfire of appropriate muscular response. That neural misfire can mean, in turn, a crash resulting in anything from a twisted knee to death. Do I take nutrition seriously for alpine skiers? You better believe it! Perhaps that's why, to date, no alpine skier has ever suffered a ski-produced injury while under my supervision! The choice is yours. Feed your body crap, and your ski performance will reflect that choice. Nourish your body by the principles outlined in this book, and you will experience higher levels of ski performance than ever before.

Alpine skiers must make certain to take a high-quality amino acid and vitamin/mineral supplement each day, plus supportive nutrition for joint health. Consider Siberian ginseng, Muscl-Flex, and/or a cycle of creatine load/maintain as per Chapter Eight. And if you are still carrying some unwanted body fat, this is the time to jettison it by keeping fat intake to 15 percent of total calories per day and doing the higher range of CV volumes as per the Quantum Tao Master Sheet. These choices are all yours. How badly do you want it?

RESOURCES

Contact the following associations for qualified instruction in alpine skiing.

Professional Ski Instructors of America (PSIA): 133 South Van Gordon Street, Suite 101, Lakewood, CO 80228; 303-987-9390; fax: 303-988-3005.

U.S. Skiing: P.O. Box 100, Park City, UT 84060; 801-649-9090; fax: 801-649-3613.

Magazines

Powder: P.O. Box 1028, Dana Point, CA 92629.

Skiing and *Ski:* Both are at 929 Pearl St., Boulder, CO 80302; 303-448-7600; www.skinet.com.

Mountain Sports and Living: 810 7th Ave. 4th Floor, New York, NY 10019; 212-636-2700.

Outside: 400 Market Street, Santa Fe, NM 87501; 800-678-1131.

Books

Alpine Skiing: Steps to Success, John Yacenda. 1992. $15.95. Human Kinetics Publishers.

Centered Skier: Skiing as a Moving Meditation, Denise McCluggage. 1983. $6.95. Bantam New Age Publishers. (This classic can be hard to find; ISBN 0-553-34020-4).

Cold Comfort: Keeping Warm in the Outdoors, Glenn Randall. 1987. $10.95. Lyons & Burford Publishers.

Wholistic Fitness® Winter Performance Training Quantum Tao Cycle Summation

Cycle's Dates: _____

Athlete's Name: _____

Please address each category as openly as possible.

STRENGTH TRAINING

1) Note your consistency during this discipline. How were your energy levels?

_____

_____

_____

_____

_____

2) What were your strengths? What were your weaknesses? Identify them and describe how you will deal with them this in-season.

_____

_____

_____

_____

_____

3) The most important teaching of this strength-training discipline that I can use in my alpine skiing performance is:

_____

_____

_____

_____

_____

CV TRAINING

4) Did you have any standout reactions in this discipline? Were you able to do the volumes as prescribed?

_____

_____

_____

_____

_____

5) Which dryland training activities did you do the most? How will this help you this season?

_____
_____
_____
_____
_____

6) The most important teaching of this CV-training discipline that I can use in my alpine skiing performance is:

_____
_____
_____
_____
_____

KINESTHETIC TRAINING

7) Did you have any standout reactions in this discipline?

_____
_____
_____
_____
_____

8) Comment on how the past fifteen weeks of intense study in this discipline has shifted your awareness compared to previous years.

_____
_____
_____
_____
_____

9) The most important teaching of this kinesthetic-training discipline that I can use in my alpine skiing performance is:

_____
_____

_____

_____

_____

MEDITATION

10) Note your consistency with your meditation practice this cycle.

_____

_____

_____

_____

_____

11) On a scale of one to ten, with ten being the highest, judge your mental focus during meditation:

_____

_____

_____

_____

_____

During everyday life:

_____

_____

_____

_____

_____

12) What are you doing to resolve this difference while skiing?

_____

_____

_____

_____

13) The most important teaching of this meditation discipline that I can use in my alpine skiing performance is:

_____

_____
_____
_____
_____

NUTRITION

14) How did this cycle's workload affect you nutritionally?

_____
_____
_____
_____
_____

15) Describe *exactly* what you ate and drank yesterday and the manner in which you ate it. Note any cravings.

_____
_____
_____
_____
_____

16) What could you have done to better nourish yourself? Why didn't you? How will you make the adjustment over this in-season?

_____
_____
_____
_____
_____

17) Overall, what did you learn from your Quantum Tao training cycle?

_____
_____
_____
_____
_____

30

Area Telemark Skiing

"Relax, pare down, let go, and simplify. Chuang Tzu speaks of 'fasting of the mind.' Let the mind fast, and learning happens."
—Denise McCluggage in "The Centered Skier"

Telemark skiing near where it all began ... Carving sunset turns at Salla Ski Area, Finland. Photo by Mike Powell/ ALLSPORT.

FREE THE HEEL, FREE THE MIND

First, make sure you are reading the right chapter. It's not for backcountry ski tourers who enjoy making an occasional telemark turn through a bowl or glade during their ski excursion. This chapter concerns itself with aggressively linked telemark turns done at established ski areas. That's right, we nordic types are mixing it up with the alpine, fat-ski boys and girls on the double-diamond runs. Area telemark skiing is about chairlifts, holding aggro fall lines, and mogul bashing! It's fast and dynamic, and it's a splendid sight to see when a good tele skier whups it up on a hard run. Heads

345

turn from the chairlift and alpine skiers, those beasts with their heels clamped down on their skis, can only shake their heads and wonder, "How did she do that?"

We do it by freeing the heel! Free-heeling is where the sport of skiing began! In the 1850s people in the town of Telemark, Norway, invented a special turn to do downhill while on their cross-country skis. In this turn was the epitome of aesthetic athletics: arcing gracefulness, sweeping speed, and fast-twitch turns in tight runs.

TELEMARKING AND PHYSICAL REALITY

Somewhat unfortunately, today's telemark skiers are getting too carried away by the fanfare generated by equipment manufacturers. In other words, the contemporary area telemark skier is looking more and more like an alpine skier. Many tele skiers now use alpine skis as well as stiff plastic boots not dissimilar to alpine ski boots. The old three-pin bindings, once our hallmark (those bindings are what inspired the nickname "pinheads" for telemark skiers), have been replaced by beefy, bombproof cable bindings complete with "heel locators." I mean, really, why don't we just go alpine skiing?

If we want to know *genuine* telemark skiing, then dump all that fancy stuff, go and get some edgeless nordic track skis and low-cut leather boots and head for the

chairlift! This flimsy set-up forces you to find true balance in the fore-to-aft stability of such a feeble ski at high speed. Wholistic Fitness sport philosophy always questions technological advances. Gandhi once said that technology should have stopped at the spinning wheel. I wonder what he'd think of parabolic skis?

Do technical advances really "advance" the sport, or do they subtract from it by replacing inner skills with greater reliance on equipment? Have I depressed you? Will you ever look at your Terminator Tele Boots and parabolic skies the same way again? My intent here is certainly not to depress or impress. The intent is a Wholistic Fitness principle of authenticity: look within to find your skills, not in equipment or technology. Do this: Every third time you go tele skiing, do so on your track skis! Not only will this improve your ski feel, balance, and responsiveness, it will add new challenge to your local ski area and increase your fitness. I'm not saying, throw away your fancy tele gear, I'm just asking you to get back to the shining fundamentals.

Since telemark skiing was not covered in Part Three, let's take a moment and do a little info skiing.

TECHNICAL SKILLS

The technical skills of area telemarking are rooted in spirituality. To be technically proficient on tele skis means being free from the bonded heel, free to the art of letting go and being fully open and receptive to the mountain. So long as we force the telemark turn, we will not know its essence. The moment we stop *trying* to telemark is the moment the telemark finds us. I recall a poster in one of my elementary school classrooms that depicted the image of a butterfly resting on a flower. The writing on the poster said:

> Happiness is like a butterfly.
> The more you chase it
> The more it will elude you.
> But the moment you put attention
>   elsewhere,
> It comes and lands softly on
>   your shoulder.

The technical skills of telemarking allow us to put our attention elsewhere, so the telemark comes into us on its own accord. Allow the turn to happen naturally; don't make it a goal. Instead, concentrate on the following technical aspects of the telemark in order to create that inner opening for it to manifest. I work with four phases: the preparation phase, drop phase, steering phase, and recovery phase.

Preparation Phase

Glide downhill with both skis parallel, then slowly stride into the telemark position. For the purposes of this discussion, let's have the right leg be our lead ski. Keep the head and upper body quiet. Your body weight should be centered between the lead and trailing ski. Lower your center of gravity (COG), keeping even your body weight distribution. The arms mimic the lower body, keeping a 90-degree flexion at the elbows. The shoulders are slightly flexed to create a more stabilized position for poling.

Drop Phase

As the name implies, drop assertively into a lower stance by flexing both knees. Rotate the right knee in the direction of the turn (in this example we are turning left) and flex the right hip. Extend the left hip, and as the body sinks lower into the telemark position, your pelvis should rotate to the left. Really get low here—that's why I mandate so much flexibility and yoga work for tele skiers. The lower your position, the more stable you become, because your COG allows the body closer proximity to its support base. The arms should abduct only slightly and stay low. The higher you keep your arms and the farther away from the upper torso, the more reduction in lateral stability. Meanwhile the pelvic girdle needs to flex laterally to the right, allowing proper body lean into the mountain. Balance is tricky during these rotary movements. Keep the eyes soft and focused on a stationary object down the mountain. This does two things: It keeps you centered, and it forces the upper torso to twist in the opposite direction of the turn. This counterrotation maximizes efficient COG positioning.

Steering Phase

Push the right toe down into the snow and allow the trunk to compress into the turn. This body position and compression accomplishes the edging effect from which the turn arises. Beginning tele skiers tend to overcommit to this edge, causing the ski to push out instead of down, like the front tire of a mountain biking washing out. Keep pressing weight into the right toe to increase the beneficial friction between ski and snow. Poling during the steering phase transfers speed and momentum into the turn. Plant the right pole just before you turn. As you complete the turn, bring the left arm and pole forward to complete the follow through in smooth form. At the same time, push down on the lead ski and turn the body to the left. Push off the right pole to carry the body through the turn. This entire phase lasts but a few seconds, before you find yourself in the recovery position.

Recovery Phase

Once your trunk has rotated back to center and the left knee, right hip, and right knee are extended, you have reached the recovery phase. Here the arms mimic the preparation phase, but with the left arm and pole anticipating the pole plant. Beginning pinheads will tend to rise during the recovery phase to aid in balance, while advanced pinheads stay low to keep their COG contributing to momentum.

PHYSICAL SKILLS

Tele skiers tend to be a pretty fit bunch. Most are not outwardly competitive but often display significant inner drive to perform at their best. Area telemarking is fatiguing stuff, way harder than alpine skiing. I regularly keep my heart rate at my Zone 3 level when tele skiing on my track skis. When I use my bigger Kazama boards, my heart rate lowers. One of my favorite half-day Santa Fe winter workouts begins with a body- and spirit-opening morning yoga class, then a prefatigue of my thighs and lungs with a fifty-minute snowshoe run on the Borrego Trail (a four-mile, hilly loop), into three hours of tele skiing on the poma at Santa Fe Ski Basin. That final hour of tele skiing just torches my legs. I ride the poma to keep my heart rate up and to really push my thighs to the max. I might not have the most beautiful telemarking form in the world during that last hour, but my training effect is sky high!

The program in this book targets the kinesiology of area telemark skiing, according to the phases discussed earlier.

Preparation Phase

Striding into the telemark position means rectus femoris and vastus lateralis activity as well as stabilization via the hamstring group. A little bit lower, the gastrocnemius is working to help keep the plantar flexion sound. I like training the erector spinae and trapezius to keep the head and upper body quiet. Deltoids need preparatory work since the shoulders are slightly flexed.

Drop Phase

The knee extensors have to flex the right and left knees, which means priority training for the quadriceps. At the right hip, eccentric contraction occurs with the hip extensors, namely my favorite muscle—the gluteus maximus. Some of the adductors and medial rotators have to work as well to adduct eccentrically the hip and inspire concentric medial rotation. Extending the left hip will activate the glutes as well as the hamstrings in an eccentric fashion. The ankle muscles, the gastrocnemius, soleus, and tibialis group are quite involved during the drop phase as they flex the ankle. Up in the trunk, both eccentric and concentric contractions occur to rotate and laterally flex the trunk. This is why you'll see a lot of oblique and midsection work in the following program.

Steering Phase

The big deal from a kinesiological perspective in the steering phase is the force applied to the lead ski via the knee extensors and lateral trunk flexion. I like my tele skiers to have superstrong ankle joints due to the concentric eversion occurring repetitively at the subtalar joint on both sides. This is what the big, plastic boots strive to achieve: isometric contraction of the plantar flexors during dorsiflexion as well as

the eversion movement at the subtalar joint. Wholistic Fitness philosophy says just get in the gym and train this area instead of looking to equipment to act as a Band-Aid for what should come from within! It is also during this phase that the arms are most active, mostly flexion at the shoulder joint, protraction and depression of the scapula, and a little extension at both elbows.

Recovery Phase

We need good training targeting the serratus anterior, external obliques, and rectus abdominals to rotate the trunk. The vastus lateralis and medialis will take care of the knee extension in this phase while the hip extensors concentrically contract. Basically, every involved muscle is in a concentric state of contraction, save for the lead leg, whose ankle is isometrically contracted. This is why we call this phase a recovery phase since eccentric contractions always require more effort than concentric contractions.

MENTAL SKILLS

I have previously touted the technical value of spiritually "letting go" to discover fluid, effective telemark form. Your mental training should facilitate this concept of letting go while also focusing on technique-specific movement. William Blake wrote, "If one is to do good, good must be done in minute particulars." Though Blake was speaking of humanitarian gestures, the same holds true for tele skiing. If we are to discover the goodness of our tele turns, we must focus on the details of our skiing to allow the flow to evolve. My kinesiological evaluation of tele skiing gives you plenty on which to focus. I know from experience that should my analysis be taken to the mountain, the words will melt into a jazz-like rhythm that will produce skiing at a level you've only dreamed about. The magic of the Wholistic Fitness way is such. We can create complexity in our minds, but we learn to breathe with simplicity. If we allow the play of analysis its freedom, we discover the spirit of direct presence in our sport performance. All mental training in the following program is directed toward this playful presence.

The following program is to be engaged immediately after the Perfect Power phase recovery week. This program is appropriate for all recreational and expert-level area telemark skiers.

This program does not cover specific telemark technique but prepares the body, mind, and spirit for the pursuit of performance telemark skiing. Specific telemark technique should be studied under the guidance of a qualified instructor. Recommended instruction is available via the organizations, magazines, and books listed in the resources section that concludes this chapter.

Now, let's get to training!

THE FLUID EDGE PROGRAM

The Fluid Edge program is to be followed for five consistent weeks. This phase enhances telemark ski performance while decreasing injury potential. Appropriate transpersonal power development is also designed into the program.

Length of cycle: five weeks.
Frequency: seven-day cycle.
Next cycle: in season.
Primary goals: refine all prior mental, physical, and spiritual fitness gained from previous training cycles for telemark skiing performance.

Wholistic Fitness® Training Precepts

1) Be prepared.
2) Be on time.
3) Give 110 percent.

FLUID EDGE MASTER SHEET

All workouts are described in the next section, Wholistic Notes.

Zip Bowl Monday: Day One

Off-day on *all* disciplines. Get massage/bodywork if possible.

Big Tesuque Tuesday: Day Two

Strength training: Fluid Edge Workout One.
CV training: None, or sixty minutes of a CV activity of your choice at Zones 1–2.

Kinesthetic training: Medium Form Flexibility before strength training.

Meditation: Early-morning zazen practice.

Whiteout Wednesday: Day Three

CV training: Run, cycle, or inline ski for one hour at Zone 2 with cruise intervals.

Kinesthetic training: Medium Form Flexibility before CV training.

Meditation: 3 x 30 assignment.

Hop Telemark Thursday: Day Four

Strength training: Fluid Edge Workout Two.

CV training: None, or sixty minutes of a CV activity of your choice at Zones 1–2. Cross-train from Wednesday.

Kinesthetic training: Yoga class or Short into Medium Form Flexibility.

Meditation: Sanskrit Skillfulness meditation.

Fluid Edge Friday: Day Five

CV training: Inline ski for one hour at Zones 1–2. Focus on telemark ski technique during all descents. Option: Set up a street slalom or GS course and run "gates."

Kinesthetic training: Yoga class or Short into Medium Form Flexibility.

Meditation: Early-morning zazen practice.

Off-Piste Saturday: Day Six

CV training: Pick one or a combo of running, cycling, hiking, inline skating and do it at Zones 1–2 for one to two hours.

Perform Minutes Are Forever workout. The intervals should be done on moderate (5–7 percent grade) uphill terrain.

Kinesthetic training: Yoga class or Short into Medium Form Flexibility.

Meditation: Let your kinesthetic and your intervals be your meditation.

Sastrugi Sunday: Day Seven

Strength training: Fluid Edge IWT/IWCT full-body workout.

EEE-GAD full-body workout (alternate weekly).

CV training: None, but keep the heart rate elevated during your strength training.

Kinesthetic training: Yoga class or Short into Medium Form Flexibility.

Meditation: Pre-event meditation; passive meditation for ten to twenty minutes; visualize your upcoming week of training. Schedule bodywork and yoga, plan mealtimes, etc.

WHOLISTIC NOTES

This section provides the specific workouts prescribed in the Fluid Edge Master Sheet.

Strength-Training Workouts

Effective skiing involves staying relaxed during difficult sections. Practice staying relaxed during each set; that is, really focus on the body part under attention but relax all the others. Cultivate full-body awareness and isolate the specific body part being trained.

For each of the following workouts adhere to these three guidelines:

1) Limit the recovery phase to thirty seconds.
2) Perform all sets to momentary muscular failure or failure of elegance, unless otherwise noted.
3) Refer to the Appendix for instructions on all movements and techniques.

Fluid Edge Workout One

Bench Presses: Three sets of ten reps.

Dumbbell Flat Bench Flyes: Three sets of twelve reps.

Bent Arm Dumbbell Pullovers: Four sets of ten reps with Ku Top Form recovery.

Seated Rows: Four sets of eight reps with Ku Top Form.

High Pulls: Three sets of ten reps with Ku Bottom Form.

Seated Dumbbell Presses: Two sets done with Three-Stage Technique.

Seated Dumbbell Side Lateral Raises: Three sets of twelve reps.

Barbell Curls: Four sets of fifteen reps.

Two-Bench Triceps: Two sets of one minute each. Pace yourself; I want the final fifteen seconds at tempo!

Upper-Body Plyometric Superset:
1) Double Pole Plyos for fifteen seconds.
2) Dumbbell Horizontal Swings for fifteen seconds.
3) Recover for fifteen seconds.
Repeat twice.

Superset for Two Times:
a) Wrist Curls for forty-five seconds.
b) Reverse Wrist Curls for thirty seconds.
c) Recover for thirty seconds.
Repeat.

Fluid Edge Workout Two

Squats: Four sets of six reps. Visualize strong knee joints for the slopes!

Leg Curls: Three sets of six reps. Develops leg bicep strength.

Leg Extensions: Three sets of eight to ten reps. Develops more connective tissue health for those long runs!

Gunther Hops: Two sets of sixteen reps. Focus on gluteal power.

Superset for Two Times:
a) Jump Squats: Ten. Keep the heart high and power in the legs!
b) Scissor Jumps: Ten. Improves the neural pathway to the legs, which means more coordination!

Standing Calf Raises: Use Envelope Technique.

Oblique Twists: Three sets of one minute each. Midsection fitness means strong tele skiing!

Suspended Leg Raises: Three sets of forty-five seconds each. Dissolve into Knee Ups if you must—just keep moving!

Stiff Leg Deadlifts: Two sets of four reps. Keep a strong spine; take this posture to the slopes!

Fluid Edge IWT/ICWT Program

This two-part workout prepares the mind/body/spirit for performance teleskiing. This workout offers exceptional biochemical training besides the obvious spiritual benefits of tenacity and confidence. Your enriched inner power will bring on the training effect necessary for complete physiological and spiritual transfer. Good luck and remember: There is nothing like Wholistic Fitness strength training!

Part One: The IWT (Interval Weight Training) Program

Back Squats: Fifteen reps.

Stationary Cycle (or Versa-Climber or Elliptical Trainer): Two minutes at Zones 3–4.

Back Squats: Fifteen reps.

Stationary Cycle: Two minutes at Zones 3–4.

Pull-Ups: Go to muscle failure.

Split Jumps: Thirty seconds each leg.

Dips: Go to muscle failure.

Scissor Jumps: Twenty seconds each leg.

Part Two: ICWT (Interval Circuit Weight Training) Program

Bench Presses: Fifteen reps.

Speed Cleans: Fifteen reps.

Upright Rows: Fifteen reps.

Barbell Curls: Fifteen reps.

Handstand: Go until you blow; keep feet up against wall, elegance!

Oblique Twists: One minute.

Gunther Hops: Twenty jumps.

Recover for one minute then repeat: two times for recreational pinheads; three times for serious pinheads; four times for serious pinheads who want enlightenment *now!*

Fluid Edge EEE-GAD Full-Body Workout

Pull-Ups: Two sets of however many you can do.

Front Lat Pulldowns: One set done with Staccato Technique; three sets of eight to ten reps.

Dumbbell Flat-Bench Flyes into Dumbbell Bench Presses: Flyes for ten reps to failure, then crank out high-frequency Dumbbell Bench Presses until you puke black blood. Do two sets.

Back Squats Superset with Leg Extensions: Do Squats for twelve reps to failure, then run over and perform Leg Extensions with Staccato Technique. Do two supersets.

Seated Dumbbell Presses: Two sets done with Three-Stage Technique. Commit to fluidity.

Two-Bench Triceps: Two sets of one minute each. See each rep in a "clean" top and bottom position. You should feel the contraction in the triceps up top. Bring chi to the triceps.

Barbell Curls: Three sets done with Shivaya Technique. Be beautiful; be elegant.

Abdominal Crunches Directly into Leg Raises: Three sets of one minute each.

CV Training

Minimum weekly hours range from three to a max of six. The higher your skill level as a skier and the more ambitious your winter goals, the higher those weekly hours should be!

Minutes Are Forever Workout

Run or hike hard for one minute (at Zones 3–4), then do a recovery walk for one minute at Zone 1. Keep doing this until you throw up or ten minutes have gone by. Recover for ten minutes, then repeat the sequence. Do these intervals on steep uphills to increase lactate threshold and leg stamina.

Cruise Intervals

While on a Zone 1–2 workout, perform four to six intervals of two minutes each, with a full recovery between. During the intervals, focus on smooth, powerful mechanics. Bring your intervals to Zone 3 as soon as possible and finish at Zone 4. During the last thirty seconds of each interval increase the tempo. After each interval, go at Zone 1 until your heart rate drops down to Zone 2. Resume fluid form, then pop off another interval. Repeat.

Kinesthetic Training

Notice the high priority given to yoga and flexibility training. It will come back to you a hundred times over in the form of injury prevention, mental focus, and spiritual development. Stay consistent with the Master

Sheet in this discipline, and you will be astounded at your ski performance. Note: This strength-training program has significant kinesthetic transfer for your skiing. Work with pure devotion during each strength-training session for optimal ski performance. Run active visualizations of skiing when performing ski-specific strength-training movements such as Scissor Jumps.

Meditation

Early-Morning Zazen Session. Wake up, relieve yourself, then assume the zazen posture. Sit for eight minutes. Perform Kin Hin (walking meditation); it should be performed with hands in a "gassho mudra," or prayer hand, position. The meditation is designed to mindfully place each step with awareness and not to let the mind wander from the walking. It is best done in an environment where you are not likely to be interrupted in any way. The walk can be as short as one minute to as long as several minutes in duration. Sit for another eight minutes. End the session and take mindfulness with you.

Beeper Guru Breath and Posture Assignment. Set your watch alarm to go off every hour. Upon the beep, take note of where your breath, posture, and mind are. Make adjustments in alignment. Note how often the Beeper Guru catches you in random thought, out of posture, or with the breath high and shallow instead of low and deep.

3 x 30 Assignment. This is taken from a Theravada Buddhist mindfulness exercise.

At each mealtime (assume three sit-down meals per day) I want you to chew your first bite of food thirty times. During this chewing, feel the significance of the food being eaten. Appreciate the fact that you are not different from the food you eat and that one day, you too will be "eaten" by the universe. Use this time to honor and revere your food and "tell" the food that you will do your best to use its life-giving energy to refine yourself in order to help others.

Wholistic Fitness®
Pre-Event Meditation

Assume zazen posture;
perform ten cleansing breaths;
perform ten filling breaths.
Recite the following:

As I release my breath, I release my body.

As I release my breath, I let go of any physical, mental, or emotional tensions.

Relaxing into my breath, I realize no separation between myself and the world around me. Nor am I separate from the easy or difficult circumstances in my life. They are all me. I am all them. And it's all appropriate.

As I breathe, I realize that Joy is my natural state.

As long as I breathe, I know that nothing can interfere with this Joy.

Upon my inbreath, I sense a rush of beautiful, comfortable energy. This is my Divine Source. I allow this energy to flow into and out from my body. Relaxing ... feeling empty ...

When I relax, I perform better. When I am empty, I perform better. I will use my breath in my upcoming event in order to relax. In order to empty. I will surrender into the Universe. I trust completely that the Universe will power me into my best effort. Everything that I will go through during my event will be precisely what I need to learn most.

I can already sense how powerfully I will compete because I will have the Universe charging through my emptiness ... all I need to do is breathe and relax into my effort.

As long as I breathe, my performance will be an elegant and strong expression of the Universe.

Recite three times. Go into a visualization of your event for three to five minutes; perform five cleansing breaths; perform five filling breaths; end the session.

Sanskrit Skillfulness Meditation

Assume zazen posture ...
Take ten Cleansing Breaths
Recite the following:

All skillfulness, all strain, all intention is contrary to ease.

Practice a thousand times and It becomes difficult.

Practice a thousand thousand and It becomes easy.

Practice a thousand thousand times a thousand thousand, and It is no longer thou that doeth It, but It that doeth Itself through thee.

Only then, is that which is done well done.

Take ten Filling Breaths
Repeat two more times.

Nutrition

Area telemarkers need to be aware of consistent high-quality nutrition if higher levels of ski performance are desired. Especially at elite levels in extreme situations, one second of poor neural service resulting from sloppy nutrition can mean a misfire of appropriate muscular response. That neural misfire can mean, in turn, a crash resulting in anything from a twisted knee to death. Do I take nutrition seriously for teleskiers? During the writing of this book, two skiers perished at a nearby ski resort within the same month. Both were "accidents." Was inadequate awareness due to fatigue a factor in these deaths? Inadequate nutrition spells premature fatigue. Yes, I take nutrition seriously for my athletes. The high rate of injury prevention in my athletes all goes back to nutrition.

Nourish your body by the principles outlined in this book, and you will experience higher levels of ski performance than ever before. Make certain to take a high-quality amino acid and vitamin/mineral supplement each day plus supportive nutri-

tion for joint health. Consider Siberian ginseng, Muscl-Flex, and/or a cycle of creatine load/maintain as per Chapter Eight. If you are still carrying some unwanted body fat, this is the time to jettison it by keeping fat intake to 15 percent of total calories per day and doing the higher range of CV volumes as per the Fluid Edge Master Sheet. These choices are all yours. How much do you want it?

RESOURCES

Contact the following associations for qualified instruction in and information about telemark skiing.

Professional Ski Instructors of America (PSIA): 133 South Van Gordon Street, Suite 101, Lakewood, CO 80228; 303-987-9390; fax: 303-988-3005.

www.winterworld.com/ussi (a collective site for ski resources)

Magazines

Back Country: 7065 Dover Way, Arvada, CO 80004; 303-424-5858.
Cross Country Skier: 1823 Fremont Ave. South, Minneapolis, MN 55403; 612-377-0312.
Outside: 400 Market Street, Santa Fe, NM 87501; 800-678-1131.

Books

The ABC's of Avalanche Safety, Edward R. LaChapelle. 1985. $6.95. Mountaineers Books.

Cold Comfort: Keeping Warm in the Out-doors, Glenn Randall. 1987. $10.95. Lyons & Burford Publishers.

Cross-Country Skiing: A Complete Guide (Trailside Series), Brian Cazeneuve. 1995. $17.95. W.W. Norton & Company.

Good Glide: The Science of Ski Waxing, Leif Torgersen. 1985. $9.95. Human Kinetics Publishers.

Equipment

Black Diamond Equipment, Ltd.: 2084 East 3900 South, Salt Lake City, UT 84214; 801-278-5533.

Eagle River Nordic: P.O. Box 936, Eagle River, WI 54521; 800-423-9730.

Fischer Skis: Geneva Road, Brewster, NY 10509; 800-525-0153.

New Moon Ski Shop: P.O. Box 591XC, Hayward, WI 54843; 715-634-8685.

Reliable Racing Supply, Inc.: 800-223-4448; www.reliableracing.com; e-mail: nordic@reliableracing.com.

Wholistic Fitness® Winter Performance Training
Fluid Edge Cycle Summation

Cycle's Dates: _____

Athlete's Name: _____

Please address each category as openly as possible.

STRENGTH TRAINING

1) Note your consistency during this discipline. How were your energy levels?

_____

_____

_____

_____

_____

2) What were your strengths? What were your weaknesses? Identify them and describe how you will deal with them this in-season.

_____

_____

_____

_____

_____

3) The most important teaching of this strength-training discipline that I can use in my ski performance is:

_____

_____

_____

_____

_____

CV TRAINING

4) Did you have any standout reactions in this discipline? Were you able to do the volumes as prescribed?

_____

_____

_____

_____

_____

5) Which dryland training activities did you do the most? How will this help you this season?

_____

_____

_____

_____

_____

6) The most important teaching of this CV-training discipline that I can use in my ski performance is:

_____

_____

_____

_____

_____

KINESTHETIC TRAINING

7) Did you have any standout reactions in this discipline?

_____

_____

_____

_____

_____

8) Comment on how the past fifteen weeks of intense study in this discipline has shifted your awareness compared to previous years.

_____

_____

_____

_____

_____

9) The most important teaching of this kinesthetic-training discipline that I can use in my ski performance is:

_____

_____

_____

_____

_____

MEDITATION

10) Note your consistency with your meditation practice this cycle:

_____

_____

_____

_____

_____

11) On a scale of one to ten, with ten being the highest, judge your mental focus during meditation:

_____

_____

_____

_____

_____

During everyday life:

_____

_____

_____

_____

12) How will you find softness while skiing difficult terrain this winter?

_____

_____

_____

_____

13) The most important teaching of this meditation discipline that I can use in my ski performance is:

_____

_____

_____

_____

NUTRITION

14) How did this cycle's workload affect you nutritionally?

_____
_____
_____
_____
_____

15) Describe *exactly* what you ate and drank yesterday and the manner in which you ate it. Note any cravings.

_____
_____
_____
_____
_____

16) What could you have done to better nourish yourself? Why didn't you? How will you make the adjustment over this in-season?

_____
_____
_____
_____
_____

17) Overall, what did you learn from your Fluid Edge training cycle?

_____
_____
_____
_____
_____

31

Ice Climbing

"The voice of Nature loudly cries,
And many a message from the skies,
That something in us never dies."
—Robert Burns

SERIOUS STUFF

Of all the sports covered in this book, ice climbing is the most technical and carries the most serious injury potential. The margin for error is slim. Given the popularity of indoor rock climbing, there is a generation of climbers growing up on synthetic walls, where the environment can provide a false sense of safety in the climbing arts.

When I was doing difficult ice climbs in Canada in the '80s, my climbing felt free and uninhibited. It had to. The form of mental training I chose to pursue was formal Tibetan meditation. Much of this inner work pivots upon preparation for death. The Buddha taught,

> In the end, these things matter most:
> How well did you love? How fully did you live?
> How deeply did you learn to let go?

I needed to learn just how deeply I could let go. The Rigid Designator, Vail, Colorado. Photo courtesy George Bracksieck.

363

My journey into ice climbing was a living practice of my meditation. I needed to learn just how deeply I could let go. That meant everything, including my attachment to life. Since I focused primarily on free-soloing (climbing without a rope), to be encumbered by emotional or material baggage while climbing would—for me—clutter intuitive, graceful movement.

Of course, the following program does not require you to test your mental fitness by free-soloing the Rigid Designator or Polar Circus. However, through the following program, which includes meditations that you may feel uncomfortable with, your fitness will advance through mental, physical, and spiritual realms, enabling you to ice climb at your highest level.

Ice climbing is *not* a safe sport. Understand that from the beginning. There is nothing natural about a human being scaling vertical walls of fragile ice. Therefore, it requires extraordinary measures of body/mind awareness and preparation to do it safely.

THE GADD AND ILG SHOW

I would like to introduce a climber and adventure athlete whom many of you may already know, Will Gadd. Will first climbed ice with his father when he was twelve years old. By eighteen, he had climbed most of the Canadian classics, such as Polar Circus and the Weeping Wall. Will stopped climbing ice for a few years to compete in sport climbing and paragliding competitions, but has lately melded sport-climbing techniques and skills to produce new "mixed" routes that have helped establish a new standard at the extreme end of difficulty in the alpine arts. I've known Will for a long while, and it is an honor to have him contribute to this chapter. Let's listen to what this leading ice climber has to share.

Steve: Will, I guess I'm dating myself here, but I'm a little concerned with the younger, indoor sport climbers taking to the ice and high mountains. There seems to be general lack of mindfulness, or respect, or perhaps both for the outdoor elements. It's like they don't realize how different the outdoor environment is, and, as a result, there are a lot of foolish injuries and even deaths occurring.

Will: Occasionally I'll be in a rock gym and someone will ask me, "How come you ice climb? It's all cold and scary and hard and dangerous." I usually say, "Yes, you have it exactly right!" I think it goes without saying that the people reading this book understand that climbing ice must be approached with respect. You know, Yvon Chouinard has a great quote that kind of expresses the importance of respect, not only for the mountains but for the elders in our history. He said, "The rules of the game must be constantly updated to keep up with the expanding technology. Otherwise we overkill the classic climbs and delude ourselves into thinking we are better climbers than the pioneers."

Steve: How much of ice climbing is art, and how much is sport?

Will: That may depend on your goals. The first step in training for anything is deciding what you want to accomplish. Open up your mind, think about what you want to find—not necessarily achieve—in ice climbing. Picture it, then come up with a strategy to get there. Even if the strategy doesn't work you'll still learn something, instead of hiding behind fear or ignorance.

Steve: So much of Wholistic Fitness training is about first accepting, then learning from failure. There is so much growth from failure. What went wrong in our upbringing that makes us so afraid of failure?

Will: Perhaps that is the art in sport? My goals in winter, for instance, revolve around climbing the most aesthetic lines I can find, icicles hanging in the middle of caves, connected with cracks or pockets like notes in music. For this type of climbing, I not only have to be strong, I have to instinctively use techniques borrowed from many sports, equipment made especially for the task, and, most importantly, a belief that I can climb the route because

my training is working! Even with all of that, I'm always going to fail more often than I succeed. But here is the fascinating part: I rate most of my training and climbing sessions not by how many of this or that I did, but by how many good failures I had! Fail lots. A good, successful failure is when you learn something. Sometimes it's physical, like a new way to drop your knee or move, but the best failures enlarge your mind and tell you what to do differently in life or next time in order to succeed.

Steve: I invited you to contribute to this chapter because not only do you have beautiful technique on the ice, but you also validate the importance of a proper strength base, and not at the expense of technique.

Will: I was at my absolute strongest when my performance just stopped. So I spent a month in France. As I climbed with the best climbers in the world, as I observed their training, as I competed against them in the World Cup, I had a near-religious revelation: All climbing is fundamentally based on technique and mental skill, *not* strength! Think about it. My wife can do exactly six pull-ups on a good day, but she climbs overhanging 5.11 better than most people who can do thirty. If you want to move from WI4 to WI7, it's technique, not strength that will take you there. Jeff Lowe can only do ten pull-ups, but he climbs the hardest ice in the world after months of not touching an ice tool. He has simply got great technique and the mind to go with it.

> *We took risks. We knew we took them. Things have come out against us. We have no cause for complaint.*
> —Robert Scott, found in his diary after his exploration party froze in Antarctica

Steve: So rock gyms and craggin' are an ice climber's best friend?

Will: Absolutely. The best ice climbers are now almost always accomplished rock climbers. The drop-knees, stems, dynoes, and other techniques of rock climbing translate perfectly to ice and mixed climbing. I think rock gyms are the best places to learn modern movement, mainly because climbing plastic forces you to meld your moves to the route. The rock gyms are open late, which is good since most people, even you, Ilg, have to work for a living! Rock gyms also allow the less-experienced climber to watch very good climbers in action.

Steve: What about climbing on real rock? We've done some of that together years ago.

Will: One advantage to climbing a lot of traditionally protected crag routes before ice season is that you'll learn how to place gear and manage your fear in a relatively safe environment. Gyms teach you great movement skills, but placing gear and being comfortable on lead are also really important!

Steve: How about ice performance via mental imagery? Providing those images to the undeveloped mind/body quickly accesses heightened performance.

Will: Exactly. Old guys like you *(smiles)* who grew up climbing aid routes and 5.6's all day didn't have the advantage of being weaned in a performance-oriented environment alongside seasoned masters. But it's never too late to develop new climbing skills, and doing so in a gym is usually a lot of fun. Sometimes I think climbing is the process of forgetting everything society has taught us as "adults" and just remembering how it was to climb as a child. Children often have near-perfect technique and flexibility, but we somehow lose those abilities as we age.

Steve: Old guys like me, huh? Remember bucko, I'm only five years older than you! Describe the best way to taper this rock-gym fitness into a season of ice.

Will: As the season approaches, focus your plastic and rock workouts around longer workouts (at least a hundred moves, on big holds) or laps on shorter routes. Most ice leads last about fifteen minutes, so you'll need to be able to hang on and move for at least that long. If you can crank out four continuous thirty-minute sessions in three hours on a gently overhanging traverse wall, I can guarantee that you are not going to have physical problems leading even very hard ice. As you develop your stamina base climbing plastic, you'll also develop the movement patterns to climb ice.

Steve: This book outlines a fifteen-week approach to ice season. It sounds like the amount of climbing-specific training you advocate doesn't include general strength training in a normal gym, right?

Will: If you have time for only one or the other in life, climbing will make you better at climbing faster than anything else. However, too much of anything leads to injuries and mental burnout. I do strength train in the offseason, not so much to get strong for climbing as to maintain a balanced body and because I like the sound of steel. The weight room also teaches me a lot about pushing myself harder when I think I can't, which is a very important mental skill for climbing. Also, when I'm working way too hard and can only get an hour a day to train, then I lift weights for the simplicity and, you of all people will understand this, the joy that I find there! However, any strength training needs to be apart from your climbing volumes; otherwise elbow injury is likely.

Steve: So, once the general strength base has been established, drop it entirely and just climb, climb, climb, eh?

Will: Climb, climb, climb is right. For several months before the ice forms and even during ice season, because most people can only ice climb a couple of days per week.

Steve: Readers of this book should plan accordingly. Finish the enclosed fifteen-week program at least two to three months before ice season.

Will: Right. There is one ice-specific exercise that I do like, but it should be done in moderation after having developed a good strength base: Hang a sling from a pull-up bar and stick your tool through it. Stack your other tool on top of the first, and crank a pull-up. If you can, lock off on one arm and practice swinging your free tool before slowly lowering back down. Repeat, alternating arms. This is strength training, but it's also getting you comfortable with hanging in space from one wrist loop. If you can do this, then how hard can ice climbing be, when you can use your crampons?

Steve: Up at the practice ice in Canmore, Canada, we used to do laps up and down ice columns in our tennis shoes so we couldn't use our feet.

Will: That sounds like you, Ilg. It's funny, though; that's actually a great example of being inventive and fun in training, plus I'll bet it taught you to use the ice intelligently with your feet rather than just kicking randomly.

Steve: Oh, it was inventive all right (laughs). Talk to us about mental training for ice climbing.

Will: The climbing arts put huge amounts of real survival pressure on the participant; runners seldom fear running off the edge of the path and dying, but every time you rope up, you have to climb in a way that keeps you alive. This skill is also far more important than strength, although it's much more difficult to train. Fear and ice climbing go together like whiskey and ice; the best way to reduce fear while climbing ice is to climb it a lot, but at a grade you feel very comfortable on. Rather than pushing yourself to climb hard because you "should," wait until you have a strong desire to climb harder. If you don't, then enjoy where you are. More people quit ice climbing because they try to climb routes that are too hard for them than for any other reason. Be patient with your mind; it has evolved over thousands of years to keep you alive, and climbing ice doesn't really fit into the pattern. On the other hand, climbing ice makes a whole lot more sense than the rest of this modern mess called civilization, and your mind will come to recognize this if allowed to do so slowly.

Steve: Wholistic Fitness philosophy at work: Practice patience. Things take time!

Will: Many climbers will fail climbing because they can't figure out how to do a move or a route, rather than really analyzing a nice failure and developing their minds or technique. For example, if you fall off 'cause you're pumped, it's easy to think, "Hey, I'll just get stronger," rather than, "I failed because my technique sucked, and I got pumped out of mind as a result." Those who fail to analyze their failures are doomed to repeat them. To be a good climber you first have to train your mind to run your body while climbing. Only then does extra strength help. Again, going to the rock gym or a good crag and training climbing motions will pay big dividends come ice season! Plus, you can do a lot cooler routes if you can Egyptian and backstep with the best of them.

The following program is to be engaged immediately after the Perfect Power phase recovery week. This program is appropriate for all beginning and expert level ice climbers.

This program does not cover specific ice-climbing techniques but prepares the body, mind, and spirit for the pursuit of technical ice climbing. Specific ice-climbing technique should be studied under the guidance of an qualified instructor. Recommended instruction is available via the organizations, magazines, and books listed in the resources section that concludes this chapter.

Now, let's get to training!

THE ANDROMEDA ICE-CLIMBING PROGRAM

The Andromeda program is to be followed for five consecutive weeks. This phase enhances ice-climbing performance for beginners to experts. Appropriate transpersonal power development is also designed into the program.

Length of cycle: five weeks.
Frequency: seven-day cycle.
Next cycle: in season.
Primary goals: refine all prior mental, physical, and spiritual fitness gained from previous training cycles for ice-climbing performance.

Wholistic Fitness® Training Precepts

1) Be prepared.
2) Be on time.
3) Give 110 percent.

ANDROMEDA MASTER SHEET

All workouts are described in the next section, Wholistic Notes.

Make It Easy, Monday: Day One

Off day on *all* disciplines. Get massage/bodywork if possible.

Brideveil Tuesday: Day Two

Strength training: Andromeda Workout One.

CV training: None, or sixty minutes of a CV activity of your choice at Zones 1–2.
Kinesthetic training: Medium Form Flexibility before strength training.
Meditation: Early-morning zazen practice.

Weeping Wall Wednesday: Day Three

CV training: Run for one hour at Zone 2 with with cruise intervals; preferred terrain is off-road, gradual uphill.
Kinesthetic training: Pick one—beginning ballet class, yoga class, or Short and Medium Form.
Meditation: 3 x 30 assignment.

Thermal Cracking Thursday: Day Four

Strength training: Andromeda Workout Two.
CV training: None, or sixty minutes of a CV activity of your choice at Zones 1–2.
Kinesthetic training: Yoga class or Short into Medium Form Flexibility.
Meditation: Beeper Guru breath and posture assignment.

Ophir Ice Hose Friday: Day Five

CV training: Cross-train from yesterday for one hour at Zones 1–2.
Kinesthetic training: Pick one—beginning ballet class, yoga class, or sport climbing.
Meditation: Tibetan death meditation.

Silk Tassel Saturday: Day Six

CV training: Pick one or do a combo of running with hand weights or inline skiing at Zones 1–2 for one to two hours. Perform Minutes Are Forever workout.

Kinesthetic training: Pick one—beginning ballet class, yoga class, or sport climbing.

Meditation: Discretionary.

Polar Circus Sunday: Day Seven

Strength training: Andromeda IWT/IWCT full-body workout.

CV training: Cross-train from yesterday, but keep it easy, Zone 1 for one hour. This workout must follow strength training. No intervals.

Kinesthetic training: Medium Form either before strength training or after CV training.

Meditation: Pre-event meditation; passive meditation for ten to twenty minutes; visualize your upcoming week of training. Schedule bodywork and yoga, plan mealtimes, etc.

WHOLISTIC NOTES

This section provides the specific workouts prescribed in the Andromeda Master Sheet.

Strength-Training Workouts

Survive these workouts, and you will experience unprecedented ice-climbing performance and mental focus. Master these workouts, and you will experience ice enlightenment! Before every set, mentally preplay the entire set in your mind before doing it physically. This type of mental training prepares the body to perform in a neurospiritual realm that is conducive to success. Such mental training will see you to the top of ice climbs. Once you win the mental game, the rest just follows along for the ride!

For each of the following workouts adhere to these three guidelines:

1) Limit the recovery phase to thirty seconds.

2) Perform all sets to momentary muscular failure or failure of elegance, unless otherwise noted.

3) Refer to the Appendix for instructions on all movements and techniques.

Andromeda Upper-Body Workout

Pull-ups: Perform six to eight sets at body weight. Do these Pull-ups as if your life depends on them. It does! Note: Unless your facility does not allow it, bring your ice tools into the gym, place them over the pull-up bar, and get cranking! Use the wrist loops and just keep pulling! You must turn your arms into total endurance pistons during the next five weeks!

Dips: Perform four sets at body weight with only a twenty-second recovery!

V-Handle Pulldowns: Two sets of eight to ten reps each, then four sets of eight to ten reps with Ku Bottom Form recovery.

Bench Presses: Three sets of fifteen reps done in total, utter, completely poetic beauty.

Seated Dumbbell Presses: Three sets done with Three-Stage Technique.

Seated Dumbbell Side Lateral Raise: Two sets done with Staccato Technique.

Barbell Curls: Four sets of fifteen reps.

Two-Bench Triceps: Two sets of one minute each. Pace yourself; I want the final fifteen seconds at tempo!

Upper Body Plyometric Superset:
1) Dumbbell Arm Swings for fifteen seconds.
2) Double Pole Plyos for fifteen seconds.
3) Recover for fifteen seconds.

Repeat twice.

Superset for Two Times:
a) Wrist Curls for sixty seconds.
b) Reverse Wrist Curls for forty-five seconds.
c) Recover for thirty seconds.

Repeat.

Andromeda Lower-Body Workout

Stiff Leg Deadlifts: Two sets of five reps. You must make the spinal muscles strong to resist fatigue during sustained pitches; no postural collapse!

Superset for Three Times:
a) Squats: Six. I want these to be deep! Think scuba squats.
b) Leg Extensions: Use Staccato Technique.

Superset for Three Times:
a) Leg Curls: Eight.
b) Squat Jumps: Sixty seconds, baby— no whining! Strive for elegance through difficulty!

Superset for Three Times:
a) Standing Calf Raises: One minute— no funny stuff, just get high up on the extension phase! Strong feet are essential for your ice climbing foundation.
b) Seated Calf Raises: Use Staccato Technique. "Stick" the top position only, but vary your foot position to really promote strong ankles and powerful calves.

Tri-set for Three Times:
a) Suspended Leg Raises for one minute.
b) Oblique Twists for one minute.
c) Twist Crunches for one minute.

The Andromeda IWT/ICWT Program

This two-part workout prepares the mind/ body/spirit for performance ice climbing. This workout offers exceptional biochemical training besides the obvious spiritual benefits of tenacity and confidence. Your enriched inner power will bring on the training effect necessary for complete physiological and spiritual transfer. Good luck and remember: There is nothing like Wholistic Fitness strength training!

Part One: The IWT (Interval Weight Training) Program

Squats (Full or Back Squat preferred): Fifteen reps.

Stationary Cycle (or Versa-Climber or Elliptical Trainer): Two minutes at Zones 3–4.

Squats: Fifteen reps.

Stationary Cycle: Two minutes at Zones 3–4.

Pull-ups: Go to muscle failure.

Jump Squats: Forty-five seconds.

Dips: Go to muscle failure.

Jump Squats: Forty-five seconds.

Part Two: ICWT (Interval Circuit Weight Training) Program

Pull-ups: Go to muscle failure.

Dips: Go to muscle failure.

Speed Cleans: Fifteen reps.

Seated Barbell Presses: Fifteen reps.

Barbell Curls: Fifteen reps.

Handstand: Until you drop; find elegance in the difficulty!

Gunther Hops: Twenty jumps.

Recover for one minute, then repeat: two times for recreational climbers; three times for serious climbers; four times for serious climbers who want enlightenment!

CV Training

Minimum weekly hours range from four to a max of eight. The higher your skill level as a climber and the more ambitious your winter goals, the higher those weekly hours should be! Also, the fatter you are at this time of the year, the higher those weekly hours *need* to be! Beginning climbers must follow the low range. Even intermediate-level athletes will be torn up by Andromeda unless all disciplines (especially nutrition) are followed with conviction of self.

Ice climbing is all about confidence—confidence borne from centered, strong, and committed practice!

Minutes Are Forever Workout

Run or hike hard for one minute (at Zones 3–4), then do a recovery walk for one minute at Zone 1. Keep doing this until you throw up or ten minutes have gone by. Recover for ten minutes, then repeat the sequence. Do these intervals on steep uphills to increase lactate threshold and leg stamina.

Cruise Intervals

While on a Zone 1–2 workout, perform four to six intervals of two minutes each, with a full recovery between. During the intervals, focus on smooth, powerful mechanics. Bring your intervals to Zone 3 as soon as possible and finish at Zone 4. During the last thirty seconds of each interval increase the tempo. After each interval, go at Zone 1 until your heart rate drops down to Zone 2. Resume fluid form, then pop off another interval. Repeat.

Kinesthetic Training

Notice the high priority put on outside kinesthetic training in this program. Andromeda wants you to really use these five weeks to tap into new activities that will stimulate neural response. Basically, Andromeda uses strength and kinesthetic training to teach your central nervous system how to recruit more muscle fibers, thus helping improve power and endurance simultaneously. The lower the percentage of your maximum effort you require to sustain an effort (like leading a hard ice-climbing pitch), the better your endurance. Your effort in Andromeda's kinesthetic program will come back to you a hundred times over in the form of injury prevention, mental focus, and spiritual development.

Meditation

The Andromeda Program offers the most varied and frequent meditation volumes of any program in this book. Your mental fitness is a training priority. Each day you will have a different meditation session to follow, and I expect full compliance. Being consistent for the next five weeks is imperative to your ice-climbing performance.

The ability to mentally preplay your actions is extremely important in ice climbing. That is, train your mind to see the ice axe biting cleanly and solidly into every placement. See the protection going in smoothly, without error; see the clipping of protection happening fluidly. Run these types of mental images during your strength-training sessions and pre-event meditations, and then, of course, once you are climbing rock, plastic, or ice.

During the strength-training workouts, train your mind to focus on seeing the entire set done easily, as though you were lifting Styrofoam barbells and dumbbells!

Successful sport performance begins in the spirit and is performed by the mind; the body merely completes the task that has already been done in the ethereal planes.

Early-Morning Zazen Session. Wake up, relieve yourself, then assume the zazen posture. Sit for eight minutes. Perform Kin Hin (walking meditation); it should be performed with hands in a "gassho mudra," or prayer hand, position. The meditation is designed to mindfully place each step with awareness and not to let the mind wander from the walking. It is best done in an environment where you are not likely to be interrupted in any way. The walk can be as short as one minute to as long as several minutes in duration. Sit for another eight minutes. End the session and take mindfulness with you.

Beeper Guru Breath and Posture Assignment. Set your watch alarm to go off every hour. Upon the beep, take note of where your breath, posture, and mind are. Make adjustments in alignment. Note how often the Beeper Guru catches you in random thought, out of posture, or with the breath high and shallow instead of low and deep.

3 x 30 Assignment. This is taken from a Theravada Buddhist mindfulness exercise. At each mealtime (assume three sit-down meals per day) I want you to chew your first bite of food thirty times. During this chewing, feel the significance of the food being eaten. Appreciate the fact that you are not different from the food you eat and that one day, you too will be "eaten" by the universe. Use this time to honor and revere your food and "tell" the food that you will do your best to use its life-giving energy to refine yourself in order to help others.

Wholistic Fitness®
Pre-Event Meditation

Assume zazen posture;
perform ten cleansing breaths;
perform ten filling breaths.
Recite the following:

As I release my breath, I release my body.

As I release my breath, I let go of any physical, mental, or emotional tensions.

Relaxing into my breath, I realize no separation between myself and the world around me. Nor am I separate from the easy or difficult circumstances in my life. They are all me. I am all them. And it's all appropriate.

As I breathe, I realize that Joy is my natural state.

As long as I breathe, I know that nothing can interfere with this Joy.

Upon my inbreath, I sense a rush of beautiful, comfortable energy. This is my Divine Source. I allow this energy to flow into and out from my body. Relaxing ... feeling empty ...

When I relax, I perform better. When I am empty, I perform better. I will use my breath in my upcoming event in order to relax. In order to empty. I will surrender into the Universe. I trust completely that the Universe will power me into my best effort. Everything that I will go through during my event will be precisely what I need to learn most.

I can already sense how powerfully I will compete because I will have the Universe charging through my emptiness ... all I need to do is breathe and relax into my effort.

As long as I breathe, my performance will be an elegant and strong expression of the Universe.

Recite three times. Go into a visualization of your event for three to five minutes; perform five cleansing breaths; perform five filling breaths; end the session.

Tibetan Death Meditation

Assume zazen posture and perform ten Cleansing Breaths into ten Filling Breaths to deeply relax.

Imagine a green sphere in your heart center. Picture it growing bigger and bigger until the sphere is so large that your entire body is bathed in its green energy. Take a few moments to "float" in this green. You feel unconditional love as well as comfort and safety. There is a feeling that everything is all right, that your true nature is spirit that is endless.

Invoke the image of a loved one, a

parent, or a sibling. Imagine this person dying in a calm, peaceful setting. See yourself caring for this loved one, holding his or her hand, and just being present. Know in your heart that you need to help this loved one die a peaceful death so he/she may take on the Next Step with love in their spirit.

Imagine the loved one taking the last breath ... breathe with him or her. Help make the transition as comfortable as possible. Feel now what your life will be like without this person's physical presence. Prepare yourself fully for this situation.

Imagine yourself dying. Prepare to take your last breath with as much poise and assurance as possible. The body is only a shell for our spirit. Death is a time to drop this shell and move into another realm. Invoke the image of your Higher Source and at the moment of death, exhale into the heart of that Higher Source. Allow that dying breath to be a radiant white light into the heart of your Higher Source.

Bring your awareness back to the green heart center. Feel the love, the comfort, and safety of this heart center. When you are ready, come out of this meditation determined to make the most of every minute. Commit yourself to your spiritual awakening before you—or someone you love—dies.

After coming out of this meditation recite the following phrase three times:

We have so much anguish and difficulty facing death because we ignore the truth of impermanence. To practice death is to practice freedom.

Nutrition

Deserve success, the saying goes, and you shall command it. Nourish your body by the principles outlined in this book, and you will command a body and mind that are as bombproof against injury as possible. Eat well during Andromeda or suffer the consequences. This program is designed to separate the wannabe climbers from the real ones. Lack the self-discipline to eat appropriately during Andromeda and training injury could be the result.

Take a high-quality amino acid and vitamin/mineral supplement each day plus supportive nutrition for joint health. Consider Siberian ginseng, Muscl-Flex, and/or a cycle of creatine load/maintainas per Chapter Eight. If you are still carrying unnecessary body fat, drop it now! Allow only functional body weight; the lighter you can be, the better. Ice climbs are not to be muscled, but danced. If you need to drop body fat, limit fat intake to 15 percent of total calories per day and do the higher range of CV volumes as per the Andromeda Master Sheet. And when you finally get on the ice, think light!

RESOURCES

Contact the following associations for qualified instruction in and information about ice climbing.

The American Alpine Institute: 1212 24th Street, Bellingham, WA 98225; 206-671-1505.

American Avalanche Institute: P.O. Box 308, Wilson, WY 83014; 307-733-3315.

National Outdoor Leadership School (NOLS): 288 Main Street, Dept. R, Lander, WY 82520; 307-332-6873; fax: 307-988-3005.

Magazines

Climbing: P.O. Box 339, Carbondale, CO 81632; 303-963-9449.

Outside: 400 Market Street, Santa Fe, NM 87501; 800-678-1131.

Rock & Ice: 603A S. Broadway, Boulder, CO 80303; 303-499-8410.

Books

The ABC's of Avalanche Safety, Edward R. LaChapelle. 1985. $6.95. Mountaineers Books.

Climbing Ice, Yvon Chouinard. 1979. $15.00. Sierra Club Books.

Cold Comfort: Keeping Warm in the Outdoors, Glenn Randall. 1987. $10.95. Lyons & Burford Publishers.

Equipment

Black Diamond Equipment, Ltd.: 2084 East 3900 South, Salt Lake City, UT 84214; 801-278-5533.

Mountain Tools: 140 Calle Del Oaks, Monterey, CA 93940; 408-393-1011.

Patagonia: 8550 White Fir Street, Reno, NV 89523; 800-638-6464.

Wholistic Fitness® Winter Performance Training
Andromeda Cycle Summation

Cycle's Dates: _____

Athlete's Name: _____

Please address each category as openly as possible.

STRENGTH TRAINING

1) Note your consistency during this discipline. How were your energy levels?

_____

_____

_____

_____

_____

2) What were your strengths? What were weaknesses? Identify them and describe how you will deal with them this in-season.

_____

_____

_____

_____

_____

3) The most important teaching of this strength-training discipline that I can use in my ice-climbing performance is:

_____

_____

_____

_____

_____

CV TRAINING

4) Did you have any standout reactions in this discipline? Were you able to do the volumes as prescribed?

_____
_____
_____
_____
_____

5) Which dryland training activities did you do the most? How will this help you on the ice this season?

_____
_____
_____
_____
_____

6) The most important teaching of this CV-training discipline that I can use in my ice-climbing performance is:

_____
_____
_____
_____
_____

KINESTHETIC TRAINING

7) Did you have any standout reactions in this discipline?

_____
_____
_____
_____

8) Comment on how the past fifteen weeks of intense study in this discipline has shifted your awareness compared to previous years.

_____

_____

_____

_____

_____

9) The most important teaching of this kinesthetic-training discipline that I can use in my ice-climbing performance is:

_____

_____

_____

_____

_____

MEDITATION

10) Did you have any standout reactions in this discipline?

_____

_____

_____

_____

_____

11) On a scale of one to ten, with ten being the highest, judge your mental focus during meditation:

_____

_____

_____

_____

_____

During everyday life:

_____

_____

12) When fear creeps into your hard leads on the ice, what will you do?

13) The most important teaching of this meditation discipline that I can use in my ice-climbing performance is:

NUTRITION

14) How did this cycle's workload affect you nutritionally?

15) Describe *exactly* what you ate and drank yesterday and the manner in which you ate it. Note any cravings.

16) What could you have done to better nourish yourself? Why didn't you? How will you make the adjustment over this in-season?

_____

_____

_____

_____

_____

17) Overall, what did you learn from your Andromeda training cycle?

_____

_____

_____

_____

_____

32

Snowboarding

*"There is something better in us because of our feats
in these mountains. . . . After a descent, my heart is open
and free, my head is clear. . . . All the beauty of the world
is within the mad rhythm of my blood."*
—Extreme winter athlete Patrick Vallencant

JUST A FAD

"Oh, they'll go away soon ... it's just a fad," was the cavalier hope of countless alpine skiers in the late '70s. Today, there are well over two million devoted board-heads across the world. Dude, we're just beginning! Of all the sports covered in this book, snowboarding is the fastest growing. We snowboard fanatics, also known as riders (or knuckle-draggers by skiers), have gotten our marketing act together over the past decade. We have emerged with our own World Pro Tour as well as Olympic recognition, and we are fawned over by a smitten media eager to expose, express, and explode the sport of snowboarding into mainstream appeal.

It's working. Although a few idiotic ski resorts still cop an archaic attitude by prohibiting riders on "their" mountains, most

... all the beauty of the world is within the mad rhythm of my blood. Photo by Mike Powell/ALLSPORT.

areas gladly embrace boardheads. Hey, the color of money is the same, be it from the pockets of skiers or riders! And the anticipated war between alpine skiers and riders never really materialized. The common ground was fun. Skiers, perhaps due to

383

battered knees or just plain boredom, took up the challenge of the single board and discovered a most aesthetic joy. The edge-to-edge, graceful glide over the crystal lattice turned many skiers away from their heavy alpine skis, boots, and poles. After riding a board, such stuff seems like way too much clutter!

I, like a number of my generation, immediately answered the call of the board in those early days. As a competitive skier, my season went from early November into April. By April, I was sick of skiing, tired of having heavy equipment dangling from my knees on long chairlift rides. I was totally psyched to try something different. Snowboarding was and remains a wonderful gift to my life.

Some of my most transcendent experiences in sport have occurred while riding. Standing above a sunlit bowl, I see in my mind's-eye an unwritten script of linked turns below me. The snow whispers to my soul. The deep powder urges me to caress it in a sensual glide. Jumping into my first turn, I begin carving clean, unbroken lines through aspen and pine-studded glades. Falling into and away from the lean of each turn is to me a form of divine music: the sound of snow, the rush of trees, the meeting of wind and skin.

Additionally, some of my most heart-stopping, life-passing-before-my-eyes moments have come while committed to a steep couloir descent, tethered to my board, attempting to be at one with cliff, gully, and avalanche glade. This, then, is what I love most about snowboarding: commitment to a flow. The board and self are two entities merging into fluid unity upon oceans of snow.

Since snowboarding was not covered in Part Three, let's take a moment and do a little info riding.

TECHNICAL SKILLS

In my first book, *The Outdoor Athlete*, I used a quote from Plato to underscore a coaching point for boarders: "The most beautiful motion is that which accomplishes the greatest results with the least amount of effort." Unlike alpine ski, in which weighting, unweighting, rotation, and counterrotation must occur at each of the four independent limbs, the technical skills of a rider are less complex. The rider balances over the front foot. If you ride with your left foot forward, then you have a "regular" stance. If you ride with the right foot forward, you have a "goofy foot." Me? I'm goofy (but you already knew that, didn't you?). Steering is primarily accomplished by the rear leg, but to unlock the elegance of the board you must stay forward. Herein lies one of riding's greatest metaphysical teachings. To control your board (and the same holds true for life), devote yourself to moving forward. On the slopes (especially moguls and steeps), however, instinct sends the wrong message: "Get back!" The moment you throw your weight back over the rear foot, you lose the ability to effectively edge the board. Isn't life the same way? The moment "gunky stuff" comes into our lives we tend to shy away, losing control of the situation. In riding and in life do this: Stay forward, and control will be all yours.

Two other qualities, steering and pressure control, come much easier after you've trained yourself to stay forward. Steering is simply changing the direction of the board by pivoting it under you during unweighting. Unweighting, which is difficult at slow speed, involves a rising movement. Pressure control involves compressing the board—especially the edges—into the snow to achieve good lateral resistance from which crisp, sure turns may be carved. Pressure the board by adopting a surferlike crouch, but stay forward, not back. Soon the hiss of snow will sing beneath you, a manifestation of good board-to-snow pressure. Novice boardheads often try to turn by muscling their boards, or overrotating their upper bodies. They whip the upper body back and forth in a futile, energy-sapping attempt to transfer that rotation into a pivot of the board. Let gravity do the technical skills! Stay forward and play with the rear foot, moving it forward, backward, and side to side to discover svelte transitions and precise board control.

PHYSICAL SKILLS

Few recreational riders actually train in the sense of fitness conditioning. The younger freestyle riders (a.k.a., "jibbers") who hang out in half-pipes and above jumps waiting for inspiration to do aerial tricks often spend their summer months "tramp jumping" (wearing snowboards on a trampoline to practice maneuvers) or skateboarding. This type of cross-training is effective for sport-specific skills, but lacks overall conditioning in terms of strengthening joint structure, enhancing chemical components of muscular fitness, and cardiovascular conditioning. Chronic skateboarding (because it involves pushing off on one leg) can even develop a structural imbalance that may come back to haunt you in later years. The following program is specifically designed for alignment and symmetry to iron out any such imbalances that may be incurred by high-volume snowboarding.

According to my personal files, competitive slalom racers and extreme riders are the snowboarders who seek out qualified training counsel. The program in this book targets the kinesiology of snowboarding, which involves the following three positions.

- Neutral or preparation stance: The rider is in a flexed, transitional stance, with the center of body mass over the lead foot. The gluteals as well as the abdominals stabilize this position, while the quadriceps (vastus lateralis in particular), biceps femoris, anterior tibialis, gastrocnemius, and peroneals all contribute to proper postural positioning, from which the more active phases of weighting, unweighting, and pressure control are performed. The upper torso contributes to this position via muscular assistance delivered courtesy of the rotational muscles. I like my riders to prioritize training of the oblique, serratus, abdominal, and erector spinae muscles. Inadequate upper-body conditioning means a collapse of forward body position on the board.

- Steering: The emphasis falls on the quadriceps as the rider rises to unweight the board. The entire erector spinae group, rotators, and psoas must be well trained and strong to produce and maintain an effective body position while steering. The arms and head meanwhile are kept forward toward the fall line. Not much muscular force is generated by the upper body during any phase of snowboarding.

- Pressure control: The rider commits to either a toe-side or heel-side edge. The intent is to carve a smooth turn with nominal lateral drift in the snow. Good riders use radical body lean and skeletal bracing on toe-side turns, allowing their upper torsos to nearly scrape the snow! Such movements, especially when performed in deep powder conditions, are one of the

most mystical, beautiful sensations in all of sports. Consistent flexion and extension at the knee are greatly imbalanced to the lead foot. The hamstrings produce flexion, while the quadriceps extend the knee during unweighting. The most dramatic stabilization stress falls upon the vastus complex, especially the vastus medialis and lateralis. The tensor fascia latae is also called into play, as is the illipsoas to flex the hip as the rider deepens his or her body lean. The rectus abdominus flexes the midtorso during crouching, and the erector spinae extends the torso during unweighting. For freestyle riders doing aerial tricks, all this kinesiology is amplified.

MENTAL SKILLS

As in alpine skiing, the ability to relax and to ride from a centered mental and physical core is fundamental to optimal snowboard performance. Real mental fortitude comes from the confidence gained through experiencing a wide variety of riding conditions and styles. Accomplished riders handle all slope environments with poise and effortless control. Such artistry comes not so much from physical conditioning but from constant mental training in the forms of awareness, acceptance, and faith in oneself. The commitment factor is higher in riding than in alpine skiing, however. For one thing, snowboard bindings do not prerelease. Where the board goes, you go. Also, riders can't just "step out" from a fall line like skiers can. Finally, in snowboarding, safety is in speed, for that's where edge control is maximal. In view of these factors, a very confident mental and physical stance is even more necessary for the rider than for the alpine skier. I emphasize mental training with my riders because it builds confidence. A rider's greatest ally is his or her mental strength, because the key to performance in snowboarding is a powerful transpersonal meditation: Stay forward! And that requires confidence.

The following program is to be engaged immediately after the Perfect Power phase recovery week. This program is appropriate for all types of recreational and expert level boardheads (snowboarders), including alpine, freestyle, and freeride.

This program does not cover specific snowboard techniques but prepares the body, mind, and spirit for the pursuit of performance riding. Specific snowboard technique should be studied under the guidance of a qualified instructor. Recommended instruction is available via the organizations, magazines and books listed in the resources section that concludes this chapter.

Now, let's get to training!

THE RIDING LIFE PROGRAM

The Riding Life program is to be followed for five consecutive weeks. This phase en-

hances snowboarding performance while decreasing injury potential. Appropriate transpersonal power development is designed into the program.

Length of cycle: five weeks.
Frequency: seven-day cycle.
Next cycle: in season.
Primary goals: refine all prior mental, physical, and spiritual fitness gained from previous training cycles for riding performance.

Wholistic Fitness® Training Precepts

1) Be prepared.
2) Be on time.
3) Give 110 percent.

RIDING LIFE MASTER SHEET

All workouts are described in the next section, Wholistic Notes.

Mogul Field Monday: Day One

Off day on all disciplines. Get massage/ bodywork if possible

Tweak It Tuesday: Day Two

Strength training: Riding Life Workout One.
CV training: None, or sixty minutes of a CV activity of your choice at Zones 1–2.
Kinesthetic training: Medium Form Flexibility before strength training.
Meditation: Early-morning zazen practice.

Wipeout Wednesday: Day Three

CV training: Run, cycle, or inline skate for one hour at Zone 2 with with cruise intervals.

Kinesthetic training: Medium Form Flexibility before strength training.

Meditation: 3 x 30 assignment.

Stale Fish Thursday: Day Four

Strength training: Riding Life Workout Two.

CV training: None, or sixty minutes of a CV activity of your choice at Zones 1–2.

Kinesthetic training: Yoga class or Short into Medium Form Flexibility.

Meditation: Let your kinesthetic training be your meditation.

Flying Kilometer Friday: Day Five

CV training: Inline ski or skate for one hour at Zones 1–2. Focus on downhill ski technique during all descents. Option: Set up a street slalom or GS course and run "gates."

Kinesthetic training: Yoga class or Short into Medium Form Flexibility.

Meditation: Early-morning zazen practice.

Off-Piste Saturday: Day Six

CV training: Pick one or a combo of running, cycling, hiking, or inline skating and do it at Zones 1–2 for one to two hours. Perform Minutes Are Forever workout.

The intervals should be done on moderate (5–7 percent grade) uphill terrain.

Kinesthetic training: Skateboard, play racquetball, jump on a trampoline, mountain bike, play basketball, or do a combo of these for one hour.

Meditation: Let your kinesthetic training and your intervals be your meditation.

Shred Betty Sunday: Day Seven

Strength training: Riding Life IWT/IWCT full-body workout or EEE-GAD full-body workout (alternate weekly).

CV training: None, but see kinesthetic training.

Kinesthetic training: Skateboard, play racquetball, jump on a trampoline, mountain bike, play basketball, or do a combo of these for one hour.

Meditation: Pre-event meditation; passive meditation for ten to twenty minutes; visualize your upcoming week of training. Schedule bodywork and yoga, plan mealtimes, etc.

WHOLISTIC NOTES

This section provides the specific workouts prescribed in the Riding Life Master Sheet.

Strength-Training Workouts

Much of effective riding involves staying relaxed during difficult sections. Practice staying relaxed during each set; that is, really focus on the body part under attention, but relax all the others. Cultivate full-body awareness and isolate the specific body part being trained.

For each of the following workouts adhere to these three guidelines:

1) Limit the recovery phase to thirty seconds.
2) Perform all sets to momentary muscular failure or failure of elegance, unless otherwise noted.
3) Refer to the Appendix for instructions on all movements and techniques.

Riding Life Upper-Body Workout

Bench Presses: Use Envelope Technique.

Bent Arm Pullovers: Four sets of ten reps with Ku Top Form recovery.

Seated Rows: Use Envelope Technique.

High Pulls: Three sets of ten reps with Ku Bottom Form recovery.

Seated Dumbbell Presses: Two sets done with Three-Stage Technique.

Seated Dumbbell Side Lateral Raises: Three sets of twelve reps.

Barbell Curls: Four sets of fifteen reps.

Two-Bench Triceps: Two sets of one minute each. Pace yourself; I want the final fifteen seconds at tempo!

Upper-Body Plyometric Superset:

1) Dumbbell Arm Swings for fifteen seconds.
2) Dumbbell Horizontal Swings fifteen seconds.
3) Recover fifteen seconds.

Repeat twice.

Superset for Two Times:

a) Wrist Curls for forty-five seconds.
b) Reverse Wrist Curls for thirty seconds.
c) Recover for thirty seconds.

Repeat!

Riding Life Lower-Body Workout

Seated Good Mornings: One set of ten reps. Keep a strong lower back.

Overhead Squats: Two sets of ten reps. Find balance, open the hips, and make the spine strong!

Squats: Four sets of six reps. Visualize strong knee joints for the slopes!

Leg Curls: Three sets of six reps. Develops leg bicep strength.

Leg Extensions: Three sets of eight to ten reps. Develops more connective tissue health for hoofin' it!

Gunther Hops: Two sets of sixteen reps. Focus on gluteal power.

Jump Squats: Three sets of ten reps. Keep the heart high and power in the legs!

Knee Tuck Jumps: Two sets of ten reps. Improves the neural pathway to the legs, which means more coordination!

Standing Calf Raises: Four sets of fifteen reps. Deep and strong.

Abdominal Crunches: Three sets of one minute each. Midsection fitness means strong riding!

Suspended Leg Raises: Three sets of forty-five seconds each. Dissolve into Knee Ups if you must—just keep moving!

Stiff Leg Deadlifts: One set of six reps. Keep a strong spine; take this posture with you all day!

Riding Life IWT/ICWT Program

This two-part workout prepares the mind/body/spirit for performance riding. This workout provides exceptional biochemical training besides the obvious spiritual benefits of tenacity and confidence. Your enriched inner power will bring on the training effect necessary for complete physiological and spiritual transfer. Good luck and remember: There is nothing like Wholistic Fitness strength training!

Part One: The IWT (Interval Weight Training) Program

Overhead Squats: Fifteen reps.

Stationary Cycle (or Versa-Climber or Elliptical Trainer): Two minutes at Zones 3–4.

Overhead Squats: Fifteen reps.

Stationary Cycle: Two minutes at Zones 3–4.

Pull-Ups: Go to muscle failure.

Knee Tuck Jumps: Thirty seconds.

Dips: Go to muscle failure.

Jump Squats: Forty-five seconds.

Part Two: The ICWT (Interval Circuit Weight Training) Program

Bench Presses: Fifteen reps.

Speed Cleans: Fifteen reps.

Upright Rows: Fifteen reps.

Barbell Curls: Fifteen reps.

Handstand: Go until you blow; feet up. Fifteen reps.

Inversion Crunches or Oblique Twists: One minute.

Gunther Hops: Twenty jumps.

Recover for one minute, then repeat: two times for recreational riders; three times for serious riders; four times for serious boardheads who want enlightenment *now*.

Riding Life EEE-GAD Full-Body Workout

Pull-Ups: Two sets of however many you can do.

Front Lat Pulldowns: One set done with Staccato Technique; three sets of eight to ten reps.

Dumbbell Flat-Bench Flyes into Dumbbell Bench Presses: Flyes for ten reps to failure, then crank out high-frequency Dumbbell Bench Presses until you puke black blood. Do two sets.

Back Squats Superset with Leg Extensions: Do Squats for twelve reps to failure, then run over and perform Knee Tuck Jumps for twenty jumps. Do two supersets.

Seated Dumbbell Presses: Two sets done with Three-Stage Technique. Commit to fluidity.

Two-Bench Triceps: Two sets of one minute each. See each rep in a "clean" top and bottom position. You should feel the contraction in the triceps up top. Bring chi to the triceps.

Barbell Curls: Three sets done with Shivaya Technique. Be beautiful; be elegant.

Abdominal Crunches Directly into Leg Raises: Three sets of one minute each. Really stay concentrated in the abs!

CV Training

Minimum weekly hours range from three to a max of six. The higher your skill level as a rider and the more ambitious your winter goals, the higher those weekly hours should be!

Minutes Are Forever Workout

Run or hike hard for one minute (at Zones 3–4), then do a recovery walk for one minute at Zone 1. Keep doing this until you throw up or ten minutes have gone by. Recover for ten minutes, then repeat the sequence. Do these intervals on steep uphills to increase lactate threshold and leg stamina.

Cruise Intervals

While on a Zone 1–2 workout, perform four to six intervals of two minutes each, with a full recovery between. During the intervals, focus on smooth, powerful mechanics. Bring your intervals to Zone 3 as soon as possible and finish at Zone 4. During the last thirty seconds of each interval increase the tempo. After each interval, go at Zone 1 until your heart rate drops down to Zone 2. Resume fluid form, then pop off another interval. Repeat.

Kinesthetic Training

A high volume of yoga and flexibility training is mixed in with some kinesthetic activities such as basketball and racquetball. I've prescribed this because I want as much ath-letic influence as possible coming from other sports to enhance your kinesthetic feel on the board. Note: This strength-training program has significant kinesthetic transfer for your riding, especially in terms of injury prevention. Work with pure focus during each strength-training session for optimal knuckle-dragging performance!

Meditation

Early-Morning Zazen Session. Wake up, relieve yourself, then assume the zazen posture. Sit for eight minutes. Perform Kin Hin (walking meditation); it should be performed with hands in a "gassho mudra," or prayer hand, position. The meditation is designed to mindfully place each step with awareness and not to let the mind wander from the walking. It is best done in an environment where you are not likely to be interrupted in any way. The walk can be as short as one minute to as long as several minutes in duration. Sit for another eight minutes. End the session and take mindfulness with you.

Beeper Guru Breath and Posture Assignment. Set your watch alarm to go off every hour. Upon the beep, take note of where your breath, posture, and mind are. Make adjustments in alignment. Note how often the Beeper Guru catches you in random thought, out of posture, or with the breath high and shallow instead of low and deep.

3 x 30 Assignment. This is taken from a Theravada Buddhist mindfulness exercise. At each mealtime (assume three sit-down meals per day) I want you to chew your first bite of food thirty times. During this chewing, feel the significance of the food being eaten. Appreciate the fact that you are not different from the food you eat and that one day, you too will be "eaten" by the universe. Use this time to honor and revere your food and "tell" the food that you will do your best to use its life-giving energy to refine yourself in order to help others.

Wholistic Fitness®
Pre-Event Meditation

Assume zazen posture;
perform ten cleansing breaths;
perform ten filling breaths.
Recite the following:

As I release my breath, I release my body.

As I release my breath, I let go of any physical, mental, or emotional tensions.

Relaxing into my breath, I realize no separation between myself and the world around me. Nor am I separate from the easy or difficult circumstances in my life. They are all me. I am all them. And it's all appropriate.

As I breathe, I realize that Joy is my natural state.

As long as I breathe, I know that nothing can interfere with this Joy.

Upon my inbreath, I sense a rush of beautiful, comfortable energy. This is my Divine Source. I allow this energy to flow

into and out from my body. Relaxing ... feeling empty ...

When I relax, I perform better. When I am empty, I perform better. I will use my breath in my upcoming event in order to relax. In order to empty. I will surrender into the Universe. I trust completely that the Universe will power me into my best effort. Everything that I will go through during my event will be precisely what I need to learn most.

I can already sense how powerfully I will compete because I will have the Universe charging through my emptiness ... all I need to do is breathe and relax into my effort.

As long as I breathe, my performance will be an elegant and strong expression of the Universe.

Recite three times. Go into a visualization of your event for three to five minutes; perform five cleansing breaths; perform five filling breaths; end the session.

Nutrition

Riding does not deplete the physiological component of fitness too much, but what is important to the rider is joint health. Boardheads must make certain to take a high-quality amino acid and vitamin/mineral supplement each day plus supportive nutrition for joint health. Consider Siberian ginseng, Muscl-Flex, and/or a cycle of creatine load/maintain as per Chapter Eight. If you are still carrying some unwanted body fat, this is the time to shed it. Limit fat intake to 10 percent of total calories per day and do the higher range of CV volumes as per the Riding Life Master Sheet. Too often, riding injuries, such as tweaked knees, torn shoulders, and wrenched lower backs come from poor nutritional intake. If you want to be the best rider you can be, eat like a warrior, not a couch potato!

RESOURCES

Contact the following associations for qualified instruction in snowboarding.

American Association of Snowboard Instructors: 133 South Van Gordon Street, Suite 101, Lakewood, CO 80228; 303-987-9390; fax: 303-988-3005.

United States Snowboard Instructors: 332 Broadturn Road, Scarborough, ME 04074; www.winterworld.com/ussi.

Magazines

Snowboard Life: 353 Airport Road, Oceanside, CA 92054; 760-722-7777; www.twsnow.com.

Mountain Sports and Living: 810 7th Ave. 4th Floor, New York, NY 10019; 212-636-2700.

Transworld SNOWboarding, P.O. Box 469019, Escondido, CA 92046; 800-334-8152.

Books

Snowboarding, Outdoor Pursuits Series, Rob Reichenfeld and Anna Bruechert. 1995. $13.95. Human Kinetics Publishers.

Wholistic Fitness® Winter Performance Training Riding Life Cycle Summation

Cycle's Dates: _____

Athlete's Name: _____

Please address each category as openly as possible.

STRENGTH TRAINING

1) Note your consistency during this discipline. How were your energy levels?

_____

_____

_____

_____

_____

2) What were your strengths? What were your weaknesses? Identify them and describe how you will deal with them this in-season:

_____

_____

_____

_____

_____

3) The most important teaching of this strength-training discipline that I can use in my riding performance is:

_____

_____

_____

_____

_____

CV TRAINING

4) Did you have any standout reactions in this discipline? Were you able to do the volumes as prescribed?

_____

_____

_____

_____

5) Which dryland training activities did you do the most? How will this help you this season?

_____

_____

_____

_____

_____

6) The most important teaching of this CV-training discipline that I can use in my riding performance is:

_____

_____

_____

_____

_____

KINESTHETIC TRAINING

7) Did you have any standout reactions in this discipline?

_____

_____

_____

_____

_____

8) Comment on how the past fifteen weeks of intense study in this discipline has shifted your awareness compared to previous years.

_____

_____

_____

_____

_____

9) The most important teaching of this kinesthetic-training discipline that I can use in my riding performance is:

_____

_____

_____

_____

_____

MEDITATION

10) Note your consistency with your meditation practice this cycle.

_____

_____

_____

_____

_____

11) On a scale of one to ten, with ten being the highest, judge your mental focus during meditation:

_____

_____

_____

_____

_____

During everyday life:

_____

_____

_____

_____

12) How will you find softness while riding difficult terrain this winter?

_____

_____

_____

_____

_____

13) The most important teaching of this meditation discipline that I can use in my riding performance is:

_____

_____

_____

_____

_____

NUTRITION

14) How did this cycle's workload affect you nutritionally?

_____

_____

_____

_____

_____

15) Describe exactly what you ate and drank yesterday and the manner in which you ate it. Note any cravings.

_____

_____

_____

_____

_____

16) What could you have done to better nourish yourself? Why didn't you? How will you make the adjustment over this in-season?

_____

_____

_____

_____

_____

17) Overall, what did you learn from your Riding Life training cycle?

_____

_____

_____

_____

_____

Part VIII

Appendices

photo by Roy Wilkinson

Two Wholistic Fitness® Flexibility Routines: Short and Medium Form

It is my great honor to share with you two of my most popular and effective flexibility routines. These forms, which I introduced professionally in 1983, have produced tremendous flexibility gains for my students. They have also spurred many students to explore my more advanced flexibility routines: Long Form; WhirlWind Dancer; and two breathing katas, Ten Sho, from the Go Ju Kido karate system as taught to me by Sensei Kaoru Kishiyama, and the Sitting Kata, another of my creations. (These forms are available on videotape through the Wholistic Fitness website at wholisticfitness.com-us.net.)

Since I based these routines on the philosophy of Eastern movement art, each position contributes toward self-healing. These forms influence organ health and enhance life force. Pain erasure and inner peace are common training effects. The forms will be most beneficial if you regularly practice them with mindfulness. Your participation is what moves the *chi*—or life force—throughout your body. By practicing these forms, you will experience greater kinesthetic awareness, which leads to improved energetic recognition (the ability to sense varying degrees of energy vibrations or energy fields) both in yourself and in others. This sensitivity is critical to transpersonal sport performance.

The beauty of these forms is that you can do them fluidly when time is short or hold each position statically for an extended period when you have more time to practice. The trigger words and phrases make it easy to memorize the forms within a few sessions. When done fluidly, the forms inspire energetic flow, loosen joint and muscle adhesions, increase joint mobility, and strengthen the bones. When done statically, the forms impart elasticity and plasticity within the musculature and connective tissue. They also elongate the muscles while toning internal organs, deepening respiration, and stimulating circulatory fitness as well as reduce tension in the sympathetic nervous system and enhance the parasympathetic aspect.

How do these forms help sport performance? The ways are many. Whenever we relax, we do better. As discussed in Chapter 4, flexibility training is paramount to long-term health and sport performance. Unlike conventional, Western models of robotlike stretches, my stretching routines speak of inner and outer dancing. They heighten inner listening. A kind of moving meditation, these forms allow for what the Taoists call *wei wu wei,* or "not-doing." As in so many winter sports, we learn that by conscious awareness a type of "effortless action" arises from our movement. Within your execution of the forms, *wei wu wei* will arise naturally if you are listening. Finding and nourishing this conscious awareness during flexibility practice invites effortless action to visit you during sport performance. Simple but provocative choreography animates these basic forms. It is a source of ongoing delight for me to hear that students discover their own dancing within the forms.

The following forms quiet the body, still the mind, and soften the spirit. They allow space for our best winter performance to come singing through. Enjoy!

Note

Each Wholistic Fitness Flexibility Form has been approved and enthusiastically embraced by a number of physicians, coaches, and healing arts practitioners for more than thirteen years.

WHOLISTIC FITNESS®
SHORT FORM FLEXIBILITY

Trigger Word or Phrase

These trigger words identify each major pose in the flexibility form. The form is described in detail in the next section.

1. Butterfly posture, three Cleansing Breaths
2. Pick a leg; extend into Janu Sirasana
3. Janu Sirasana: Yin
4. Janu Sirasana: Yang
5. Create a Window
6. Reach Through Window
7. Rotate back into Janu Sirasana: Yang
8. Janu Sirasana: Yin
9. Ten Leg Raises into
10. "Baryshnikov" pose
11. Hold for a pause; bring heart forward, spine straightens, into
12. Butterfly posture, three Cleansing Breaths

Repeat numbers 1 through 12 for opposite leg

25. Sun Pose Balance posture
26. Lower both legs into Pascimottansana: Yin
27. Pascimottansana: Yang
28. Pascimottansana: Yin
29. Do Ten V-Sit Leg Raises or Knee-Ups
30. Palms forward; legs lower to earth
31. "Creep into" Front Shoulder Stretch

32. "Creep back through" hips, legs in Yin
33. Repeat numbers 31 and 32
34. Unfold to finish!

Short Form Flexibility Routine

1) Butterfly posture: Sit on the earth with spine straight. Really ground through the sitting bones. Draw both heels in toward groin, as close as possible, keeping both shins parallel to the plane of the hips. Grasp feet with hands. Take three Cleansing Breaths; on the exhale, draw your forehead toward your feet; on the inhale, return spine to upright posture.

2) Pick a leg; extend into Janu Sirasana. For this example, let's select the right leg. Keep the left leg folded in toward your groin, while extending the right leg slightly off to the side in front of you. Square your hips to the extended right leg.

3) Janu Sirasana: yin. Press the right leg fully straight, moving the rear thigh into the earth. Lean forward from the waist, and reach forward for the back of the right knee, the calf, or the toes as long as your spine remains *flat!* No rounded spine on the yin movements.

4) Janu Sirasana: yang. With each inhalation lift the torso up and away from your waist, and upon each exhale—with the help of your arm muscles—soften deeper into the pose, gradually drawing the upper body down and over the extended right leg. The back can now round, but prioritize bringing the navel to the thigh, then the heart to the knee, then the chin to the shin as a sequence.

5) Create a Window. Take the left hand and trace an imaginary arch up and over the left side of the body. This motion opens up and stretches the left side of the body while the right side of the body collapses toward the right leg. The left hand attempts to catch the right toes.

6) Reach Through Window. From pose #5, take the right hand toward the left-knee. Twist the heart under the left arm so that it attempts to face the sky.

7) Rotate back into pose #4, just like the trigger phrase says.

8) Janu Sirasana: yin. Rise elegantly into pose #3.

9) Ten Leg Raises. Bring both hands to the abdominals. Lean away a bit and perform ten Leg Raises or Knee Ups with the extended leg. The former is more difficult (see Strength Training Descriptions in Appendix B) and Knee-Ups involve the less-intense movement of flexing the knee toward and then away from you without letting the heel touch the earth.

10) "Baryshnikov" pose. Upon the tenth and final repetition of either your Leg Raises or your Knee-Ups, take your hands and lift the right leg while extended into a high position, higher than what you could voluntarily lift the leg by itself.

11) Hold for a pause; bring heart forward, spine straightens. Take your hands away and don't let the leg drop!

12) Butterfly posture and take three Cleansing Breaths. This is a return to pose #1.

Now, repeat the choreography of numbers 2 through 12 for the left leg.

25) Sun Pose Balance. With both feet still gathered near your groin, grab your toes with your hands and exhale, at the same time bringing both legs to extension in mid-air. You will need to rock back on your tailbone to allow the feet, legs, and hands to release toward the sky. Hold for a moment and then slowly bring your legs back to the earth, extending them directly in front of you.

26) Lower both legs into Pascimottansana: Yin. Press both legs fully straight, moving the rear thighs and the back of the knees into the earth. Reach forward for the back of the knee, the calf, or the toes as long as your spine remains *flat!* No rounded spine on these yin movements. This is a nonaggressive movement. Posture is what is important.

27) Pascimottansana: Yang. Grab the bottom of your feet and use your arm muscles to draw your forehead to your shin, with legs still straight. The back can now round, but prioritize bringing the navel to the thigh, then the heart to the knee, then the chin to the shin as a sequence. Use determined energy.

28) Pascimottansana: Yin. Come out of the Yang position and go into the Yin position as in movement #26.

29) Do ten V-Sit Leg Raises or Knee-Ups. Put both hands on your abdominals and with your legs still out in front of you, raise your feet off of the earth. Now bring your knees to your chest and then back to the starting position for ten repetitions.

30) Palms forward; legs lower to earth. Have your legs out in front of you and place your palms forward right next to your hips.

31) "Creep into" front shoulder stretch. Bend your knees and raise your hips off of the earth and slowly walk your feet forward and feel the stretch in the shoulders.

32) "Creep back through" hips, legs in Yin. Walk your feet back until your hips pass by your forearms. Discover elevation to the shoulder girdle as you hold this pose for a moment, keeping your spine straight and your legs extended in front of you.

33) Repeat numbers 31 and 32.

34) Unfold to finish. Lower your body down until your "sit bones" are resting upon the earth. Slowly unfold your fingers out of the palms in a forward position, bring them overhead, and then down slowly. You are finished!

Short Form Flexibility Notes

1. Butterfly Pose

This is an extremely effective pose for spinal and postural awareness. It is traditionally performed to strengthen the entire nervous system (particularly the sciatic nerve) and relieve urinary difficulties. It's also good for opening the hip joints and lengthening the lower-back musculature.

3 and 4. Janu Sirasana Yin and Yang

Training effects include abdominal muscle strengthening and increased circulation of internal energy to the pelvis and throughout the lower back. The rounded back common among most people during Janu Sirasana reflects inner obstacles that must be overcome, by repetition, to achieve an open, flat back.

6. Reach Through Window

This low, twisting side stretch is essential training for the often ignored intercostal muscles. Note how much tension is released from the upper back and shoulder areas as you come out of this pose. This pose is also good training for the vertebrae, rendering them more limber and open to subtle energy flows. Lateral mobility to the spine is the first type of flexibility to be lost. This pose restores lubrication to the spine and awakens latent energy. As the yoga saying goes, "We are only as old as our spines."

27. Pascimottansana: Yang

This classic stretch is incredibly important for Westerners. Complete extension throughout the spine creates much needed intervertebral disc space. This is especially appropriate for athletes whose concussive activities tend to compact the spine. You must overcome a rounded back to liberate full-body energetics.

29. V-Sit Leg Raises

The quest here is to study your center of balance. Try to eliminate jerky motions or superfluous muscle activity.

WHOLISTIC FITNESS® MEDIUM FORM FLEXIBILITY

See accompanying photos, with author Steve Ilg. Photographer: Mike Powell/ ALLSPORT. Location: Pacific Athletic Club, Pacific Palisades, California.

Trigger Word or Phrase

1. Sarvasana (Corpse Pose)
2. Pick a leg; Knee Squeeze
3. Ankle Swirls
4. L Pose: Yin (lowest vertebra to earth, passive arm extends to side, palm down)
5. L Pose: Yang (nonactive leg heavy, relaxed, extended)
6. Roll onto active hip, extend active leg, passive arm extends to side, palm down
7. Roll over to opposite side, switch hands at midposition; extend active leg, passive arm extends to side, palm down (nonactive leg heavy, relaxed, extended)
8. Chipko: catch lateral aspect of foot with opposite elbow (or wrist); then do two subtle positions: 1) draw forehead to toe, then 2) reconnect all vertebrae to earth.
9. Unfold Chipko and extend active leg overhead

10. Back to Knee Squeeze
11. Ankle Swirls
12. Extend working leg into Sarvasana
Repeat numbers 2 through 12 for opposite leg
25. Sit up into a comfortable Sitting Split position
26. Lower Back "Gunk Up Scan"; reach forward and rotate side to side from lower back awareness
27. Pick a leg; sit up and out of hips
28. Both hands on outside of leg; Spinal Twist
29. Yin attitude over near leg into

30. Yang attitude
31. Create a Window
32. Reach Through Window
33. Back to Yang attitude to
34. Yin attitude
Repeat numbers 27 through 34 for opposite leg
43. Rise as elegantly as possible into Strength Split
44. Switch sides; Strength Split
45. Come to center; Hang from Flat Back
46. Balance into V-Sit
47. Unfold to finish!

Medium Form Flexibility Routine

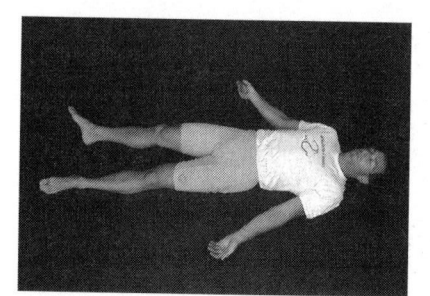

Sarvasana (Corpse Pose)

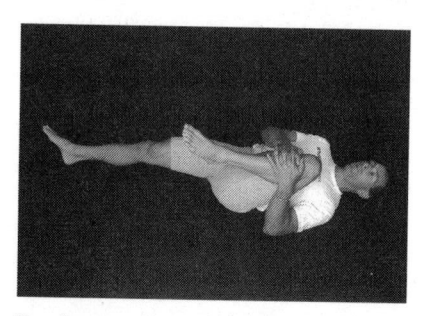

Knee Squeeze with Ankle Swirl

1) Sarvasana (Corpse Pose). Lie flat on your back with your body totally relaxed. Your arms are at your side, palms up, at about 45 degrees from your body. Your legs are apart, heels about shoulder width, toes having fallen out to the sides. The abdomen rises and falls with nasal inhalations and exhalations. Your mind is focused on the breath.

2) Pick a leg: knee squeeze. We will use the left leg for this discussion. Bring the left leg up to your chest and hold it with both hands, fingers interlocked two inches below the knee. Really squeeze the thigh into the belly to massage the internal organs as you breathe; the breath will force the belly up against the thigh bone as you keep focusing on drawing the left knee toward left armpit. Keep your other leg extended and relaxed as possible. Tuck chin toward chest.

3) Ankle Swirls. Keeping your knee to your chest, do ankle swirls. Pretend your ankle is in a vat of molasses and move it very slowly. Do a few ankle swirls in a clockwise rotation and then a counter-clockwise motion.

4) L-Pose: Yin (lowest vertebra to earth, passive arm extends to side, palm down). From the corpse pose bring the left leg up and grab the arch of the foot on the inside and create an L with your leg. The bottom of your foot faces the sky and is not turned over at the ankle. Keep grounding through the tailbone into the earth.

L-Pose: Yin

5) L-Pose: Yang (the non-active leg heavy, relaxed, extended). From the L-Pose Yin position, aggressively bring the knee to the earth by using your arm muscles. Do not force the knee down, but rather deepen it toward the earth upon the exhalations. Try and close the gap between your knee and the earth, and make sure your non-working leg stays relaxed and extended. Keep grounding through the tailbone. Tuck chin toward chest.

L-Pose: Yang

Roll onto active hip, extend active leg, passive arm extends to side, palm down.

Roll over to opposite side, switch hands at mid position; extend active leg, passive arm extends to side, palm down. (Non-active leg heavy, relaxed, extended).

6) Roll onto active hip, extend active leg, passive arm extends to side, palm down. So now just roll onto the left hip and work on extending the left leg as fully as possible. After this leg extension, keep the left hand holding the left foot, then reach back to the right with the right hand. Press your right shoulder into the earth as much as possible. The left foot may be flexed or extended depending upon your flexibility in this pose.

7) Roll over to opposite side, switch hands at mid-position; extend active leg, passive arm extends to side, palm down. Your non-active leg is heavy, relaxed, extended. The primary objective is to first roll onto the right hip and extend the left leg fully while holding the left foot with the right hand. After this leg extension, keep the right hand holding the left foot, then reach back to the left with the left hand, and look back to the left. Press your left shoulder into the earth as much as possible and breathe into the lower back.

Chipko: opposite elbow (or wrist) catches lateral aspect of foot.

Unfold Chipko and extend active leg overhead.

8) Chipko. Roll back to a supine position and grasp the left foot with the left hand. Reach forward with the right arm and then tuck the heel of the foot into the cradle of the right elbow. Encourage your forehead toward your big toe. Hold that position and then slowly reconnect all vertebra back to the earth. Tuck chin toward chest.

9) Unfold Chipko and extend active leg overhead. Grab the hamstring, knee, or toes of the left leg and unfold the leg into an overhead extension upon an exhale. Keep drawing the left leg closer to your head. Tuck chin, draw shoulder blades toward the earth.

10) Back to knee squeeze. Bend the left knee to bring the left leg back into Pose #2.

11) Ankle Swirls. Swirl the left foot clockwise, then counter-clockwise.

12) Extend working leg into Sarvasana. Release the left leg to the earth.

Repeat numbers 2 through 12 for the right leg.

Sit up into a comfortable Sitting Split position and reach forward and rotate side-to-side from lower back.

25) Sit up into a comfortable Sitting Split position.

26) Lower Back "Gunk Up Scan." Reach forward and rotate side to side for lower back awareness. When reaching forward, do so by emphasizing the navel toward the earth, then the heart center. The spine stays relatively flat throughout this movement.

Pick a leg; sit up and out of hips, place both
hands on outside of leg and do a Spinal Twist.

Yang attitude over same leg.

27) Pick a leg; sit up and out of your hips.
For this discussion, let's begin with the right leg.

28) Both hands on outside of leg: Spinal
Twist. When twisting to the right, lead from the
heart and ground through the sit bones. Elongate your core all the way through the spinal
twist, lengthening the spine upon inhales, and
deepening the twist upon exhales. Keep head
pulled up.

30) Yang attitude. With each inhalation lift
the torso up and away from your waist and
upon each exhale—with the help of your arm
muscles—soften deeper into the pose, gradually
drawing the upper body down and over the extended right leg. The back can now round, but
prioritize bringing the navel to the thigh, then
the heart to the knee, then the chin to the shin
as a sequence. You just want to drape the upper
body over the right thigh.

Yin attitude over near leg.

29) Yin attitude over near leg. Square your
hips to the extended right leg. Press the right leg
fully straight, moving the rear thigh into the
earth. Both legs, still extended, must be in knee-
to-toe alignment. Reach forward for the back of
the right knee, the calf, or the toes as long as
your spine remains *flat!* No rounded spine on
the yin movements.

Create a Window and reach through it for opposite inner thigh.

31) Create A Window. Take the left hand and
trace an imaginary arch up and over the left side
of the body. This motion opens up and stretches
the left side of the body, while the right side of
the body collapses toward the right thigh. The
left hand attempts to catch the right toes while
keeping the left elbow pointed skyward.

32) Reach Through Window. From pose
#31, take the right hand toward the left inner
thigh. Once attained, use a pulling motion from
the right hand under the left inner thigh to assist in twisting the heart under, through, and
eventually skyward beneath the left elbow.

Back to Yang attitude.

Back to Yin attitude.

33) **Back To Yang Attitude.** Release the right arm from the left inner thigh, retracing the arch, then rotate the torso back to pose #30.

34) **Yin Attitude.** Raise the torso with a flat back into pose #29.

Repeat numbers 27 through 34 for left leg.

Rise elegantly as possible into Strength Split.

The toes on the right foot point forward and the toes on the left foot point laterally.

43) Rise as elegantly as possible into Strength Split. This may take some time to do elegantly. Square the hips to the left leg. Place the right hand, palm down, in front of your groin. Place the left hand in back of your left buttock. Lean the torso forward to gather some kinetic energy, flex both elbows to store even more energy in the arms. Now, on an exhale, blow yourself up into a Strength Split, which is a wide, standing stance. The toes on the right foot point forward and the toes on the left foot point laterally. Only the heel of the left foot should be in contact with the earth. The spine is directly over the center of your hips. To increase the stretch throughout the inner thighs and legs, keep the right foot as your anchor foot and inch the left heel away from you.

44) Switch sides: Strength Split. You can put your hand on the earth in front of you and rotate or pivot on both heels until you are facing the right leg. Bring the arms and hands back to the hips or at the sides. Keep both legs at extension, but do not force the depth. Allow the depth to gradually emerge as you keep inching the right foot away from you as the weeks go by.

Switch sides: Strength Split.

45) Come to Center: Hang from a Flat Back. Pivot back to center, then imagine a clothesline being strung across your waist. Upon an exhale, simply fold or drape your upper torso over the clothesline and hang yourself out to dry! Your hands can grab the opposite elbows. Make your skull heavy and limp. Breathe deeply. Press the rear, thigh and the back of the knees away from you as you work on elevating the hips skyward and coercing the spine away from the pelvis.

Come to Center: Hang from a Flat Back.

46) Balance into V-Sit. Crux move for many students. From pose #45, reach way back under your groin and place both palms backward on the earth beneath you. Flex both knees to accomplish this. Keep scooting the palms backward as the knees flex even more, until only the heels of both feet are in contact with the earth. Create as much space as possible between the shoulders and the ears in order to find the skeletal bracing. Once you have found the support from the upper skeleton, not the muscles, just lever back as the heels now leave the earth and you sit into a V-Sit. The top of the forearms are supporting the inner thighs. Hold for as long as possible (probably only a nanosecond, but that's okay!).

Reaching back to find balance for V-sit.

47) Lower (try not to crash down) the buttocks back to the earth and unfold your hands which are trapped beneath you, to finish. Congratulations, you've done Medium Form!

Holding V-sit for a nanosecond? Unfold to finish!

Medium Form Flexibility Notes

1. Sarvasana or Corpse Pose

This is a traditional restorative hatha yoga pose. The body is supported; the mind no longer needs to "worry" about it. A deep state of relaxation may be quickly achieved. Even lions need rest to regain their strength.

2. Knee Squeeze

Derived from Pavanamuktasana, this position's benefits may include relief from abdominal dis-ease (bloatedness, gas, constipation), and lower-back tension. Positions 4 and 5 also address these benefits. While holding this pose, study residing distractions in the mind and body, and squeeze them out.

8. Chipko position

I named this pose in honor of a women's movement in the Himalayan foothills. In the mid '70s, villagers hurried into forests slightly ahead of loggers to *chipko* (to hug or cling to) the trees to save them. The yoga of this position opens major energy channels servicing the liver, spleen, and gall bladder. It also opens the hip joint, excellent for all types of athletes.

9. Extend active leg overhead

Derived from Supta Padangusthasan, this asana (pose) is said to promote growth and development of bones and muscles in legs as well as relieve sciatica. Additionally, a lower back subject to weakness or pain is rejuvenated by the nerves and muscles in the hips and pelvis. The leg *must* be extended fully. You may wish to loop a towel or strap around the active foot until it can be grasped with the hands.

28. Spinal Twist

This gentle self-chiropractic adjustment strengthens the rib cage and chest area, improves digestion, tones spinal nerves, and may help relieve chronic constipation and other urinary, bladder, and prostate difficulties. Spiritually, one should use this posture to look only briefly to the past (physically symbolized by looking behind you). By acknowledging our past, but not dwelling on it, we empower our present and positively affect our future.

29 and 30. Yin and Yang over near leg

Another variant of Pascimottanasana, this posture strengthens the abdominal viscera and diaphragm, stretches the legs and spine, and aids the digestive and eliminative organ systems.

43 and 44. Strength Split

Gymnastically speaking, a split is not a split unless you can do something while holding it. In other words, flexibility must be functional! The ability to "do" the splits is meaningless if you are just holding your spine straight by placing your hands on the floor. Remain high enough in the split to keep the inner thighs engaged.

45. Flat Back Hang

This is a variant of Prasarita Padattana-sana. To be stooped, rounded, and collapsed is to weaken your spinal energies. A flat back is imperative to long-term health and vitality. This inverted posture stimulates the digestive and reproductive systems as well as activates the lymph system.

46. V-Sit

This is a gymnastic move. Let go and trust in yourself. Find the skeletal bracing in this move; do not rely on muscle! By physically reaching into your center, you reach into your most hidden fears. And by finding your balance in this place, you free latent energy in a positive, growing manner.

Wholistic Fitness®
Strength-Training Movements

The movements in this section have been organized into Lower Body, Upper Body, and Midsection categories. They are further divided according to their relative size (i.e., back, chest, shoulders). They are listed in alphetical order according to their name within their category. The models are author Steve Ilg, with Robin Horsfield. Photographer: Mike Powell/ALLSPORT. Location: Pacific Athletic Club, Pacific Palisades, California. Various clothing provided by Verve™, Boulder, CO.

LOWER BODY MOVEMENTS

Back Squats

Physical: Using a power rack, situate a barbell across the back of the neck, low on the upper trapezius muscles. Stance is wider than shoulders, toes point slightly out. Begin a controlled descent, tracking the knees over the toes. When top of thigh is parallel to the earth, begin explosive phase up to start position. Knees are slightly flexed up top. Never bounce in the bottom position. Heart center stays up while the hips remain low throughout.

Top position: note the flexed knees ready to "track" directly over the toes, the heels down, heart center is forward, and the head pulled up. Herein lies great beauty and power if this form is maintained during the motion.

Robin demonstrates an ideal bottom position with the tops of each thigh parallel to the earth, the face and neck are relaxed, the spine is flat, and look at the alignment of knees-to-toes.

Metaphysical: Back squats are the king of all transpersonal exercise. They singlehandedly develop enormous reservoirs of inner power, spiritual tenacity, and mental focus. Their performance stimulates growth in physical, spiritual, and mental planes. Back Squats are the most potent tool I know of for self-knowledge and self-healing. How a person Squats is how a person is. A true character builder. There are a million ways to cheat or take it easy during a set of Back Squats. You must take responsibility for every nuance of this lift. Character, remember, can be lost by a single act.

Bottom position must reveal high elbows, super strong spine, composed facial demeanor, and integrity of knee-to-toe alignment.

Front Squats

Physical: Using a power rack, sandwich a barbell between throat and upper shoulders by crisscrossing the hands over the barbell and maintaining a high elbow position. An alternative hand placement is the same as the top position of a Hang Clean. Stance is wider than shoulders, toes point slightly out. Begin a controlled descent, tracking the knees over the toes. When top of thigh is parallel to the earth, begin explosive phase up to start position. Knees are slightly flexed up top and never bounce in the bottom position.

Metaphysical: All the spiritual benefits of a Back Squat plus added emphasis for the spine. Builds spinal strength remarkably fast while promoting intense balance. Imparts self-confidence and trust in oneself. Many fail because they have a wishbone where their backbone ought to be.

Start position for meeting Mr. Gunther. If it looks like I am praying to the Gunther gods ... that's because I am. You will too when you do these. From this position, my left thigh is my "drive" thigh and I will explode directly upward, not sideways to reach ...

Gunther Hops

Physical: Quarter squat with one leg out to the side. Hands in a "prayer position" near heart. Explode UP off the supporting leg. At max height, switch legs laterally so supporting leg becomes the one off to the side. Repeat this leg switch for the prescribed time or reps. Focus on height, not frequency.

Metaphysical: This plyometric movement inspires tremendous lower body power. Enhances lateral mobility. As fatigue sets in, upper body will collapse forward; instead, keep heart center high. Mental tenacity and inner conviction are the spiritual qualities associated with Mr. Gunther. Be courageous—do your best.

Top position: here both legs are quickly brought together in mid-air while strong hip extension is being done. My position here is about two feet above dear Mother Earth. At top position, I switch legs so that my right leg will become my "drive" leg for the next rep.

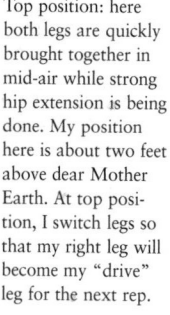

Bottom position: now I am ready to drive off my right leg and repeat this alternating leg sequence for prescribed amount of time or reps. Do not collapse the upper torso forward, keep the heart center pulled up. Be elegant through difficulty.

Jump Squats

Physical: Stand with hands behind head, fingers interlocked, elbows wide. Do not push head forward. Drop into a half-squat and explode upward as high as possible. Lead from the heart, do not allow hips to come up as spine needs to be as upright as possible throughout the movement. Get off the earth as fast as possible. Repeat for prescribed number of reps or time.

Metaphysical: Allow pain to come ... when everything is comfortable we get complacent. There is no spiritual growth in complacency. Awareness is heightened by pressure. Take responsibility for the preciseness and power of your practice. Use breath to courageously complete each set in as elegant a form as possible.

Start and bottom position: steady your focus and get ready to explode ...

Top position: notice the extremely powerful hip extension—this is key.

Knee Tuck Jumps

Physical: Assume upright stance and place arms palms down at chest height. Tuck thumbs under armpits. Keep elbows high. Rapidly dip into a quarter squat then explode upward, driving both knees toward the elbows. Upon landing, repeat as fast as possible for required reps. Keep head as stationary as possible.

Metaphysical: Work in this plyometric involves increasing our grounded movement nature. If we are feeling insecure about the direction of our lives, this movement will loosen our insecurity of self. If this movement is particularly difficult for you, examine what you are resisting in order to move forward into the next phase of your life.

Nearing top position: my feet are well above Mother Earth.

Top position: in mid-air, my knees are "slapping" my elbows.

Top position should be attained with constant contraction of the glutes and the abdominals. This pre-contracted state is vital for hamstring authenticity.

Leg Curls

Physical: Can be done seated or lying or standing depending upon apparatus. Pretty straightforward; curl the heels toward the butt. Purity of movement comes when the abdominals and gluteal muscles are pre-contracted. Very important movement to heighten the integrity of the thigh muscles and their attachments.

Metaphysical: Energetic sciences tell us the thighs represent movement in our lives. Sexuality issues can be held here resulting in tight hamstrings and illiotibial bands. The journey of strengthening the thighs while increasing their flexibility is a tremendous one, bringing up many aspects of our lives. Leg curls help facilitate such inner work.

Top position: note relaxed hands and face. Keep hips quiet and the toes in alignment with the knees.

Leg Extensions

Physical: Not very technical. Find a Leg Extension machine. Sit in it. Select a resistance appropriate to your prescribed repetition range. Extend the leg. Repeat. Refrain from overgripping the seat handles.

Metaphysical: When using some Wholistic Fitness Strength Training Techniques, this exercise will make you see God. Or Allah, or Buddha, or Shiva, or all of them combined! Mental focus is steadfastly increased here since it becomes very easy to get sloppy near the end of a difficult set. Best form comes from resting hands on thighs and listening inwardly for the utmost contraction and lengthening of the quadricep muscles.

Leg Press

Physical: Can be done on a Horizontal, Vertical, or Diagonal Leg Press Apparatus. Take a shoulder-width stance, heels in, toes out. Knees track over toes during execution. A slow yin phase is mandatory to feel every inch of this great frontal thigh movement. During yang phase, bring attention to glutes. Can you tap into the seat of power residing there? Never bounce the weight or be jerky mentally or physically.

Metaphysical: Seated like a god (or goddess) on a throne, this apparatus is truly a temple empowering all spiritual athletes to look deeply within. At extreme moments only breath remains steady in tempo, leading to panoramic awareness. The best use of breath comes from being present with it. Cultivate a sensitivity to it and the breath herself will teach you.

Top position.

In bottom position, maintain a firm tempo and poetic transition from yin (lowering) to yang (upward) energetics. Keep the knees tracked over the toes and relax the upper body and face.

Overhead Squats

Physical: Stand upright and extend a barbell overhead using a wide overhand grip. Wide foot stance. *Slowly* squat down, tracking knees over toes. From bottom, be aggressive on ascent and rise upward until the knees are nearly extended. Repeat for prescribed repetitions.

Metaphysical: Commit to the flow. Initiate descent immediately. Balance and fluid movement. Find the glutes and use them! Arms fatigue and quiver. Must still pump up and down like piston. Ego retaliates, wants to stop. Use mind to keep going. Find skeletal bracing. Keep breath low in belly. Overhead Squats teach perseverance of mind and body.

Top (start) position with barbell taken with a wide overhead grip. Note how the barbell will remain in back of the head and over the heels throughout the movement.

Bottom position unveils a classic strength training image that has been lost in today's chronic reliance upon expensive machines.

Start Position.

Scissoring the legs in the top position.

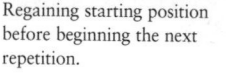

Regaining starting position before beginning the next repetition.

Scissor Jumps

Physical: Assume lunge position. Explode off both legs as high as possible. At the apex of your jump, scissor the legs once. Upon landing, retain the same leg-split position. Upper torso rock solid like mountain. Arms spread wide like eagle soaring. Repeat for required repetitions before training the other leg.

Metaphysical: Much activity and force must be generated from the knees, the energetic root of our ability to be giving. Allow the energy to flow through both knees by maintaining soft power, like a cat, upon landing. This yin energy must be countered by forceful yang, explosive energy on the jump phase. Use breath to find harmony in both.

Bottom position again reveals no bouncing or jerky movement. Really elevate the heels to reach a peak contraction in the top position.

Seated Calf Raises

Physical: Seated at the appropriate apparatus, allow the spine to be straight and head pulled up. Elevate the heels until a definite pinching sensation occurs in the calf area. Squeeze that pinch, then lower the heels providing a healthy, full stretch to Achilles Tendon. Form must remain poetic.

Metaphysical: Improves mental concentration and determination. Ability to work through difficulty. Visualize cable-like tendons stabilizing the ankle joint. Principal injury-prevention training. Ankles are another very important energetic vent in the body, so keep the energetic river flowing strongly through this area.

Side Hops

Physical: Find something to hop over, in a side-to-side manner. A pylon is best. Stand to one side of the pylon. Instantly drive thumbs, arms, and knees up and laterally to clear the pylon. Immediately upon landing, hop to the other side. Repeat for prescribed repetitions or time.

Metaphysical: Think, "Thumbs Up, Knees Up." Enhances neural coordination, mental concentration, and fast-twitch development. Work on even mindedness. Do not judge each rep, but rather commit to the entire set. Judge each day, not by the harvest, but by the seeds you plant.

Nothing but fast-twitch fun here. Hop back and forth over a non-threatening obstacle to inspire reaction fitness. Use the mantra, "Thumbs Up, Knees Up," while enjoying this fantastic movement.

Split Jumps

Physical: Assume lunge position. Explode off both legs as high as possible. Upon landing, retain the same leg-split position. Upper torso rock solid like mountain. Arms spread wide like eagle soaring. Repeat for required repetitions before training the other leg.

Metaphysical: Much activity and force must be generated from the knees, the energetic root of our ability to be giving. Allow the energy to flow through both knees by maintaining soft power, like a cat, upon landing. This yin energy must be countered by forceful yang, explosive energy on the jump phase. Use breath to find harmony in both.

Start position.

Nearing the "high as possible" top position.

Approximately mid-position: note slightly flexed knees and straight spine. Commit to elegant fluidity, not bouncing about or using herky-jerky movement.

Standing Calf Raises

Physical: Employing the appropriate apparatus, stand in alignment with knees slightly flexed. Elevate the heels until a definite pinching sensation occurs in the calf area. Squeeze that pinch, then lower heels to provide a healthy, full stretch to Achilles Tendon. Form must remain poetic.

Metaphysical: Improves mental concentration and determination. Ability to work through difficulty. Visualize cable-like tendons stabilizing the ankle joint. Principal injury prevention training.

UPPER BODY MOVEMENTS

CHEST/BACK

Bent Arm Dumbbell Pullovers

Physical: Place a dumbbell perpendicularly on a flat bench. Position yourself at a perpendicular angle to the bench. Rest the rear of your skull on the far edge of the bench, hips suspended and low. The feet stabilize the body, placed at shoulder-width. Reach over, cup the inside top plate of the dumbbell and bring it overhead. Slightly flex elbows. This is start (top) position. Yin phase begins as you lower the dumbbell in back of your head during a nasal inhale. Feel a great stretch to ribcage. Don't allow hips to rise. From bottom position, initiate Yang phase on an exhale. Quickly raise the dumbbell to top position. Establish a strong groove.

Metaphysical: Hips are the big guru here; the entire pelvis must remain soft. Getting into and out of this exercise requires awareness. This prominent movement expands the chest/ribcage fascia as well as training the central back musculature and deepening respiration. Feel the tightness dissolve in the upper torso. This movement may prove difficult until our heart center opens. Difficulties are intended to make us better, not bitter.

Top position: keep the hips soft.

Bottom position: feel the tightness dissolve in the upper torso. Difficulties are intended to make us better, not bitter.

Dips

Physical: Mount a Dip Bar apparatus. Curl heels toward butt. Drop chin to chest. With control, descend into the Dip until the upper arm bones break parallel to earth. Fire like a cannonball from bottom position back to start. Must use breath vigorously, exhale on explosive yang phase.

Metaphysical: A beautiful dance between a controlled descent and super aggressive ascent which must be done with total conviction. Very powerful anecdote for those who do not believe in or trust in their own power.

Top (start) position of the king of all upper body movements: chin on chest, "eye of the tiger" focus on the ground, heels brought toward glutes. Begin slow descent, feeling every centimeter of the lowering phase.

Bottom position: when done for chest, exaggerate the forward lean to really put pressure on the pectoral muscles. From here, one must call upon every fiber of self to achieve proper detonation to get back to top position. Repeat with elegance and steadfast determination.

Dumbbell Flat Bench Flyes

Physical: Lie supine and connect lowest vertebrae on a flat bench. Feet may need to be raised into the air to achieve this. Hold a pair of dumbbells overhead. Slightly flex elbows. Palms face each other. Begin with a slow, controlled yin phase as dumbbells are lowered to the sides of the body. Do not flinch the elbows. Once dumbbells are flush to bench, raise them upward in aggressive but disciplined manner to top position.

Metaphysical: Major heart center work. If done acknowledging each phase of each rep, honoring the female and male energies involved, there are few finer movements to develop personal balance and transpersonal depth. The spiritual athlete does more than necessary, and keeps on doing it. Activate every fiber in your chest, activate even more than those necessary.

Top position: note "ultra-yin" leg position.

Mid position with integrity throughout the motion.

Bottom position: do not flinch elbows at any time.

Front Lat Pulldowns

Physical: At a Lat Pulldown machine, position lower body so good compression is transferred from the earth through your foot for a solid

Start and top position: there is a slight elbow flex and the torso leans away from the machine.

Bottom position: notice elbows trying to meet the spine.

connection with the knee pad. Lean away from the machine at the waist, arching the lower back by rotating the pelvis forward. Spine energy very active, head pulled up. Engaging a wider-than-shoulder grip, initiate a yang, downward phase to the bar until it touches the heart center. Allow the heart to come forward to make this rendezvous. Slowly control the ascent of the bar until the elbows are nearly locked out but not quite. Explode down, control up.

Metaphysical: Offers ample stimulation of Anahata (heart center) energies. Inspires balance in relationships of all kinds; how you relate to your sport, loved ones, friends, nature, etc. Must envision drawing the elbows together in bottom position. Lower body ever so still while upper body so active. Classic yin and yang contained here.

Some students actually think I am kidding when I prescribe this movement! The point is to fatigue the back and arms, so use a wall or a partner to support the legs.

Hand Stand

Physical: Find a wall. Face the wall. With arms overhead, lunge forward and plant both hands 12″ from the wall as you swing one or both feet to the wall. Supporting yourself at arms length, straighten legs. Only the heels touch the wall. Remain in this position for required time or until you drop.

Metaphysical: For some odd reason, some of my students think I am kidding when they see this exercise prescribed. This movement teaches skeletal bracing, mental tenacity, emotional equanimity, provides cardiac and circulatory restoration, and imparts equilibrium (the foundation for all physical and spiritual pursuits) to the mind, body, and spirit. Why would I kid about that? Do not worry about failing ... the fear of failure is the father of failure.

Hang Cleans

Physical: A relative of the full PowerClean whereupon the barbell starts on the earth. Fortunately, you get to start with the bar held at mid-thigh. Literally jump up while simultaneously shrugging the barbell. Allow the hips to extend. This jump phase imparts big velocity to the barbell. As the barbell takes off toward the ceiling, keep the elbows high, point them toward the ceiling. As the bar travels up, it should remain close to the body. Next comes the Catch Phase. Once the bar reaches max height, quickly squat under the barbell and catch it on the upper chest with an inverted overhand grip. Stand up, keeping the barbell sandwiched between throat and upper shoulders. Drop the barbell back to start by simply drawing the elbows back, passing the midline of the body.

Start and bottom position.

Metaphysical: Stay with it. It will come. A baffling lift for many people. It combines extraordinary speed, inner acceleration, and quick foot movement. A sublime lift, second only to Back Squats for developing full-body power. The transpersonal effects of Hang Cleans clears the etheric ground from which we can begin or intensify our journey Higher. Don't be afraid to go out on a limb on this one. That's where the best fruit is!

Jump Phase: note how my feet have left the earth.

Catch phase ... or top position.

High Pulls

Physical: Perform an Upright Row but with these two differences: load on more weight and do it dynamically. A High Pull is a very aggressive movement whereupon the athlete jumps a loaded barbell from mid-thigh to chin. Elbows are driven toward the sky. A jerky stop to the upward momentum must be counteracted by a super controlled yin phase, lowering the bar right from the trapezius muscles of the upper back.

Metaphysical: A dynamic movement amazingly ignored by mainstream fitness people. This lift imparts yin/yang energetics beautifully throughout the body/mind/spirit. Physically, you'll feel it the next morning. Erases chronic tension from upper back.

Start position: body strong like a plank.

Top position with hands having left the earth.

Plyo Push Ups

Physical: Assume traditional Push Up position. Upon exhalation, dynamically push off from the earth with both hands and feet. Upon landing, rocket back off. Continue for as long as you are able, then you may wish to dissolve into standard Push Ups until failure.

Metaphysical: People generally have too many opinions and not enough convictions. As you blast away from the earth, reach down, dig down into that deep, powerful space within to find and develop your conviction. What some call genius or gifted is simply someone developing an infinite capacity to take life by the horns.

Pull Ups

Physical: Grasp a Pull Up bar using an overhand grip. Using an explosive upward movement, bring heart to the bar as elbows draw out to the sides. Curl heels toward butt. Descend with control to a near lock-out position. Repeat for prescribed repetitions. Exhale on yang phase.

Robin set up for a Pull Up.

Nearing top position: bring heart center, not the chin to the bar!

Metaphysical: Must have clear purpose here, know precisely what you are targeting. To hit spiritual goals, must aim at yourself. How do you expect to master your life if you cannot master a Pull Up? Life is very simple during Pull Ups, just pull! Zero timidity! Pull Ups bring forcefulness to life. Each set you will push yourself to the point of giving out. That is fine. Giving up, however, is *not* fine. As John Wooden taught, "Never let what you cannot do interfere with what you can do."

Rear Lat Pulldowns

Physical: At a Lat Pulldown machine, position lower body so good compression is transferred from the earth through your foot for a solid connection with the knee pad. Lean forward, toward the machine. Spine energy very active, head pulled up. Engaging a wider-than-shoulder grip, exhale and initiate a yang, downward phase to the bar until it reaches the back of the neck. Slowly control the ascent of the bar until the elbows are nearly locked out but not quite.

Start and top position: note the aggressive, leaning-in toward the machine.

Bottom position.

Metaphysical: This exercise influences anahata chakra, the heart center. Invoke an image of your favorite sport or a loved one during the performance of the Rear Lat Pulldowns. Stay open to whatever arises without judgment or analysis. This movement also activates the thymus gland which strengthens the immune system, especially the T-cells that have been shown to attack and destroy cancerous cells and viral infections.

Seated Rowing

Physical: On a Seated Row machine, attach the V-Handle article. Position body so several inches of tension is in the cable leading to you. Grasp handle between both knees which bend the legs in an inverted "V" position. Bring lower back in by rotating pelvis forward. Heart center forward, and lean toward the machine keeping spine straight and head pulled up. There is a stretched sensation in central back. Pull handle toward you, push chest outward, and slide into a flat, upright back position. Elbows must be driven backward for peak contraction of the back muscles. The yin phase must be done with elegance and precise control. Slowly control the retreat of the handle until the elbows are nearly locked out but not quite.

Top position: elbows must be driven backward for peak contraction of the back muscles.

Metaphysical: Gracefulness is a must. Practice with preciseness. This is what leads to enhanced awareness. Strive for full-body harmony and accept no short cuts. Allow the hips to oscillate a bit, but in doing so create more productive tension in the back, not less. This exercise helps "break down" resistances and adhesions in the scapular area, a vital energy center.

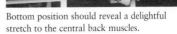

Bottom position should reveal a delightful stretch to the central back muscles.

(Photo 1) Start position.

(Photo 2) Jump Phase: One explosive, highly technical movement now occurs as you whip the barbell overhead ...

(Photo 3) and jump under it ...

(Photo 4) to enter the Catch Phase, landing in a full Asian Squat holding the barbell directly overhead.

Snatches

Technical: Perhaps the most technical movement in this book. Using an overhand grip, grab an Olympic barbell that has been raised on blocks to a mid-shin height. Wide grip, significantly wider then shoulders (good idea to do some Overhead Squats as a warm up to determine proper hand spacing). Bring chest forward, settle hips very deep, almost assuming an Asian Squat position. Look forward, preferably not in a mirror. One explosive, highly technical movement now occurs as you whip the barbell overhead and jump under it, landing in a full Asian Squat holding the barbell directly overhead (bottom position of an Overhead Squat). Now, squat up while holding the bar overhead to a standing position. From standing, lower the barbell to mid-thigh, then to floor, re-find your start position and repeat.

Metaphysical: Pure explosion. Must be "out of your mind" during execution since everything happens so fast. Visualization is enhanced as the movement must be visualized in its entirety before execution. Teaches transpersonal qualities of balance under explosion.

Speed Cleans

Physical: Read my description for Hang Cleans, then do it faster with a lighter weight. I mean *fast!!!!!*

Metaphysical: Read my description for Hang Cleans, then multiply the spirituality times two.

Standing Cable Flyes

Physical: Stand between two High Pulleys, a handle in each hand. Place one foot slightly in front of the other, toes straight ahead, knees slightly flexed. Torso: significant forward lean. Heart pulled up and in front of hips. Hands (with handles) face toward you in front of the groin. One hand is closer to your body than the other. Elbows slightly flexed. Begin a yin phase, allowing each arm to travel upward and laterally without elbow involvement. Top position is when the arms are parallel to the earth, palms facing down. Now initiate yang phase, really squeezing the chest in the bottom position. Repeat for prescribed amount of reps and sets.

Metaphysical: Chest training symbolizes ego-identification like when Tarzan pounded his chest. Strength training in this area must be done with careful meditation on opening the heart, not armoring it.

Top position is when the arms are parallel to the earth, palms facing down.

Really squeezing the chest in the bottom position.

Start and top position: there should be no stress at the back of the neck.

Bottom position is when the handle just "kisses" the chest without engagement from the hips or upper torso.

Detail: bottom position. This exercise helps "break down" resistances and adhesions in the scapular area, a vital energy center.

V-Handle Pulldowns

Physical: At a Lat Pulldown machine, position lower body so good compression is transferred from the earth through your foot for a solid connection with the knee pad. Lean well away from the machine. Spine energy very active, head pulled up. Initiate a yang, downward phase bringing the V-Handle to the heart. Allow the heart to come forward to meet the handle, really pinching the shoulder blades. Slowly control the ascent of the bar until the elbows are nearly locked out but not quite. Aggressive pulling the bar down, slow and controlled ascent of the bar from bottom to top.

Metaphysical: This exercise helps "break down" resistances and adhesions in the scapular area, a vital energy center. Mental focus must be top notch here as the hips wish to oscillate. Do not allow them to. Keep everything rock solid by using kinesthetic awareness. Movement is generated only from the arms and shoulders. There is slight movement at the heart center as it greets the V-Handle at bottom position.

V-Handle Pull Ups

Physical: These are Pull Ups done with a V-Handle apparatus placed over a Pull Up bar. As the heart is pulled toward the bar, slightly twist right shoulder to clear the left handle. Alternate sides with each rep.

Metaphysical: Increases stimulation of muladahara or solar plexus chakra. Activates issues of self-will.

Start and bottom position.

Nearing top position, Robin will soon turn one shoulder to meet the bar then alternate shoulder twists with each rep.

Weighted Pull Ups

Physical: These are Pull Ups done with weight attached. I just use a climbing sling and loop it around the inside plate of a dumbbell and go for it. Many gyms have a leather belt with a chain for this movement. Sounds kinky, eh?

Metaphysical: Far from kinky, this movement is like attending church ... chances are likely you will see God. Weighed Pull Ups amplifies all heart center energies. Do not even grip the Pull Up bar until you have mentally pre-played each set in your mind with explosive determination. The first few inches are the most difficult. The going gets tougher after that!

Refer to Pull Ups on page 426.

SHOULDERS

Repetition Jerks

Physical: Stand with an Olympic bar resting atop the chest, grip slightly wider than shoulders. Squat down a few inches to store energy in the legs, then *jerk* the barbell overhead as fast as possible! This is a fast-twitch movement. *Do not push* or *press* the barbell! *Jerk* it directly to arms length. Catch and hold it overhead for a moment, then *slowly* lower the barbell back to start position (atop the chest). Repeat for prescribed amount of reps.

Metaphysical: This is a full-body expression of the shoulders. Develops mental pre-play abilities. Teaches self-growth through confidence of execution. A powerful transpersonal exercise grossly underused by the mainstream. Taking good leadership of your life requires strong, powerful shoulders. This leadership is not a right. It is a responsibility which you must develop.

Start by storing energy in the lower body.

In mid-position my feet have left the earth as I "jump" the barbell overhead using speed, not strength.

Finish position.

Bottom (start) position.

Mid position, do not waver the hips.

Top position.

Reverse Curls

Physical: Stand and hold a barbell with an *overhead* grip near mid-thigh. Bring heart in front of hips. Elbows pressure the sides of your body. With unmatched discipline and artful elegance, curl barbell toward chin. Nearing the top, elbows naturally elevate. Pin them back to the sides of the body as yin phase begins. As barbell reaches bottom position elbows roll forward, providing deep stretch to brachialis and brachioradialus.

Metaphysical: Similar to Barbell Curls.

Seated Barbell Press

See Seated DB Press on the next page.

Seated Behind Neck Press

Read description for Seated DB Press. This movement differs only in that a barbell is used that is raised and lowered behind the neck. Enhanced forward lean is required.

Seated Dumbbell Bent Over Lateral Raises

Physical: Sit with knees pressed together on edge of a flat bench holding a pair of dumbbells. Emphasizing a flat back, bring chest toward thighs. Dumbbells meet under the hamstrings, palms facing each other. Elbows flexed at about 60 degrees. Look forward. Raise both dumbbells laterally and *keep the upper torso near the thighs.* As you raise the dumbbells, rotate the wrists so you turn the palms downward (pronate). Top position is when both arms reach parallel and both wrists are turned to the back of you. There is little activity at elbow; just at shoulder. Slowly lower dumbbells back to start position. Don't look up, head looking down, keep neck in alignment with the flat spine.

Metaphysical: Same as Seated Dumbbell Side Lateral Raises.

Bottom (start) position.

Top position: note backward facing palms.

Seated Dumbbell Press

Physical: Sit on the edge of bench in front of a mirror. Use reflection as posture guru. Holding a pair of dumbbells, begin in top position by raising both dumbbells overhead. Look up. Make sure both dumbbells are directly overhead, not pushed forward. Palms face mirror. Begin with yin phase, slowly lowering dumbbells until they hover just off each shoulder. Elbows are low but directly out to the side, not collapsed forward. Press dumbbell back to start position. This movement can also be done using a barbell or machine.

Metaphysical: Imbues body, mind, and spirit with irreparable work-ethic capacities. Grounds overly-cerebral constitutions by bringing them back into the shoulders where we accept the fact that life without discipline is no life at all.

Top (start) position: look up. Make sure both dumbbells are directly overhead, not pushed forward. Palms face mirror.

Bottom position: note refined foot/leg placement. Keep this posture. When the going gets tough, the tough get elegant. See how the dumbbells hover just off each shoulder. Elbows · are low but directly out to the side, not collapsed forward.

Seated Dumbbell Side Lateral Raises

Physical: Sit with knees pressed together on edge of a flat bench holding a pair of dumbbells. Bring chest toward thighs. Dumbbells meet under the hamstrings, palms facing each other. Elbows flexed at about 60 degrees. Look forward. Raise both dumbbells laterally. Top position is when elbows pass parallel. There is no activity at elbow; just at shoulder. Slowly lower dumbbells back to start position.

Bottom (start) position.

Top position is when elbows pass parallel. There is no activity at elbow, just at shoulder.

Metaphysical: Stay fluid here. Allow rhythm to emerge. Shoulders need to express heart energy. Tight, restricted shoulders restrict personal growth. Free the shoulders by strengthening them. A wise movement for dissipating inner conflict and stress regarding the direction or calling in your life.

Top position: strive to keep upper torso elegant with the head pulled up. Don't futz or gunkle the feet or legs. Just remain steady and smooth.

Seated Dumbbell Front Raises

Physical: Sit on the edge of a flat bench holding a pair of dumbbells, palms face one another. Use a mirror for form check: spine straight, head pulled up, elbows slightly flexed. Raise one dumbbell forward rotating the wrist so that when arm reaches parallel to earth, palm faces down. There is no activity at elbow; just at shoulder. Slowly lower dumbbell back to start position then raise the other one. Alternate and repeat for prescribed amount of repetitions.

Metaphysical: Minimize excessive body movement by concentrating on each shoulder, making it take responsibility for each repetition. Upper body remains as still as desert air. Remember our discussion of differentiation? Here is a perfect workshop to practice!

Upright Rows

Physical: Stand in alignment with the heart in front of hips while holding a barbell at arms length using an overhand grip. Slightly flex the elbows. Raise the barbell toward the chin in a perpendicular ascent. Elbows point at sky during upward phase. Once the barbell reaches chin and elbows are pointing up, begin a controlled descent, keeping the heart in front of the hips. Bottom position maintains slight elbow flexion. Repeat for prescribed amount of reps.

Bottom (start) position should promote strong posture with flexed elbows.

Top position: elbows high and proud.

Metaphysical: A movement that questions our vulnerabilities while increasing strength in the deltoids where we "shoulder our burdens." Stay poetic throughout this exercise and take note of psychological activity. Breath is tricky, I like to exhale during the descent of the barbell and aggressive nasal inhalation as barbell rises.

ARMS

Barbell Curls

Physical: Stand and hold a barbell with an underhand grip near mid-thigh. Bring heart in front of hips. Elbows pressure the sides of your body. With controlled verve, curl barbell toward chin. Nearing the top, elbows naturally elevate. Pin them back to the sides of the body as yin phase begins. As barbell reaches bottom position elbows roll forward, providing deep stretch to biceps.

Start and bottom position.

Top position: keeping elbows on or at the midline of the body.

Metaphysical: Arms express how we choose to reach out and grab life. Arm training transfers inner power forward and out where it can be used practically. As you perform this movement realize that the elegant strength with which you perform this exercise can help you elegantly strengthen your actions in daily life. Be enthusiastic, but your form must drive the enthusiasm.

Bench Press

Physical: Lie supine on a flat bench (preferably a dedicated Bench Press apparatus with two uprights to support a barbell). Top position reveals a barbell being held at arm's extension. Grip is slightly wider than shoulder width. Movement begins with a yin (lowering) phase done with *impeccable* control, as the barbell just touches the chest below the clavicle, an explosive yang (or upward) phase is performed. Link your repetitions together aiming for a harmonic flow sure to torch your pectorals. Note: Keep legs and lower spine completely quiet. If your hips are moving about, you are not doing a bench press. Use a Yin Foot Position (feet suspended in air with knees at a right angle) to achieve purity and your real authenticity in this movement.

Metaphysical: This overly popular lift is a study in contradiction. Most people who do "Benches" do so only in an ego-reiterating, body-glorification attitude that completely severs true inner power development. Bench Presses, when done with a sensitivity to the breath and energetics instead of the ego are a magnificent movement to open anahata, the heart chakra, and teaches us that peace and power come from within, not from without.

Start and top position: most WF Students use this "ultra-yin" leg position to throw more direct concentration upon the pectoralis instead of the hips. Purity is duty number one in WF strength training.

Bottom position.

Start and bottom position.

Top position: attention must be given to keeping shoulder girdle relatively parallel to earth, back is flat.

Start and bottom position.

Top position: attention must be given to keeping shoulder girdle relatively parallel to earth, back is flat.

Concentration Curl

Physical: Sit on the edge of a flat bench. Let's train the right arm first: The left arm is the "passive arm": its elbow rests on the left knee. The left palm is placed on the inside of the right knee, creating a "nesting place" into which the lower tricep/elbow of the right arm is placed. Keeping the back flat, reach down and grasp a dumbbell with the right hand. Underhand grip. Keep shoulders squared. Begin with an explosive curling movement toward chin. The yin phase begins as you slowly lower the dumbbell back to start. Repeat for prescribed reps.

Metaphysical: Greatness lies not in being strong, but in the right use of strength.

Deadman Curls

Physical: Grab a dumbbell and place feet wider than shoulder width. Bend over with a flat back and place one hand up against a wall, dumbbell rack, whatever. The other arm is active. While holding the dumbbell, the active arm hangs (like a "dead man") straight down from the shoulder. *Keep the elbow still* and curl the dumbbell toward chin, really squeezing the top couple of inches ... *slow* yin (lowering) phase back to start. Repeat for prescribed amount of reps.

Metaphysical: Keep clean, clear angle in this movement. Commit to the straight line. Every crooked turn delays our arrival at success.

Dumbbell Kickbacks

Physical: Place right hand and right knee on a flat bench. Keep back as flat as a kitchen table. Left leg is placed slightly off to the side. Active left arm grasps a light dumbbell. Bring right elbow to form a right angle so that the left forearm is perpendicular to earth. Left palm faces body. Extend left forearm backward until the entire left arm is parallel to earth. Lower to bottom position slowly and in control. Repeat for prescribed repetitions then train the right arm.

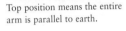

Bottom (start) position: keep back as flat as a kitchen table.

Top position means the entire arm is parallel to earth.

Metaphysical: Lots of attention here to maintain clean angles. When performing this movement, observe how difficult structure is to maintain. What structure in your life are you getting lazy with? How can you improve the various structures in your life?

Lying Triceps Extensions

Physical: Lie supine. Hold a barbell at arm's length using an overhand, false grip. Hand placement is narrow, no more than shoulder-width. Upper arm bone remains perpendicular to the earth throughout entire exercise. Flex elbows, slowly bring the barbell to the hairline of the head. Smoothly exhale into an aggressive yang phase as you extend the elbows until barbell reaches arms length.

Metaphysical: Fine tunes inner listening skills to hear the fabulous details of how breath affects strength. Lower back will want to arch, keep feet high in air to prevent this. Simplicity and purity. Repetition and perseverance of mind.

Start and top position: note Robin's use of the "ultra-yin" leg position and how perpendicular her upper arm bones are to the earth.

Bottom position: upper arm bones have not moved, just the forearms. Go strict, or go home.

Top (start) position: upper arm bones are brought close to the head and keep a clean line of energy running from the hips up the spine to the hands.

Bottom position: the battle dance here is to keep the elbows close to the head while generating controlled power to raise the dumbbell back to top position. The elbows will want to wander as much as the mind. Do not allow either to do so.

Overhead Dumbbell Triceps Extension

Physical: Perform seated with spine straight. Hold a dumbbell overhead, palms pressed against the topmost inner plate. Dumbbell handle is perpendicular to earth. Bring upper arm bones perpendicular, elbows press against ears. This requires scapular flexibility. Yin phase: lower the dumbbell in back of head. Elbows wish to wander; don't let them! Exhale on yang phase.

Metaphysical: Prioritize perpendicular upper arms and elbows in! Yin phase is a slow descent, feeling the triceps stretch. An advanced movement because of the flexibility required and total focus on the strict form. You must stay pure. Wandering elbows are a manifestation of wandering mind. A stable mind equals a stable posture.

Reverse Wrist Curls

Physical: Place the underside of the forearms on a flat bench, wrists overhanging the edge, grasping a barbell with an overhand grip. Extend and flex the wrist while holding the barbell for a stupendous burn in the forearm extensors.

Metaphysical: The whole forearm and wrist area is an important energetic vent to the body. It is where thought energy finally expresses itself in action. Strengthening this body part contributes to elegance in expression and an increased ability to handle daily circumstances with authority. Is it any wonder why arthritis strikes so frequently at this area? Some bodyworkers consider arthritis a manifestation from chronic pulling away from our true self.

Bottom position.

Top position: place fire extinguisher nearby "cuz those forearm muscles may catch fire if this movement is done well."

Triceps Pressdowns

Physical: Face a High Pulley and a Tricep Attachment (an inverted "V" bar, a rope, or straight bar), stand in elegant alignment. Bring bar down until forearms are just above parallel to earth. Engage an overhand, false grip. Pressure elbows against your sides. Extend elbows fully to feel a static, intense contraction at the triceps located in the back of the arm. Working away from that contraction (keep the contraction in your mind), flex elbow until top position is attained. Repeat. Exhalation (yang phase) as elbows extend.

Top position with elbows firmly stabilized at the sides of the body.

Bottom position: you are not at bottom until you feel the "pinch" of the triceps at the back of the arm.

Metaphysical: All lower chakras are active during this movement which urges us forward into our lives by improving our grip on our actions! Remain pulled up here, heart in front of hip always. Do not allow any extra body movement. You may enjoy a narrow foot stance for enhanced energetic flow. Have you ever tried Undergrip Pressdowns?

Bottom position: note the solid, extended leg demeanor.

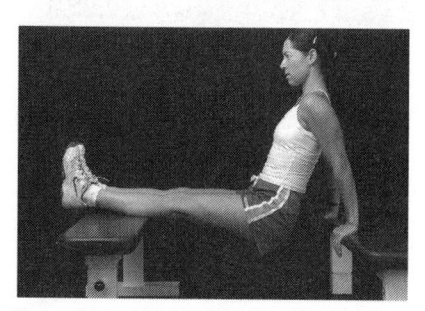

Top position with relaxed facial and hand energy.

Bottom position.

Going for the pump in the top position.

Two Bench Triceps

Physical: Place two flat benches side-by-side, approximately 3 feet apart. Place palms down on the edge of one bench, then place both calves on the opposite bench. Top position is with elbows locked out, heart center forward, and head pulled up. Bring ankles together, knees together. Lower your glutes toward the earth via elbow flexion. At bottom position, extend at elbows assertively to get back to top position. Link your repetitions together as fluidly as possible. And never, ever quit.

Metaphysical: Often, I will prescribe minute sets on this exercise. You are never allowed to quit, but I will allow you to use "escape plans" to complete your minute. Escape Plan A) upon stalling in optimal form, remove one foot from bench and place it flatly upon the earth. Continue to exercise. Escape Plan B) upon stalling in Escape Plan A, remove the other foot from the bench and place it flatly upon the earth. Continue to exercise. Escape Plan C) upon stalling in Escape Plan B, get yourself up to top position and just hold it there until you recover enough to do another rep. Repeat this hold-and-go process until you reach the required time or repetition limit.

Wrist Curls

Physical: Place the top of the forearms on a flat bench, wrists overhanging the edge, grasping a barbell with an underhand grip. Flex and extend the wrist while holding the barbell for a stupendous burn in the forearm flexors.

Metaphysical: Don't compete with the forearm burn. Don't try harder. Try softer. Explore the mystery of the forearm burn with the breath as your guide. This movement increases grip strength and overall hand energy. Development of hand strength increases our intimacy with the world. A handshake with infinity ...

MIDSECTION

Abdominal Crunches

Physical: Lie on a bench or on the floor. Cradle the back of your head in your hands, fingers interlocked. Draw elbows wide, feel shoulder blades retract. Place feet in air. Maintain a right angle at ankle and knee joints. Upper thigh bone perpendicular to earth. Curl shoulder girdle toward knees without moving the thighs. Short range of motion. Lower the head to earth via the abdominals.

Top position: don't lose the intense contraction in the abdominals when coming down from this position.

Metaphysical: Some ask why I require this simplistic movement when contemporary gyms are adorned with so many expensive abdominal machines. If done with *mindfulness*, not many reps can be done of this simple exercise. If done like most people, hundreds of reps can be done without feeling anything. True character comes through on simple movements. Character is like glass—even a little crack shows.

Abdominal Pulldowns

Physical: Face a High Pulley apparatus. Kneel on floor about 3 feet from the machine. Grasp both ends of a Rope Attachment about level with your ears. Upper thigh bone remains perpendicular to earth throughout exercise. Curl the head downward, driving elbows past knees. Feel a crunching effect in the abdominals. Keeping the abdominal contraction, lengthen the torso away from the contraction providing a stretch to the abdominals. At top position, lower back is flexed. In bottom position, upper back is extended.

Top position with elbows firmly stabilized at the sides of the body.

Metaphysical: Rumi said, "Allow the beauty of what you are to be what you do. There are a hundred ways to kneel and kiss the ground." This movement superbly affects all midsection muscles and its neural transfer means high production in all sport performance. The beauty here is that you can increase resistance.

A crunching movement attains bottom position, thighs have remained steady.

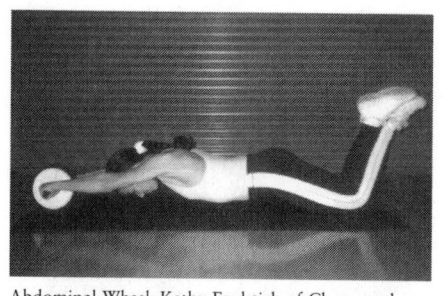

Abdominal Wheel: Kathy Faulstich of Chatsworth, California, rolls into a perfect bottom position. From here, Kathy rolls the wheel toward her until it is directly beneath her chin, arms kept at extension. Beginners and intermediates *should not* extend into such an extreme bottom position until midsection strength reaches well-developed levels. Photo by the author.

Ab Wheel

Physical: Grasp both ends of an Ab Wheel and assume a hands and knees position on the earth, ankles together, heels in the air. Roll out halfway then roll back home. Progressively flirt with full extension as the abdominals and lower back muscles strengthen.

Metaphysical: Quickly sharpens all voluntary attention skills. Quickly sharpens all athletic activity by producing a midsection pillar of strength and power like no other. After you get the hang of the Ab Wheel, try this choreography to fulfill prescribed timed sets: Roll out to full extension and come up to two-thirds position, roll back out to extension. Perform this 3 times then roll back to start position (with wheel directly under you). Repeat until prescribed time limit is attained.

Top position: countering upward momentum, preparing to explode both hands downward.

Bottom position: overcoming downward momentum before firing both hands upward.

Double Pole Plyos

Physical: Stand with two light dumbbells in a shoulder-wide stance. Raise both arms explosively until hands are at eye-level, elbows wide, then counteract that upward momentum and drive both arms down until hands pass the hips. Counteract that momentum, and explode back up to top. Repeat sequence as fast as possible until prescribed reps or time is reached. Exhale on downward phase.

Metaphysical: Really, really fast exercise and for God's sake, don't lose your grip on the dumbbells! This Ilg original teaches us not to hesitate in reaching ever higher for our loftiest dreams. The meditation here is pure velocity!

Left arm is in top position, while right arm is in bottom.

In transition, very explosive, lightning fast through here.

The finish of one complete cycle as left arm gets back to top position.

Dumbbell Arm Swings

Physical: Stand with a light dumbbell in each hand. Assume a quarter squat position with feet apart and hands at the sides. Keep head straight. Tilt the shoulders slightly forward. Drive one arm forward and up above the head while punching the opposite elbow backward. Then reverse as fast as possible. Repeat this high-speed, alternating sequence for the prescribed time or reps.

Metaphysical: Very aggressive. High speed. Focus eyes straight ahead. Envision sprinting across a finish line. Meditate upon speed, speed, and more speed for fast arm turnover. What inner weakness must be overcome before your arm turnover can increase? Drive with force into your goals and dreams!

Dumbbell Horizontal Swings

Physical: Stand with a light dumbbell clasped by both hands. Fingers interlock. Quarter squat position with feet shoulder width apart. Extend arms, holding dumbbell at chest level in front of the body. Elbows slightly bent. Keep head straight. Tilt the shoulders slightly forward. Initiate a torquing motion by pulling to one side with shoulder and arm. As momentum increases, check the motion by pulling in the opposite direction with the other shoulder and arm. Begin the checking action before the torso has swung fully in one direction. Use the momentum in one direction as the load for eliciting a plyometric response in the other direction. The work comes from the shoulders and arms, as well as the torso, using minimal hip and leg involvement. Repeat this alternating sequence for the prescribed time or reps.

A fast-twitch, super speedy movement that generates tremendous power in the upper torso. Swinging the dumbbell side-to-side fashion will force you to counteract and overcome the velocities created by the motion. Keep elbows high and the hips facing mostly forward.

Metaphysical: Midsection work improves the processing of our reality … our "gut check," our "gut reaction." Do we have the "guts" to meet and walk our dragons? Fiery midsection training as in this movement enhances intuitive wisdom for knowing what is most appropriate to our highest truth.

Top position: really crunching the abdominals to prepare for a slow, controlled descent.

Bottom position: fill yourself with inner conviction gained from seeing your life upside-down.

Inversion Sit Ups

Physical: Advanced movement for superior midsection development. Using some type of inversion "boots," hang upside down from a Pull Up bar. Perform a Sit Up maneuver. Be explosive going up and very controlled on the descent. Exhalation on explosion.

Metaphysical: Helps correct energetic and structural dysbalance by decompression of the spine thus harmonizing one-sided and poor habitual postural patterns. Develops self-observation and mental acuity. Calms the mind. Drains the lymph system. Excellent for flushing fatigue toxins from the cells after a workout.

Lying Leg Circles

Physical: Lie face up and raise legs to perpendicular position. Bring legs neatly together with slight flexion at knee. Maintain that neatness and begin tracing an imaginary circle in the air above you with your feet. Top of the circle should be above the neck. Bottom of the circle should be just off the floor. Be sure to work the circle both directions. Smooth circles.

Trace large, imaginary circles with both legs pressed together for wholistic toning effect for the abdominal musculature.

Metaphysical: Emily Dickinson said, "My business is circumference." While performing this movement, so too, is yours. Midsection work accelerates the processing of our reality ... our "gut check," our "gut reaction." Do we have the "guts" to meet and walk our dragons? Midsection training can help enhance instinctive wisdom.

Oblique Twists

Physical: Lie supine on a Bench Press apparatus. Stabilize upper body by grasping the upright bars. Raise legs to perpendicular position. Bring legs neatly together with moderate flexion at knee. Drop both legs to your right side. Counteract the downward momentum as the legs reach parallel to earth by raising them back up to start position. Drop to other side and repeat for prescribed amount of time or reps. Superb conditioning for all rotators, obliques, and serratus. Inhale as legs descend, exhale as legs rise.

Metaphysical: More than we realize, the alignment of the body and breath during training affects the course of our spirit. This is why I stress so much form and alignment. As Dogen says, "Practice and enlightenment are one." Unite body and breath during this fantastic midsection movement. Visualize internal organs being squeezed and wrung like a wet towel. This internal massage cleanses the organs and strengthens their visceral connective tissues. Very good for digestive system.

Using utmost control, slowly bring the legs from left to right and back again without too much activity at the knees. Unite body and breath during this fantastic midsection movement. Visualize internal organs being squeezed and wrung like a wet towel.

Seated Good Mornings

Physical: Sit on the edge of a flat bench with a barbell across the top of the shoulders behind the neck. Sit with spine straight and eyes soft. Feet are placed slightly wider than shoulder-width. Bend forward prioritizing a high heart center. Maintain spinal integrity during descent. At maximum depth, raise up to start position concentrating on the erector spinae muscles to do the work.

Start (top) position requires a pulling up of spinal and hip energy.

Near bottom position of this spinal-strengthening classic.

Metaphysical: This is a close relative to the Stiff Leg Deadlift but reduces hamstring involvement making for pure spinal satisfaction! Form and alignment before depth of posture. This movement trains the spine, the core of our human incarnation. Develops the psychospiritual spine while stabilizing the structure of entire vertebral column.

Bottom position: if one movement defines WF attention to form and posture, this one is it. Note Robin's beautiful flat back and the wonderful elongation effect of the rear thigh which this elegant movement produces. There can be no rounding of the back otherwise the whispers of the teachings from this movement will be lost.

Stiff Leg Deadlifts (SLD)

Physical: Stand in alignment with barbell held at arms length near mid-thigh. Bring heart center forward, pinch shoulder blades together. Head pulled up as if suspended from above. Begin super slow descent but *do not* let hips travel forward. Keep them directly over the heels. Back *must remain flat* the whole way down. The moment the back rounds, go back to start position and try again. Genuine bottom position is when the *flat back* breaks parallel to earth. Raise slowly, studying every inch of the ascent for possible postural flaws, back to start. Good luck and listen well. Repeat for prescribed amount of reps.

Metaphysical: The SLD taps us into the present like no other movement. Remember, you must be present to win! Total mental focus in the SLD opens the door for spiritual awareness. SLD is the most powerful postural teacher I know. Each time resistance is added, the spine gets stronger, the mind becomes more fruitful, and life deepens as the spine flattens. The SLD is a journey into oneself by releasing chronic tension in the back and hamstrings, two areas that dramatically restrict personal growth. The performance of this movement brought me back from paralysis and has saved my life on at least two occasions since. Warriors do not pray for lighter burdens. They train hard to create stronger backs!

Suspended Leg Raises

Physical: These can be done using an "AbOriginal Strap" that is hung from a Pull Up bar, or they can be done off a Suspended Leg Raise apparatus. Center your mass by drawing the heels behind your hips with only a slight bend at the knee. Now, swing both legs up to horizontal, then lower with control from the abdominals to prevent inelegant swinging of the upper torso.

Top position.

Metaphysical: This movement annoys most people when they cannot control the dynamic balance involved. Interestingly, this exercise inspires activity at swadhisthana chakra, an energy center that, when undeveloped, keeps us stuck in sensory pleasure. Strengthening this area by Suspended Leg Raises can help balance this chakra leading to more focus on spiritual growth instead of just doing what our ego desires want. May sound silly, but the majority of people remain stuck at the lower chakra levels and their sport performance suffers because of it.

Wholistic Fitness®
Strength-Training Techniques

"The art of life is to know how to enjoy a little and to endure much."
— William Hazlitt

The following strength-training techniques, which I formally introduced in 1982, transform the sterile and predictable gym workout into a colorful, challenging, and creative explosion of inner and outer strength. The techniques are divided into two categories, *stimulative phase techniques*, which are used during the actual lifting of weights, and *recovery phase techniques*, which take place in between sets. These techniques are copyrighted, but I urge you to share them with your training partners. Just be sure to tell them where they came from: Wholistic Fitness, the original transpersonal training system! Have fun exploring these techniques and may they bring you rich insight and high performance!

STIMULATIVE PHASE TECHNIQUES

ENVELOPE TECHNIQUE®

This technique increases muscular endurance and deep-fiber recruitment. It also teaches perseverance and mental stamina. "Open the envelope" by performing a first set for one minute. Recover for thirty to forty-five seconds. Then perform two heavy sets of five to six reps each. Recover for thirty to forty-five seconds. "Close the envelope" by doing a final set for another minute. Take each set to momentary failure.

STACCATO TECHNIQUE®

This technique is designed to enhance the blood flow in muscle tissue and prevent associated hypoxic mechanisms, as well as teach elegance through difficulty. It also improves mental concentration. A set is performed for one minute, divided into ten-second "splits." Begin the set by "sticking" the first rep in the top position and holding it there for ten seconds Then "move" during the next ten-second split by performing the exercise movement throughout its full range. Repeat this procedure for one minute. Always focus on posture.

THREE-STAGE TECHNIQUE®

This technique was created to improve mental focus, lifting form, rhythm, and postural awareness during work output. An exercise is performed for one minute, divided into twenty-second "splits." Perform the first split, or "stage," by executing only the *top half* of the movement. During the second split, do only the *bottom half* of the movement, in accelerated tempo. For the third split, perform the movement throughout its *full range* with total conviction. Repeat the sequence for one minute.

SHIVAYA TECHNIQUE®

This is structured as a pre-exhaustive technique to fatigue a specific muscle at its strongest contractile range. The choreography of set is as follows: Perform the first three repetitions for the full range of the exercise. For reps four through nine, train only the *top half* of the movement. For rep ten, take the full range of the movement to failure (the optimal range of this final set should be five to six reps).

SWAN MEDICINE TECHNIQUE®

Grace and fluid movement are two aspects of Swan Medicine. This technique increases

mental concentration while promoting muscular endurance and isometric strength. Note that it's only for use with dumbbells or machines with independent arm levers. Select a resistance heavy enough so that momentary failure will be reached within six reps. While holding the resistance in the top, mid-, or bottom position with one arm or leg (the contraction intensity will be high), perform the standard range of movement for the exercise with the other limb. Upon failure of the working limb, repeat the sequence in the opposite manner.

> "Without haste, but without rest."
> —life motto of
> Johann Wolfgang Von Goethe

RECOVERY PHASE TECHNIQUES

KU

Method: Upon the completion of a set, keep holding the weight as effortlessly as possible. Hold this position for five Cleansing or Filling Breaths in one of the two positions described below:

Ku Top Form: The exercise movement is held at its top position (i.e., after Front Lat Pulldowns, take five breaths while holding the bar with the arms extended).

Ku Bottom Form: The exercise movement is held at its bottom position (i.e., after Front Lat Pulldowns, take five breaths while holding the bar at the chest).

Meditation: Intensely void. Feel the energy of the inner power now under attention. Your musculature is still contracting. "He who has never failed somewhere, that man cannot be great," Herman Melville wrote, "and it is better to fail in originality than to succeed in imitation." Find your truth in this originality and in this failure.

ENTRÉ NOUS

Method: After performing the final repetition of a set, decrease the resistance so that it does not produce a contraction within your musculature. Then simply grasp the weight, without clutching it. The point is to maintain touch with the apparatus on the physical level to access the spiritual level. Take ten Cleansing Breaths, then initiate the next set.

Meditation: Be at one with the movement. By maintaining a touch with the apparatus, you keep the mind from wandering. It's just you, your apparatus, and your breath. Upon breath number ten, perform the movement again for the required repetitions.

KIN-HIN

Method: This recovery technique mandates a slow, rhythmic walk between sets. The walk should be well prepared and take approximately thirty seconds to complete. Do not let your mind wander from the feeling of your feet upon the earth.

Meditation: Develop a pure, uncontested mind. Accept the moment, whatever it brings. Walk upright and breathe from the belly during the walk. Accept the next set regardless of how you feel. You may have to lower the weight resistance during extended sets.

Nutrition: A Few
Wholistic Fitness® Recipes

The following dishes were selected from two Wholistic Fitness cookbooks *First Course* and *Second Course*, by Deborah Ilg. The books, which grew out of requests from students seeking specific recipes, are available from Wholistic Fitness.

There is not another, more potent spiritual workshop than our nutritional discipline. The senseless war of aggression and domination is too easily embraced by the typical American diet. Though there is no way around each of our unique personal predicaments, we *can* choose to lead clearer, more insightful, and more harmonious lives through our work and our joys in the nutritional discipline. Special thanks to Deborah Ilg.

MORNING MEALTIMES

Tofu Scramble

preparation time: five to ten minutes
serves: two

  1 tsp. safflower oil
  1 clove garlic, crushed
  ¼ cup onion, chopped
  ½ lb. (½ package) tofu
  ¼ tsp. raw sesame seeds
  2 tsp. tamari (to taste)
  garnishes: salsa, catsup

Saute oil, garlic, and onion in a heavy skillet on medium/high heat. When onions are clear, add tofu (putting the whole cube into the skillet and mashing it into small pieces with a fork). Add the sesame seeds and tamari. Cook on medium/high heat for three to five minutes, or until slightly brown. Garnish and serve.

Crispy Granola

preparation time: forty-five minutes
makes: 7–8 cups

  4 cups rolled oats
  1 cup oat bran
  1 cup raw sunflower seeds (you may grind half of them to assimilate easier)
  ½ cup pumpkin seeds (optional)
  1–1½ cups raisins
  ½ cup dried apple or apricot, chopped (optional but tasty)

3 T. sunflower oil

¼ cup apple concentrate (you may need to get this at a health food store)

2 T. cinnamon

½–1 tsp. dry ginger

¼ tsp. ground cloves

Preheat oven to 325°F. Mix dry ingredients together. Combine the oil and the apple concentrate in a separate large bowl; whisk together. Mix all the spices, then add the dry ingredients, stirring well until the oats are coated. Spoon the mixture onto one or two ungreased baking sheets. Bake until golden brown, about thirty minutes. Cool until crisp. Store in an airtight container.

MIDDAY MEALTIMES

Tofu Sandwich

preparation time: ten minutes
serving: one sandwich

½ tsp. safflower oil (or any light oil)

¼ pound hard tofu (cut into 2 slices)

½ tsp. tamari

2 slices of your favorite bread

suggested garnishes: mustard, lettuce, sprouts, tomato, onions, pickles, chilies, soy cheese, catsup, avocado, pepper

In a skillet add the oil, then brown both sides of the tofu on medium/high heat. If you're using soy cheese you can melt it on the tofu after the first side is browned.

When the tofu is browned put it on plain or toasted bread and add your favorite garnishes.

Electra Lentil Soup

Named for Electra Lake, located north of Durango, Colorado, a beautiful playground of my childhood.

preparation time: sixty minutes
serves: six

1 cup lentils

6 cups water

3 T. olive oil

1 medium potato, cut into ½-inch cubes

½ tsp. black pepper

1 cup celery, chopped

1 cup swiss chard, chopped

¼ cup cilantro, chopped

½ tsp. cumin

2 T. lemon juice

¼ cup parsley, chopped

1 tsp. ground coriander

sea salt, to taste

In a large soup pot over medium heat, cook the lentils in the water. Bring to a boil. Simmer for thirty-five minutes. Meanwhile in a small frying pan saute the potato and pepper in oil for two minutes. Add the celery and continue to saute for another minute. Add the saute mixture to the lentil broth and boil for ten minutes. Add the chard, cilantro, cumin, and lemon juice; cook for another ten minutes. Add the parsley, coriander, and salt to taste. Serve.

EVENING MEALTIMES

Bok Choy and Rice

Sounds like an Asian law firm! A great dish: subtle, cleansing, and invigorating on all planes.

preparation time: twenty minutes
serves: two to three

  1 T. safflower oil
  ½ lb. tofu
  ½ small onion
  1 clove garlic, minced
  ¼ cup water
  1 med. stalk bok choy, chopped
  2 T. lite soy sauce
  2 T. mustard
  2–3 tsp. curry powder
  2 cups basmati rice, precooked

Add the oil and tofu to a heavy skillet and brown slightly on medium/high heat. Add the onion and garlic. Cook for one minute, then add the bok choy and water (you may need to add more water if the bok choy gets too dry). Cook for five minutes, or until the bok choy has softened. Add the soy sauce, mustard, and curry powder; simmer for three more minutes. Serve over rice.

Spinach Staple

If you stopped by my house during meal-time, we would most probably be having this meal. It's an especially valuable meal for vegetarian-types. The dark-green, leafy nutrition is an important energetic choice. The simplicity is astounding. Please feel free to experiment with the seasonings.

preparation time: twenty minutes
serves: two to three

  1 T. safflower oil
  ½ lb. firm tofu, sliced or cubed
  1 clove garlic, chopped
  ½ small onion, chopped
  ¼ cup water
  2 bunches fresh spinach
  ¼ cup yellow mustard
  2 T. lite soy sauce
  1 T. Bragg® liquid aminos
  ¼ tsp. ground ginger
  2 cups cooked basmati rice
  garnish: soy sauce, mustard, or Bragg

Place the oil and tofu into a frying pan. Brown both sides of the tofu on high heat. Add the garlic and onion. Add the spinach and water, then cover. When the spinach softens, add the mustard, soy sauce, liquid aminos, and ginger (you may need to add more water if the spinach is drying out). Cover for one minute, stirring frequently. Garnish and serve over rice.

Glossary

Aerobic. In the presence of oxygen; normally refers to the metabolism utilizing oxygen.

Alpine skiing. Downhill skiing activity in which the heel of the boot is fixed to the ski.

Anaerobic. In the absence of oxygen; normally refers to nonoxidative metabolism.

Asana. A physical yogic exercise done to enhance mental and bodily control. In Sanskrit, means posture or position.

Asian squat. A common body position that involves squatting close to the ground, heels flat, buttocks near the earth.

Backcountry. Wilderness that is ungroomed, untracked, and often remote.

Blade. The wide, flat part of an oar or paddle that contacts the water.

Boardhead. A snowboarder.

Bonk. To experience exhaustion or fatigue caused by glycogen depletion in the muscles.

Chakras. Energy centers in the subtle body.

Chi. Chinese word meaning the vital energy, life force, or cosmic spirit that animates all things.

Concentric. A contraction involved in shortening muscle fibers.

Dharma. Usually relates to the central notion of Buddhism, which sees Dharma as the cosmic law expressing universal truth.

Dhyana. A stilling of the mind, or any absorbed mental state brought about by concentration. In yogic terms, Dhyana is the seventh of eight steps in Raja Yoga that lead to Samadhi.

Drala. Tibetan word meaning natural wisdom.

Dryland training. Sport-specific winter preseason training activities.

Eccentric. A contraction involved in lengthening muscle fibers.

Ego. That aspect of the mind that delineates reality into notions of personal separateness, such as "I" and "mine." It is the thought form of duality that sees reality as self and other.

Extreme. In outdoor athletics, a term that is used to describe a situation or sport where severe injury or death will occur if one screws up. Nowadays, the term means "out of the ordinary" as in "extreme golf" where one runs between holes. Whatever.

Fall line. An imaginary line down a slope that represents the course a rolling ball or stream of water would follow down the hill.

False grip. In strength training, where thumbs are placed on the same side of barbell as the fingers.

Free-heeling. Telemark skiing.

Gassho mudra. A prayer hand posture in which the palms are held together at the level of the chest. A traditional gesture in Zen for greeting, gratitude, a request, veneration, or supplication. In yoga, this gesture is known as Namaskar.

Green Tara. In Tibetan Buddhism, Green Tara is the female aspect of enlightenment. Green Tara guides novice practitioners along the path of awakening. She encourages victory over inner obstacles and fear.

Higher self. Opposite of ego; true knowledge. The intuitive wisdom that sees no separation between self and reality.

Kin Hin. In Zen, a walking meditation done between periods of formal sitting practice. Can be done slowly or rapidly or in between.

Kundalini. The primordial cosmic energy that lies dormant within each individual until it is awakened by meditation techniques. Also known as Shakti in Hinduism.

Lactate threshold. During exercise, the point at which blood lactate accumulates above resting levels. Also known as the anaerobic threshold.

Macronutrients. Protein, carbohydrates, and fats.

Meridians. Subtle energy channels in the body.

Metaphysical. That which is beyond the known laws of physics. Refers to the unknown but intelligent forces latent in the human mind.

Micronutrients. Nutritional elements that are not classified as macronutrients, such as vitamins, minerals, enzymes, enzymatic cofactors, and antioxidants.

Nadis. Yogic term for the 72,000 meridians of the astral body. The primary three are the Ida, Pingala, and Sushumna.

Nordic skiing. Skiing in which the heel is not fastened to the ski. Often called cross-country skiing. Nordic skiing also includes free-heel ski jumping.

Plyometrics. Athletic training system that concentrates on the development of fast-twitch muscles and explosive power.

Prana. Sanskrit term meaning breath of life. The cosmic energy that animates all living things.

Pratyahara. Withdrawal of the senses. In yogic terms, the fifth of eight steps in Raja Yoga that lead to Samadhi.

Periodizational training. A process of cyclic, structured training periods to produce a desired training effect.

Rider. A snowboarder.

Samadhi. The culmination of many yogic traditions that results in a superconscious state. Blissful absorption; the end of the dualistic mind.

Serial distortion. A state of malalignment resulting from a loss of functional integrity.

Sesshin. In Zen, extended formal sitting practice over several days.

Ski feel. A developed ski-to-snow sensitivity.

Supine. Lying on the back or having the face upward.

Taoist. A person practicing the mystical teaching of *wu-wei*, or unmotivated action. There are two movements of Chinese taoism: the wu-wei teachings and teachings on how to attain immortality.

Telemark. Used in this book to describe a downhill technique in nordic skiing.

Wu-wei. Taoist term meaning unmotivated action.

Yang. Chinese term meaning the sunny side of a mountain. Relates to masculine, active, creative, bright, and hard. In Wholistic Fitness terms, yang also means the explosive, forceful, and rising qualities of an exercise movement.

Yin. Chinese term meaning the shady side of a mountain. Relates to feminine, passive, receptive, dark, and soft. In Wholistic Fitness terms, yin also means the more controlled, poetic, or lowering qualities of an exercise movement.

Zazen. In Zen, formal sitting practice. Main vehicle used to attain enlightenment.

Bibliography

Annapurna: A Woman's Place, Arlene Blum. 1980. Sierra Club Books: San Francisco. An excellent, moving account of an ascent of a classic Himalayan peak.

Beginning To See, Sujata. 1987. Celestial Arts: Berkeley. A handwritten collection of insights and sketchings that delightfully steers the reader toward the value of meditation.

Being Nobody, Going Nowhere, Ayya Khema. 1987. Wisdom: Boston. Through this book and Khema's other, *When The Iron Eagle Flies*, the path of meditative insight is available to anyone.

Discovering the Body's Wisdom, Mirka Knaster, 1991. Bantam New Age: New York. A pragmatic and well-researched guide to body-centered therapies.

The Inner Athlete, Dan Millman, 1994. Stillpoint: New Hampshire. A compact reading on useful, transformative techniques for athletes.

In The Zone: Transcendent Experience in Sports, Michael Murphy. Penguin, 1995 (formerly titled *The Psychic Side of Sports*). A pretty impressive work of research.

Meditation in Action, Chogyam Trungpa, 1991. Shambala: Boston. Keep this little jewel near you at all times. It is full of insights that will enable you to stay awake throughout your day.

Plyometrics: Explosive Power Training, James Radcliffe and Robert Farentinos. 1985. Human Kinetic Publishers. An ideal guide for understanding plyometrics. Includes routines for many sports and excellent descriptions. Yep, that's me as one of those figurines in the illustrations.

The Prophet, Kahlil Gibran. 1980. Alfred A. Knopf: New York. And speak to me of beautiful inspiration through some of the most wonderful writing in the world.

Returning to Silence: Zen Practice in Daily Life, Dainin Katagiri. 1988. Shambala, Boston. Katagiri Roshi says, "Don't expect enlightenment—just sit down!" His book is based on this Zen Master's dharma talks to his students at the Minnesota Zen Meditation Center.

Shambala: The Sacred Path of the Warrior, Chogyam Trungpa. 1988. Shambala: Boston. A beautiful but very practical articulation of principles that guides one toward enlightened conduct in an often troubling and chaotic world.

The Tibetan Book of Living and Dying, Sogyal Rinpoche. 1993. Harper Collins: New York. Mandatory reading for those genuinely interested in learning how to live and die elegantly and consciously.

Training for Cycling, Davis Phinney and Connie Carpenter. 1992. Perigree: New York. I like Davis and his great stories from the golden era of his 7-Eleven racing years.

Yoga: Mind and Body, Sivananda Yoga Vedanta Center. 1996. Dorling Kindersley, London. An absolutely gorgeous, big book that details the Sivananda approach to yoga.

"The Ilgster" has been a nationally sponsored multisport athlete for thirteen years. Known for performing at high levels in physiologically divergent sports, *Ultra-Cycling* Magazine called him, "The world's fittest human" and Steve was the cover feature of *Outside* Magazine in 1992.

Some of Steve's athletes include Penny Davidson, two-time MTB Downhill National Champion; Michael Richter, MVP World Champion and goaltender for the New York Rangers and Stanley Cup Champions; Gerry Roach, Everest Summiteer, among hundreds of others across the world.

Steve holds Coaching License #00185 from the United States Cycling Federation.

His winter sport background includes numerous difficult Canadian and Colorado ice climbs, and skiing on the U.S. Jr. National Nordic Combined Team; he is a multi-champion in nordic skiing in both classic and skate skiing, a competitive alpine, tele, and snowboard racer, backcountry skier, and is a top contender in Rocky Mountain winter du, tri, and quadrathlons.

During the writing of this book, Steve split his time between racing bikes and teaching yoga in New Mexico and working with private clients in Los Angeles, California.

We don't know where he is now ...

*For more information on becoming a student of Wholistic Fitness®
or attending a Wholistic Fitness workshop, seminar, or retreat, visit*
www.wholisticfitness.com-us.net